MW01257070

"Few issues in contemporary, especially Western, society engender as much impassioned debate as immigration. In this biblically assessed and nuanced accounting, Markus Zehnder provides a needed corrective to all one-sided and overly generalized treatments of the foreign 'other.' His analysis is clarifying, courageous, and contrarian. Readers appreciative of an alternative point of view will find this book comprehensive in scope, compelling in force, and circumspect in application."

—DAVID L. MATSON
Hope International University

"Markus Zehnder is a cherished colleague, a top-tier, careful scholar, and a biblically faithful, fair-minded exegete. It is hard to overestimate the importance of his new book, *The Bible and Immigration*. It is never healthy for discussion of a significant cultural issue, especially one that engages God's people, to be dominated by one side. So it is especially important for a person of Zehnder's stature to provide a rigorous case for a position that is underrepresented. After reading this book, it is hard not to agree with Zehnder's case. But for those who hold the dominant position, intellectual integrity now demands that they interact with Zehnder. I highly recommend this work."

—J. P. MORELAND
Talbot School of Theology, Biola University

"*The Bible and Immigration* is an indispensable, rich resource which provides a solid basis for informed discussion around the contentious and complex issue of immigration. This excellent, comprehensive study not only deals with the biblical data but also applies any relevant extra-biblical principles to the present debate in a very nuanced, careful, and sensitive way. Zehnder avoids simplistic analysis and conclusions and challenges many current assumptions. This well-researched and perceptive work is highly recommended!"

—CORNELIS VAN DAM
Author of *God and Government*

"This is a very discerning book written by a scholar with longstanding interest and serious previous work in the field of immigration/migration. Markus Zehnder has managed to sort out the various biblical, social, and ethical issues raised in the complex discussion of immigration and migration today. He distinguishes between justice and compassion for those immigrants who have been admitted as opposed to public policies that require open admission at the borders. The Bible supports the former, but not the latter. Zehnder pushes back against the selective use of Scripture used by many to support their position without serious consideration of all that the Bible teaches on the matter in its ancient context. This is a badly needed and important contribution the discussion of the immigration issues we are facing today in the USA and around the world."

—RICHARD E. AVERBECK
Trinity Evangelical Divinity School

The Bible and Immigration

The Bible and Immigration

A Critical and Empirical Reassessment

MARKUS ZEHNDER

PICKWICK *Publications* · Eugene, Oregon

THE BIBLE AND IMMIGRATION
A Critical and Empirical Reassessment

Pickwick Publications
An Imprint of Wipf and Stock Publishers
199 W. 8th Ave., Suite 3
Eugene, OR 97401

www.wipfandstock.com

PAPERBACK ISBN: 978-1-7252-9798-2
HARDCOVER ISBN: 978-1-7252-9799-9
EBOOK ISBN: 978-1-7252-9800-2

Cataloguing-in-Publication data:

Names: Zehnder, Markus, author.
Title: The Bible and immigration : a critical and empirical reassessment / Markus Zehnder.
Description: Eugene, OR: Pickwick Publications, 2021 | Includes bibliographical references and index.
Identifiers: ISBN 978 1-7252-9798-2 (paperback) | ISBN 978-1-7252-9799-9 (hardcover) | ISBN 978-1-7252-9800-2 (ebook)
Subjects: LCSH: Emigration and immigration—Biblical teaching | Emigration and immigration in the Bible | Emigration and immigration—Religious aspects—Christianity | Hospitality—Biblical teaching
Classification: BS680.E38 Z44 2021 (paperback) | BS680.E38 (ebook)

08/06/21

Contents

Preface

CHALLENGES CONCERNING IMMIGRATION AND integration of foreigners are of critical interest in the current situation, on a local as well as on a national level in most countries in the Western world, and even in a global horizon.

The current discussion about migration (which is a concept that is broader than immigration)[1] is very often characterized by the dominance of strong, in many instances emotionally charged, views that either advocate for (quasi-)open borders and a "welcoming culture," or reject such notions. In this debate, the Bible is frequently used (or misused) to support the view of one side or the other. In fact, it is used in the current debate predominantly to support arguments in favor of liberal immigration policies.[2] In order to move forward in a positive direction and overcome unnecessary divisions, it is crucial to step back and to analyze the various and rich biblical traditions more closely and carefully and to rethink how these traditions can inform our understanding of the current situation and can help addressing it, such as to prevent us from heading into dead-ends, and enhance the flourishing of our communities.

---

1. The two terms will be distinguished in the following way: "Migration" refers to the movement of people from one place to another, regardless whether the movement is voluntary, semi-voluntary, or forced, and regardless whether it includes crossing national borders or not. "Immigration," on the other hand, will be used in the more narrowly defined context of people moving into a country that is not their country of origin, and only in cases in which the entering and settlement at the new place are being focused on, not in cases that deal with movement of persons more generally. Unfortunately, in the English-speaking world, especially in the U.S., "immigration" and "immigrant(s)" have mostly replaced the broader terms "migration" and "migrant(s)" in the discussion of these topics.

2. Among the rare exceptions are Edwards, "A Biblical Perspective," and Hoffmeier, *The Immigration Crisis.*

It is the aim of this book to contribute to this task, by (1) enhancing the understanding of the various biblical models concerning the dealing with (im)migrants, (2) identifying historical parallels *and* especially divergencies between the social and historical circumstances reflected in biblical texts and the current situation in our communities, and (3) recovering the broader ethical principles and specific practical measures found in the Bible that can be applied to positively shape our dealing with the current situation.

A large part of my research in the last two decades has been dedicated to the study of issues related to migration. Initially my focus has been on Israel's inclusion (and in fact, in some cases exclusion) of migrants, analyzing historically and exegetically the relevant biblical material, culminating in the monograph that was accepted as a *Habilitationsschrift* by the Theological Faculty of the University of Basel.[3] In the current study that is presented in this book, I am looking at ways in which historical findings related to the Bible can be transferred and applied in a responsible way to the contemporary challenges that (mass-)migration poses.

Hopefully, also my personal biographical experiences will be an asset in pursuing the goals just outlined: I am born in one of the European countries that in the last several decades had a very high percentage of immigrants among its population, and after leaving my home country I have lived in five different countries in Europe and the Middle East before moving to the U.S. a couple of years ago. These experiences have given me a rich opportunity to observe first-hand how various approaches to questions of migration lead to differing results, some of them more successful and some quite problematic. It is my hope that this study located at the interface of Bible and migration will be a useful contribution to strengthening responses that are helpful and contribute to reframing and moving the current discussion both in the U.S. and Europe—and even beyond—in a positive direction.

As the reader will find, most of the finding collected in this book are "counter-cultural" in the context of the current situation, in the sense that they cast a critical light on many of the assumptions dominating the discussion on migration issues both in official church documents and in the field of academic theology, and indeed in the broader social and political sphere.

3. See Zehnder, *Umgang mit Fremden*.

It is a pleasure to extend my thanks to the leadership of Talbot School of Theology for granting and partially financing a seventh semester leave that made writing this book possible. I also thank a group of friends back in the "sending country" of Switzerland for the necessary additional financial support that was needed to accomplish the project.

Abbreviations

AB	Anchor Bible
AJS	*American Journal of Sociology*
AJSL	*American Journal of Semitic Languages and Literature*
BBR	*Bulletin for Biblical Research*
BWANT	Beiträge zur Wissenschaft vom Alten und Neuen Testament
BZAR	Beihefte zur Zeitschrift für altorientalische und biblische Rechtsgeschichte
BZAW	Beihefte zur Zeitschrift für die alttestamentliche Wissenschaft
CBN	Christian Broadcasting Network
EJT	*European Journal of Theology*
ERT	*Evangelical Review of Theology*
FRLANT	Forschungen zur Religion und Literatur des Alten und Neuen Testaments
HTR	*Harvard Theological Review*
ICC	International Critical Commentary
IVP	InterVarsity Press
JBL	*Journal of Biblical Literature*
JBQ	*Jewish Bible Quarterly*
JSOT	*Journal for the Study of the Old Testament*
MIT	Massachusetts Institute of Technology
NAC	New American Commentary
NCBS	New Century Bible Commentary

NIBC	New International Biblical Commentary
NICNT	New International Commentary on the New Testament
NICOT	New International Commentary on the Old Testament
NovT	*Novum Testamentum*
NPG	Negative Population Growth
OTL	Old Testament Library
PEQ	*Palestine Exploration Quarterly*
RB	*Revue biblique*
TNTC	Tyndale New Testament Commentaries
VT	*Vetus Testamentum*
WBC	Word Biblical Commentary
WUNT	Wissenschaftliche Untersuchungen zum Neuen Testament
ZAW	*Zeitschrift für die alttestamentliche Wissenschaft*

Introduction

1. CURRENT SITUATION

MIGRATION IS ONE OF the most important topics with which the West (and in various ways also many other parts of the world) are wrestling. Many branches of academia, including theology and biblical studies, are trying to address this issue, with an ever-growing amount of studies produced in recent years. Sociology, anthropology, ethnography, history, demography, geography, economy, law, political science, psychology, medicine, public health are just some of the most salient major players in the debate. Given the complexity of the matter, it is positive that some attempts at transdisciplinary collaboration to address various issues connected with migration are being made.[4]

There are good reasons why also biblical studies and theology are involved in the debate, given the fact that the biblical material related to migration of various kinds is rich. However, as far as the contributions by biblical and theological scholars are concerned, the majority of them fail—as far as I can see—to fully appreciate the complexity of the biblical material and the implications of the considerable historical differences between ancient Israel and the current situation.[5] Therefore, a comprehensive new study on the topic that specifically focuses on the complexity of the biblical material on migration and on the historical differences between then and now is required. The present study will also try to remedy another lack in most biblical and theological studies, which is an insufficient recognition of extra-biblical data, by taking into

---

4. See, e.g., Brettell and Hollifield, *Migration Theory*.

5. This is observed also by Brett ("Forced Migrations," 123); he is, however, within the limits of a short paper, not able to remedy this deficiency properly.

consideration findings collected by other disciplines that are crucial in addressing ethical questions about dealing with (im)migration issues.[6]

2. HORIZON

As far as the current situation is concerned, the main focus of this study is on the large-scale movements from non-Western places of origin to the U.S. and to the Schengen-Dublin area in Europe (that is, the European Union plus Norway and Switzerland), as some of the main countries of destination in the West.[7] This means that internal migration within one and the same country, migration movements within the global South, or types of migration that can—as of now—clearly be labelled minority phenomena (like the temporary migration of managers or diplomatic personnel etc.) are not part of the background that informs the present investigation. Nor will it deal with a specific group of migrants in different parts of the world who are labeled "returnees."[8] Since mass-(im)migration to the West is currently more a phenomenon related to economic issues, and only in second place to cases that clearly fall in the category of "refugees" according to the definition found in the 1951 (Geneva)

---

6. The repetitiveness and large overlap between various studies on the topic is remarkable. As one randomly chosen example one can point to the extraordinary parallels in the use and interpretation of biblical material by Carroll (*Christians*) and Houston (*You Shall Love*). The main body of the analysis presented in these two monographs is largely identical; the only real difference is the focus on specific refugee issues at the beginning of Houston's book, together with a detailed study of Ezra–Nehemiah, and the particular interest for Hispanic immigration to the U.S. in Carroll's. In her treatment of specific cases of refugees, Houston includes a chapter on Palestinian refugees (see *You Shall Love*, 13–15); the lack of historic accuracy and nuance in this chapter is emblematic for problems that arise when deficient analyses of historical or contemporary circumstances are used as a basis for ethical assessments. On the other hand, her notes on the special case of Christian converts (see *You Shall Love*, 45–47) are very helpful in my view.

7. Canada, Australia, and New Zealand will not be taken as examples for detailed studies of current issues dealt with in chapter 6, both because of limits of space and because of a lesser degree of personal familiarity of the author with the situation in these countries. However, most of the findings presented in this study are relevant also for them.

8. For glimpses into the special challenges that these groups of persons are facing see, e.g., Houston, *You Shall Love*, 121–22.

Refugee Convention, the main focus will be on economic migration rather than the specifics of refugeehood.[9]

The horizon of this study is limited in some additional ways: (1) Migration and diversity(/multiculturalism) are related topics, but they are also—in spite of partial overlap—distinguishable.[10] In this book, matters pertaining to diversity will only be dealt with where necessary for the understanding of migration. Further questions concerning diversity will need to be dealt with in more detail in a separate study. (2) The philosophical, sociological, and political question about the role and position of mass-(im)migration within the cluster of related challenges and especially within the ongoing transformation of the fundamental tenets of Western societies will not be pursued. (3) The spiritual dimension of migration issues—adding to the historical-exegetical and the ethical dimensions—will not be taken up in this book. (4) There is no attempt to sift through all the relevant theological publications and documents. This is impossible given the fact that each denomination has by now published its own statement on (im)migration, sometimes even updating older versions; and very often innumerable individual congregations and individual biblical and theological scholars and pastors have done the same.

It is obviously not possible to make a distinction between (im)migration in general and the more specific phenomenon of large-scale or mass-(im)migration in absolute quantitative terms. On the other hand, it is not difficult to recognize the distinction between individual cases and large-scale movements when looking at the realities on the ground in most cases. In the current situation, one might use the expression "large-scale" when roughly one thousand persons or more of a specific group are involved, migrating either to the U.S. or to Western Europe.[11]

9. Some introductory information concerning the specifics of refugeehood can be found in, e.g., Houston, *You Shall Love*, 1–68. It has to be pointed out that the relatively narrow definition of "refugee" found in the 1951 Refugee Convention is no longer broadly accepted in the Western discourse. The widespread use of the expression "economic refugees" (or more recently also "climate refugees") is an indicator of this change on the semantic level. The new Global Compact for Migration (see *Global Compact for Safe, Orderly and Regular Migration, Final Draft, 11 July 2018*) is one of the newer documents that changes the legal perception and administration of migration and refugee issues profoundly. Cf. also Houston's statement that "[s]ome human rights violations do not necessarily meet the refugee definition of persecution" (*You Shall Love*, 43).

10. These matters are routinely treated together in ecclesiastical documents; see, e.g., John Paul II, *Message for the Celebration of the World Day of Peace*.

11. Alternatively, one might use the expression when the resulting change in population in a receiving country moves beyond 1 percent.

3. RESEARCH PROCEDURE AND METHODOLOGY

The main body of the study applies standard historical/critical methods of exegetical research to analyze the biblical texts that are relevant for the investigation. The analysis is, however, restricted to aspects that are relevant for the use of the texts in the current migration debate; a special focus will be, where appropriate, on their ethical message. Besides this, studies made by sociologists on aspects of migration in the past and in the present that are important to understand the general framework of migration and the differences between migration in biblical times and in the present are also used. This includes, among other things, the relationship between ethnicity and identity. In addition, migration research done in the fields of psychology, demography, economy, and security studies are also taken into consideration; in these cases, with the exception of psychology, the macro-level perspective is the dominant one, because in the frame of the current study it is not possible to deal with more than the general overview perspective. The integration of the data presented in these chapters is important because ethical assessments of current (im)migration issues cannot be developed in a responsible way without taking them into consideration.

Comparison is a continuous element of the present study, applied to the various texts within the Hebrew Bible, the Bible as a whole, the situations reflected in the biblical texts and current issues, and finally between various (country-)specific examples in the chapter dealing with demographic, economic, and security aspects of migration in the current circumstances.[12]

What will not be focused upon are the gender-specific aspects of migration.[13] This does not mean that they are not important. For the present purposes, however, focus on this specific aspect would complicate the analysis beyond a degree that is appropriate for the investigation at hand.

---

12. For the importance of comparison in migration studies see, e.g., Brettell and Hollifield, "Migration Theory," 15.

13. These aspects have gotten a great deal of attention in the last couple of decades; see, e.g., Timmerman et al., *Gender and Migration*. See also Brettell, "Theorizing Migration," 126–31.

1

Pitfalls in Approaching
Migration Issues

1. GENERAL OBSERVATIONS

ATTENTION MUST BE PAID to the fact that migration is a socio-politically sensitive issue. Doing research on this topic is commonly not as unaffected by a variety of agendas as—to choose a random example—would be the case in the area of the botanical analysis of the variety of roses or the historical analysis of the clashes between Egypt and Assyria in the Iron Age. Therefore, special attention must be given to critically question *a priori*-assumptions of all kinds and to identify distortions in the application of scientific standards that may turn the research process into a support engine for a politically (or otherwise) driven agenda.

The identification of some of the most important problems and pitfalls in the current discussion on migration may be used as a map that points to the areas in which further research and careful discussion are needed. A good number of these points will be dealt with in the subsequent parts of the present volume, especially those that are connected to the use of the Bible in the migration debate.

2. PITFALLS NOT PRIMARILY OR EXCLUSIVELY RELATED TO THE USE OF THE BIBLE[1]

2.1. A Priori Positive or Negative Views of Migration/Migrants

In many cases, as a matter of basic assumption, (im)migration (either generally or in unspecified terms) is seen as either *a priori* positive or *a priori* negative. Related to this is the notion that migrants per se are either an enrichment or a threat.[2] These problems are related to the fact that (im)migration is a topic that highly engages observers both politically and religiously.[3]

---

1. The list is by no means comprehensive.

2. Both in the scholarly and in the religiously oriented debate the first of the two alternatives dominates. This view is sometimes formulated in elevated theological language. For examples, see Carroll, *Christians*, 25–26, 40; Castillo Guerra, "A Theology," 243 (claiming that "migrants represent a major sign of the presence of God within our contemporary history"); Campese, "¿Cuantos Más?" 283–85, 292, asserting that migrants "are chosen by God," "carrying the sins of those who are really responsible," and in this way "become the 'light of the nations'"; they are "the crucified peoples" who are "the sign of the times"; "they are the body of the crucified Christ," "saved and saviors . . . because they make present in history the Savior par excellence"; they "offer hope" and "generate solidarity"; they are also "the carriers of truths and values that make them the prophets and protagonists of a better society"; Fornet-Betancourt, "Hermeneutics," 210; Groody, "Fruit," 311, writing that, "In the Eucharist, we see in faith not only the body and blood of Christ. In the Eucharist, we also see the body and blood of the migrant"; Schreiter, "Migrants," 113. Among the church documents see "A Wesleyan View of Immigration," *The Wesleyan Church* (2013); the Preamble contains the assertion that, "We model His compassion when we offer charity and hospitality to strangers He sovereignly brings to our shores to offer talents, skills, and labor that can contribute positively to our society." Sometimes, this line of reasoning is given a specific turn by asserting that the Christian immigrants are God's instrument to revive the church in the receiving countries and to evangelize these countries (see, e.g., Carroll, *Christians*, 40). For a similar view, encompassing also further aspects relating to the theologically positive role of migration, see "A Wesleyan View," The Sovereignty Principle (offering the following statement: "As Wesleyans, we view immigration as an aspect of God's larger plan to bring salvation to the world. Immigration can and Empirical be used through God's wisdom to introduce many to Jesus who might not otherwise hear the gospel message"; interestingly, this statement is related to Acts 17:26–28; Rev 7:9–12; Dan 4:35; and Gen 50:20—passages that in no way bear out the message deduced from them in the Wesleyan document).

3. Favell notes that the situation is complicated by the fact that "leading academics are almost always also highly politically engaged, and their careers and appointments are themselves often political" ("Rebooting Migration Theory," 265).

2.2. Migration as an Uncontrollable Process

In many cases, again as a matter of basic assumption, migration (either generally or in unspecified terms) is seen as an unavoidable and largely uncontrollable process, in much the same way as processes in nature.[4] This is normally related to the view that globalization has to be accepted as a fact that cannot or should not be critically questioned.[5]

2.3. Migrants as Victims

In many cases, migrants (or at least the vast majority of them) are primarily or almost exclusively perceived as victims.[6] A frequent corollary of this view is that the receiving societies in the West are seen as exclusionary and discriminating.[7]

---

4. An example would be the following statement: "When the rivers of wealth flow in one direction, it is only natural for population to flow in the same direction" (Gonzales, *For the Healing*, 83); see also, e.g., Battistella, "Migration," 180; Gutiérrez, "Poverty," 76; Hoover, "The Story," 172. Similar statements can also be found in Carroll, *Christians*, 73 ("migration is a human condition to be appreciated"), 98 ("the reality of continual immigration is a fact"). Carroll published an updated version of *Christians at the Borders* in 2020, unde. the title *The Bible and Borders*. Identical or near-identical formulations to those just quoted from *Christians* can be found on pp. 49 (identical) and 81 (near-identical: "the reality of continual immigration is an indisputable fact"). In the remainder of this study, references to *The Bible and Borders* will only be given in cases of notable departure from the previous edition of his study.

5. See, e.g., Battistella, "Migration," 179–80; Carroll, *Christians*, 23, 32; Groody and Campese, "Preface," xx–xxi; Gutiérrez, "Poverty," 79 ("to be against globalization per se is like being against electricity"); Groody, "Fruit," 312; Hoover, "The Story," 172; Schmitter Heisler, "The Sociology," 91. It is, however, obvious that globalization has also negative aspects; see, e.g., Tverberg's article on "12 Negative Aspects of Globalization;" cf. also Castillo Guerra, "A Theology," 258.

6. As a random example, one can point to the articles collected in Groody and Campese, *A Promised Land*. See also Beck, "Sanctuary," 132–45. A special nuance is found in Battistella who defines the migrant as "our helper," with reference to Gen 2:18–20 ("Migration," 189).

7. See, e.g., Battistella, "Migration," 178, 180–81; Campese, "¿Cuantos Más?" 276–82, 286; Castillo Guerra, "A Theology," 244; Carroll, *Christians*, 119; Groody and Campese, "Preface," xxi; Gutiérrez, "Poverty," 76; Groody, "Fruit," 302–3; Kerwin, "The Natural Rights," 193–203; Rodríguez, "A Witness to Hope," xiv; Schreiter, "Migrants," 118. Cf. also Carroll, *Christians*, 6–9.

2.4. Extreme Views of Ethnic and National Identity

Ethnic and national identity, which are affected by large-scale immigration, are seen as either static or completely fluid.[8]

2.5. Lack of Differentiation between Various Kinds of Migration

Migration issues are frequently addressed with a lack of differentiation between various kinds of migration.[9] Distinctions are often—and with good reasons, in my view—made between "refugees" and "economic migrants." It is, however, a matter of dispute—both on the theoretical level and in practice—who qualifies as "refugee," and one has to admit that the polar distinction between "refugees" and "economic migrants" is in many cases not adequate enough to reflect the complexities of reality.[10]

8. This topic will be discussed further in the section devoted to sociological aspects below. Those arguing for liberal immigration policies usually stress the aspect of fluidity—especially as far as the receiving societies are concerned, while at the same time tendentially more stability is allowed for the migrants (and their home countries); see, e.g., Carroll, *Christians*, 25–26.

9. As a random example, one can again point to the articles collected in Groody and Campese, *A Promised Land*. A telling specific example is found in the shift between "pursuing a career" and "flying" in Hagan's description of a Mexican family who migrated to the U.S.; see Hagan, "Faith," 3. In his treatment of the implications of the biblical reports on immigrants, refugees, and exiles, Carroll summarily refers to people being "compelled to go to another place" (*Christians*, 70), though the element of compulsion cannot be applied in such a general way. Various types of migrants are consistently lumped together in Beck, "Sanctuary," 133, 136, 140, 144; Gonzales, "Sanctuary," 36–47. The Wesleyan statement speaks of "persons who have fled countries of origin in which they suffered persecution, poverty, or political oppression" (Preamble). See also "Southern Baptist 2018 Resolution on Migration," second and twelfth paragraph. Houston for the most part refers to "refugees" and "persons seeking asylum"; it is, however, clear that in many cases those in view are really persons whose main incentive to migrate are economic reasons (cf. also her remarks on the necessity of finding a broader definition of "refugee," one that relates more generally to "the absence of state protection of the citizen's basic needs" [*You Shall Love*, 11]).

10. Cf., e.g., Brettell, "Theorizing Migration," 115. Kerwin observes: "The refugee definition . . . does not apply to the millions who flee civil war, generalized violence, natural disaster, or poverty" ("The Natural Rights," 199). A similar distinction is often made between "forced" and "voluntary migration" (see, e.g., Castillo Guerra, "A Theology," 247). As in the case of the distinction between refugees and economic migrants, however, the line between the two types is not clear-cut and a matter of debate—which does not mean that there is no heuristic value in the distinction. Even if such distinctions are made, many authors still advocate for liberal immigration policies whatever the specific category a migrant might fall in; see, e.g., Escobar, "Refugees," 102–8, and the authors mentioned in the footnote on legal and illegal migrants.

In recent times, new types of migration have appeared, among them such types that are marked by an increasing importance of trans-national identities in which traditional concepts of one-way movements no longer apply (cf. the previous category of "guest workers").[11] The causes or motivations for migration are subject to changes as well.

One of the most contentious issues in this lemma is the distinction between legal and illegal types of migration.[12] This issue is complicated by the fact that "legality" is a relative concept, exposed to the constant change that takes place in the legal system. The challenge to navigate between the importance of the rule of law and the fact that all positive law is not "eternal," and the tension between positive laws and "laws of nature" and "divine law," will never be solved once and for all. In the current debate, the notion of "human rights" often plays a prominent role in discussions related to the legal domain. However, it should be admitted that the introduction of this notion does not "solve" the problem either.

A lack of differentiation is also apparent where immigration to distinct countries of destination by distinct types of migrants is not taken sufficiently into account. Within the horizon of the present investigation, this is especially pertinent with a view to the differences between the situation in many countries in Europe as compared to the situation in the U.S.

11. This relates to the important distinction between permanent and semi-permanent migration; see, e.g., Castillo Guerra, "A Theology," 247. See also Brettell, who refers to the distinction between seasonal, temporary non-seasonal, recurrent, continuous, and permanent types of migration, and enforced migration as a special category (Brettell, "Theorizing Migration," 115; cf. also pp. 117–18).

12. Often, authors relativize or do not acknowledge the distinction; see, e.g. Battistella, "Migration," 181, 184–85; Beck, "Sanctuary," 132–45 (in some ways, legal immigration does not even appear as a real possibility in his article); Brett, "Forced Migrations," 136; Campese, "¿Cuantos Más?" 272, 276–77; Carroll, *Christians*, xxviii–xxix; Groody, "Fruit," 305; Hagan, "Faith," 4–5; Hoover, "The Story," 160–73; Houston, *You Shall Love*, 154; Kerwin, "The Natural Rights," 192–205; Schreiter, "Migrants," 117; "A Wesleyan View," Preamble (and most of the eight Principles); "Southern Baptist 2018 Resolution on Migration," eleventh paragraph; in its overall tendency also "Immigration 2009," *The National Association of Evangelicals*. For a different approach see, e.g., Hoffmeier, *The Immigration Crisis*, 15–16, 19–22.

2.6. Migration as the Preferred Instrument in the Fight against Poverty

Migration is often presupposed to be the best option to alleviate poverty for people in developing countries.[13] As we shall see in chapter 6, this presupposition is not in accordance with reality. The problems related to migration and mass-immigration must not be ignored.

2.7. Focus on Either Micro-Level or Macro-Level Perspective

In many cases, the focus is either on a micro-level perspective (individual migrant and his/her family),[14] or on a macro-level perspective (macro-economic systems; institutions; state policy), instead of both.[15]

2.8. Focus on Perspectives of the Migrants or Perspectives of the Receiving Societies

In many cases, the focus is either almost exclusively on the perspective of the migrants, or almost exclusively on the perspective of the receiving society.[16] Often, the first perspective will lead to the promotion of a more liberal, and the second perspective to the promotion of a more restrictive view on immigration.

2.9. Lack of Holistic Perspective

A holistic perspective is mostly lacking. It is, however, important that all the factors involved in and affected by migration must be scrutinized: Culture, economy (including costs and benefits), human rights, particular laws (or the absence of specific laws) and the broader concept of the

13. See, e.g., Hoover, "The Story," 162, 172. Sometimes, authors who share this view in principle nevertheless admit that the situation is more complex; see, e.g., Groody who observes that "the desire to provide for the family" through migration "in many cases ends up breaking up the family" ("Fruit," 310).

14. See, e.g., Hagan, "Faith"; Schreiter, "Migrants."

15. This is also observed by Brettell and Hollifield, "Migration Theory," 2, 8–12.

16. So also Brettell and Hollifield, "Migration Theory," 5. In fact, in biblical and theological studies, it is the first perspective that overwhelmingly dominates. As a random example, one can point again to the articles collected in Groody and Campese, *A Promised Land*.

rule of law in general, politics (including questions of sovereignty and citizenship), religion, demography, ecology, psychological and physical health, education, security, social cohesion, etc., with respect to all parties involved, including not only the individual migrants and the receiving society, but also the situation in the sending societies.[17] The situation in the sending countries need to be analyzed not only in terms of how their societies are affected by emigration, but also in terms of an identification of the factors that lead to emigration in the first place.[18] In all cases both the personal micro-level and the macro-level of broader structures within which the individuals operate must be looked at.

2.10. Lack of Long-Term Perspective

Current migration issues are frequently debated without a long-term (future) perspective. However, the questions about future possible or likely consequences especially of mass-immigration, both with respect to the receiving and the sending societies, are important to consider.

2.11. Lack of Historical Perspective

The other side of the same coin is the lack of a historical perspective. An analysis of earlier periods marked by large-scale migration, with a special view on the causal factors and the long-term results of such movements, is an important contribution to the understanding and assessment of current migration issues. One has to ask what the historical parallels are with the present situation that can help to understand it better and inform policies to tackle it in ways that may be seen as helpful by a majority of people in all societies involved.

17. See, e.g., Brettell and Hollifield, "Migration Theory." The lack of a holistic approach is also noted by Amstutz, *Just Immigration*, 225–26.

18. When this factor is taken into consideration, it is normally confined to pointing to economic distress in the sending countries which provides the incentive for people to leave. Much rarer are cases in which responsibility for deficiencies is directly related to misconduct of the ruling elites of the sending countries. As one of the exceptions we may mention Battistella's observation that abuse of human rights is found in many of the sending countries ("Migration," 183). Beck, on the other hand, not only ignores the responsibilities of the ruling elites in the sending countries completely (as many authors do), but locates the causes for mass-migration fully on the Western countries, pointing explicitly to meddling in other countries, free trade agreements, and demand for drugs ("Sanctuary," 143).

The discussion in the U.S. is special in this respect because routinely reference is made to the U.S. being historically a country of immigrants.[19] While this is obviously true in many ways on the surface, it obfuscates the fact that immigration was handled very differently in the course of the history of this country. At least as important is the point that a past history of immigration can in no ways be used as an argument to determine how immigration is to be handled in the present.

2.12. Logical or Ethical Inconsistencies

Logical and/or ethical inconsistencies can often be found in the context of the migration debate; but they should be avoided. Here are some randomly chosen examples of such inconsistencies:

- In the U.S., some groups (mostly on the right of the political spectrum) are opposed to large-scale immigration by undocumented migrants; and yet members of the same groups will hire such migrants as cheap labor.[20]

- The protection of migrant children is given special weight in the migration debates in the West; at the same time, forced marriages of children are sometimes accepted on grounds of cultural respect by the same groups (mostly on the left of the political spectrum).[21]

- The separation of families at the borders is often highlighted as a major problem; at the same time, societal developments of various kinds that take away children from their parents—culminating in the ultimate "separation" through abortion—will routinely be supported by the same groups (usually on the left of the political spectrum).

- Some groups propagate the idea that everyone should be allowed to settle wherever he/she wishes, and that "no human being is illegal"; at the same time, the same people will in fact be opposed to the settlement of specific groups of people in other parts of the world for various political reasons.[22]

19. See, e.g., "Immigration 2009," National Realities.

20. See, e.g., Lemon, "Ann Coulter."

21. See, e.g., Kelek, "Zwangsehen."

22. For more details on this point see chapter 4 below.

2.13. Name-Calling

It is perhaps not particularly surprising, given the importance of the issue and its vast emotional dimension, to encounter name-calling very often, especially instances in which compounds with the final element "-phobia" are used. In the case of (im)migration, this would primarily apply to the term "xenophobia" for positions that do not embrace liberal immigration policies. One of the main problems with such terms is the implied pathologization of persons holding different views from one's own, since a "phobia" is something irrational. Another important example is the now widely expanded use of the term "racism," which is often levelled at anyone taking a critical stance against liberal immigration policies.[23] Instead of name-calling, rational debates based on as much knowledge as possible would be preferable, even if it is clear that—based on deep-rooted differences in world-view—it is not likely that one will find common positions with which all can agree.

2.14. Manipulation of Language

Language is under pressure and used as a partisan instrument not only in terms of name-calling. One can also observe rhetoric that is coined to conceal reality, or to stir up emotions and suggest clear-cut realities where in fact the situation is more complex. Randomly chosen examples are fights over the expressions "undocumented" vs. "illegal,"[24] "extremists" or "militants" vs. "terrorists," the borders as places where migrants are "slaughtered"[25] or "crucified,"[26] and of course, perhaps most importantly, questions about the use of the term "refugee."[27] It would certainly be helpful to seek and use the terms that come closest to the facts as we

23. An example can be found in Escobar, "Refugees," 104.

24. Campese speaks of the "construction of the 'illegal alien'" ("¿Cuantos Más?" 275). Cf. the remarks made by Carroll in defense of the use "undocumented (immigrants)" instead of "illegal (aliens)" in *Christians*, xxviii–xxix.

25. Campese, "¿Cuantos Más?" 271.

26. Campese, "¿Cuantos Más?" 287. Such terms imply willful and wanton cruelty on the side of law enforcement, which is unwarranted in the overwhelming number of circumstances. They also imply that persons trying to enter a country illegally had no other choice, which again is a false claim in most cases.

27. Another example is the use of the term "slaves" for "undocumented migrants in the United States" as long as they have not been granted legal status (see Hoover, "The Story," 171).

know them, and in cases where these facts are disputed to make the fault-lines of the disagreements visible instead of hiding them behind some smoke-screen rhetoric.

3. PITFALLS PERTAINING TO THE RELIGIOUS/ THEOLOGICAL DIMENSION OF THE DEBATE, PARTICULARLY THE USE OF THE BIBLE

3.1. General Overview

In this section, we will try to address the two following questions:

1. What are the main problems and misunderstandings in the *understanding* of the biblical material that deals with various aspects of migration?

2. What are the main problems and misunderstandings in the *application* of the biblical material to the current debates on migration?

Very often, the two areas of misunderstanding are directly connected with each other. The following section briefly deals with the major issues involved here.[28]

3.2. Random Selection of Biblical Texts

Often biblical passages are interpreted in isolation from their literary context—and then transferred one-to-one to present-day circumstances.[29] Such procedures are of course scientifically not defensible, because

28. A good (though rare) example for a study that avoids these deficiencies is Hoffmeier's *The Immigration Crisis*.

29. See, e.g., *"und der Fremdling, der in deinen Toren ist:" Gemeinsames Wort*; "A Wesleyan View"; "Refugee Highway Partnership," *World Evangelical Alliance* (selecting Lev 19:34 and Matt 25:35–36). Amstutz rightly observes: "Despite the acknowledgment that Scripture should not be used to directly advance specific public policies, most of the Evangelical immigration documents that I examined do just that, implicitly if not explicitly. They do so by using specific biblical texts to emphasize certain themes, such as hospitality and compassion, and by selectively using biblical principles to advance particular policy goals" (*Just Immigration*, 131). In the scholarly literature see, e.g., Beck, "Sanctuary" (applying passages that talk about support of the sojourner and the regulations for asylum cities to illegal immigrants in the U.S.) and Van Nguyen, "In Solidarity," 224 (using Exod 23:9 as a general rule, together with Gen 18:1–10; 1 Kgs 17:1–16; Matt 2:13–15).

they violate the integrity of the source text and ignore the historical gap between the ancient Near East and the Graeco-Roman world on the one hand and the present-day world on the other.

Besides the problem of single verses being taken out of their immediate literary context, there is another shortcoming that one encounters often: The reduction of the complexity and diversity of the biblical material on (im)migration by selecting only those texts that fit one's already established assumptions or agenda, which in many cases will be texts that exhibit a positive assessment of (im)migration/(im)migrants.[30] Texts that do not square well with such a view are then simply overlooked, or subjected to the modern interpreter's *a priori* criticism, as happens for example to the relevant passages in Deuteronomy 23 or Nehemiah 13, where the text is denounced without being given a fair hearing.[31] In order to make such a criticism possible, foundational biblical concepts such as the divine election of Israel are sometimes ignored or questioned.[32]

3.3. Identifying Migration-Issues with the Core of the Gospel

Many biblical and theological scholars, and especially many representatives of various churches and faith-based NGOs view migration-issues—and especially advocacy for liberal immigration policies—as a core gospel issue, where only one approach can be accepted as the right one.[33] As we

---

30. See, e.g., Carroll, "Welcoming the Stranger," 444, 447. More precisely, Carroll's article mentions, with a view to Deuteronomy, both welcoming and less welcoming passages; but it is only the first that are given weight in the chapter on "Lessons for Immigration from Deuteronomy" (see "Welcoming the Stranger," 447–61). For further examples see Gonzales, "Sanctuary," 45–47; Maruskin, "The Bible," 77–90.

31. An example can be found in Houston, *You Shall Love*. As opposed to other authors, she does indeed look at Ezra–Nehemiah in quite some detail (see *You Shall Love*, 117–33). She rejects, however, the views expressed in these books—as far as the treatment of non-Israelites is concerned—as unacceptable ideology.

The problem pointed out here can also be observed in the following case where it is not Deuteronomy 23 or passages from Ezra–Nehemiah that are at stake. Strine ("Embracing Asylum Seekers," 480) rejects the views presented in Ezekiel as "neo-national" and therefore incompatible with a Christian approach to the Bible (see also pp. 485–86). He connects what he calls "the strongly nationalistic and ethnocentric approach" promoted by Ezekiel directly to the isolated context of the Judahite exiles in which Ezekiel lived ("Embracing Asylum Seekers," 486).

32. For examples see O'Neill, "'No Longer Strangers,'" 228–31.

33. See, e.g., Koenig, "What Does the Bible Say."

shall see in the following chapters, this position is based on a reductionist understanding of the Bible.

3.4. Neglect of the Theological Dimension of Biblical Texts

The *theological* dimension of biblical texts pertaining to migration can be neglected by overemphasizing social, economic, psychological, or other non-theological aspects. It makes, however, a difference when a migrant's journey is driven by the search for improved living conditions or by a direct call from God (as, e.g., in the case of Abraham). In the *application* of the biblical material, concomitant reductionist approaches will focus more or less exclusively on material and humanitarian aspects, at the expense of spiritual aspects.[34]

3.5. Conflation of Exegesis and Activism

This point is closely connected to the previous one. A majority of authors who try to look at migration issues through the lens of the Bible focus almost exclusively on the aspect of compassion towards immigrants,[35] sometimes even as a matter of presupposition. For example, in his influential study *Christians at the Border*, Daniel Carroll states in the Preface that, "The people of God will need to continue to be informed about the call to welcome the outsider and to grow in divine hospitality."[36] Another example is Escobar, who in a recent article, entitled "Refugees: A New Testament Perspective," introduces his analysis by identifying a threefold

34. This is the basic thrust in Carroll, "Immigration," 1–21; Maruskin, "The Bible"; O'Neill, "'No Longer Strangers.'"

35. So Amstutz, *Just Immigration*, 216. For examples of this one-sidedness see Beck, "Sanctuary," 132–45; McKinney et al., "Welcoming the Stranger," 50–55; Van Nguyen, "In Solidarity," 219–24; "A Wesleyan View." Sometimes, lip service is given to the necessity of the state's role as a guarantor of law and order, including border protection, while the whole weight of the argument focuses on compassion, mercy, and liberal immigration policies; see, e.g., "Committee to Study the Migration of Workers," *Christian Reformed Church* (2008); "Immigration 2009," Biblical Foundations.

36. Carroll, *Christians*, xiv. On the same page, he uses the phrase "gracious commitment to the stranger." He concludes the Preface by expressing the hope that his book "will be . . . a helpful resource for orienting Christians toward welcoming the strangers in our midst" (*Christians*, xv). In the Introduction to his book, he identifies the "truly Christian perspective on immigration" with activism supporting the "call for openness toward outsiders" (*Christians*, xxvi).

challenge:[37] challenge to Christian compassion and sensitivity; need for the churches to take a prophetic stance in the face of injustices in the way in which society treats immigrants;[38] migration as an avenue for the evangelistic dimension of mission. What transpires in such an attitude is a principled rejection of the clear demarcation between scholarly analysis of the biblical texts and practical action, in this case action on behalf of migrants. This attitude is characteristic of the broad movement called liberation theology. One of their well-known representatives, Gutiér-rez, maintains, in his article on the connection between migration and the option for the poor: "[T]he Good News must be . . . translated from scripture into daily life. . . . Announcing and giving witness to the gospel message of the kingdom of God is also the goal and meaning of any theo-logical consideration. Outside of such service, theology is meaningless."[39] Similarly, Castillo Guerra states that theological reasoning must be "compassionate," informed by a commitment to the poor in general and the migrants in particular, aiming at "the transformation of reality."[40] In order to achieve this, it is necessary "to start from the faith, experience, and sapiential knowledge of the migrants."[41]

In my view, because of the complexity of the biblical witness and the historical differences between biblical times and the present, and in order not to distort the cautious investigation of the historical sources in any way, it is important to clearly distinguish the tasks of analysis from practical action.

---

37. See Escobar, "Refugees," 102–3.

38. In his explanation of this challenge, Escobar identifies "a militant advance of paganism with an attitude in which there is no room for solidarity or compassion in the face of human need and suffering" ("Refugees," 103). He does, however, not offer any supporting data for this far-reaching claim. The problem with a sweeping statement such as this is that it does not leave room for the possibility that in the eyes of some it might be wiser, depending on the circumstances, to help people in need in other ways than by encouraging migration.

39. Gutiérrez, "Poverty," 77. He also maintains that, "The option for the poor . . . is a way of doing theology," and that we must "commit ourselves to our migrant brothers and sisters" ("Poverty," 81). See also Castillo Guerra, who identifies and constructs "the theology of migration as a specific liberation theology" ("A Theology," 245; cf. also pp. 249–53).

40. Guerra, "A Theology," 252.

41. Guerra, "A Theology," 253. He also states that it is necessary to construct "a theology that tries to be an expression of the human situation of the migrants" ("A Theology," 251).

3.6. Lack of Semantic and Conceptual Precision

The complexity of the biblical data may be unduly reduced by neglecting the nuanced distinctions that the biblical texts make between different types of migrants. This is related to the biblical use of specific terms. Sadly, in many cases the question of the precise meaning of crucial biblical terms that are related to the topic of migration, especially the nouns "*ger*" and "*nokri*," is not addressed. Such nouns are simply identified with generic modern notions of "foreigner" or "migrant," which is misleading.[42] Rather, these terms refer to social categories that function within a specific social system, and therefore cannot be transferred one-to-one to a different system. The problem can be illustrated by looking at another biblical term from a different semantic and conceptual field: The Hebrew noun *bushah* is normally translated in English with "shame." This translation is, however, in many cases misleading, because in spite of some overlap in meaning, *bushah* and "shame" are distinguished by considerable differences in connotations and associations.[43]

3.7. Misunderstanding of Genre

As part of the broader issues of context, one has to keep in mind that the collections of what is generally called "legal" material in the Hebrew Bible cannot simply be understood as legal texts in the modern sense of the word. There was in all likelihood no "Law Code" as we know it in ancient Israel, and in all events the biblical law collections cannot be classified as "Law Codes" in the modern sense of the term.[44] This is often overlooked, which leads to a wrong analysis of the situation in ancient Israel, and from there to misconceptions in how these "laws" might be applied today.

3.8. Negative Effects of Speculative Historical Reconstructions

In many cases the analysis of the biblical picture on migration is influenced by speculative source-critical presuppositions that read the relevant

---

42. For a random example see "Immigration 2009," Biblical Foundations. Here, the *ger* of Deut 10:18–19 is identified with a generic "foreigner" of any given era.

43. See, e.g., Avrahami, "שוב in the Psalms," 295–313.

44. This is also rightly stressed by Houston, *You Shall Love*, 79–80.

texts against the grain in terms of historical localization, for example by dating the book of Ruth in the Persian period or by identifying the "so-journer" in some priestly legal texts with the proselyte of early Second Temple Judaism.[45] Such historical reconstructions may distort the real picture and affect the understanding of these texts in an unhelpful way. In this respect, caution is needed, which in many instances means to abstain from definitive historical judgments.

3.9. Unwarranted Generalizations

Proper analysis of the biblical material and transfers to current issues building on the biblical analysis can also be distorted by unwarranted generalizations. Claiming, for example, that the presence of sojourners "was fundamental to . . . the very meaning" of "Israel's national identity"[46] goes beyond the exegetically observable data. Nor would it be hermeneutically appropriate to simply jump from the past to the present in a generalizing way. The situation is similar in the case of the following statement, written by Groody: "The story of the Israelites in Egypt is an ancient story but it is also a recurring story; as the Word of God the Passover contains an enduring metaphorical truth. . . . In many respects, we might say the Passover narrative is the prototypical migration story."[47] He adds that many migrants of today "see in the Exodus story their own stories."[48]

3.10. Ignoring the Historical Differences between Then and Now

In terms of the historical interpretation of the biblical material, but even more so in terms of its application to current issues, differences between the historical situation in ancient Israel and the present-day world are sometimes neglected.[49] This leads to all too sweeping identifications of

45. For the former see, e.g., Villiers and le Roux, "The Book of Ruth," 1–6; for the latter see, e.g., Nihan, "Resident Aliens," 129–32. We also note that the description of the position of the *ger* ("sojourner") in the book of Deuteronomy in some of the recent studies on the topic is dependent on hypothetical historical reconstructions of the development of the postulated layers of Deuteronomy; see, e.g. Bultmann (*Der Fremde im antiken Juda*) and Glanville (*Adopting the Stranger*).

46. Carroll, *Christians*, 97; the formulation used in *The Bible* (p. 80) is near-identical.

47. Groody, "Fruit," 303.

48. Groody, "Fruit," 304.

49. Hoffmeier's observation hits the nail on its head: ". . . we must recognize the

biblical migrants (either the Israelites themselves or the non-Israelite *ger* ["sojourner"]) with various types of present-day migrants.[50] Especially common in the identification of the *ger* ("sojourner") with modern immigrants; care for them is understood as one of the "enduring ethical ideals" that "continue to be valid and should be made concrete in the contemporary world."[51]

3.11. Identification of the People of God with Society at Large

In many cases the distinctions between the ancient people of Israel or the church on the one hand and modern people not belonging to these entities on the other hand are blurred. As a consequence, what is understood as right for the church—especially with a view to internal diversity—is transferred one-to-one to the realm of society at large; that is, an internal ecclesiastical program is transposed into political action.[52] A lack of historical distinction may also be in display when ordinances given to ancient Israelite individuals or the Israelite people as a whole are simply transferred to modern political entities or church bodies, thereby conflating church and state and/or the levels of personal ethical and collective responsibility.[53]

3.12. Sanctuary Cities

The concept of sanctuary cities (or the use of churches as sanctuary) for asylum seekers whose application was rejected is a relatively widespread phenomenon in various Western countries. It is often justified by

---

vast differences that exist between the cultural, economic, and social milieu of ancient Israel three thousand years ago and present western culture" (*The Immigration Crisis*, 25).

50. See, e.g., Carroll, *Christians*, 71–73; Carroll, "Immigration," 3, 10 (cf. also pp. 15–16); Carroll, "Welcoming," 457–58; Maruskin, "The Bible," 77–90; O'Neill, "'No Longer Strangers,'" 228; Wünch, "Gast, Mitbewohner, Fremdling," 101–2; "A Wesleyan View"; "Southern Baptist 2018 Resolution on Migration," third paragraph.

51. Carroll, *Christians*, 96; the formulation in *The Bible* (p. 79) is near-identical. Similar statements can be found, e.g., in Houston, *You Shall Love*, 73.

52. So also Amstutz, *Just Immigration*, 227, 229. For an example see, e.g., O'Neill, "'No Longer Strangers,'" 228–30.

53. For examples see Carroll, "Welcoming," 456, 460; Groody, "Fruit," 303; Maruskin, "The Bible," 87, 89; O'Neill, "'No Longer Strangers,'" 228–29.

recourse to the Hebrew Bible.[54] And in fact, the institution of sanctuary cities is found there; see Exod 21:12–14; Num 35:11–16, 20–30; Deut 19:1–13; and Josh 20:1–6, 9. In the Hebrew Bible, however, the institution is meant only for the protection of someone who accidentally killed another person, to prevent the manslayer from being killed by a kin of the person who lost his life in an act of retaliation outside of the judicial system. The defendant was temporarily protected in this way so that his case could be heard by an impartial body of elders. As Hoffmeier concludes: "Sanctuary was never intended as a place to avoid the law but to allow the law to takes [sic] its proper course."[55] In the Bible, sanctuary cities never had the function to protect illegal immigrants or immigrants who had been found guilty of a crime in court.[56] Moreover, the regulations concerning asylum cities were applicable only to Israelites and persons who were already established in the land (for some time) as sojourners; they had no role in deciding the question whether a new arrival had to be admitted to the land.[57]

3.13. An Example

The interpretation and use of Num 15:16 is an example for several of the deficiencies mentioned in this paragraph. The text reads:

> There is to be one law and one ordinance for you and for the alien who sojourns with you.[58]

This verse is often understood along the following lines:[59] The Israelites were supposed to grant general judicial equality to foreigners; and this is what should be done in modern societies as well. This interpretation

54. See, e.g., Beck, "Sanctuary," 132–45; Gonzales, "Sanctuary," 36–47. Cf. also Houston, *You Shall Love*, 160–62. While she basically supports the concept, she also notes that it is not sufficient and may have negative consequences, by potentially associating refugees with homicide (see *You Shall Love*, 161). What is ultimately needed, according to Houston, is "to challenge asylum policy and practice when it is seen to be unjust or inhumane" (*You Shall Love*, 161), and to fight inhospitable attitudes towards asylum-seekers on all levels (*You Shall Love*, 162).

55. Hoffmeier, *The Immigration Crisis*, 84.

56. *Pace* Beck, "Sanctuary," 136.

57. It is exactly the latter aspect that is promoted by advocates of the sanctuary movement; see, e.g., Gonzales, "Sanctuary," 36–37, 40. See also Beck, "Sanctuary," 138.

58. All translations are, if not indicated otherwise, based on the NASB 1977.

59. For examples see the comments on this and related verses in chapter 2 below.

is, however, not tenable. The Hebrew text uses the specific term *ger* ("so-journer"), a term that does not designate a "foreigner" in general, but a certain type of foreigner only: One who has come to Israel with the aim to settle for an extended period of time and to assimilate into the Israelite society. Furthermore, the verse, seen in context, does not refer to a general, sweeping judicial equality in the sense of the foreigner of the *ger*-type having exactly the same status before the law as the native Israelite. The formula "one law for the alien" only points to equal duties in those clearly defined areas in which the formula is used, not anything beyond this. And lastly, as mentioned before, the fact that this verse is part of a biblical law collection does not imply that it can be understood as positive civil law in the modern sense of the word.

2

Complexity of Views on Migration Attested in the Hebrew Bible

1. INTRODUCTION

THERE IS A DANGER to reduce the complexity and diversity of the biblical material concerning migration, by selecting only those texts that fit one's assumptions or agenda. For example, texts like Exod 22:20 ("you shall not wrong a stranger or oppress him") or Num 15:16 ("there is to be one law and one ordinance for you and for the alien who sojourns with you") are often dealt with as the only important texts deciding the matter, while texts that do not square well with such a view are sometimes left aside or overlooked, or subjected to the modern interpreter's *a priori* criticism, for example Deut 23:2–9 or Nehemiah 13, where the views expressed in the respective texts are denounced without being given a closer or fair hearing.[1]

What are basic concepts collected in the Hebrew Bible that deal in some way or another with migration—or more specifically with immigration, or more broadly with "otherness"? The remainder of this chapter presents a selection of important aspects that are pertinent to the issue.[2]

1. Such an approach can be found in, e.g., Bedford-Strohm, "Den Fremdling sollt ihr nicht bedrücken" [accessed September 23, 2016]); Carroll, "Welcoming," 441–61.

2. For reasons of space, it is not possible to explain the various aspects mentioned here in any detail or to discuss the relationship between them. The main point is more modest: To demonstrate the wide spectrum and variety of aspects that are represented by the diverse biblical voices.

These aspects will be studied on the literary-conceptual level only; this means that questions about the relationship between the texts and the historical situation in ancient Israel will generally not be investigated.

The Hebrew Bible as a whole and noticeably single literary entities within it make a clear distinction between different types of foreigners coming into contact with or living in Israel. Most often, differences are made between individuals without reference to their specific ethnic background—most noticeably the distinction between the *ger* ("sojourner") and the *nokri* ("foreigner); in some instances, however, specific ethnic labels are used, mostly—but not exclusively—when reference is made to groups of people as opposed to individuals. How far these two types of differentiation are thought to reflect one coherent system is difficult to assess. This question, however, cannot be investigated further in the present context.

Most studies on migration in the Hebrew Bible focus on the legal passages in the Pentateuch which mention the *ger*, a term that is translated variously as "resident alien," "sojourner," "stranger," or "immigrant." It is normally pointed out how much protection this type of (im)migrant receives in various legal texts. Regularly, the simple conclusion is that contemporary immigrants should receive the same benevolent treatment. While not wholly wrong, it is argued here that such a procedure is too simplistic and needs considerable modification. One of the reasons why this is the case is the observation that the texts dealing with migrants in the Hebrew Bible are much more complex than is normally perceived.

2. THE *GER* ("SOJOURNER") IN THE LEGAL COLLECTIONS AND BEYOND

2.1. General Remarks

As far as individuals are concerned, the two terms that are most prominent when it comes to reference to foreign person are *ger* and *nokri*.[3]

---

3. Another important term is *zar*. This term, however, is not used in the same way as *ger* and *nokri* with a clear combination of social and ethnic connotations, but rather as an adjective denoting foreignness and strangeness of various kinds. In a few cases, the plural *zarim* is used in ways that are more or less synonymous with *nokrim*. It may be that the noun *toshab* (often translated as "sojourner" or the like) which is often used in combination with *ger*, has a semantic range that comes close to *ger*; it is, however, used only infrequently and does not alter the overall picture.

More or less all biblical text corpora make a clear distinction between these two types of foreigners.

The *ger* is mentioned in all legal collections found in the Hebrew Bible, as well as in narrative and prophetic texts (and in fact also sporadically in Psalms and Job). For reasons of space, the following investigation will be restricted to the most important aspects appearing in the respective texts.

The noun *ger* likely refers to a person of foreign origin who immigrates into Israel because of war, famine, poverty, or impending debt slavery or the like. He is typically a person who has come to stay in Israel for an extended period of time; it seems that in many cases it is implied that he intends to become part of the Israelite society.[4] This implies a willingness to assimilate on all levels. On the other hand, the repeated references to the Israelites' stay in Egypt with the use of the term *ger*[5] can also intimate that a *ger* was expected to go back to his country of origin once the circumstances would allow him to do so, unless he decided to fully assimilate into Israelite society.

2.2. The Decalogue

The *ger* is mentioned once in the Decalogue, in a relatively marginal way (Exod 20:10; cf. Deut 5:14): The commandment concerning the Sabbath urges the addressee—likely the landowning adult free Israelite—to abstain from work on the seventh day; in the second part of the sentence that prohibits work, children, servants, chattel, and the *ger* are also included. It is possible to see this regulation as beneficial for the *ger*: As much as the members of an Israelite household, he may participate in the rest which the Sabbath grants. It is, however, also possible to reckon with an element of obligation: As much as the free Israelite man is prohibited to work on the Sabbath day, so is the *ger*. It is likely that the first aspect, granting rest, is more dominant than the second.[6] If there is an element

---

4. It must be pointed out, however, that there is an ongoing discussion as to whether the term *ger* in most of its attestations in Deuteronomy as well as in the Covenant Collection really refers to an ethnically non-Israelite person. The question is answered positively by, e.g., Krauss ("The Word 'GER' in the Bible," 264–70), and negatively by, e.g., Bultmann (*Der Fremde im antiken Juda*).

5. See Exod 22:20; 23:9: Lev 19:34; Deut 24:18, 22; 26:5.

6. For details see Zehnder, *Umgang mit Fremden*, 313–14.

of obligation, the simplistic view that the legal regulations are all about supporting the *ger* is already disturbed at this point.

2.3. The Covenant Collection

There are three verses in the Covenant Collection in which the *ger* is mentioned. In Exod 22:20 and 23:9, the addressees are enjoined not to "oppress" the *ger*. In Exod 23:12, the *ger* is mentioned, together with ox, donkey, and the son of the maidservant, as belonging to those who must be granted participation in the rest of the Sabbath. All three cases are clear instances of legal regulations that aim at protecting the *ger* from abuse.[7]

2.4. The Deuteronomic Laws

The Deuteronomic law collection (Deuteronomy 12–26), together with the stipulations found in additional parts of the book of Deuteronomy, contain the highest density of regulations that mention the *ger*.[8] These regulations can be classified in terms of topics as follows:[9]

- general measures of protection of the weak, with special focus on the judicial sphere (Deut 1:16; 24:[14.]17; 27:19);

- economic measures of promotion of the weak (Deut 14:28–29; 24:14, 19–22; 26:11–13);

- foundational principles of ethics: Command to love the *ger* (Deut 10:18–19);

- cultic regulations (Deut 14:21; 16:11, 14);

- establishment of the covenant and public reading of the Torah (Deut 29:10; 31:12–13).

---

7. For details see Zehnder, *Umgang mit Fremden*, 316–19. See also Houston, *You Shall Love*, 71–72. Her formulation that oppression "implies depriving a person of what is his or hers by right" (*You Shall Love*, 71) may be problematic insofar as it anachronistically imports current human-rights notions into the biblical texts.

8. For details see Zehnder, *Umgang mit Fremden*, 356–69.

9. Slightly different classifications can be made. See, e.g., Glanville, *Adopting the Stranger*, 43–263.

It is clear that the main interest of the Deuteronomic laws concerning the *ger* lies in the areas of economic promotion and judicial protection. Even the cultic laws have a social dimension: The fact that carcasses (*nebelah*) may be given to the *ger* (Deut 14:21) opens access to cheap meat for him; and the inclusion of the *ger* in the Feast of Weeks and the Feast of Booths (Deut 16:11, 14) has both socially and materially beneficial consequences for the *ger*. As Deut 24:14–15 shows, not heeding the prescriptions that protect and promote the *ger* is deemed a sin, and the abused *ger* can appeal directly to YHWH. Very importantly, the prohibition to oppress the *ger* found in the Covenant Collection is topped by the command to "love" him, which is explained as giving him bread and clothing (Deut 10:18).[10]

It has been claimed recently that the thrust of the Deuteronomic laws concerning the *ger* is to include him into the community of Israel.[11] It would go too far in the present context to discuss the merits and problems of this proposition in any detail.[12] The aspect of inclusion can perhaps best be seen in Deuteronomy 16, where the *ger* is included in the celebrations of the Feast of Weeks and the Feast of Tabernacles. The laws in Deuteronomy as a whole, however, do not open a path to full membership for anyone coming from outside, unless the person fully assimilates to Israel, including Israel's religion based on the covenant with YHWH. In practical terms, circumcision of males and intermarriage will be the main means through which someone transitions from the status of *ger* to the status of Israelite and member of the assembly of the Lord.

Besides the aspects of protection, support, and inclusion, there are, however, also other tendencies: In Deut 14:21, the *ger* is distinguished from the people of Israel, which is characterized as an *'am qadosh*, a "holy people"; and the inclusion in the covenant ceremony in Deut 29:10 and the public reading of the Torah in Deut 31:12–13 has clear connotations of obligation.[13] It is also noteworthy that the *ger* is not mentioned in the Passover celebration in Deut 16:1–7. Finally, in Deut 28:43 the *ger* is mentioned in the context of the curses which Israel has to face if they

10. See Zehnder, "Literary and Other Observations," 194–200. Cf. Glanville, *Adopting the Stranger*, 124–27. It is not clear why Houston (*You Shall Love*, 75) detaches the command to love the *ger* from the provision of material support.

11. See Glanville, *Adopting the Stranger*, 43–263.

12. For some remarks on Glanville's thesis see Zehnder, Review of *Adopting the Stranger*, 79–81.

13. See Zehnder, *Umgang mit Fremden*, 367–69.

do not follow the Lord's commandments: He will be elevated over the Israelites, a situation which is seen as a reversal of the normal state and the opposite of the situation in which the Israelites will find themselves when they are under God's blessing. This verse also does not reflect a view that either presupposes or envisions the inclusion of the *ger* as part of the Israelite community.[14]

In sum, protection, support, and inclusion (under certain conditions) are important aspects; on the other hand, they are not all there is in Deuteronomy as far as the *ger* is concerned.

2.5. The Priestly Laws (/Holiness Collection)

The regulations dealing with the *ger* in the priestly laws (Leviticus and Numbers, probably also some passages in Exodus) can be classified in terms of topics as follows:[15]

- general measures of protection of the weak (Lev 19:33);
- economic measures of promotion of the weak (Lev 19:10; 23:33);
- foundational principles of ethics: to love the *ger* (Lev 19:34);
- morals (Lev 18:26);
- civil law, relating to issues of bodily injury and inadvertent homicide (Lev 24:22; Num 35:15);
- cultic regulations (Exod 12:19, 43–49; Lev 16:29; 17; 18:26; 20:2; 22:18–25; 24:16; Num 9:14; 15:14–16; 19:10).

While, as in the case of the Deuteronomic laws, measures of protection and promotion of the *ger*, together with the command to love him, are found in the priestly laws (or more precisely: in the Holiness Collection) as well, the main focus is clearly on regulations concerning cultic issues.[16] As far as the latter are concerned, the picture may be summarized in the following way: Some of the stipulations in which the *ger* is mentioned open a door for him to participate in the Israelite cult, and

14. In an interesting twist, Houston in her reference to the verse stresses that "the author conveys a pointed awareness of where the *ger* is currently situated: at the bottom of the social scale" (*You Shall Love*, 76), implying that this situation should be amended.

15. Again, different classifications are possible.

16. For details see Zehnder, *Umgang mit Fremden*, 323–50.

regulate how this participation is to be enacted, in most cases by assigning him the same rights and duties as apply to the native Israelite. In these cases, participation in the cult of YHWH is an *optional* choice that the *ger* is offered. A second group of stipulations *oblige* the *ger* to follow some of the fundamental cultic laws that a native Israelite has to observe, irrespective of how much he wants to integrate into the congregation of the Israelites on the religious level. The obligation to follow a minimal amount of Yahwistic cultic prescriptions does not, however, imply that the *ger* is compelled to accept or practice the YHWH-religion as a whole. The stipulations that the *ger* has to observe mainly deal with the avoidance of any kind of "abomination" and with the extermination of every kind of guilt and impurity which, if not removed, would cause the land to "vomit" all of its inhabitants.[17] The *ger* is also requested to follow legal stipulations in cases where a deviant course of action on his side would affect the Israelite community as a whole and endanger the Israelites' faculty to keep God's commandments, which in turn would have negative consequences for the existence of Israel before God in the Promised Land. In practical terms, this means that generally the *ger* is included in the prohibitions, but not forced to observe the positive commandments.[18]

An example for the group of commandments that are optional for the *ger* to follow can be found in Lev 17:8–9, the regulations concerning burnt offerings and peace offerings: The *ger* is allowed (but not requested) to offer these sacrifices; if he decides to do so, he has to take them to the entrance of the holy tent, as all Israelites have to. Among the second group of cultic stipulations, the ones that are binding on each *ger*, we find especially the prohibition not to work on the Sabbath[19] and on Yom Kippur.[20]

It is in the context of the passages that offer the *ger* the option to participate in the Israelite cult if he wishes to do so that we find formulations such as "there shall be one law for you and the *ger*."[21] Formulations such as these are often understood as an expression of a complete judicial equality of the *ger* with the native-born Israelite, either generally or in the

---

17. See especially Lev 18:25, 28.

18. For details see Zehnder, *Umgang mit Fremden*, 327–40, 348–50.

19. See Exod 20:10; Deut 5:14. These commandments are part of the Decalogue and as such do, of course, not relate directly to the priestly laws.

20. See Leviticus 16.

21. See especially Lev 24:22; Num 9:14; 15:16.

(later layers of the) priestly laws.[22] These "inclusion formulas," as they are often called, are, however, not as sweepingly inclusive as it might appear: They refer to the *ger* only, not to any kind of foreigner, and they only state that in cases in which the *ger* wants to participate in the Israelite cult, in areas in which this is only a question of personal choice and not an obligation, the same rules apply to him as to the native Israelite, not stricter or more lenient rules.

The general focus of the regulations concerning the *ger* in the priestly laws is not on protection and support—even if these elements are not absent—, but on regulating his options and indeed duties in the cultic area.

There is an additional passage that has to be mentioned in this section in which the *ger* appears: In Lev 25:47–55 there is an extended paragraph that regulates the case in which an Israelite is compelled by adverse economic circumstances to sell himself to a *ger* who is in a strong position economically. If the financial means are made available, the respective Israelite can be redeemed without any waiting period, and he will go free in any event in the Year of Jubilee.[23] This points to a treatment of the *ger* that is distinct from the treatment of a native-born Israelite brother, and less favorable than in the case of dealings between Israelites. A similar pattern can be found in Lev 25:45, where Israelite landowners are permitted to acquire sojourners as slaves.[24]

2.6. General Observations on the *ger* in the Law Collections

Summarizing the legal injunctions concerning the *ger* in the various law collections, the following can be said:

To the degree that the *ger* is perceived as a person belonging to the socially weak, he is safeguarded by the law. The *ger* is entitled to many of

22. For a recent example see Beck, "Sanctuary," 134. For more details see Zehnder, *Umgang mit Fremden*, 340. Among those who misunderstand these passages in generalizing terms is also Hoffmeier (see *The Immigration Crisis*, 76–77, 154). On the other hand, his remark that the resident aliens "could not pick and choose which laws to obey" (*The Immigration Crisis*, 78) is obviously correct in general terms, particularly with a view to non-cultic regulations (and the obligatory part of the cultic regulations).

23. See also Zehnder, *Umgang mit Fremden*, 347–48.

24. Houston (*You Shall Love*, 79)—as opposed to most other commentators—does point to this last verse; however, it is treated by her as an isolated exception that only proves the rule of a "generally egalitarian nature of the relationship" between *ger* and Israelite.

the same measures that are meant to protect and further the well-being of the potentially weak members of the Israelite society, especially orphans and widows (and sometimes Levites). However, this does not imply a full legal equality with native Israelites, especially insofar as he is generally not an independent legal subject and not allowed to acquire land.[25] With respect to religion, the *ger* is prohibited to follow visibly deviant forms of worship and obliged to respect the basic rules of the Yahwistic religion; he is also invited to actively participate in the Israelite cult. As opposed to the former, however, the latter option is not compulsory. In practical terms, this means that generally the *ger* is included in the prohibitions, but not forced to observe the positive commandments. This system can be said to be one in which freedom of religion is granted *partially*. This is what one can expect in a society in which ethnic and religious identity are not clearly separated. The degree of freedom is, of course, lower than in modern liberal societies,[26] but higher than, e.g., in states that strictly follow(ed) the principle of *cuius regio eius religio* (lit. "whose realm, his religion").

The measures of support for the *ger* do not, with the exception of the tithe, include free gifts handed out to the recipients without any activity of their own; nor are certain amounts of the income given to central or local authorities to be redistributed by them.[27] The right to glean, for example, presupposes that the *ger* himself goes out on the fields and gathers what is necessary for his support. In the case of the tithe, the support consists of agricultural produce, shared with the *ger* and other persons of need locally, not redistributed nationally.

There are several cases in which the injunctions to treat the *ger* well are related to the Israelites' own experience as *gerim* in Egypt: Exod 22:20; 23:9; Lev 19:34; Deut 10:19; 24:18, 22. The reference to the stay of the forefathers as *gerim* in Egypt functions as a motivation to empathize with those who dwell among the Israelites as *gerim* and to heed the commands

25. See also Carroll: "Inheritance of property went along kinship lines . . . . As foreigners, they [i.e., the *gerim*] were excluded from the land-tenure system" (*Christians*, 88). On the other hand, he—wrongly—speaks about "their equal standing before the law" (*Christians*, 93). The latter formulation is replaced in *The Bible* by "their equal standing in the community" (*The Bible*, 71).

26. On the other hand, the degree of freedom of religion and worldview in general is obviously shrinking considerably under current circumstances both in the West and in various ways also in other parts of the world.

27. For a similar observation see Houston, *You Shall Love*, 74 (with specific reference to the tithe).

that aim at their protection and support.[28] It may also imply the expectation that once the situation allows the *ger* would leave Israel again.

2.7. The *ger* outside of the Law Collections

As we have seen, to the extent that the *ger* is perceived as a person belonging to the socially weak, he is safeguarded by the law, especially in the Covenant Collection and in Deuteronomy. This approach finds its correspondence in prophetic statements that criticize the abuse of the *ger* and other weak persons. The relevant passages are found in Jer 7:6; 22:3; Ezek 22:7, 29; Zech 7:10; and Mal 3:5.[29]

There are two passages in Psalms and one on Job which also express the thought that the *ger*, together with other weak persons, needs protection or receives special protection by God; see Ps 94:6; 146:9; Job 31:32. In addition, 2 Chr 30:25 notes that *gerim* were present at the celebration of the Feast of Unleavened Bread during the reign of Hezekiah.

On the other hand, according to 1 Chr 22:2 and 2 Chr 2:17, *gerim* were used to perform forced labor under both David and Solomon. It is not fully clear, however, whether this is seen as ethically commendable by the narrator(s) or not.

Some valuable information about the *ger* can also be gleaned by looking at the patriarchal stories. Abraham calls himself a *ger* in Gen 23:3–4. This passage makes clear that he "recognized that he was an immigrant or alien who needed to accommodate to the laws and norms of the land."[30] The implication is also that permission for the temporary settling is needed. This is confirmed in the case of the settling of the extended family of Joseph in Egypt, see Gen 47:1–6.[31]

---

28. In a critical reconstruction of the history behind the texts, it is the experience of exile in Babylon that informs the readers, rather than the stay of the patriarchs and the nascent people in Egypt; see, e.g., Houston, *You Shall Love*, 75. Such reconstructions remain, however, speculative.

29. See also Zehnder, *Umgang mit Fremden*, 422–25.

30. Hoffmeier, *The Immigration Crisis*, 48.

31. See Hoffmeier, *The Immigration Crisis*, 55. He also observes that the pharaoh "did not want a group of people entering Egypt to become financially and economically dependent on the governmental resources" (*The Immigration Crisis*, 56), as can be seen from the king's questions about their occupation and the references to the flocks and herds of Jacob's family.

3. THE *NOKRI* ("FOREIGNER") IN THE LEGAL COLLECTIONS AND BEYOND

3.1. General Remarks

Besides the *ger*, there is another type of migrant, called *nokri* or *nekar* or *ben-(ha)nekar*. These terms are usually translated as "foreigner" or "stranger." Such foreigners, much like a *ger*, are not legal subjects who could stand for themselves in court; and the acquisition of land within the areas allotted to the Israelite tribes is not open to them.[32] The social position of the *nokri* becomes clear mostly from his appearance in the Deuteronomic laws. The noun *nokri* refers to a type of foreigner who comes to Israel not to seek permanent residency, but to stay there temporarily, in a typical case as a person involved in trade. He remains emotionally, culturally, and religiously in some distance to the receiving society.

3.2. The Deuteronomic Laws

The *nokri* is mentioned four times in the Deuteronomic laws:[33]

The *nokri* is the one to whom, according to Deut 14:21, the corpses of animals that have not been ritually slaughtered may be sold for him to eat, while this kind of meat may be given to the *ger* without him being charged for it; the Israelite, on the other hand, is forbidden to eat such meat. In this passage, the *nokri* is seen as being further removed from the community of Israel than the *ger*, and not being in a materially weak position.

The *nokri* is also mentioned in Deut 17:15 where it is stated that no *nokri* must be allowed to become king over Israel. Again, the aspect of distance from the community of Israel is apparent.

According to Deut 15:3, the remission of debt that must be granted to the fellow Israelite in the Sabbatical Year does not apply to the *nokri*. And according to Deut 23:20–21, it is permitted to charge interests on loans granted to a *nokri*, while this is not allowed with loans given to a

---

32. There is one attestation of *nokri*, in the compound *'am nokri* ("foreign people"), in the Covenant Collection (Exod 21:8). It does not add anything to the discussion below; *nokri* simply introduces the notion of foreignness, standing outside the people of Israel.

33. For more details see Zehnder, *Umgang mit Fremden*, 358–59, 369–73.

fellow Israelite, called "brother" ('ach).[34] These last two commandments
have the same thrust: The *nokri* must not be covered by regulations that
aim at protecting the fellow Israelite. The rationale behind this regulation
is clear: The *nokri* stands in a relatively distanced position both to the
people of Israel and to Yahwism; therefore, special measures aimed at
protecting the members of the ethnic-religious community of Israel—
and by extension the *ger*—economically do not apply to him. Rather, he
is treated according to the internationally valid conditions informing the
ancient Near Eastern credit system. If the specific measures intended to
protect the Israelites economically were extended to the *nokri*, he would
in fact be granted a one-sided economic advantage; for the *nokri* himself,
by not being bound by the laws of Deuteronomy, did not have to observe
a prohibition on interests vis-à-vis an Israelite loan taker, and he did not
have to forgo debts in the Sabbatical Year. Moreover, it is possible that the
nokri continued to entertain close relations with his country of origin,
which would mean that he was not dependent on the internal economic
situation in the same way as his Israelite neighbor. In this case, the difference being made between an Israelite and a *nokri* can be explained by the
necessity to grant special economic protection for those being confined
to the interior Israelite economy and prevent their being exploited by
high interest rates in times of crises by persons wielding more financial
resources. It is also possible that the difference between a *nokri* and an
Israelite in terms of regulations of economic protection is based on the
perception that loans granted to a fellow Israelite are usually measures
to grant survival in situations of pressing need, while loans to a *nokri* are
typically granted in the framework of ordinary business relations.[35]

On a more general level, the exclusion of the *nokri* from the economic measures of promotion and protection for the Israelites and the
gerim can be explained as follows: The regulations concerning these measures are rooted in the special covenantal relationship between YHWH
and his people. The natural consequence of this relation is that special
measures of promotion and protection as much as cultic obligations only
apply to the elected people. The restriction of such measures to Israelites
and *gerim* and the concomitant exclusion of the *nokri* from them can
therefore not be described as expressing a "discriminatory" attitude in

---

34. It is possible that Lev 25:35 implies or ordains that also a *ger* must not be sub-
mitted to interest payments for loans; but this is not certain. Cf. the comments in
Milgrom, *Leviticus 23–27*, 2204–12.

35. See Zehnder, *Umgang mit Fremden*, 370–71.

the negative meaning of the term; for we are not dealing with a case of random exclusion of foreigners, but rather with a correspondence between promotion and protection on the one hand and integration on the other hand, with the degree of integration into the Israelite community being left at the foreigner's discretion.

3.3. The Priestly Laws (/ Holiness Collection)

The *ben-nekar* is mentioned twice in priestly laws or laws commonly reckoned as "priestly." According to Exod 12:43, he is not allowed to eat of the Passover. Leviticus 22:25 forbids the Israelites to buy (defect) animals from a foreigner to offer them to YHWH.[36] What transpires primarily is again the distance between a *ben-nekar* and the community of the Israelites.

3.4. General Observations on the *nokri* in the Law Collections

As opposed to a *ger*, a *nokri* (/*ben-nekar*) remains in greater distance to Israel both socially and religiously. However, even if a foreigner decides to do so, this does not mean that he can just do what he wants and live in a wholly independent parallel society. The civil law is certainly binding on him as well in its entirety, and even in the religious realm he is likely to be subject to a number of regulations that will limit foreign religious practice to a considerable degree. When special rights are conceded to foreigners on the practical level that encourage them to continue non-Israelite religious practices, this is regularly condemned by the biblical authors.[37] Nor, in fact, are there cases in which they are seen as promoting any kind of interreligious dialogue in the (post)modern understanding of this expression.

3.5. The *nokri* outside of the Law Collections

The terms *nokri* and *nekar* are used much more frequently outside of the law collections than within them. In most cases, they have the connotation of foreignness in the sense of distance towards Israel. There

36. On these two passages see the comments in Zehnder, *Umgang mit Fremden,* 333–35, 339–40.

37. See, e.g., 1 Kings 11; 16:29–33.

are almost no instances that add to the picture that can be gained from looking at the attestations of *nokri* (or *ben-nekar*) within the law collections. Nevertheless, there are some occurrences that are noteworthy: In 1 Kgs 8:41, 43,[38] in the context of Solomon's prayer of dedication for the newly built temple, he (or the author of this passage) expresses the expectation that a *nokri* will come from a distant country and will pray to YHWH. The *nokri* is here still conceived of as a non-Israelite foreigner, but it is envisioned that he will enter in a (relatively) close relationship with YHWH. Importantly, however, this relationship is not combined with a permanent residence in the land of Israel. A different picture is drawn in 1 Kgs 11:1, 8: The foreign women whom Solomon marries do not let go their non-Yahwistic religious affiliations, and instead of turning to YHWH induce Solomon to become a syncretist and support their foreign cults. As far as the prophetic writings are concerned, the general tone of the use of the terms is negative: *nokri* and *nekar* denote things or persons that Israel should distance itself from, but fails to do so; see Isa 2:6; Jer 2:21; Ezek 44:7, 9; Zeph 1:8.[39] Turning to the book of Psalms, we find the most noteworthy attestation of *nekar* in Ps 144:7, 11, where the psalmist cries out in supplication to God to deliver him from the hands of *beney-nekar*. In Proverbs, the term *nokri* is used predominantly in its feminine form (*nokriah*), to denote the "strange woman"; see Prov 2:16; 5:20; 6:24; 7:5; 23:27; 27:13. Also the attestation of the term in Ruth 2:10 is interesting. Ruth refers to herself as *nokriah*, though she would in fact be a prime example of a *ger*, given the fact that she attaches herself completely to the people of Israel and the God of Israel, taking permanent residence in the land of Israel. It is likely that she uses the term as a way to express humbleness and modesty.[40] One should also note that the noun *ger* is not attested in the feminine, and is never explicitly used to refer to a woman.[41] Foreign women are also referred to with the term *nokriah*

38. See also 2 Chr 6:32–33.

39. For the uses of *nekar* in prophetic texts that can be classified as eschatological, see below.

40. Hoffmeier explains the use of the terms in the following way: "Perhaps Ruth did not realize that in Israel, thanks to the special protective status of the alien in biblical law, she had a right to glean the fields. Alternatively, she may have used the term in self-deprecating manner in order to accentuate the generosity of Boaz" (*The Immigration Crisis*, 105).

41. This does not in itself exclude the possibility that there might have been women included in the category of *ger*, as for example Glanville proposes (see Glanville, *Adopting the Stranger*, 230). The matter is, however, difficult to decide.

several times in Ezra 10:2–18, 44 and Neh 13:27. These women are the wives of Judahites, who are summoned to send them away, in order to protect the integrity of the congregation. The reason must be that the foreign wives were not willing to let go their non-Yahwistic religious affiliations.[42] Separation from "all foreigners" and "all things foreign" is the topic of Neh 9:2 (*kol beney nekar*) and 13:30 (*kol nekar*).[43]

3.6. General Observations on the Use of the Terms *ger* and *nokri*

a) The distinctive use of the terms *ger* and *nokri* (/*nekar*) demonstrates that there is in the Hebrew Bible no real general category of "foreigner" that does not take into consideration differences of background on the one hand and assimilation on the other when it comes to the regulation of the status of foreigners. This stands in contrast to the postmodern theoretical principle of a general prohibition against "discrimination," that is, to treat differently people with different ethnic or other backgrounds and different dispositions towards the receiving society.[44]

b) In the case of ancient Israel, assimilation is seen as positive and necessary for those who have come to stay (*ger*).

c) Depending on the realm of life and on the degree of assimilation, entitlements given to and obligations laid upon a foreigner vary. Foreigners of the *nokri*-type who do not commit themselves fully to a life in Israelite society are exempted from specific measures of support and promotion like debt relief in the Sabbatical Year or prohibition of interests on loans (Deut 15:3; 23:20–21). There is a clear correspondence between the degree to which a foreigner is willing to assimilate, and the degree to which the Israelites will absorb and integrate him. This is different from current models that attempt to use the giving of rights to unadapted or barely adapted foreigners as a *means* to promote their integration.

---

42. For more details see below.

43. For more details see below.

44. This principle, however, is often more theoretical than practical, because in all cases of a state's attempt to guarantee factual results and not only equal opportunities, by implementing various kinds of affirmative action, an element of different treatment, that is, "discrimination," based on different ethnic or other backgrounds, is necessarily involved.

d) The laws concerning the *ger* and the *nokri* cannot in any direct way be transferred to the present, because they make sense only within the social and theological system of ancient Israel as a whole, and because they have in view a very limited number of individuals, not scenarios involving mass-(im)migration.

4. SOME OBSERVATIONS CONCERNING ISRAEL'S DEALINGS WITH OTHER FOREIGNERS/MIGRANTS[45]

4.1. Legal Prescriptions

4.1.1. Law concerning Admission to the Assembly of the LORD (Deuteronomy 23:2–9)

A text such as Deut 23:2–9 shows that distinctions could be made not only on a general level between an individual *ger* and an individual *nokri*, but also with respect to specific ethnic groups.[46] In this passage, Ammonites, Moabites, and Egyptians are singled out for special treatment, based on historical encounters between them and Israel in the past, either of a negative or a positive character. Also the Edomites are referred to in this passage, with the treatment prescribed for them based on ethnic proximity. Remarkably, theological criteria are not mentioned explicitly in these cases, which gives the passage a somewhat "nationalistic" outlook as seen from a modern perspective. The Israelites seem to feel free to "discriminate," that is, make distinctions, based on both ethnic considerations and historical experience.

Deuteronomy 23:2–9 is important also in other respects. The passage seems to regulate admission to the religious community of Israel, which would be at the same time admission to the class of "citizens" enjoying full rights, presupposing that people may live on Israelite territory and yet not be full members of the congregation. If this interpretation is

---

45. In this section, observations will be adduced concerning passages in the Hebrew Bible that deal with cases that are not covered by the terms *ger* or *nokri*. It is neither possible nor necessary in the present context to aim at comprehensiveness; rather, the observations will demonstrate the complexity of the dealing with various types of foreigners reflected in the relevant texts.

46. For a more comprehensive discussion of this passage see, e.g., Tigay, *Deuteronomy*, 210–13; Zehnder, "Anstösse aus Dtn 23,2–9," 300–314; Zehnder, *Umgang mit Fremden*, 373–80.

correct, it would point to the fact that there was a distinction between right of residence on the one hand and full citizenship on the other hand, a distinction which in some cases would be tantamount to the indefinite exclusion of some people groups from "citizenship" based on their ethnic background. There is no political program in view here dictating that the receiving society must guarantee full integration for everybody at least in the long term. On the other hand, the implicit message seems to be that no one is in principle prohibited from taking residence in Israel.

While Ammonites and Moabites—perhaps only male Ammonites and Moabites—are excluded from the "assembly of the LORD" in perpetuity, things look different for Edomites and Egyptians: they are given permission to join in the third generation. This is one of the relatively few passages that explicitly open avenues for outsiders to be grafted into Israel, showing that ethnic boundaries are by no means seen as insurmountable.

Finally, the point that one element of the reason why Ammonites and Moabites are not allowed to enter the "assembly of the LORD" is their failure to support the Israelites on their way to the Promised Land with food and water may well be taken as relevant for migration issues in general: Migrants—as long as they do not pose a threat to the security of the places through which they transit—must be treated decently and provided with the basic supplies for survival. On the other hand, this is clearly not the same as an obligation to accept them as permanent immigrants.

4.1.2. Law concerning Amalekites (Deuteronomy 25:17–19)

Besides the ethnic groups that are mentioned in Deuteronomy 23, we find other groups singled out for special treatment. A prime example are the Canaanite peoples and the Amalekites, also mentioned in the book of Deuteronomy. As far as the Amalekites are concerned, the Israelites are requested to destroy their "remembrance" (*seker*). The main reason given for this is that Amalek behaved in a treacherous and insidious way when they opposed the Israelites after the latter had left Egypt. In Deuteronomy 25 their action was seen as opposed to fundamental humanitarian and moral rules, attacking a fleeing people, and especially non-combatants, on their way. The addition in v. 18b "and he did not fear God" (*welo' yare' 'elohim*) adds the nuance of a lack of basic fear of God which can be expected also from non-Israelites. Similarly to what can be found in Deuteronomy 23, past historic experience is used as a determining factor in organizing the relationship with a specific ethnic group both in the present and in the future, in this case not only in terms of exclusion from "citizenship," but even extinguishing their remembrance from the face of the earth. This is one further case in which the concept of "welcoming the stranger" is clearly not at work.

4.1.3. Laws concerning Canaanites (Exodus 23:23–33; 34:11–16; Numbers 33:50–56; Deuteronomy 7:1–5; 20:15/16–18)

According to a number of passages in the books of Exodus, Numbers, and Deuteronomy, the Israelites are requested to expel the Canaanite peoples and destroy their cultic installations.[47] Abstention from treaties and intermarriage are also commanded. According to some passages in Deuteronomy, they even have to subject the Canaanite peoples to the "ban" (cherem),[48] which probably implies the annihilation of these peoples at least if they do not submit themselves to Israel and her God.[49] The main reason for the command to treat the Canaanite peoples in this way is double-edged: God's punishment shall be enacted on a group of peoples who have sinned against him in a particularly odious way;[50] most importantly, the Israelites are prevented from being snared by the Canaanites' deviant but potentially attractive religious practices—which of course is a precondition for the Israelites being able to serve as God's model people for other nations.[51] This shows that the rationale for the special treatment of the Canaanite peoples has nothing to do with their ethnicity—and the concomitant protection of "ethnic purity" on the side of the Israelites—but is related to the religious level. This is confirmed by the observation that the ban is also imposed on Israelites in case of

---

47. For details see Zehnder, *Umgang mit Fremden*, 388–400. As far as the destruction of the cultic installations of the Canaanite peoples is concerned, see also Deuteronomy 12.

48. See Deut 7:2, 26; 20:17; cf. also Num 21:3; Deut 2:34; 3:6.

49. For details see, e.g., Cowles et al., *Show Them No Mercy*; Hess, "War," 19–32; Hoffman, "The Deuteronomistic Concept," 196–210; Zehnder, "The Annihilation of the Canaanites," 263–90; Zehnder, *Umgang mit Fremden*, 388–93.

50. See Deut 9:4–5; cf. Gen 15:16. The use of the term *toʿebah* ("abomination") in Deut 7:25–26 and 20:18 points in the same direction. Walton, however, rejects the view that there is any notion of punishment present in the commands to expel the Canaanites; see Walton and Walton, *The Lost World*, 50–63, 137–56.

51. Cf. especially Exod 19:6; Isa 42:1, 4, 6; 49:6.

apostasy, see Deut 13:13–19.[52] The religious dimension, while dominant, is likely not the only one. According to Num 33:55, if the Canaanite peoples are not expelled, they "will become as pricks in your eyes and as thorns in your sides, and they shall trouble you in the land in which you live." This points to a military-political motive.

There are good reasons for the argument that not only the killing, but also the expulsion of the Canaanites was only a conditional ordinance: Only if they were not willing to submit themselves to Israel, accept their rule over the country, and assimilate at least to a considerable degree also religiously, would they face expulsion. What needed to be terminated was not the Canaanite peoples as such, but Canaanite religion and their political, military, and social dominance.[53] This view is supported by the commandments found in Josh 23:7, 11–13. They enjoin only separation from the Canaanite peoples, not expulsion or extinction. While this reading of the laws points to a higher degree of clemency towards the Canaanites, it still remains the case that the transition of ownership of the country was non-negotiable.

The importance of the religious separation is underlined by the fact that it is mentioned numerous times in the legal collections, also outside of the passages pointed to above.[54] What is important is that the separation can normally not be restricted to what is called in our context "religion," but also includes "culture" more generally, at least to the degree that it has religious and moral implications.

As opposed to the cases of the *ger* and the *nokri*, it is clear that the special treatment envisioned for specific ethnic groups cannot be generalized and taken as a model that can be applied one-to-one in other circumstances even within the context of the biblical framework. This is true not only for the nations mentioned in Deuteronomy 23, but also for the Amalekites and the Canaanite peoples.

---

52. See also Exod 22:19. Both the execution of Achan and his family in Joshua 7 and of the Ba'al-worshippers in 2 Kings 9–10 point in the same direction, even if the root *ch-r-m* is not used.

53. See Zehnder, "The Annihilation of the Canaanites," 278–79.

54. See especially Exod 20:3–5, 23; 22:19; 23:13; 34:17; Lev 18:21; 19:4; 20:2; 26:1; Deut 4:16–19, 23, 25; 5:7–9; 6:14; 8:19; 11:16, 28; 12:2–3, 29–31; 13:3, 7, 14; 14:1–2; 16:22; 17:3; 18:9–14, 20; 27:15; 28:14; 29:17, 25; 30:17; 31:18, 20; 32:16–17, 21, 37–38. In many cases, it is not just Canaanite cultic installations and practices that are in view, but non-Yahwistic cults in general.

4.1.4. Laws concerning Warfare against Foreign Nations (Deuteronomy 20:1–14/15, 19–20; 21:10–14)

Deuteronomy 20 deals with issues of war, both in general and also specifically wars against the pre-Israelite inhabitants of the Promised Land.[55] The first verse opens with the particle *ki*, which can best be interpreted as "when." This means that it is assumed that war is likely to occur once the Israelites set foot on the Promised Land and establish themselves in it. The main thrust of vv. 1–4 is to exhort the Israelites not to be afraid when they (have to) go to war, because YHWH will be with them and will fight for them himself. The introduction in v. 1 that points to the fear-inspiring numerical superiority of the enemy makes it likely that defensive wars are in view. According to Deut 20:10–14/15, the Israelites have to offer *shalom* ("peace") to cities outside of the Promised Land in the case of war. This *shalom* includes the unconditional surrender of the enemy and the imposition of *mas* ("forced labor"). In effect, the enemy city would become a kind of vassal of the Israelites. If the respective city does not accept these conditions, the Israelites are enjoined, if they win, to subject the city to the following treatment: killing of its adult male inhabitants, and taking as booty the other inhabitants as well as livestock and material possessions. This is relatively humane in comparison to what seems to have been common praxis outside of Israel in the ancient Near East, namely, to kill not only adult men, but also non-combatants such as women and children.[56] Verses 19–20 add a regulation concerning the dealing with fruit trees in the surroundings of a beleaguered city: They may be used as providers of food, but it is forbidden to cut them. This is again much more humane than what we find outside of Israel: "It was common practice in ancient warfare to destroy the enemy's fruit trees and fields. This weakened its economic potential and hampered its ability to fight again in the near future. It may also have been intended to pressure besieged cities into surrendering before they suffered such long-term damage."[57]

While it may seem at first sight that Deuteronomy 20 does not have to say much about migration issues, it is nevertheless related to the topic in two important ways: The chapter demonstrates that the assertion of

55. That is, the "Canaanites."

56. Cf. 2 Kgs 8:12; Hos 14:1; Amos 1:3, 13. For details see Zehnder, *Umgang mit Fremden*, 102–12, 120–90, 385.

57. Tigay, *Deuteronomy*, 190. See also Zehnder, *Umgang mit Fremden*, 103.

the sovereignty of Israel as a fully independent nation and the protection of her borders, if necessary by the use of military means, is completely legitimate, and in fact divinely ordained. Secondly, the fact that the regulations stand out as particularly humane in the historical context of the ancient Near East is also important, because it testifies to a perspective of the "other," even the enemy "other," as someone who has to be treated with a remarkable degree of fairness and decency, and even some concern for their future well-being.

A second law that needs to be mentioned in this section is the law concerning the dealing with female prisoners of war, Deut 21:10–14. This law is closely related to Deut 20:12–14. It presupposes a situation in which the Israelites are at war with a city outside of the Promised Land and conquer it. It regulates the case in which an Israelite wants to take one of the female prisoners of war as a wife.[58] The law presupposes that such a way of action is in principle legitimate, but subject to the observance of certain procedures: The respective woman has to cut her hair and nails and change clothes, and then be granted a period of roughly one month during which she will weep for her father and mother. Only afterwards can she be taken as a wife and the marriage be consumed. "The object of the provision is evidently . . . to give her time to become reconciled to her separation from her parents . . . and her own people, and to accustom herself to her new surroundings, into which she has been brought against her will."[59] The last part of the law (v. 14) stipulates that in case the respective Israelite man gets weary of his wife, he is not allowed to reduce her to slavery or sell her; rather, he has to divorce her legally so that she is free to go where she wishes.

As in the case of the regulations in Deuteronomy 20, it seems at first sight that the law of Deut 21:10–14 has little to do with migration. It is, however, connected to the topic in two ways: It demonstrates that even the particular group of forced migrants/immigrants that is constituted by (female) prisoners of war has to be treated with an unusual degree of respect and dignity. On the other hand, it shows not only that Israel felt entitled to defend herself with the use of force, but also to force individuals

58. The term *ishshah* ("woman," "wife") used in vv. 11 and 13 likely implies that she has the position of a full wife, not just a concubine. There are, however, those who assume that she might in fact be a *pilegesh*, a wife of second degree, which would liken her position to the captive women of cuneiform documents (see Feigin, "The Captives," 244–45).

59. Driver, *Deuteronomy*, 245.

who belonged to a people who was an enemy in war to fill roles assigned to them regardless of their individual consent. Finally, it supports the view that the prohibition against intermarriage was really only directed at members of the Canaanite peoples.

4.2. Select Observations concerning the Dealings with Other Foreigners/Migrants through History

4.2.1. Pre-Monarchic Period[60]

From the very beginning of the patriarchal stories, we see the patriarchs dwelling as strangers in various places, both in Syria, Canaan, and Egypt. The stories depict them as hospitable and being in friendly relations with the various owners of their dwelling places.[61]

Several texts mention the presence of foreigners among the Israelites during the exodus from Egypt and the subsequent period of wanderings through the desert on the way to the Promised Land: Exodus 12:38 ("a mixed multitude"), Lev 24:10–12 (a case of mixed marriage between an Israelite woman and an Egyptian man), Num 11:4 (a "rabble" of foreigners among the Israelites), Num 10:29–32 (the Midianite Hobab), Num 12:1 (a case of mixed marriage involving Moses and a Cushite woman), Num 32:12 (Caleb, the son of Jephunneh the Kenizzite; see also Josh 14:6, 14). The Kenites, who are depicted as descendants of the Midianite Hobab, assimilate into Israel. In addition, Josh 8:33–35 and 20:9 mention the *ger* as being present among the Israelites.

Besides this, many stories tell about violent encounters with various foreign rulers and peoples: Amalekites (Exod 17:8–16); the king of Arad (Num 21:1–3);[62] Sihon of Heshbon (Num 21:21–31; Deut 2:26–36); Og of Bashan (Num 21:33–35; Deut 3:1–13); Moabites and Midianites (Numbers 25); and Midianites alone (Numbers 31). The military clashes are either of a defensive character or part of the divinely ordained conquest of territory in the area of the Promised Land. The encounters with

---

60. For details see Zehnder, *Umgang mit Fremden*, 402–7, 448–54, 482–92.

61. For examples of hospitality see Genesis 18 (Abraham and the three unknown visitors) and 19 (Lot and the two unknown visitors).

62. This is the first incident in which reference is made to the execution of the *cherem* ("ban").

Edomites, Ammonites, and Moabites show hostility from the side of these peoples against the Israelites, but God does not allow a violent response (Num 21:14–21; Deut 2:1–9, 19, 29). In the case of the Moabites and Midianites in Numbers 25, the main issue is mixed marriages combined with syncretism and apostasy—which (in the view of the main protagonists as depicted by the biblical author[s]) cannot be tolerated. Numbers 31:18, referring to the violent revenge taken on the Midianites, is important in the sense that it shows that foreign virgins could be accepted as wives into the people of Israel—much in line with the regulation found in Deut 21:10–14.

Most room is given to the reports concerning the conquest of the Promised Land, found in the book of Joshua.[63] While the *cherem* ("ban") is mentioned already in the context of the first campaign, directed at Jericho (see Josh 6:17–18, 21), this incident is important also in a different way: Much space is given to the special treatment of Rahab and her family (see Joshua 2; 6:23, 25). Because of her allegiance to the Israelites and their God, she and her family are not only spared, but actually integrated into the people of God, even if in a somewhat distinct position.[64]

The report of the conquest of Jericho is followed by the one of Ai (Joshua 7–8). After this follows the lengthy story about the encounter with the Gibeonites (Joshua 9). Again, as in the case of Rahab and her family, Canaanites who submit themselves to the Israelites are spared and integrated into the people of God in a distinct position.[65] Both examples demonstrate that it is possible to join Israel regardless of ethnic background; the condition is acceptance of the rule of Israel on the territory of the Promised Land and of Israel's God.

Joshua 10 and 11 describe how the Israelites under the leadership of Joshua manage to defeat those Canaanite rulers who resist the shift of ownership of the land from the Canaanites to the Israelites, with the execution of the ban mentioned several times.[66] The passage found in Josh 11:16–20 is of particular importance. The execution of the ban is explained as a consequence of the respective towns not to be willing to

---

63. For details see Zehnder, "The Annihilation of the Canaanites."

64. For details see Zehnder, *Umgang mit Fremden*, 483–85.

65. For details see Zehnder, *Umgang mit Fremden*, 490–92. According to 2 Sam 21:2, Saul attempts to exterminate the Gibeonites. His position is, however, not approved of by the biblical author.

66. For details see Zehnder, "The Annihilation of the Canaanites," 283–86; Zehnder, *Umgang mit Fremden*, 486–87.

accept Israel's rule in a peaceful way. The negative response of the Canaanites, in turn, is related to YHWH's hardening of their hearts. What transpires here is that there was no genocidal intention to annihilate all the Canaanites, based on ethnic differences. Rather, despite ethnic differences, Canaanites would have been allowed to remain in the Promised Land, had they been willing to submit to the Israelites and their God. The real issue, then, is not of an ethnic, but of a political and a religious nature. As long as foreigners do not pose either a political or religious threat, that is, as long as Israel's sovereignty and religious integrity are not endangered, foreigners are tolerated and my indeed become part of the people. Translated into modern categories, it is not ethnic background, but religious and cultural assimilation and politico-military subordination that determine the relationship between Israel and the foreign "other."

Mention of various Canaanite groups or individuals in biblical texts still living in the country after the invasion of the Israelites demonstrate that there was no complete expulsion or annihilation of the pre-Israelite inhabitants of the Promised Land;[67] archaeological evidence of the centuries-long coexistence of Canaanite with Israelite settlements points in the same direction.[68] Eventually, these Canaanite groups and individuals obviously assimilated into Israel, with intermarriage being very likely one of the most important means by which this state was achieved.[69]

With regards the period of the judges, the main pattern looks as follows: Because of the disobedience of the Israelites, YHWH allows foreign peoples to oppress them on the territory of the Promised Land: Philistines (Judg 3:31; 10:7–8; 13–16); Midianites (Judges 6–8); Ammonites (Judg 3:13; 10–11); Aramaeans (Judg 3:8–10); Moabites (Judg 3:12–30); and Amalekites (Judg 3:13; 6:3). YHWH uses inspired judges to lead the Israelites to—mostly violent—resistance against the oppressors. Evidently, there is a clear sense of ethnic difference that distinguishes the Israelite tribes from the non-Israelites, and a desire to defend their political independence. Except for the Danites' conquest of the city of Laish all the violent encounters are defensive in character. In addition, we read about further cases of mixed marriages. Shamgar's mother is likely a Canaanite

67. See, e.g., Josh 16:10; 17:13; Judges 1; 2 Sam 5:6–10; 1 Kgs 9:16, 20–21.

68. See, e.g., Faust, "Ethnic Complexity," 2–27.

69. See, e.g., Pitkänen, "Ethnicity," 179. For intermarriage see especially Judg 3:6. Other means may also have been at play; however, neither the biblical texts nor extra-biblical evidence provide clear information about this.

woman (Judg 3:31).[70] Probably, also Gideon's *pilegesh* ("concubine") from Sichem is a Canaanite woman. Later, in Judges 14, Samson wants to marry a Philistine woman (14:2); his parents, however, would prefer him to take an Israelite wife (14:3); but he does not listen to them and proceeds with his original plans.

Very instructive is the story contained in the book of Ruth.[71] The book is often referred to as an example for the importance of a welcoming attitude towards immigrants in the current situation;[72] this interpretation needs, however, considerable modification, as we shall see. According to the storyline of the book, a couple from Bethlehem, in order to avoid starvation, settles in Moab, and their two sons marry Moabite women (Ruth 1:4). Finally, one of these women, Ruth, widowed in the meantime, accompanies her mother-in-law when she resettles in Bethlehem (Ruth 1:16). Ruth will eventually be married by a Judahite. In the context of the present investigation, this story is important especially in two ways: It shows the willingness to accept non-Israelites as marriage partners, and the willingness to accept a foreigner as a permanent resident of the own country (Judah). As far as the former is concerned: Clearly in the case of the marriage between the Bethlehemite Boaz and Ruth, both partners share the Yahwistic religion. It is likely that in the case of the marriage between the two Judahite expatriate men and their Moabite women, their households would also be Yahwistic, regardless of the inner convictions of the wives.[73] As far as the acceptance of Ruth in Bethlehem goes: Her case is special in the sense that it concerns only one person, and a person who is already part of a Judahite family through marriage, and—in addition—has professed loyalty to the God of Israel.[74] All of these elements

70. As can be deduced from her name which refers to the Canaanite goddess Anath. Summarily, Judg 3:5–6 mentions, in the context of a negative evaluation, mixed marriages between Israelites and Canaanites.

71. The book claims to inform the reader about circumstances during the period of the Judges. Whether this is historically plausible is a matter of ongoing debate.

72. See, e.g., Carroll, *Christians*, 55–58; cf. also Houston, who devotes a lengthy paragraph to this book (see *You Shall Love*, 83–91). Houston underlines, i.a., the live-giving potential of the immigrant (see *You Shall Love*, 86, 92).

73. This point is, however, not absolutely certain.

74. It is extremely unlikely that there is a tension between the acceptance of Ruth in Bethlehem and the regulation concerning the admittance of Moabites into the *qehal YHWH* ("the congregation of the LORD") in Deut 23:3 (*pace*, e.g., Carroll, *Christians*, 56, 93); see Zehnder, *Umgang mit Fremden*, 406.

make her case in fact rather distinct from the overwhelming circumstances in current cases of immigration.

In fact, it may well be that the story contains elements that are more critical towards both migration and intermarriage: If the analysis that the book of Ruth follows the sequence of laws found in Deut 24:6 through 25:7 is correct,[75] the reports concerning the death of Elimelekh on the one hand and his sons Machlon and Chilion on the other may not be as neutral as is commonly assumed. Rather, these deaths can be interpreted in light of Deut 24:16,[76] and therefore connote some kind of punishment: Elimelekh's death is related to him having abandoned his land and people, while the death of his sons is related to them having married Moabite women.[77]

4.2.2. Monarchic Period[78]

The topic of violent clashes with the Philistines, who control parts of the territory of the Promised Land, continues after the period of the judges, into the reigns of Saul and David (see 1 Samuel 13–14; 17–18; 23; 27–29; 31). Also Saul's campaigns against Edom, Moab, Ammon, Zoba, and the Amalekites are summarized under the sentence "and he delivered Israel from the hands of those who plundered her" (1 Sam 14:48). There are many reports about military conflicts also after the reign of David; they can all be classified as either wars undertaken in self-defense, or in some cases as wars to reconquer lost territories. Things look more complicated when it comes to David's campaigns other than against the Philistines. Details about these campaigns, as those about the ways in which David and his successors organized the control and administration of conquered territories, need not be investigated here, because they are not immediately related to the topics of migration or ethnic identity. On the other hand, it must be noted that in several cases kings of Israel and Judah are reported to rebel against the neo-Assyrian and neo-Babylonian overlords, which points to a lasting will to political self-determination.[79]

---

75. Thus Berman, *Inconsistency*, 138, 142–43.

76. See Berman, *Inconsistency*, 142.

77. See Hubbard, *Ruth*, 91.

78. For details see Zehnder, *Umgang mit Fremden*, 407–23, 454–73, 492–98.

79. See, e.g., 2 Kgs 17:4 (Hoshea); 2 Kgs 18:7 (Hezekiah); 2 Kgs 24:1 (Jehojakim); 2 Kgs 25:1 (Zedekiah).

There are many examples of foreigners living among the Israelites and Judahites; here is a selection of the most salient ones: It transpires from 2 Sam 4:3 and 24:7 that Canaanites were among the inhabitants of both Saul's and David's kingdoms. According to 1 Kgs 9:15, 20–22 (and similarly 2 Chr 8:7–9), the descendants of the Canaanites whom the Israelites were not able to put under the ban are subjected to forced labor (*mas*) by Solomon. According to 1 Chr 22:2 David uses *gerim* ("sojourners"), likely people of Canaanite descendance, for preparatory works in the context of the temple building project. A similar note is found 2 Chr 2:16–17, to the effect that Solomon used the *gerim* for forced labor. It is likely that not only descendants of the Canaanites, but also other people with foreign backgrounds were subject to forced labor, notably prisoners of war and members of subjugated neighboring nations.[80]

Besides the Canaanites, we find a good number of other people with foreign backgrounds referred to in texts describing the situation in Israel and Judah during the monarchic period. The first example is the Edomite Doeg, who appears as a high ranking official in Saul's administration (1 Sam 21:8; 22:9, 18, 22). It may well be that this arrangement is in tension with Deut 23:8–9, though this is not absolutely sure. In any case, the narrator views Doeg in a tendentially negative way.

Things look differently in the case of the Hittite Uriah (2 Sam 11:3; 23:39), an officer in David's army. His name points to a Yahwistic affiliation, but it seems that he was ethnically of Hittite descent. As opposed to Doeg, he is depicted in a fully positive light.

It is likely that some or all of David's "heroes" mentioned in 2 Sam 23:36–39 were of foreign origin. They ranked certainly very high in David's army, and are valued positively.

Part of David's army consisted of contingents of Cherethites and Pelethites (2 Sam 8:18; 15:18; 20:7, 23; 1 Kgs 1:38, 44; 1 Chr 18:17), foreign mercenaries perhaps of Cretan and Philistian background who seem to have formed a kind of personal guard of the king and therefore fulfilled a very important function. Besides them, we find Ittai from Gath and his 600 men, also foreign mercenaries in David's service (2 Sam 15:18–22). Ittai is, not too surprisingly, called a *nokri* ("foreigner," 2 Sam 15:19). This may well mean that he and his men were not integrated into the Israelite people in any deeper way either socially or religiously. Foreign mercenaries, probably of broadly Greek background, in the service of Judahite

---

80. For details see Zehnder, *Umgang mit Fremden*, 493–97.

kings are also attested for the late pre-exilic period in the letters from Arad.[81] During the reign of Solomon, a very important role was played by Hiram, a man with an Israelite mother and probably a Phoenician father (1 Kgs 7:13–14; 2 Chr 2:12–13). He was in charge of the artistic design of the temple.

Much space is devoted in the biblical writings to the large number of foreign wives that Solomon had. While the description of Solomon's marriage with the daughter of Pharaoh in 1 Kgs 3:1 is relatively neutral, things look differently in 1 Kgs 11:1–4, where the author mentions Solomon's marriage with 700 main and 300 secondary wives of Moabite, Ammonite, Edomite, Sidonian, and Hittite background in negative terms. The passage not only mentions that these wives were allowed to follow their own religions, but that they even enticed Solomon to become a syncretist himself in the later days of his life. On the surface, the condemnation of these marriages is clearly focused on the religious, not the ethnic level. Connections with the king's law in Deut 17:14–20 make it possible, however, that also social issues are at stake, with the king elevating himself unduly over his compatriots and using too many economic resources in the process.[82]

After Solomon, it is Ahab, ruler of the Northern Kingdom, who is reported as having a foreign wife, the Sidonian princess Jezebel (1 Kgs 16:31). In this case, the major negative consequence is the state-promotion of Ba'alism on a broad scale, combined with a widespread persecution of Yahwistic opponents (see, e.g., 1 Kgs 16:32; 17–18). The problem is, however, not confined to the religious level. The story of Naboth and his vineyard in 1 Kings 21 is indicative of a social conflict: Jezebel promotes an absolutist position of the king that is not checked by legal restrictions, undermining the Israelite concept of kingship which puts much more restriction on the power of the king. The policies of Ahab and Jezebel find vehement opposition first in the prophets Elijah and Elisha and their followers, later—on the political level—in Jehu, who violently eradicates the members of the house of Ahab and the functionaries of Ba'alism (see 2 Kings 9).

81. See Renz and Röllig, *Handbuch der althebräischen Epigraphik I*, 353–82; Smelik, *Historische Dokumente*, 91, 99–104.

82. Criticism of Solomon's marriage with foreign wives is taken up in Neh 13:26–27. For a recent assessment of the relationship between the depiction of Solomon in 1 Kings and Deut 17:14–20 see, e.g., Vang, "The Non-Prophetic Background," 215–18.

Besides the foreigners mentioned so far, there is only a very limited amount of cases in which other foreigners are mentioned, among them the Amalekite *ger* ("sojourner") who transmits the news of Saul's death to David (2 Sam 1:13). We also note that extra-biblical epigraphic evidence does not point to a large number of foreigners during the monarchic period residing either in Israel or Judah.[83]

Not only are there notes in the Hebrew Bible about various foreigners living among the Israelites and Judahites, but also about foreign, non-Yahwistic cults being practiced in Israel and Judah, beyond the examples during Solomon's and Ahab's reigns just mentioned.[84] This points to an openness among broader societal groups to foreign cultural influence. In some cases, it is explicitly noted that the adherence to non-Yahwistic cultic practices was related to contacts with foreigners both inside and outside of Israel/Judah.[85] Canaanite and Aramean influences were particularly strong. On the other hand, the Hebrew Bible also mentions that time and again reform movements arose that encouraged more rigid separation from foreign practices, especially non-Yahwistic cultic practices.[86] In some cases, such reforms could take on violent forms, and among the targets of the violence also foreigners or immigrants could be found.

Evidently, biblical writers routinely criticize the tolerance or promotion of non-Yahwistic cults in Israel and Judah. In some cases, however, their criticism is not clearly restricted to religious matters, but is also directed at foreign cultural elements more broadly or at diplomatic relations with foreign powers that aim at securing Israel's or Judah's survival—instead of relying on YHWH. Hosea 7:8–9, for example, deplores the mixture (root *b-l-l*) of Israel with other peoples. Israel has allowed foreigners to enter its fabric like oil into flour. Israel's identity is undermined

---

83. See Renz and Rӧllig, *Handbuch der althebräischen Epigraphik II/1*, 55–87 (only 7 percent out of the 263 personal names attested in inscriptions are non-Israelite; only just under 5 percent of the ca. 1,000 bullae contain non-Israelite names).

84. See, e.g., 1 Kgs 12:28–33; 13:2, 32–33; 14:9, 23–24; 15:13–14; 16:13, 26; 22:44–54; 2 Reg 1:2; 12:4; 14:4; 15:4, 35; 16:3–4; 17:7–35; 21:2–7, 21; Isa 17:8–11; 30:22; Jer 1:16; 2–3; 5:19; 7:6, 9, 18, 30–31; 10; 11:10–17; 13:10; 16:11; 17:2–3; 19:4–5, 13; 22:9; 25:6–7; 32:29, 34–35; 35:15; 44:3–5, 8, 15–19; Ezek 6:3–6; 16:15–59; 20:27–32; Hos 2:8; 3:1; 4:12–13, 17; 13:1–2; 14:8; Amos 5:26; 7:9; Mic 1:7; Zeph 1:4–5, 9.

85. See, e.g., 1 Kgs 14:24; 2 Kgs 16:3; 17:8, 15; 21:2–3; Ezek 20:32.

86. See, e.g., 1 Kgs 15:11–13 (Asa); 2 Kings 9–10 (Jehu); 11:17–18 (Jehoiada the priest); 18:4 (Hezekiah); 22–23 (Josiah).

because of political alliances that are combined with processes of cultural and religious assimilation to foreign elements.[87] The situation is similar in Jer 2:25 and Ezek 16:32.

Some texts focus on cultural elements without any clear connection with the political realm. In Hos 12:8–9, the author exhibits a negative attitude towards the economic behavior of Phoenician tradesmen. Verse 13 of the same chapter implicitly calls the Israelite addressees to abstain from all mixture with foreign peoples, which includes their religious practices, but is not limited to them. Isaiah 2:6 criticizes that the house of Jacob is filled with things from the east, and with soothsayers as the Philistines; they are also accused of having inappropriate relationships with foreigners (*nokrim*). In other words, instead of walking in the ways of the Lord, Israel walks in the ways of the nations.[88] Another example can be found in Zeph 1:8, where judgment is announced over "all those who wear foreign clothes." The persons in view are likely members of the wealthy elite,[89] who express their inner predilection for foreign cultural, political, and religious models through their choice of clothing. The following verse (Zeph 1:9) mentions people who leap over the threshold. This habit must also refer to some foreign custom, likely of a religious/superstitious nature.[90]

Prophetic books are full of indictments of foreign nations, based on their negative behavior ethically or religiously, in many cases also based on their adversity against Israel. The expectation is that, because of their misbehavior, God himself will bring punishment on them.[91] Similar sentiments can be found in various psalms.[92] While these phenomena are most widely attested in the pre-exilic period, they are not restricted to it.

Criticism of foreigners, or of members of God's people following foreign religious or cultural practices or entering in too close relationships with them, is not the only perspective found in biblical texts. For example, David's and Solomon's close relationships with Tyrus are for the most

87. Political alliances are also criticized in Isa 30:1–5; 31:1–3; Jer 27:3; Hos 7:11; 8:9–10; 12:2.

88. See Oswalt, *The Book of Isaiah, Chapters 1–39*, 128.

89. Because the types of clothes in view must have been expensive.

90. For details see Zehnder, *Umgang mit Fremden*, 469–71.

91. Many chapters in prophetic books are devoted to these topics; see, among others, Isaiah 13–23; Jeremiah 46–51; Ezekiel 25–32.

92. See, e.g., Psalms 79, 83, and 137.

part not criticized, and Isaiah 16 testifies to a compassionate view on the distress of the Moabites, expressed especially in verses 9 and 11. This chapter also seems to point to a willingness to at least temporarily accept a larger number of Moabite refugees in Judah.[93] This acceptance is, however, predicated on a clear subordination of the Moabites under the ideal Judahite king in Zion.[94]

Moreover, it is clear that orthodox Yahwism itself shows many traits of foreign influence both on the material and linguistic levels, and to some degree even on the religious level through adaptation and transformation.[95]

4.2.3. Exile and Postexilic Period[96]

The Babylonian exile has some importance for the topic of this study in the sense that a certain number of Judahite exiles retained (parts of) their cultural and religious identity in Babylonia.[97] This can be seen as suggesting that current immigrants must be allowed to behave in similar ways.[98] From a biblical perspective, however, the problem with this view is that the people of God cannot be put on the same level as other people(s); also, the biblical texts referring to both the pre-exilic and the postexilic periods show that for the people of God, assimilation was the normal expectation for people living among them permanently on the territory of Israel/Judah.

Turning to the postexilic period, the following picture emerges: Ezra 2:43–54 mentions the *netinim* ("[temple] servants") among those who returned from exile in Babylonia. According to Ezra 8:20, they had been

93. See the comments in Smith, *Isaiah 1–39*, 332–34. Houston, on the other hand, focuses on what she considers to be a rejection of the plea for protection in v. 7a (see *You Shall Love*, 84–85); her interpretation seems, however, not to appreciate enough the compassionate elements in the chapter as a whole.

94. See especially verses 1, 3, and 5.

95. For the reception of Egyptian and Canaanite-Phoenician-Syrian models in the temple of Solomon see, e.g., Dever, *What Did the Biblical Writers Know*, 144–57; Kitchen, *On the Reliability*, 122–27. Concerning supposed influences of Canaanite, Egyptian, and Syrian perceptions of God see, e.g., Smith, *The Early History*; Mathys, "Fremde Religionen," 40–42; Müller, "Gott und die Götter," 99–142.

96. For details see Zehnder, *Umgang mit Fremden*, 424–47, 473–81.

97. See, e.g., Senior, "Beloved Aliens," 21.

98. Thus, e.g., Strine, "Embracing Asylum Seekers," 479.

servants of the Levites since the time of David. Some of their names point to a foreign background. Their position in post-exilic times is a respected one—in Neh 11:3 they are even related to the "heads of the province"—even if they are placed behind priests and Levites. Their willingness to join other Jews in the return to Yehud proves the high degree of integration into the Jewish community. The situation is similar with the "servants of Solomon" mentioned in Ezra 2:55–57, although it is not clear whether they also served at the temple.[99]

The main topic dealt with in biblical texts concerning foreigners in the postexilic period is mixed marriages between Jewish men and foreign women.[100] According to Ezra 9:1–2, Israelites have married women from the "peoples of the land," who contextually are to be interpreted as Canaanites, Hittites, Perizzites, Jebusites, Ammonites, Moabites, Egyptians, and Amorites. Ezra himself is reported to condemn these marriages as a breach of the commandments that YHWH had given through his prophets (Ezra 9:10–11). Ezra, as much as Nehemiah, criticizes the mixed marriages of their time because they estimate that the prohibitions found in Exod 34:12–16 and Deut 7:2–5, 16, as well as Deut 23:2–9, can be transferred to their own situation. The main reason must be the fact that the foreign wives are non-Yahwistic and therefore pose a threat to the religious identity of the people of God. Connections with Leviticus 18 (to'ebah ["abomination"], tame' ["unclean"], niddah ["impurity"]) point to the realm of sexual ethics in addition to the cultic one. The solution to the problem proposed by Sechanja and approved by Ezra consists in sending away the foreign wives, together with their children (Ezra 10:3, 5, 11, 44). Most likely, this way is chosen because the wives were not willing to join the Yahwistic faith.[101]

The second passage that deals with the issue of mixed marriages at some length is Neh 13:23–27. Nehemiah encounters Jews who are married with Ashdodite, Ammonite, and Moabite women. The offspring of these marriages do not speak "Judahite" well. Nehemiah goes on to curse the men in question and to beat them—likely a "conventional expression of public humiliation."[102] Nehemiah's main measure consists in requesting

99. For details see Zehnder, Umgang mit Fremden, 427–28.

100. For details see Zehnder, Umgang mit Fremden, 428–47.

101. See Zehnder, Umgang mit Fremden, 435. Houston can be mentioned as a recent commentator who rather sees racial considerations (or even racism) on the side of Ezra (and Nehemiah) at work (see You Shall Love, 123–27, 129–30).

102. Blenkinsopp, Ezra-Nehemiah, 364.

the Jewish men not to give their daughters into marriage to foreign men and not to take foreign women for their sons.

A second paragraph in Nehemiah also deals with the problem of mixed marriages: Nehemiah 13:28–29 contains the note that Nehemiah chases away one of the sons of Joiada, the son of the high priest Eliashib, because he had married a daughter of Sanballat, thereby contaminating the priestly covenant. In this case, the background is probably Lev 21:14–23.

It is very likely that the rejection of mixed marriages in Ezra and Nehemiah is based on the fact that the non-Israelite wives were not adherents of Yahwism. The religious contamination has to be avoided in order to preserve the religious identity and holiness of the people. The situation was particularly dangerous because of the lack of political independence and the existence of powerful competing ethno-religious groups on the same territory in the province of Yehud.

The issue of mixed marriages is also dealt with in a third major passage, found in Mal 2:10–16.[103] Verse 11 likely intimates that some Jewish men have married women who are not only ethnically, but also religiously foreign, and that as a consequence a syncretistic culture takes root in Yehud, because many of these women stay loyal to the traditions of their families of origin. Based on v. 14 it can be deduced that in many cases the marriage with foreign women was related to a divorce from a prior Jewish spouse. It is probable that the exchange of the marriage partner was done by the Jewish men to attain a higher social position.

Separation from foreigners is not restricted to the foreign wives in mixed marriages and their offspring. Ezra 4:1–4 mentions that the community of the returnees does not allow the "people of the land" ('am-haʾarets) to participate in the rebuilding of the temple in Jerusalem.[104] The people in view describe themselves as descendants of deportees who were brought to the land by the Assyrian king Esarhaddon (v. 2). It is likely that the rejection of the offer of the "people of the land" has both political and religious reasons: Politically, there was a danger that the community of the returnees would open the path for their subjugation under the authority of the Samaritans; and religiously, the "people of the land" were certainly perceived of as syncretistic, in line with 2 Kgs 17:24–41.

---

103. For details see Zehnder, "A Fresh Look," 224–59.

104. Tensions between the community of the returnees and the "peoples of the lands" are already mentioned in Ezra 3:3.

Nehemiah 2 and 4 also contain reports about clashes between the community of the returnees and inimical groups who try to thwart the project of the rebuilding of the walls of Jerusalem. These groups are led by Sanballat the Horonite, Tobia the Ammonite, and Geshem the Arab; Neh 4:1 also mentions Arabs, Ammonites, and Ashdodites more generally.

The enmity of the persons and groups just mentioned is matched by the wish of the community of the returnees to separate themselves from others not just as far as marriage relationships are concerned. This is especially obvious in Nehemiah 13. In Neh 13:1–3, Deut 23:2–9 is used as a piece of applicable law and implemented probably even on the civic level, not only on the level of the religious community, in the middle of the fifth century BC. According to this text, the application of the law is done in a way that goes beyond its literal stipulations; for restrictive measures are taken not only against the ethnic groups mentioned in Deuteronomy 23, but against all foreigners. As in the case of mixed marriages, it is not unlikely that people who joined the faith of the Israelites were not affected by the measures. If this interpretation is correct, the ethnic and historical criteria prevalent in Deuteronomy 23 were replaced by religious criteria in the time of Nehemiah.

Similar remarks are in place as far as Neh 13:4–9 is concerned. Nehemiah is reported to directly apply Deut 23:4 against Tobia, the latter being either an Ammonite or an Israelite of Ammonite descent. He is blocked from the temple because he is seen as cultically/ritually unfit to serve there. The case makes clear that there was a dynamic development in the understanding and possible use of rules regulating the dealing with immigrants. Old traditions were taken up, but applied in a way that clearly takes changes in the historical circumstances into consideration. This approach of combining reverence for traditional prescriptions with sensitivity to historical changes might open a window into possible ways of how to consider biblical and other relevant paradigms in the current debate.

Statements about a general, far-reaching separation from all that is "foreign" are also found in Neh 9:2 and 13:30, in the latter case referring to the purification of priests and Levites.

Ezra 6:21, referring to the period of the first returnees towards the end of the sixth century BC, and Neh 10:29, referring to the times of Ezra and Nehemiah, are often understood as suggestive of a position that relativizes the seemingly rigorous separation from non-Israelites to which the passages dealing with mixed marriages point.[105] These two verses seem to suggest that it was possible for persons who did originally not belong to the community of returnees to join them, through an act that would be called in later times "conversion." If this were correct, the view that the separation from foreign wives and from everything foreign only applies in cases where the respective persons do not want to assimilate to Yahwism, would receive further corroboration. However, there are strong linguistic arguments to understand the phrases "and all those who had separated themselves from the impurity of the peoples of the land" (Ezra 6:21) as well as "and those who had separated themselves from the people of the lands" (Neh 10:29) not as pointing to a separate group of people, converts as it were, but as appositional phrases that refer to the community of the returnees.[106]

More generally, the following principle seems to emerge: Foreigners are not rejected as such, but separation from them is needed where the keeping of the law is in danger of being compromised. A clear example of this can be found in Neh 10:32 and 13:16. These two verses presuppose permanent commercial interaction with resident foreigners, and there is no hint at this being seen as problematic. What is condemned, however, is doing business with these foreigners on a Sabbath. And this may well be indicative of the broader attitude.

A hint pointing in the same direction is the fact that motivating the separation from foreigners in the case of the dissolution of mixed marriages in Ezra 9 (vv. 1, 11, 14) is the concept of *to'ebah* ("abomination"), which is not—at least not primarily—a racial, but a moral(-cultic) category.[107] Besides *to'evah*, *tum'ah* ("impurity") is mentioned (Ezra 9:11); the same term is also used in Ezra 6:21, which talks about the separation of the peoples of the land on a more general level, going beyond the question of mixed marriages. Very likely, *tum'ah* cannot be reduced to ritual impurity in these cases, but also has moral connotations.[108]

---

105. See, e.g., Blenkinsopp, *Ezra–Nehemiah*, 133, 314.

106. See Thiessen, "The Function of a Conjunction," 63–79.

107. See, e.g., Feder, "Defilement," 157–89.

108. A strict dichotomy of "moral" and "ritual" is unwarranted for the conceptual world of the author of the respective texts in Ezra as much as for the related passages in the Torah, especially Leviticus. See again Feder, "Defilement."

Furthermore, Neh 10:29 mentions the positive goal of the separation from the non-Israelites, namely to cling to the Torah of the Lord. The Torah, of course, not only contains texts such as Exod 34:12–16 and Deut 7:2–5, 16 prohibiting intermarriage and other forms of covenant relationships, or Deut 23:2–9 with its restrictions concerning access the the "congregation of the LORD," but also texts that enjoin economic support and judicial protection for the *ger* ("sojourner") and open up the possibility of his joining the community of Israel. And of course, Gen 1:27 with the creation of every human being in the image of God is prominently placed at the beginning of the Torah and therefore important for its understanding generally.[109] It is hardly conceivable that all of this would be bluntly ignored by the postexilic community who is so intent on hearing and following the Torah.

Indeed, positive attitudes towards non-Israelites are in fact attested in a number of passages in Ezra–Nehemiah—besides the passages referring to the *netinim* ("[temple-]servants") and the *'abdey Shelomo* ("servants of Solomon") already mentioned—, all those other texts focusing on separation not withstanding:

- There is a spirit of positive reference to the Persian authority in many passages; see Ezra 1:1–4; 6; 7; 8:36; Nehemiah 2;

- The building of the temple and the re-institution of its cult is linked to the Persian Empire as a whole, which is thought to extend more or less to the ends of the world; see Ezra 3:7; 4:3–4; 5–7; 8:24–36.

- Nehemiah 9:6 underlines that God has made the earth and all that is on it, which is indicative of a perspective that is not narrowly nationalistic at all.

Both these last two points make clear that Israel's existence as a distinct entity serves a broader purpose, to enable God to reach the whole world through Israel.

All of this suggests that it was likely not impossible for non-Israelites to join the community of Israel if they fully assimilated especially on the religious level. However, because of the (perceived) threats to the religious and ethnic identity of "Israel" in a situation in which this identity could not be safeguarded in the same way and by the same means as in the pre-exilic situation, Ezra and Nehemiah attempted to preserve this identity

---

109. The implications of this will be taken up in paragraph 5 below.

through radical measures of separation.[110] On the theological level, it is ultimately the special calling of Israel to be the people of the Lord which is at play. And this calling has as its goal not just Israel, but implies also God's redemptive-salvific plans with the non-Israelite peoples.

5. PERSPECTIVES ON MIGRATION ISSUES RELATED TO THE CONTEXT OF CREATION AND PRIMEVAL HISTORY

a) First and foremost: Every human being, as an individual, independent of his or her racial or ethnic background, bears infinite value because of his/her *imago Dei* character.[111] This is of course true for every migrant as well, as much as for every non-migrant. The creational equality of humankind regardless of their racial or ethnic background means that there cannot be an absolute strangeness between humans that would touch the very core of human nature. It also excludes racial subordination, favoritism, or pride at the expense of others. Therefore, there is no, and has never been, a biblical-creational justification for racism.

However, it must be pointed out that the term "racism" in the current situation is used in ways that do not only refer to racial pride at the cost of others, but to virtually all types of demarcations between groups and criticism of groups that are not identical with one's own group, even if the groups in question are not racially or

110. So also Kaminsky, "Did Election Imply," 417 ("They were not trying to eliminate a threatened minority. They were trying to preserve a threatened minority").

With Dyck, the strong focus on separation from everything "foreign," as far as it is non-Yahwistic according to the definition of the returnees, can be understood as typical of a "vertical ethnicity," that is, of an ethnic group that stresses—or has to stress—the social deepening of the shared cultural elements as opposed to the extension in space (see "The Ideology of Identity in Chronicles," 99). The opposing model is the "lateral ethnicity," which is marked more by spatial extension than social depth.

111. See Gen 1:26–27; 9:6. Cf. the comments in Carroll, *Christians*, 46–48; Carroll, "Immigration," 5–6. Carroll posits that the *imago Dei* character of every person includes the possession of an "immense potential to contribute to society" (*Christians*, 48). While this is true, it does not mean that the potential can necessarily be used best just in any given society, or that a person is free to choose the society in which to use the potential. Moreover, every person also carries negative potential that cannot be simply ignored. Carroll (*Christians*, 48) makes a quick jump from the concept of *imago Dei* to the human rights perspective. The latter, however, is not simply identical with the former, especially when it comes to the question of the free choice of settlement.

ethnically defined. Along such lines, critical questioning of liberal immigration policies is per se labeled "racist." Evidently this use of the term goes far beyond its traditional semantic content and functions to discredit without further discussion divergent opinions.

b) In the larger biblical context, it becomes clear that the ascription of the status of image of God and the concomitant dignity of the human person primarily refers to individuals. It does by no means exclude the possibility of certain historical peoples or nations being evaluated and treated in different ways, often (in post-lapsarian conditions) negatively. One example among many others are the Canaanites. In accordance with the *imago Dei* concept, however, negative assessments are not related to flaws in the creation or to unredeemable flaws in human nature itself.

c) The fact that all humankind is depicted as descending from one couple, Adam and Eve, in the light of Genesis 3 also means that every person, regardless of his/her ethnicity, is a sinner before God, not simply "good." Again, this also applies to all migrants, no less than to the members of the receiving societies.[112]

This point is lost in those instances in which migrants per se are ascribed a special spiritual quality, representing the presence of God in an elevated way, or instances in which they are imagined as "more precious than gold" or the like.[113]

d) One of the striking traits of biblical Israelites' attitude towards foreigners is that while Israelite culture is marked by a high degree of self-criticism, this is not combined with an idealization of the foreign "other" as such. This seems to be untypical, since one often finds either a combination of lack of self-criticism with pejorative views of the foreign "other," or a combination of self-criticism with an idealization of the foreign "other."[114] We also note the absence of

112. See also Carroll, *Christians*, 73.

113. For examples of such views see the information given in chapter 1 above. The formulation that what refugees can contribute is "more precious than gold" was coined by German politician Martin Schulz, former President of the European Parliament (see Riemer, "Was Flüchtlinge uns bringen ist wertvoller als Gold").

114. In the continental European political context, the Nazis would be an extreme example for the first position, broad currents within the left-green camp examples for the latter. The first position is the dominating one both in the ancient Near East and in the Graeco-Roman world, though nuances can be found. For the elevation of the own

general denigrations of the foreign "other" as sub-human or barbarian or the like. This set of postures can be seen as closely connected with both the concept of equality of all humankind before God, both in terms of *imago Dei* and in terms of being sinner before God.

e) Adam (and Eve) are placed in the garden of Eden to till and protect it (Gen 2:15). The implication of this is that migration was not part of the original plan for the first couple. Only as a consequence of the Fall does (one-time, forced) migration occur: Adam and Eve must leave the garden of Eden (Gen 3:23–24).

However, according to Gen 1:28 (taken up in Gen 9:1, 7) the descendants of the first human couple are commissioned to fill the earth and subdue it, which necessarily includes movements of migration during subsequent generations. These movements, however, would be necessary only as a series of one-time events, with the purpose of settling uninhabited areas, and they would come to an end once the ends of the earth were reached.

A permanent existence as a migrant is ordained only for Cain, as part of the punishment for the killing of his brother Abel (Gen 4:14).

The result of these observations is that generally migration is not an ideal established in creation. Migration as a positive factor can only be implicitly detected as a provisional part of the process leading to the implementation of the command to fill the earth and subdue it. As opposed to this, within the first four chapters of Genesis the explicit practical examples of migration are related to human sin.

f) Plurality and diversity in terms of ethnicity is understood as something positive, not as a deficiency that has to be overcome by human endeavors to create faceless uniformity.[115] This can be seen from the connection between the blessing of humankind in Gen 1:28 and of Noah and his sons in Gen 9:1 on the one hand and the list of nations in Genesis 10 on the other. The list in Genesis 10 shows that the

culture and ethnicity and the disdain for "barbarian" cultures and ethnicities in Assyria see Zehnder, *Umgang mit Fremden*, 62–77. The tension between the classification of non-Greeks as "barbarians" and the interest for (and sometimes even appreciation of) foreign peoples and their culture in ancient Greece is well known (see, e.g., Dihle, *Die Griechen und die Fremden*, 7–53). It is also interesting to observe the (acknowledgment of the) cultural dependence of Assyria on Babylonia and Rome on Greece.

115. *Pace* Maruskin, "The Bible," 79.

blessing has come to fruition,[116] and the fruition does not consist only of a large number of *people*, but indeed of a large number of *peoples* as well. The list contains the names of 70 different nations, with 70 most likely being a symbolic number pointing to completion and fullness. What can be deduced from this is that plurality and diversity in terms of ethnicity and nationality are depicted as demonstrating God's creative power.[117] Mass-migration, on the other hand, has the potential to blur identity boundaries between peoples, and the replacement of nation-states through supra-national bodies escalates this tendency.

The alternative vision, the human desire to avoid the separation and diversity depicted in Genesis 10, by establishing a centralized and unified form of society, is explicitly and polemically rejected in the story of the city and tower of Babylon in Gen 11:1–9.[118]

g) According to Gen 10:5, 20, 31, the constitutional elements of a "people" (*goy*) consist of a particular territory (*'erets*, "land"), a specific language (*lashon*, "tongue"), and a unity and identity based on some kind of familial relationship (*mishpachah*, "family," "clan"). Biblical stories referring to later events show that the definition of a people in terms of these three components must not be understood in a rigid way. Rahab and her family, the Gibeonites, or Ruth are just some of many examples that show that ethnic—and even more so national—boundaries are not envisioned as insurmountable. The possible avenues for a *ger* ("sojourner") to become part of the people of God over time is another important example.[119] Moreover, cases like the Kenites demonstrate that while the core of a people is related to the elements of territory, language, and familial relationship, there are always groups at the fringes—especially, but not necessarily exclusively, in geographical terms—who are not defined by these characteristics in the same way. The joining of individuals and

---

116. So also Walton, *Genesis*, 379.

117. Similarly Walton, *Genesis*, 379.

118. See, e.g., Jacob, *Das Buch Genesis*, 302 ("Die Erzählung ist also die Verurteilung eines extremen Zentralismus"); similarly Brueggemann: "The narrative then is a protest against every effort at oneness derived from human self-sufficiency and autonomy" (*Genesis*, 100). For a different view see Walton, *Genesis*, 375–76.

119. Whether a *ger* would be reckoned as a full member of Israel in the first generation is unlikely, but difficult to assess. For a discussion of these matters see Zehnder, *Umgang mit Fremden*, 333–38.

groups who do not originally belong to a people is one of the key elements that show that ethnic identity is not fixed and static over time. And periods in the history of Israel where major parts of the people lived outside the ancestral lands also demonstrate that not all of the three elements mentioned in Genesis 10 necessarily need to be present at any given point in history to maintain the identity of a nation.

There are several ways in which Genesis 10 points to Genesis 11. For example, there is the element of the dispersion of the various groups, mentioned throughout Genesis 10, including the concomitant differences in language (see vv. 5, 20, 31); moreover, Gen 10:9 already mentions the town Babel and the country Shinar, which then are referred to also in Genesis 11. This means that Genesis 10 has to be read against the background of Gen 11:1–9.[120] This does not imply, however, that the distinction of various groups must be seen in negative terms, as the consequence of God's punitive reaction to humankind's failure to fulfill his plan of them filling the earth (or for other trespasses supposedly hinted at in Gen 11:3–4).[121] Rather, Gen 11:1–9 shows that God had to interfere directly to overcome human resistance to fulfill his original plan. The only element that may not be original is the difference of languages.

While all the qualifications and relativizations of the triadic pattern (territory, language, family) proposed in Genesis 10 are important, it is unwarranted to ignore the pattern itself completely and thereby neglect a foundational creational element of the definition of ethnic identity and nationhood. This is, however, what routinely

120. So also, e.g., Hartley, *Genesis*, 126; Jacob, *Das Buch Genesis*, 303.

121. There are those who do not perceive this point. By way of example, one can point to Carroll who states: "Humanity gathers in rebellion against God at Babel, but then is scattered, a dispersal that yields the multiplication of nations (Genesis 10–11)" ("Immigration," 6). The division of mankind into different nations is seen in such comments as basically negative, a position that does not only square badly with both Genesis 10 and 11, but is also incompatible with Deut 32:8 (see below). Because of the ambiguities of Gen 11:1–9, it is hardly possible to come to definitive conclusions about questions concerning the exact nature of the transgression(s) and punitive aspects in YHWH's reaction; cf., e.g., the comments in Hartley, *Genesis*, 126; Jacob, *Das Buch Genesis*, 301; Walton, *Genesis*, 374–78. It goes normally unnoticed that Genesis 10 uses the noun *lashon* ("tongue") to refer to languages, while Genesis 11 uses *saphah* ("lip"). The latter has nowhere in the Pentateuch the meaning of "language" (in the sense of English vs. French, Spanish, Russian, Mandarin, Arabic, etc.), and it is doubtful whether it has this meaning anywhere in the Hebrew Bible.

happens in theological discussions of migration issues. They normally do not ascribe any particular value to the element of natural
coherence. Mass-migration, however, has the potential to undercut
the creational order expounded in Genesis 10.

h) There is a general thematic overlap between the list of nations in
Genesis 10 and Deut 32:8, as well as a specific connection between
the two texts via the shared use of the verb *prd* ("separate") and
the number seventy as the (symbolic) numerical delimitation of
the world of nations that are governed by God. Deuteronomy 32:8
states:

> When the Most High gave the nations their inheritance, when
> He separated the sons of man, He set the boundaries of the
> peoples according to the number of the sons of Israel.[122]

The number in view is seventy, because it is seventy peoples that
are listed in Genesis 10, and because seventy was the number of
the members of Jacob's house when they migrated to Egypt. As in
Genesis 10, the number seventy has to be understood as symbolic,
representing completeness and abundance. Deuteronomy 32:8
again shows that a differentiation between different peoples is not a
deficit that humans must try to overcome, but in fact the opposite:
the differentiation and division of humanity into a variety of peoples
with specific "boundaries" or "borders" (*gebul*) is in accordance with
God's will and is related to his own actions.[123] Differentiation and
variety, not a unitary system, is God's purpose not only in the realms
of plants and animals, but also in the realm of peoples, including
the political dimensions of this realm.[124] In every realm, he does

122. Thus NASB; or, according to another textual variant, "in accordance with the
number of the *bney 'el*, the sons of God (i.e., the heavenly beings)"

123. A similar view is attested in Acts 17:26. Brett ("Forced Migrations," 124) also
points to these texts and states that they show that "there is a properly ethical status for
borders." He further explains that "there is an inevitable conceptual linkage between
affirming borders and affirming the idea of homeland" ("Forced Migrations," 125).
On the other hand, there are those who ignore this point; see, e.g., Maruskin, "The
Bible," 79, referring positively to the Brethren's slogan "God made people—people
made borders"; cf. also p. 89 ("As we read the New Testament, we see people moving
freely, without borders").

124. Rosenstock-Huessy writes: "Die Pluralität der vielen Staaten im Gegensatz
zur Universalität der Einen Kirche war der spezifisch christliche Beitrag zum poli-
tischen Leben. Wenn es nur Einen Staat gäbe, könnten wir nicht frei atmen" [The

not create just one "ideal" type, not just one flower or one mammal and so on, but a large variety; and God's aim with his creation, as expressed in the blessings in Genesis 1, is that this variety comes to full flourishing. As just mentioned, this is true also in terms of ethnic diversity.

This positive concept of pluriformity or diversity can be related theologically to a diversity within the divine realm, with Israel's God YHWH being repeatedly depicted as presiding over a kind of heavenly council.[125] Beyond this, the New Testament is explicit in the proposition of a dynamic relationship within God. In any event, the act of creation in itself means that God confines himself and opens space for an "other" different from himself; he creates plurality and difference.

As noted above, both mass-migration and the attempts to erase borders (*gebul*) for the sake of the establishment of supra-national or global political entities, at least potentially undermine the order that is set up by God at creation.

i) The importance and legitimacy of borders can not only be seen in Genesis 10 and Deut 32:8, but also in the fact that the detailed description of the borders of the territories of the individual tribes of Israel in Joshua 12–19 is given a considerable amount of space. Furthermore, Prov 22:28 and 23:10–11 demonstrate the importance and legitimacy of boundaries on the level of individual properties. Finally, Ezek 47:13–23 shows that borders are expected to be in place even in the (eschatological) future.

j) While Deut 32:8 and other texts show that it is God who has set the boundaries between the nations, Amos 1:13 makes the point that an extension—that is, a random and unjustified extension—of borders connected with the use of excessive force infringes on the divinely intended "international law" and will be prosecuted by him.[126]

plurality of the many states as opposed to the universality of the one church was the specific Christian contribution to political life. If there had been just One State, we could not breathe freely] (Des Christen Zukunft, 59).

125. See, e.g., Psalm 82. In addition, there are hints at a plurality within God. Details of this question cannot be taken up in the present context; a general hint at the description of the Lord in Genesis 18 and at the relationship between the "One like a Son of Man" and the "Elder of Days" in Dan 7:14 must suffice (for the latter see Zehnder, "Why the Danielic 'Son of Man' is a Divine Being," 331–48).

126. The fact that the Israelites are not allowed to go to war against the Edomites,

k) On the other hand, according to Amos 9:7 the divine establishment of the connection between the peoples and specific territories must not be understood in a strictly static sense and not be given quasi metaphysical status. The verse shows that there is not only a divine allotment of territories and an unjustified expansion or change of borders, but that there are also divinely induced wanderings of peoples resulting in their settlement at new places[127]—which is, as a rule, connected to some kind of loss for the people previously inhabiting the respective territory.

This means that both a (relatively stable) division of mankind into different ethnic groups living in different countries, and dynamic migration processes are part of God's plans with mankind. The first can be seen in Genesis 10 and Deut 32:8; also passages in Deuteronomy that prohibit the Israelites to attack neighboring peoples with the argument that their territories have been given to them by God himself speak to the same effect.[128] The second aspect comes to the fore in the vast amount of texts that point to God's involvement in the exodus of Israel from Egypt, but also in the passages that mention migrations of other peoples, like the Philistines and Arameans in Amos 9:7—as we have just seen—, the Edomites in Deut 2:12, 22, or the Ammonites in Deut 2:21.

6. ELECTION OF ISRAEL; GOD'S PEOPLE AS MIGRANTS

a) The election of Israel, including the assignment of a land of her own and the ascription not only of a specific religious profile, but also of a certain—though not rigid—ethnic identity,[129] plays an impor-

---

Moabites, and Ammonites, and occupy their territories when they are on the way to (take possession of) the Promised Land (see Deut 2:5, 9, 19) contains a similar message.

127. This does not automatically mean that God is "sovereignly involved in the movement of all peoples" and "present . . . in migrations we are witnessing worldwide" in the sense that all such movements are positively willed by him (*pace* Carroll, *Christians*, 53; near-identical formulations are found in *The Bible*, 18). Such interpretations are the result of generalizations that go beyond the specifics of God's involvement in historical events reported in the Bible.

128. See again Deut 2:5, 9, 19.

129. It is important to note that the story of the exodus from Egypt, which describes the moment of Israel's coming into being as a people, mentions the participation of an unquantifiable number of foreigners (see Exod 12:38). For a study of the

tant role in the Hebrew Bible as a whole, also beyond the use of the verb *prd* ("separate")[130] and the noun *gebul* ("border") that were mentioned above. There is an implication to this that must be mentioned here: Since Israel is thought to be a kind of model for the world of nations,[131] it may be assumed that a similar structuring of that world of nations, in accordance with the Israelite model, is what would be in accordance with the divine will in the perception of many layers of the Hebrew Bible. Texts like Genesis 10 and Deut 32:8 clearly support such a view. It is further corroborated by the observation that there is no call in any part of the Hebrew Bible for the construction of a transnational-multicultural type of state in the pre-eschatological horizon.

b) In many layers of the Hebrew Bible, there is a relatively clear demarcation against the "other" in the definition of the (own) Israelite identity as the elected people of God.[132] However, as opposed to the major ancient Near Eastern cultures and many others in the history of mankind, this demarcation is not—as we have already noted in the previous section—bound up with a general denigration of others as sub-humans or barbarians. This represents quite a remarkable combination. Rather, there are a number of instances in which God is seen at work positively also in the history of other peoples,[133] and passages can be found that bear witness to the interest in other peoples' history and culture,[134] or even appreciation of their material culture.[135]

---

ethnic identity of ancient Israel see Sparks, *Ethnicity and Identity*. Those elements that are usually seen as important markers of ethnic identity are clearly evident in the biblical depiction of Israel; see, e.g., Pitkänen, "Ethnicity," 169–74; Zehnder, *Umgang mit Fremden*, 293–94, 301. Pitkänen presents arguments in favor of the assumption that the ascription of these markers to Israel is at least partially rooted in actual history.

130. To this we would need to add the verb *bdl* ("separate"). Its role in the discussion of the topic of differentiation cannot be investigated here. Importantly, *bdl* is one of the keywords of the creation account in Genesis 1.

131. See Wright, *Old Testament Ethics*, 62–74.

132. This point is completely ignored by Maruskin, "The Bible," 89 ("There is no room in Christ's teachings for a 'them and us'").

133. See, e.g., Deut 2:12, 21–22 (Edomites and Ammonites); Amos 9:7 (Philistines and Arameans).

134. See, e.g., Deut 2:10–12, 20–23; 3:9, 11 (Edomites, Ammonites, Amorites).

135. See, e.g., Deut 6:10–11 (Canaanite peoples).

c) Experiences of migration deeply characterize the history both of the patriarchs and of the people of Israel[136]—a fact that is often pointed out by proponents of liberal immigration policies.[137] As far as the patriarchs are concerned, we observe that the very beginnings of their history are related to experiences of migration. However, the wanderings of the patriarchs and the Israelites are not glorified as some kind of ideal, but put in the frame of a divine historical plan in which not the wandering, but the rest in the Promised Land, be it before its first entry or beyond the exile, are described as the ultimate real goal.

It is also important to observe that while the encounters between the patriarchs and their hosts, mainly in Canaan, are depicted in peaceful terms, there is nevertheless a clear element of separation, in that intermarriage with Canaanites is looked upon negatively.[138] It also bears mentioning that the patriarchal stories advance the claim that the land of Canaan belongs to the descendants of Abraham as a divine gift, even with some explicit hints at the expulsion of the Canaanite peoples.[139]

There are some additional points that need to be stressed in the context of the current discussions about migration. The patriarchs and the Israelites of the periods of exodus and conquest are not just migrants of a generic type; they are especially—in most instances—not migrants in search of a place to find better material life conditions. Rather we are dealing here with divinely ordained cases of migration that serve a particular theological purpose.[140] These experiences are not described in terms of general models for other

136. As far as the people of Israel is concerned, these experiences are related both to the stay in Egypt and the wilderness wanderings on the one hand and to the deportations by the Assyrians and Babylonians on the other. Also David, when fleeing from Saul, spends some time among foreigners, in his case the Philistines (see 1 Samuel 27); he also has to take his parents to Moab for safety reasons (see 1 Sam 22:3–4).

137. See, e.g., Carroll, *Christians*, 51–54; Groody, "Fruit," 302.

138. See especially Gen 24:3; 26:34–35; 27:46; 28:1–2; 34.

139. See especially Gen 12:7; 13:14–17; 15:7, 18–21; 17:8; 26:3–4; 28:13.

140. "Genesis 11 tells us that Terah, the father of Abraham, takes his clan from Ur of the Chaldeans to the land of Canaan and so begins a long story of migration that in many ways would never end. God sanctions this journey for Abraham" (Senior, "Beloved Aliens," 20). There are two problems with this statement (and similar ones found in other publications): God does not simply "sanction" the migration, but he commands it; and the migration is not meant to never end.

peoples.[141] Moreover, in no case do the stories of the migration of the patriarchs involve incidents of illegal immigration; rather, the patriarchs are depicted as always seeking the permission of the owners of the land to set up their places of (mostly temporary) residence.[142] They are also described as putting great stress on paying for any goods and favors they might receive, such as Abraham in the case of the purchase of the cave of Machpelah (Genesis 23). It is exactly in these ways and in their willingness to adapt—in most areas of life and in most cases—peacefully to the existing order that the patriarchs as "sojourners" could be said to be a model for modern immigrants.[143]

On the other hand, one can argue that things are somewhat more complex: While the patriarchs do not dwell in their places of residence illegally, both Abraham and Isaac are described in a narrative trio as misrepresenting their wives to the local rulers as sisters (see Gen 12:10–20; 20:1–18; 26:6–11). These are clear cases of deception in order to survive in a foreign land to which they go in order to escape famine. It is evident that the narrator does

141. Senior (among other authors with similar views) claims that "the Bible views the Exodus as a definitive revelation: portraying God as a liberator who hears the cries of the poor; portraying Israel as a people . . . for whom the land was a gift and not a birthright" ("Beloved Aliens," 21). Both statements are not wrong, but the problem is that they cannot be generalized. Furthermore, the second argument is used inconsistently and thereby also unjustly in the current migration debate, in the sense that it is applied only to the receiving societies in the West, while there is no expectation that migrants' kin may not hold their land or successful immigrants may not hold the benefits they have accrued in their new places of residence.

142. Of course, the situation looks different when it comes to the entry of the Israelites under the leadership of Joshua into the Promised Land. This situation is, however, not directly analogue to modern cases of immigration. If parallels exist, they would rather point to the realm of conquest or colonization.

143. Of course, the relationship with the Canaanites is not always peaceful, as the story of the reaction to the rape of Dinah in Genesis 34 shows, and both morally and religiously the patriarchs did not blend with the Canaanites according to the patriarchal stories; however, these stories also present a picture according to which no active attempts to change the religion of the land were made. The willingness to pay for particular benefits granted to migrants is also demonstrated in Deut 2:6: the Israelites are admonished to buy food and water when attempting to pass through the territory of the Edomites.

not condemn this behavior. On the other hand, there are good exegetical reasons to assume that their behavior is in fact criticized
implicitly.[144]

d) There are four verses that describe human existence in terms of
being a "sojourner" (ger) with YHWH: Lev 25:23; 1 Chr 29:15; Ps
39:13; 119:19. What does this mean?[145] The last three texts express
the limitation of human control over one's own life. In addition, reference is made to the idea that the Israelites do not dispose fully of
the land that God has given them; they are really only tenants, not
owners. This aspect is the one that dominates in Lev 25:23: YHWH
is the real owner of the land and the Israelites are merely sojourners
with him. One of the consequences of this view is that landowner-
ship is not a matter of the free market, but must remain within the
extended family and cannot be transferred to foreigners. There is,
however, nothing to suggest that these texts advocate literal migration as the "real" or "better" way of life (for an average person).

e) It has been proposed by Strine that Jer 29:1–14, the letter addressing
the situation of the Judahite exiles in Babylonia, should be used as
a core text from which to extract "principles for a political theology of migration and integration."[146] The problem with this view
is, however, that God's historic dealing with his people cannot be
generalized and applied one-to-one to other cases; also, the situation envisioned in Jeremiah 29 is transitional only, not permanent,
and the instructions given to the exiles relate to this particular situation, not to general principles. One also has to bear in mind that
the addressees are not the hosts, but the migrants, while in Strine's

144. See Jacob, *Das Buch Genesis*, 355 (with caution); Waltke, *Genesis*, 216. Cf.
Houston, *You Shall Love*, 83

145. For details see Zehnder, *Umgang mit Fremden*, 302–4.

146. Strine, "Embracing Asylum Seekers," 479. He also interprets the report about
the Rechabites in Jeremiah 35 as making similar points (see "Embracing Asylum Seekers," 484). He asserts, i.a., that "the Rechabites offer a model for the Judahites forcibly
deported to Babylon" ("Embracing Asylum Seekers," 484). In his analysis of Jeremiah
29, Strine claims that settling immigrants in the midst of an open, multicultural host
society (as opposed to settlement in segregated camps etc.), leading to the unavoidable
necessity of close interactions, will quasi automatically produce positive results for
all parties involved (see "Embracing Asylum Seekers," 480–83, 493). That this is an
unwarranted oversimplification will be demonstrated in the chapters entitled "Broadening the Horizon"; the possibility of the incompatibility of cultures does not seem to
cross the minds of Strine and likeminded authors.

approach the situation is inversed and the ethical demands (which can be summarized as a call for openness towards the "other") are primarily directed at the hosts.

7. HOSPITALITY

There are a number of texts in the Hebrew Bible that point to hospitality towards strangers or people in need as a characteristic trait of the people of God; see, e.g., Gen 18:1–10; 24:25, 31–32; 2 Kgs 4:8–10; Job 31:32; Isa 58:7. Such texts are often mentioned as passages that support liberal immigration policies.[147] They are, however, not about immigration, but about the temporary accommodation of travelers, or—in the case of Isa 58:7—offering shelter to homeless people. This is part of a general ancient Near Eastern custom, according to which hospitality was expected to be shown to travelers, foreigners who passed through the territory of someone else.[148] Moreover, one has to consider that in these contexts "[h]ospitality functions primarily at the personal and familial level and on an informal basis,"[149] which is different from the administration of immigration in the current situation in the West. Finally, Num 20:16–21 indicates that permission was required to travel through other peoples' territories at least if the number of travelers was large.

8. ESCHATOLOGY AND MIGRATION ISSUES

a) As far as the future perspective on the relationship between Israelites and their God on the one hand and foreigners on the other is concerned, biblical texts do not present a homogeneous picture, but a rich variety of various colors. An important element of these variegated pictures is that there will still be a plurality and diversity of ethnic groups in the eschatological future, but gravitating around the spiritual center in Jerusalem.

   Both the attack of foreign armies is expected, as well as the peaceful pilgrimage of foreign peoples to Mount Zion; foreign peoples are subject to God's judgment, but foreign peoples are

---

147. See, e.g., Carroll, *Christians*, 77–78.

148. See Matthews and Benjamin, *Social World of Ancient Israel*, 82–95.

149. Carroll, *Christians*, 79.

also expected to participate in God's salvation of his people Israel. Some texts speak of a rule of Israel over other nations, while others envision the inclusion of foreigners into God's people on more equal terms. The details of such future expectations are elaborated in various ways. Different expectations are mentioned side by side, sometimes within one chapter of the same book.[150]

It is possible to tentatively integrate the various expectations into a complex coherent whole in the following way: God's judgment over his people, related to an attack of foreign powers against Jerusalem, precedes the salvation and ultimate re-establishment of Israel, which in turn will lead to a subordination of foreign peoples, combined with their inclusion into God's eschatological salvation. This means that those foreigners that were not destroyed by God's judgment will enjoy God's blessings that are mediated through Israel. Foreign nations, as far as they survive the eschatological judgment, will not be dissolved as such in a faceless and boundless unity, but retain distinct identities. They will, however, be united in their orientation towards Zion and her God, in the state of "servants." The term "servant" describes the fate of foreigners in a two-fold way: foreigners can choose to become "servants" in the positive meaning of the word by joining the congregation of the YHWH-worshippers;[151] or they can be subject to the less positive experience of being compelled to serve the Israelites in a subordinate position, in a complete reversal of previous conditions.[152]

b) Both with respect to the (eschatological) future and in descriptions of ideal types of government beyond Israel, there are no calls to establish a global political unity by means of conventional human politics.

On the other hand, some texts, primarily royal psalms/enthronement psalms, stress the world-wide character of the dominion of YHWH or his Messiah. This likely implies some kind of political unity, though no details about it are given. Importantly, however, there is nevertheless talk of a plurality of distinguishable nations in such texts,[153] and no program pointing to the

150. For details see Zehnder, *Umgang mit Fremden*, 502–40.

151. See, e.g., Isa 56:6.

152. See, e.g., Isa 14:2.

153. See, e.g., Ps 72:10–11.

human-political realization of the global dominion of God or his Messiah is developed.

9. BRIEF SUMMARY

The complexity of Old Testament texts that deal with issues of (im)migration—together with the historical differences between the circumstances reflected in those texts and the characteristics of the current situation—make a simple one-to-one transfer of such texts impossible. If one tries to "apply" such texts, one also has to carefully assess why some of them are better candidates than others, and how the transfer can be done in hermeneutically responsible ways.

As far as legal regulations concerning foreigners are concerned, together with their reflections in prophetic texts: There is no overarching category of "foreigner" that would ignore the specific backgrounds of the people in question and the degree of assimilation to Israel. What is foregrounded is the benefit of the rule of law for those who have been admitted, while rules for admittance are only very rarely in view.[154] There is clearly no "requirement of unlimited or uncontrolled admittance of those who are members of another nation,"[155] and of those who come to stay far-reaching assimilation that also includes the religious domain is expected. Israel is not expected to accommodate to immigrants. To this is related the fact that protection of Israel's own identity is an important aspect of biblical law in general. It is also clear that Israel is expected to treat immigrants with dignity and abstain from abusing them; this does, however, not imply or lead to liberal immigration policies. On a more general level, the various layers of the Hebrew Bible assert that persons in need must be helped; but preference is given to members of the people of God. The support that has to be offered to needy persons is minimal rather than maximal, focusing on the level of survival. Especially restrictive from a modern perspective are regulations concerning land ownership: The land was to be kept within the family or clan—which closes the land-market in principle for foreigners.

---

154. "[N]o immigration policy . . . is spelled out" (Edwards, "A Biblical Perspective," 5).

155. Edwards, "A Biblical Perspective," 3.

3

New Testament Views on Migration

1. GENERAL OBSERVATIONS

IN GENERAL TERMS, IT can be said that the New Testament texts do not "overcome" the complex picture that is painted in the Hebrew Bible. Rather, questions concerning migration are being taken up from a different perspective. The main difference consists in the fact that the new community of believers created by the gospel of and about Jesus from Nazareth does not address questions of migration based on an identity that is marked by ethnic coherence and state-like civic structuring as is the case in biblical Israel. The fact that the New Testament is for the most part silent on matters of ethnic identity and diversity of nations cannot be construed as proof for them being obsolete.[1] It is also obvious that the New Testament nowhere offers "direct teaching or law about aliens and the illegal immigrant to guide a nation."[2] This has to do with the fact that the earliest Christians did not live in or as an independent nation.

Following these general observations, we need to look at a number of texts—isolated passages or clusters of related texts—that are frequently mentioned in the migration debate or that can be identified on lexical grounds as being related to passages in the Hebrew Bible that deal with migration issues in one way or another.[3] We also need to look at some

1. *Pace*, e.g., Paynter, "Porous Borders," 126–28.

2. Hoffmeier, *The Immigration Crisis*, 131.

3. The following list of New Testament passages that are sometimes or frequently invoked by proponents of liberal immigration policies is not exhaustive; rather, it

additional passages that are normally not given consideration in discussions about the Bible and (im)migration.

2. ASPECTS OF DISCONTINUITY BETWEEN THE HEBREW BIBLE AND THE NEW TESTAMENT

The specific legal regulations concerning the treatment of *ger* ("sojourner") and *nokri* ("foreigner") are absent in the New Testament, which is related to the fact that not only no state in the world of the nations, but even not the church of the new covenant is a direct equivalent to ancient Israel. As far as the regulations concerning the *nokri* are concerned, it is interesting to note that as opposed to the Hebrew Bible, the focus of the corresponding Greek terms in the New Testament (most importantly *allotrios*, *xenos*, *paroikos*, and *proselytos*) is not on distance, but on the possibility of integration into the new assembly of God, sometimes with undertones of a beginning fulfillment of eschatological expectations of the Old Testament.[4]

Concerning the *ger* of the Hebrew Bible, there is no continuation of the specific legal measures provided in the law collections of the Hebrew Bible for his social protection and economic support, nor is there a continuation of the (partial) inclusion of this type of person into the religious rules found in the Hebrew Bible. Rather, there is only a thin connection between the two Testaments in this respect, in terms of a very general admonition to extend personal help to brothers in need. In addition to this, we note that legal requirements put on the *ger* in Leviticus 17–25 and Numbers 9, 15, and 19, together with passages such as Gen 9:4–6, seem to provide—at least in part—the criteria to determine which parts of the Old Testament laws can be seen as applicable to gentile believers.[5]

---

chooses those texts that are referred to most often. Among other passages of importance we need to mention Luke 24:13–36 and Eph 2:20–22. Concerning Luke 24:13–36, McKinney et al. state that Jesus is depicted as a stranger, who is recognized by the two disciples in Emmaus only "when they share a meal with the stranger" ("Welcoming the Stranger," 52). In Eph 2:20–22, the believers are said to be the dwelling of God in the Spirit, which—according to Margaret Aymer—means that God himself "is reinvented as a migrant who lives in . . . a diaspora space" (Aymer, "Sojourners Truths," 14; she also states that the Holy Spirit "becomes the ultimate 'naturalized' migrant," p. 15).

4. See, e.g., Eph 2:19, a text which will be dealt with below. This is true not only with a view to the attestations of the term *nokri* in legal texts, but with a view to the attestations of this term in general, as well as for the attestations of the term *zar* ("stranger").

5. See Bockmuehl, "The Noachide Commandments," 94, 96–97, 101, pointing

As far as texts in the Hebrew Bible dealing with the Canaanites are concerned (referring either to the concept of the "ban" or to expulsion), there is a linguistic connection from these texts to passages in the New Testament that deal with church discipline and the question of mixed marriages between believers and non-believers;[6] another line leads to passages in the New Testament that speak about God's judgment against his own people and the world at large.[7] As opposed to the Hebrew Bible, human agents are never summoned to use violence in these texts.

3. JESUS AND HIS FOLLOWERS AS MIGRANTS

3.1. Matthew 2:13–23: Flight from Bethlehem to Egypt, and Return from Egypt to Nazareth

One of the passages that is repeatedly seen as advocating liberal immigration policies is the story of Jesus and his parents fleeing from Bethlehem to Egypt,[8] with the flight being the result of Herod's intention to kill the baby. It is argued that this example points to the importance of migration as a divinely sanctioned or divinely ordained way of life, and that it underlines the importance of liberal immigration policies. It is also assumed that Jesus, because of this experience, would feel himself as a migrant and have a special sympathy for migrants; by the same token, migrants as such would be particularly close to Jesus and somehow reflect him in this world.

---

especially to Acts 15 and 1 Corinthians 5–10. This is in parallel with concepts found in Rabbinic Judaism; see Bockmuehl, "The Noachide Commandments," 86, 90.

6. Examples for the former are 1 Corinthians 5; 3 John 10; an example for the latter is found in 1 Cor 7:10, 15.

7. See, e.g., Acts 3:22; 1 Cor 16:22; Gal 1:8–9; 1 Thess 5:3; 2 Thess 1:9; Heb 12:29.

8. See, e.g., Carroll, *Christians*, 105–6; Gonzales, "Sanctuary," 4/; Groody, "Fruit," 302; Houston, *You Shall Love*, 134–36; Kerwin, "The Natural Rights," 193; McKinney et al., "Welcoming the Stranger," 50; Senior, "Beloved Aliens," 23. See also Van Nguyen, "In Solidarity." In his generalizing remarks, Van Nguyen also refers to Matt 25:35 (see "In Solidarity," 223). He also points to Gen 18:1–10 and 1 Kgs 17:1–16. In a way that is typical of the generalization and spiritualization found with many commentators, he concludes: "Solidarity with and generous welcome to the immigrants in our midst is not only a moral obligation but also an opportunity to meet God face to face. Furthermore, it could even have the possibility of changing the course of history, as shown in the hospitality Egypt gave to a poor immigrant Israelite family from Bethlehem" ("In Solidarity," 224).

There is in fact no doubt that Jesus—together with his parents—
would qualify as "refugee(s)" in the context of current legal standards.
Also according to current legal standards, Jesus and his parents would
not fall into the category of "illegal immigrants."[9] While the story presents Jesus and his parents as temporary refugees, one can hardly claim
that Jesus would define himself as a migrant based on this specific episode, understanding the term "migrant" in its broad general sense.[10] One
reason for this is that Matthew does not make the claim that this event
had a specific biographical importance for Jesus in the way that some of
the advocates of liberal immigration policies suggest. It is true that Jesus
is said to state that he has no place to lay his head (see Matt 8:20; Luke
9:58); but this comes closer, in the context of current circumstances and
categories, to the life of "homeless people" and is different from present-
day migrants in that it is fully a matter of personal choice on the side of
Jesus, and in that migrants in almost all cases aspire to overcome such a
situation which they may endure temporarily, while for Jesus's life it was
of permanent character. Moreover, one has to bear in mind that the flight
happened very early in Jesus's childhood, before the age of conscious remembrance. This means that the flight as such could not have become a
defining mark of Jesus's character. Whether the experience as exile lasted
long enough to assume that Jesus's character was formed by it, is difficult
to assess given the uncertainty of the relevant dates (date of Jesus's birth;
date of Herod's death).[11] It is, however, important to note two points
pertaining to this question: The issue here is exile and not migration for
economic reasons; and nowhere is there a reference to the stay in Egypt
in the reports about Jesus's later life.

It is obvious that Matthew's story of Jesus's flight to Egypt and return
to the land of Israel is heavily focused on a theological point:[12] Jesus is
the new Moses and, at the same time, the new Israel, in the context of a
new exodus. Like Moses's, his life is under threat right in the early stages
of his childhood, and like Moses he has to flee to preserve his life.[13] Jesus

---

9. This is also mentioned by Edwards, "A Biblical Perspective," 7.

10. The term "immigrant" would make even less sense.

11. Cf. the remarks in France, *Matthew*, 77.

12. See, e.g., Bruner, *Matthew*, 73–76; France, *Matthew*, 77–81; Keener, *Matthew*,
107–12. Cf. also Van Nguyen, "In Solidarity," 222–23.

13. Of course, the parallels are thought to work even if there are also differences:
There are two threats to Moses's life, one right at the moment of his birth, and a later
one originating in his killing of an Egyptian overseer of Hebrew slaves, with both

is also the new Israel, following the migratory patterns of the patriarchs from what was then Canaan to Egypt and back, and mirroring the exodus of the people from Egypt to the Promised Land—the latter being directly hinted at in the quote of Hos 11:1 in Matt 2:15, a quote which uses the Old Testament source in a typological way.[14] It is about the specific role of Jesus as the Messiah in a new exodus: as the new deliverer, he has to suffer persecution like the old one did.[15]

These theological dimensions of the story cannot be transferred to migration in general just like that. On the other hand, one can still argue that the fact that God has chosen to guide his people in a way that includes physical flight from oppression needs to be given due weight. This is certainly true on a spiritual level. On the practical physical level, however, there is nothing in the story and its broader use in the Gospel of Matthew that would suggest that it functions as a generic model encouraging migration of any kind.[16] Rather, if one looks for a general application beyond the spiritual realm, it would likely be that the first exodus and Jesus's flight and return demonstrate that flight from oppression may indeed be part of God's ways with his people. It is, however, not within the frame of proper interpretation to postulate that when God has been at work in the specific journeys of the patriarchs, the exodus of the Israelites, and the flight of Jesus and his parents to Egypt, God is present in a comparable way in all incidents of migration. Such an interpretation would also need to explain why in the case of Abraham and Jesus only the journey to Egypt has special weight and can be applied generally, but not the return to Canaan or the land of Israel respectively. This is all the more important because in the case of Jesus, it is exactly the return that establishes him as the forerunner of the new exodus.[17]

Overall, it seems clear that on the practical-physical level there is no bearing on issues of migration beyond instances of imminent personal persecution or death threats or instances of group oppression, if one goes beyond Jesus's flight to include also the first exodus. The flight of

threats originating in Egypt; he has to eventually flee that place (as an adult), while later returning to lead his people in the first exodus. On the other hand, Jesus has to flee to Egypt (as a child), and will return (still a child) to the land of Israel to lead God's people in a new—and final—exodus.

14. So also, e.g., France, *Matthew*, 80; cf. Keener, *Matthew*, 108–9.

15. So also Bruner, *Matthew*, 75.

16. Especially not "desiring a better life" (Carroll, *Christians*, 106).

17. So also Keener, *Matthew*, 108.

Jesus and his parents is an expression of the temporary political exile of an individual, not related to questions of escaping poverty nor to situations in which large-scale immigration takes place. It is also not possible to deduce any support for illegal immigration from the passage in question. The use of the episode in the current migration debate by proponents of liberal immigration policies, then, is largely a matter of over-interpretation, unwarranted generalization, and eisegesis. The only legitimate direct connection can be seen to cases of individuals flying from personal death threats. Even so, one has to bear in mind two important points: Only the fact that there was some kind of political and legal border between Judea and Egypt could guarantee the success of the escape; and according to the socio-political circumstances of that time, Jesus and his family would not have been economically supported by any state agencies, but either (in part) by donations of the large Jewish diaspora in Egypt, and perhaps more importantly by income generated by Joseph.[18]

3.2. Itinerant Life and Flight of Believers

According to all the four Gospels, Jesus, during his ministry of approximately three years, led an itinerant life.[19] From the very beginning, also the disciples of Jesus were used to an itinerant life: First, they followed Jesus in his wanderings within Galilee and the neighboring areas, and between Galilee and Jerusalem. They were also sent by Jesus to preach the gospel as wandering missionaries in various parts of the land of Israel. Other followers of Jesus, however, outside of the inner circle of disciples, remained in their home towns and did not wander about. In Acts, we read about the commission to the disciples to be witnesses "in all Judea, and Samaria, and to the ends of the earth" (Acts 1:8), and subsequently—both in Acts and various of the epistles—about believers who were forced to migrate and flee because of their faith, and in so doing spread

18. Cf. Keener, *Matthew*, 106. See also Hoffmeier, *The Immigration Crisis*, 133. Of course, no certainty as to how the ratio between these two possible modes of support may have looked like is available, since the sources do not provide any information about this point. Additionally, the gifts of the magi may also have played a role in the financial support of the family..

19. There are some particularly strong formulations about the harsh conditions that went along with this kind of life: He has nowhere to lay his head (Matt 8:20; Luke 9:58).

the gospel to new areas.[20] This begins right after the death of Stephen, when Christians were scattered throughout Judea and Samaria because of persecution (see Acts 8:1–2).[21] Others, however, seem to have ventured on missionary journeys without being forced to do so because of persecution. In the cases in which these journeys ended in a permanent change in the place of residence, one can legitimately speak of emigration/immigration. As this short overview shows, both voluntary and involuntary migration was part of the reality of the lives of early Christians—though never including illegal immigration. In several instances, there was a mixture between the two: Paul had to flee both Damascus (see Acts 9:23–25) and Jerusalem (see Acts 9:29–30); he was expelled from Antioch (see Acts 13:50), and was transferred as a prisoner to Rome (see Acts 28:14–16); but on many occasions, he ventured on missionary journeys voluntarily.[22] Aquila and Priscilla are another case in point: They had to leave Rome for Corinth because of emperor Claudius's edict (see Acts 18:2–3); later, they accompanied Paul from Corinth to Ephesus (see Acts 18:18–19), probably out of their own choosing. By the time of the writing of the letter to the Romans, the couple is back again in Rome (see Rom 16:3). In some cases the missionary journeys are directly prompted by the Lord through an angel, visions, or his Spirit (see, e.g., Acts 8:26; 16:6–7, 9), while in other cases this is not mentioned, which may point to a larger role of the missionaries' own initiative.[23] A very important element in the prompting of missionary journeys is the sending by mother churches, such as Antioch. The church of Antioch sends Barnabas in Acts 11:23 and Barnabas and Paul in Acts 13:1–3, in the latter case directly instigated by the Spirit.

The itinerant life of Jesus and his disciples is seen by some as an argument for liberal immigration policies.[24] However, again more caution

---

20. Another famous example of forced migration of a member of the early church is John, the author of Revelations, who at the time of the writing of his book was an exile on the island of Patmos.

21. Acts 8:4 notes that those who were dispersed immediately began to preach the gospel.

22. In Acts 9:32—10:48 Peter is described as "going here and there among all the believers" (9:32) in Lydda, Joppa, and Caesarea. It Is likely that also in his case the initial departure from Jerusalem was caused by the persecution after the death of Stephen.

23. Cf. Stenschke, "Migration and Mission," 173.

24. See, e.g., McKinney et al., "Welcoming the Stranger," 50; Senior, "Beloved Aliens," 23–31.

is needed. Parallels to modern forms of migration exist primarily as far as Christians who left their original places of residence because of persecution are concerned. Their fate, as far as cause and motivation for the respective migratory moves are concerned, is similar to modern refugees who have to flee their homes because of immediate threats to their lives. Indirectly, readers of New Testament witnesses of such cases are certainly encouraged to help and welcome persecuted brothers and sisters in the Lord—an encouragement that is given even more support through New Testament reports about such help being extended to the Christian refugees during that historical period. By way of extension, one might also find encouragement to help persecuted people in general. On the other hand, there are no direct links to any of the most dominant questions of current migration issues, insofar as they concern economic aspects. Also questions of large-scale immigration and state policy are not in any way directly relatable to the New Testament texts that describe the fate of Christian refugees or Christians engaged in voluntary missionary travels or emigration/immigration.

A sub-topic of the one just mentioned is the designation of the followers of Jesus as "those belonging to the Way" (Acts 9:2).[25] It is not clear how exactly the noun *hodos* ("way") has to be semantically analyzed in the present context. Most likely, however, it refers to the aspects of behavior and belief system which the Christians adopted—in other words, the way of life which leads to salvation.[26] It is much less likely, even if one can perhaps not fully exclude it, that the term refers to the itinerant life-style of the early Christians as well.[27] Even if this should be the case, nothing changes with respect to the interpretation presented above.

25. See also Acts 19:9, 23; 22:4; 24:14, 22; cf. Acts 16:17 ("the way of salvation"), 18:25 ("the way of the Lord"), 18:26 ("the way of God").

26. For a similar interpretation see Marshall, *Acts*, 168. This fits very well with the most wide-spread metaphorical use of the noun *derek* ("way") in the Hebrew Bible (see Zehnder, *Wegmetaphorik*, 324–40).

27. The latter understanding is proposed, for example, by McKinney et al., "Welcoming the Stranger," 52. Stenschke states: "'The Way' refers to their [i.e., the Christians'] identity and message" ("Migration and Mission," 170). The fact, however, that the term "way" is also used in a similar way in the documents of Qumran (see Bruce, *Acts*, 181; Marshall, *Acts*, 169) casts some doubt on this interpretation, as do the compounds "way of salvation," "way of the Lord," and "way of God," of which the simple "way" could be an abbreviation (cf. Peterson, *The Acts of the Apostles*, 302). Whether a connection exists to Jesus's self-designation as "the way" in John 14:6 cannot be established with any certainty.

3.3. The Believers as Aliens or Pilgrims

There are several texts in the New Testament that describe the believers' lives in terms of a pilgrimage or in terms of being aliens.[28] Also these passages are sometimes referred to in the argument for liberal immigration policies.[29] Let us look at some of the passages in question.

In 1 Pet 2:11, the addressees are called "aliens" and "strangers" (*paroikoi* and *parepidemoi*). The fact that the Greek text uses the particle *hos* ("like") before these nouns, together with the context, shows that they are used in a metaphorical way, not as descriptors of the addressees actual legal or social status.[30] It is unlikely that the author distinguishes in any precise way between the two terms; rather, together they point to the combination of geographical displacement and lack of rights connected to citizenship.[31] The emphasis here likely is on the distinction between the Christian addressees and the pagan majority culture in terms of their faith and the concomitant ethical behavior. In addition, especially based on the Old Testament background of the metaphor, the transient character of life is also in view, which in the case of a Christian audience implies an orientation to the goal of eternal life beyond "this world."[32]

Another example is Heb 13:13–14. In this case the stress is on the willing acceptance of being outcast from society at large as people who follow Christ, bearing the stigma of rejection by the majority and the establishment,[33] bound up with legal insecurity as well. At the same time, there is a positive note here that outside of the "camp" new opportunities

28. See especially 1 Pet 2:11; Heb 11:9, 13 (referring to Abraham and the patriarchs in general); 13:13–14.

29. See, e.g., Carroll, *Christians*, 116–19; Houston, *You Shall Love*, 145–48; McKinney et al., "Welcoming the Stranger," 52; Senior, "Beloved Aliens," 28–29; Strine, "Embracing Asylum Seekers," 488–89.

30. So also Michaels, *1 Peter*, 116, Schreiner, *1, 2 Peter, Jude*, 119–20. For a different view see Senior, "Beloved Aliens," 25; he thinks that the terms point to "the social and ethnic status of these Christians as migrant workers" ("Beloved Aliens," 25). According to him, the same is true for Jas 1:1 (see "Beloved Aliens," 26).

31. See Michaels, *1 Peter*, 116; Schreiner, *1, 2 Peter, Jude*, 119. It is likely that the combination of the two terms mirrors the same combination found both in Gen 23:4 and in Ps 38:13 in the Septuagint (MT Ps 39:13).

32. Cf. Schreiner, *1, 2 Peter, Jude*, 119.

33. Cf. Bruce, *Hebrews*, 403–4. It may well be that what is in view here is the rejection specifically by the Jewish establishment; see Bruce, *Hebrews*, 403; Michel, *Der Brief an die Hebräer*, 511, 517. But it would likely not be warranted to restrict the message of the passage to this dimension.

for building God's kingdom—especially among gentile nations—await the addressees who are willing to follow Jesus. It is also important to note that the passage has an eschatological dimension.[34]

We find in these New Testament passages the clearest line of continuity as far as the *ger* ("sojourner") of the Hebrew Bible is concerned: The handful of passages in the Hebrew Bible that use the noun *ger* to express the transient character of human existence on this earth or of the Israelites' tenure of the Promised Land find their continuation in the New Testament description of the believers' existence in terms of being aliens in this world or pilgrims. It can be said that such texts have more theological weight in the New Testament as compared to the Hebrew Bible, with the concept of "pilgrimage" being one of the main metaphors that describe core aspects of Christian life in this world. The pilgrimage texts differ from their *ger*-precursors in the Hebrew Bible in the sense that they are more directly oriented towards the final goal, which is life in the world to come. The latter concept, of course, is generally much less developed and prominent in the Hebrew Bible than it is in the New Testament.

In all of the cases under review, there is no direct relation to the question of the admission of large numbers of (im)migrants into the community of a state. Rather, it is about Christians being discriminated against on the one hand, and their inner independence of everything this-worldly that is not compatible with the world to come, the latter being understood both temporally and locally.[35] If there is any bridge that can be built to the topic of migration, it would be a call to hospitality towards and support for Christian refugees who might need a safe place of refuge, and a call to be willing to become a missionary-migrant for the sake of the gospel. As in the previous cases, any support for illegal immigration cannot be based on the passages dealt with in this paragraph. The New Testament passages in view here are basically spiritual, not political, and therefore their use for the advancement of specific policy goals is inappropriate.

Some commentators interpret the New Testament passages in question as commanding Christians to resist the temptation to try to control one's own land, and thereby avoid "the idolatry of unconditional national sovereignty."[36] While there is an element of truth in creating this

34. See Michel, *Der Brief an die Hebräer*, 510, 513–15, 518.

35. See, e.g., Michel, *Der Brief an die Hebräer*, 521.

36. Senior, "Beloved Aliens," 28–29; see also Carroll, *Christians*, 118.

connection, it cannot be taken as the central message of the passages in question, and it cannot be used as a decisive argument for liberal immigration policies. It has to be remembered that the message would be valid for all parties involved, the receiving societies as much as the sending societies and the migrants themselves; also, the distinction between personal lives and the organization of communal life on the national level need to be taken into consideration. A critical relativization of the priority of ethnicity and nation (which is right) is not the same as denying the importance of these concepts altogether.

4. GOD'S OPTION FOR THE VULNERABLE AND MARGINALIZED

4.1. Luke 4:18–21: Good News to the Poor

According to the Gospel of Luke, Jesus begins his public ministry in Galilee with a reading of Isa 61:1–3, which he declares as being fulfilled now.[37] Poor, captives, blind, and downtrodden are highlighted as those who receive special care by the One who is anointed with the Lord's Spirit. In fact, the poor are mentioned several times in the Gospel of Luke as being of particular concern for Jesus. At this point, it is important to note that no special reference is made either in the Old Testament source text or in its New Testament use of migrants of any kind. It is, however, clear, that as far as migrants are either poor or captive or blind or downtrodden—which is evidently often the case—they can also be subsumed under these categories. But again, this does in itself not determine questions about how resources should be dispensed between the various groups of persons in need, nor does it predicate specific immigration policies. The same is true for additional passages that are seen by some authors as pointing to Jesus being "in solidarity with the poor and suffering"[38] (Matt 18:6–14; Mark 6:34; Luke 12:16–21; 16:19–31).

37. This text is mentioned as one argument for liberal immigration policies for example by McKinney et al., "Welcoming the Stranger," 50.

38. Senior, "Beloved Aliens," 27. Cf. also Houston, You Shall Love, 136–39; she also includes Matt 5:1–12 and Luke 6:20–26. Houston asks: "Who is poorer than the person who is forced to flee for their life, leaving everything they own behind? Who is more destitute than the asylum-seeker denied leave to remain, refused permission to work, devoid of welfare benefits . . . ?" (You Shall Love, 138). She obviously assumes that these are rhetorical questions that should inspire immediate action by her readers. However, the situation is clearly more complex. For example, it is a well-known fact

4.2. Luke 10:25–37: The Good Samaritan

The parable of the good Samaritan, sometimes together with other texts pointing to Jesus's unusual close contact with Samaritans mentioned in various Gospel traditions (healing of the Samaritan leper, Luke 17:11–19; conversation with a Samaritan woman, John 4:7–30), also appears on the list of texts that are used by some authors to argue for liberal immigration policies or as a model for the rescue of migrants who try to reach the shores of the West.[39] It must be noted, however, that in many ways this parable is even further removed from current migration issues than, for example, the story of the flight of Jesus and his parents to Egypt. It is certainly clear that the parable demonstrates Jesus's attitude to view Samaritans in a more positive light than most of the Jews of his time would do.[40] Not a member of the Jewish religious elites, but a Samaritan is being depicted as a model for the exercise of love of neighbor. It is probably also fair to say that the parable implies that neighborly relationships exist between all persons that encounter one another, regardless of their respective backgrounds.[41] There are, however, no easy transfers to questions of large-scale immigration. After all, the parable is not about the question whether Samaritans should be accepted as immigrants. Also, it is not possible to claim that a member of a different religious group is elevated, because Samaritans were still very closely related to Judaism; in modern terms, it is a case of "denominational-religious" (and ethnic) distinction rather than a clearly "religious" one. On the other hand, it is in fact the case that Jesus commends an attitude of practical compassion towards the neighbor, even if this neighbor does not belong to one's own group. The help, however, is extended to an individual, not to large groups, and it is given on a personal level, by free choice, using one's own time and financial means—as opposed to the principle of delegation to state (or church) agencies being supported by compulsory taxes. Another

---

that the vast majority of those seeking asylum in Europe in the current circumstances are not the most destitute among the populations of the sending countries.

39. See, e.g., Carroll, *Christians*, 107–12; Gutiérrez, "Poverty," 82–83; Hoover, "The Story," 166; Houston, *You Shall Love*, 141–42; McKinney et al., "Welcoming the Stranger," 51; "A Wesleyan View of Immigration," The Hospitality Principle. In this paragraph of the Wesleyan document, several passages are added that call for hospitality among or to believers (Matt 10:24; Rom 12:13; 1 Pet 4:9), although there is nothing in these passages that refers directly to the topic of immigration.

40. See, e.g., Geldenhuys, *Luke*, 311; Stein, *Luke*, 316.

41. So also, e.g., Geldenhuys, *Luke*, 311–12; Stein, *Luke*, 319.

important aspect of the parable is that the help is given to a neighbor in the context of a personal-physical encounter, not to a distant person with whom no personal contact exists. Furthermore, it is noticeable that the help is restricted to what is necessary for survival and not comparable to life-long pensions, etc. In addition, as opposed to migrant rescue organizations, the Samaritan does not search the territory for the largest possible number of migrants, but happens to stumble on one individual. In terms of immigration policies, the implication is that a migrant who has arrived to one's neighborhood is a neighbor as much as anybody else; at the same time, the parable cannot be used as a text that encourages to "import" persons in need from other parts of the world—or even to extend help in other ways to other parts of the world.[42] And as in the case of the texts mentioned in the previous chapter, no justification for illegal immigration can be deduced from the passage.

There are also more directly theological aspects that need to be taken into account. According to the discourse that precedes and introduces the parable, love of neighbor cannot be detached from love of God, that is, faith. In the broader context of the Gospel of Luke, Jesus, by granting God's forgiving grace, is the one who initiates new life in those who believe; this is what enables believers to have real love towards both God and human neighbor.[43] This means that the parable is not supporting neighborly love of any kind independent of a faith relationship with God. The implication in the current circumstances—as already observed in our analysis of the parable of the good Samaritan—is that while Christian initiatives for helping migrants of all kinds can be rooted in the New Testament, attempts to impose such help on the whole of a (mostly secular) society through law and taxation is a different matter.

As far as the reports about Jesus's sporadic contacts with Samaritans are concerned, they can certainly be taken as proof of his attitude that does not shun from contact with people that are not accepted by the

42. This does, of course, not exclude that other—biblical or extra-biblical, pragmatic—reasons may be found to extend help to other parts of the world.

43. See Geldenhuys, *Luke*, 312. Cf. Stein, *Luke*, 316. Another theological question is whether the Samaritan of the parable has to be understood in christological terms, because showing compassion in Luke is a divine prerogative, and showing mercy in Luke is almost always associated with God or Jesus (see Parsons, *Luke*, 180–81). If this is true, the Samaritan is elevated to an even higher position; at the same time, the general thrust of the parable and especially its relationship with questions of migration is modified only insofar as following the Samaritan's example becomes a case of *imitatio Dei* or *imitatio Christi*.

majority of the "in-group." This can be seen as relevant not only, but also, for migration issues. It will, however, be most naturally relatable to questions about how the church or individual members of it treat immigrants, and not to questions about whom a state should allow to immigrate into its territory.

4.3. Matthew 25:31–46: The Division of Sheep and Goat, Referring to Help for Strangers

In this famous passage on the last judgment, the Lord makes a distinction between sheep and goats, based, among others, on the question whether they have showed hospitality to persons who are referred to with the term *xenos* ("stranger"), or not. Because of the latter element, this passage is very often quoted in support of a welcoming attitude toward immigrants in the current debate about migration.[44] It is sometimes even seen as the primary witness of the New Testament for an unconditional pro-immigrant position, building on texts from the Hebrew Bible that speak about the protection of the *ger* ("sojourner") in the judicial realm and his support in the economic realm.[45]

There are a number of extremely important and difficult questions related to this passage, such as: Who exactly are the persons being judged? Who exactly are the recipients of the acts of charity mentioned in the passage, referred to as "his brothers, even the least ones"? What does the text intimate about the relationship of work and grace? How is "eternal judgment" to be understood?[46] In the context of the present study, we have to restrict ourselves to an investigation of those aspects that are directly related to the topic of (im)migration.

44. See, e.g., Campese, "¿Cuantos Más?" 273, 288, 294; Carroll, *Christians*, 112–13 (see also his references to hospitality in the New Testament more generally on pp. 120–21); Gonzales, "Sanctuary," 47; Hoover, "The Story," 163; Houston, *You Shall Love*, 144–45; McKinney et al., "Welcoming the Stranger," 51; O'Neill, "'No Longer Strangers,'" 230; Rodríguez, "A Witness," xv; Senior, "Beloved Aliens," 23, 27, 30; "A Wesleyan View of Immigration," The Great Commandment Principle and The Grace Principle; "Southern Baptist 2018 Resolution on Migration," fourth paragraph.

45. Cf., e.g., the "Matthew 25 Movement."

46. For a detailed and balanced treatment of these questions see, e.g., Bruner, *Matthew*, 564–85.

Firstly, it is important to note that *xenos* ("stranger") is not the direct Greek equivalent to *ger*;[47] this means that there is no straightforward link to the regulations concerning the *ger* found in the Hebrew Bible. Moreover, the recipients of the hospitality described in the passage, among them the *xenoi*, are said to be from among "my brothers, even the least ones" (v. 40). While the meaning of this phrase is a matter of debate,[48] it is at least relatively likely that they are followers of Christ. It seems to me that the use of *adelphos* ("brother") in Matt 12:48–50, together with the likely parallel of the present passage with Matt 10:40–42, strongly suggest to prefer the restrictive Christian interpretation of the term against the more generic "persons in need."[49] This interpretation also has the advantage of giving the passage a function that best combines the literal meaning of the description of the final judgment with the text-pragmatic setting as a speech to current and possibly future disciples. According to a literal interpretation of the scene, there is no encouragement to good works being directed at the present audience and possible later audiences at its center; after all, these good works are just mentioned as a matter of retrospective fact, done without any specific purpose and not related to a specific command, and executed by people who are not identical with the audience of the speech. The real audience, however, is directly addressed insofar as the recipients of the good works are Christians, for in this case they receive a message of consolation that even if they will find themselves in situations of distress, Jesus is identifying himself with them. This interpretation also makes sense in terms of the broader context of Second Temple Jewish eschatological discourses. In texts such as 1 Enoch 62; 103–4; 4 Ezra; 2 Baruch 72, the oppressed people of God are encouraged by being given the promise that God will judge the nations based on how they treated God's people.[50]

47. In the Septuagint, *ger* is rendered mostly either by *proselytos* or by *paroikos*. The latter would be the natural candidate for Matthew 25 if the continuity with the texts mentioning the *ger* was to be stressed, given the fact that *proselytos* had become semantically too narrow to fulfill this role.

48. See, e.g., Bruner, *Matthew*, 564, 574–75.

49. For a summary of the main reasons in support of a generic view see Bruner, *Matthew*, 575. All the four points mentioned by him, however, do not seem to be compelling. Most importantly, nowhere in Matthew is the term "brothers" used to refer to humanity in general; rather, it refers always specifically to Jesus's disciples.

50. Cf. Keener, *Matthew*, 606.

The best alternative reading might be the following:[51] The addressees are (mainly future) followers of Jesus, who are supposed to identify
with the "sheep" of the judgment scene. In this way, they are indirectly
summoned to do good works—as a consequence of being Christians—
for the little ones who are brothers, or—somewhat less likely—for the
little ones as if they were brothers. Text-pragmatically also this interpretation seems acceptable, given the fact that Christians are the addressees
and will find themselves even more prominently represented in the scene
than under the first interpretation.[52] The problem, however, is that the
message is "hidden" and the text cannot be read in a way that is as literal
as with the first option. There is an additional problem: "Bad righteousness *expects* to be called good and is surprised when it isn't (v. 44); good
righteousness sees little righteousness in itself and is surprised when it
is considered righteous at all (vv. 37–39)."[53] How is it possible to "use"
the passage according to an interpretation that understands it in terms
of an indirect ethical exhortation and avoid the problem of circularity
just pointed out?[54] On the other hand, this reading has the advantage of
following the interpretative pattern set in the two parables preceding our
passage (Matt 25:1–13, 14–30).[55]

If one grants that the persons who receive the beneficial treatment
of those called "sheep" are Christians, the help described in the passage
of the last judgment is a case of support specifically for Christians, not a
program for the benefit of (im)migrants in general.[56] However, things

51. Of course, there are many other possibilities. Among those is the assumption
that the judgment refers only to people who will have been present at the last phase
of the end times, with the "brothers" being the final witnesses after the rapture, and
the "sheep" being those who reacted positively to their message (see Seibel, *Das Matthäusevangelium*). If one follows such interpretations, the passage has no relation to
general hospitality towards strangers at all.

52. Cf. Bruner, *Matthew*, 577–78.

53. Bruner, *Matthew*, 573.

54. The ethical posture of being on the high horse that can often be observed by
people using this text to request or support liberal immigration policies, is an indica-
tion of this problem.

55. According to another line of interpretation that can claim some plausibility, the
sheep and goats in view are persons who have not heard the gospel, who will be judged
based on their works of charity (or lack thereof) for needy persons in general. In this
case, the recipients of the good works cannot be Christians, because one would expect
them to proclaim the gospel. It can be argued, however, that this interpretation is not
easy to reconcile with the description of the future found in Matt 24:14 and 28:18–20.

56. See, e.g., Cortés-Fuentes, "The Least," 100–109. See also Keener, *Matthew*, 605.

are more complicated since one could still argue that this was not known by those who extended the help, taking into consideration the element of surprise that might point in this direction.[57]

Whichever interpretation one follows, it is clear that one cannot claim that the passage is not open for containing at least an *implicit* encouragement to doing good works for people in need. This is even more clear given the fact that good deeds are certainly part of the Matthean concept of being righteous. The blessing on everyone who shows mercy in Matt 5:7 is just one text that points in this direction.

It is important to note that the list of good works mentioned in the passage is not exhaustive.[58] It points to an attitude that is aware of all possible needs that persons—depending on the interpretation of "brothers:" Christians or human beings in general—may have and causes people to act accordingly. A consequence of this is that the text cannot be used to advocate for any kind of one-sided agenda. In the present context, this also applies for a one-sided focus on support for (im)migrants, which can in fact often be observed currently in the arguments presented by those who support liberal immigration policies. Rather, the passage would suggest that help is extended evenly and not to one group at the cost of others—if the recipients referred to in the text are not exclusively Christians. Moreover, if migration is seen as a suboptimal solution to a problem at least in some cases, the help to which readers of the text are encouraged might well consist in trying to enable the repatriation of emigrants. In addition, effective help that is oriented towards the larger context of the needs mentioned in the passage, including the aim of long-term improvements, will also deal with the root causes. As far as migration is concerned, in many cases facilitating migration will not be the strategy of choice to achieve this. One also has to take into consideration that what the text has in view is not more than the traditional duty of

---

Matthean language supports this view; see especially Matt 10:42; 12:46–50; 18:6, 10, 14; 28:10. Some would go a step further and identify the persons in view as Christian missionaries; see, e.g., Michaels, "Apostolic Hardships," 27–37; Suh, "Das Weltgericht," 217–33; cf. also Keener, *Matthew*, 606. It seems, however, that the designation of these persons is not specific enough to allow for such a narrow definition.

57. Thus France, *Matthew*, 959; cf. also p. 964. This argument is, however, certainly not decisive, because strictly speaking the surprise does not concern the fact that the recipients were "brothers" of the Lord, but that in these brothers the Lord was in some ways present himself.

58. So also Bruner, *Matthew*, 570.

personal hospitality,[59] something that is quite far removed from issues of large-scale immigration. Moreover, the Matthean passage speaks about hospitality (or, by extension, other forms of help and support) on a private level, which is not the same as judicial protection and long-term economic support in a legal and state-centered context.[60]

It is certainly adequate to close the discussion of this passage on a different note: There can be no doubt, both in the Matthean context and in the context of the Bible as a whole, that extending basic material (and other) help to any persons in need, beginning with the "brother," but not ending there, is in fact very important and valuable in God's eyes. By necessity, this also includes (im)migrants. However, helping individual (im)migrants is not the same as propagating large-scale immigration, and the question as to how best (im)migrants or potential (im)migrants can be helped needs to be addressed in each case on the merits of the given circumstances, with an openness to the possibility that leaving one's place may not be the best or wisest solution.

Somewhat similar points to the ones made in Matt 25:31–46 can be found in 3 John 5, where the author encourages his addressees to do good for and extend love to the brothers in Christ, especially the *xenoi* among them. In this instance, it is made even more explicitly clear that the beneficiaries of the help extended by the Christians are not *xenoi* in general, but fellow believers.[61] Whether in this case as well as in Matthew 25 *xenos* refers to people of a different ethnic background or just people outside the own extended family or from some not too distant village is not entirely clear. There seems no reason, however, to exclude the former possibility. This, then, would mean that in practical life, in correspondence with the spiritual character of the new people of God, distinctions between different ethnic groups are toned down, as we have already seen above. This does not mean, however, that ethnic distinctions are completely erased and altogether irrelevant.[62]

59. See, e.g., France, *Matthew*, 964.

60. So also Edwards, "A Biblical Perspective," 4.

61. It is also important to note that according to Heb 10:34, visiting prisoners— one of the elements mentioned in Matthew 25—is a mark of Christian love, and in this case, it is clear that the prisoners are fellow Christians.

62. For comments on a similar admonition in Heb 13:1 see below.

5. THE LOVE COMMAND

The command to love one's neighbor (or one's brother and sister in the Lord) is repeatedly invoked by authors arguing for liberal immigration policies.[63] Some aspects that are relevant for this topic have already been touched upon in the treatment of the love-command in the Hebrew Bible. However, more needs to be said as far as the love-command in the New Testament is concerned.[64] Let us look at some of the most important passages:

In the Synoptic Gospels, reference is made to the Old Testament commands to love the Lord and to love one's neighbor (*agapao*; see Matt 19:19; 22:37–40; Mark 12:30–31, 33; Luke 10:27).[65] The coordination of the two commands—not found in the Hebrew Bible—means that self-love has to be *subordinated* to the love of God and *coordinated* with the love of one's neighbor.[66] These commands are supplemented by the command to love even one's enemies (*agapao*; see Matt 5:43–44; Luke 6:27, 35), which goes beyond the explicit formulations in the Hebrew Bible.[67] In Luke 6:27–28, loving the enemies is related to doing them good and blessing them.[68] In both passages, persecutors are the most likely candidates for the identification of the "enemies." This means that passively accepting suffering is a central part of what love implies. Interestingly, both in Matt 5:43–44 and Luke 6:27–28 to love the enemies is directly connected to pray for those who persecute the believers.

According to Matt 22:40, the whole Law and the Prophets hang on the two commands to love God and the neighbor.[69] Most important

63. See, e.g., Gutiérrez, "Poverty," 83; Houston, *You Shall Love*, 139–41; McKinney et al., "Welcoming the Stranger," 50–51; Rodríguez, "A Witness," xiv; "A Wesleyan View of Immigration," The Great Commandment Principle.

64. For a more comprehensive treatment of love in the New Testament see, e.g., Zehnder, "Love in the Bible," 45–58.

65. It is likely that "neighbor" in these instances means "everyone," not just the fellow Jew or the member of any other restricted group (cf. France, *Matthew*, 846).

66. See Lussier, *God Is Love*, 142.

67. For an interpretation of these passages see, in addition to the commentaries, Wischmeyer, *Liebe*, 44–51.

68. On the other hand, Jesus's own attitude as reported in Matthew 23 shows that love does not exclude controversy and rebuke.

69. The meaning of the sentence is not that the specific ethical rules found in the Hebrew Bible are dispensable, but rather that "those rules find their true role in working out the practical implications of the love for God and neighbor on which they are based" (France, *Matthew*, 847). Lussier puts it this way (*God Is Love*, 143): "All the

in our context is the observation that love of neighbor—including (im)
migrants, we might add—cannot be separated from love of God; this
principle is of course valid also in the reverse direction. On the other
hand, Matt 7:12 states that the Law and the Prophets can be summarized
with the "golden rule." The latter, then—in its positive version—can be
understood as an explanation of what is meant by "love of the neighbor"
in practical terms.[70] With the command to love elevated into the highest
position, all other individual commands can be understood "as concrete
expressions of the love demand—*descendants*, as it were—of the two love
commandments."[71]

A specific aspect of interpersonal love is taken up in Luke 7:5, which
shows that love is shown in practical good deeds. Also the parable of the
good Samaritan in Luke 10:29–37, which follows the discourse on "love"
(*agapao*) in v. 27, likely underlines that love for one's neighbor is shown
in compassion and practical good deeds.[72]

All these passages are important for the present discussion because,
in light of the broader context, it is not possible to restrict love to the co-
Israelite or the fellow follower of Jesus.

In the Gospel of John, there are only a few passages that speak about
interpersonal love. In John 13:34; 15:12, 17, Jesus announces that he gives
his disciples a new commandment, that they love (*agapao*) one another,
as Jesus has loved them—which includes even the laying down of one's
life.[73] John 13:35 adds that if they have love for one another, people will
see that they are Jesus's disciples. With the love command being given in

---

other commandments are but elaborations and applications of these two fundamental
precepts." Love is what keeps the whole of the Law together and defines its inner essence, foundation and goal (cf. Wischmeyer, *Liebe*, 33).

70. See Gerhardsson, "Agape," 168; cf. also Houston, *You Shall Love*, 140. This is
only true for the positive version of the "golden rule"; the negative version merely
describes what is just, what must not be done in order to prevent the destruction of
the community; but only the positive version can be related to love, which builds up
the community. Interestingly, Hillel, faced with a similar request as Jesus to summarize
the law, uses the negative version of the "golden rule" (see b. Shabb. 31a). The same is
true for Didache 1:2.

71. Gerhardsson, "Agape," 169. Gerhardsson goes on to explain the so-called an-
titheses in Matthew 5 as pointing to the transformation that concrete commandments
of the *torah* are subject to. They are made into specific aspects of the *agape*-demand,
which requires "a total attitude, governed by an unreserved love for God and for one's
neighbor" ("Agape," 169).

72. See, e.g., Wischmeyer, *Liebe*, 10, 36–37.

73. See Moloney, *Love*, 107.

the context of Jesus's washing of his disciples' feet as a demonstration of his love for them,[74] the character of this love is identified as being serving and self-effacing. This passage also makes a direct link between the love of the disciples among themselves and their mission to the world. Only if they love one another can their mission to the world, which aims at incorporating even more people into the loving relationship between the Father and the Son, and by extension his followers, be successful.[75] This connection is relevant for the migration debate especially in the sense that showing love to (im)migrants merely on the material level would fall short of the deeper Johannine concept of neighborly love. John 17, especially vv. 20–23, shows that by loving (*agapao*) one another, the disciples continue the mission of Jesus that is driven by love, and glorify Jesus, as Jesus in his love glorifies the Father.[76] The love that the believers show for one another reflects the love between the Father and the Son, and thereby makes God known in the world. Finally, according to John 15:10, Jesus tells his disciples that to abide in his love (*agape*), which is likely both his love for them and their love for him as well as for one another, is to keep his commandments. As in the case of some passages in the Pauline letters, love is elevated to the position where all other specific commandments are included.[77]

While on the explicit surface level inter-human love in John is only commanded with respect to fellow followers of Jesus, the fact that love is made an integral and central part of the mission of the disciples to the world at large, together with the fact that the disciples' love is modeled on the example of Jesus's own love, which aims at the whole world, shows that the love to which the followers of Jesus are called is ultimately not restricted to fellow believers, even if the mutual love among believers is the first arena in which love must be practiced.[78]

74. See John 13:1.

75. Cf. Köstenberger, *A Theology*, 521.

76. See Moloney, *Love*, 127.

77. Köstenberger speaks of a "deliberate focalization of all of Jesus' ethical demands in the command to love" (*A Theology*, 511); he adds: "In fact, love is the glue that holds the ethic of this gospel together" (*A Theology*, 512).

78. See Köstenberger, *A Theology*, 511. He summarizes the point concerning love and mission in the following way: "at the heart of John's ethic is a call to evangelistic mission that is grounded in God's love for the world and undergirded by communal love and unity" (*A Theology*, 514; see also p. 516). One can also make an argument for an implicit or indirect hint at the love for the enemies in John: Jesus's love for his disciples is the model for the love that his disciples are to show to one another; however, in the foot-washing which is a practical embodiment of this love, Jesus also includes

There are many references to interpersonal love also in the letters ascribed to Paul. Here are some of the most important ones:

Romans 12:9–10 exhorts the addressees to exhibit love (*agape*) which is genuine, without hypocrisy, and to be devoted to one another in brotherly love (*philadelphia*). According to the immediate literary context, this is related to abhorring evil and clinging to what is good, as well as to giving preference to one another in honor. In the wider context of the following verses, seeking peace, blessing even enemies, showing empathy with people in all possible circumstances of life, and helping those in need are attitudes that can be associated with love.

One of the most fundamental statements about interpersonal love is found in Rom 13:8–10. In this passage, referring back to the Hebrew Bible, Paul admonishes the addressees of his letter to love one another and to love their neighbor. The general nature of both this expression ("neighbor") and of the contents of this passage makes it likely that not only fellow believers, but fellow human beings are in view here.[79] He further clarifies the character of this love by saying that it does no wrong to a neighbor. Importantly, he states that to love the neighbor is the fulfillment of the law.[80] This, in turn, very likely implies that other definitions found in the Pauline corpus of what it means to fulfill the law can be interpreted as explanations of how "love" is to be understood. If love can be identified as the fulfillment of the law, this means that love "is at the heart of what God requires" on the one hand, and that "the specific commandments show what the quality of this love is meant to be" on the other.[81] It can also be maintained that since love marks the highest level in terms of interpersonal relationships, surpassing all other demands, all specific commands in such relationships are certainly satisfied if love is exerted.[82]

The most extensive treatment concerning love in the New Testament, even in the Bible as a whole, is found in 1 Corinthians 13.[83] The

the "enemy" *par excellence*, Judas.

79. So also Moo, *Romans*, 813; Witherington, *Romans*, 315.

80. Or: To love is the fulfillment of "the other law," namely Christ's law (thus Witherington, *Romans*, 315).

81. Witherington, *Romans*, 316–17.

82. The same can be said, *mutatis mutandis*, with respect to the relationship between humans and God.

83. For an explanation of this chapter see, besides the commentaries on 1 Corinthians, Lussier, *God Is Love*, 146–51.

chapter underlines the kind, meek, patient, self-effacing and firm (in truth and hope) character of love (*agape*); it also states that without love, all gifts and good deeds are worthless.[84] As opposed to the other gifts of the Spirit, love will abide in eternity. Especially the juxtaposition with faith shows that the love spoken of in this chapter has in view also the love for God. Perhaps even more importantly on a theological level, this love can (or indeed: must) also be understood as reflecting God's own love.[85] This implies that recognizing God's love for unworthy human sinners will help both loving him back, but also loving the co-sinners.[86]

In 2 Cor 12:15, love (*agapao*) for one's neighbor is directly related to Christ's love for mankind, because it is connected with the giving of one's life for the other, specifically with Paul giving his life for his congregations.[87]

Another important treatise on love is found in Galatians 5. In Gal 5:6, Paul states that faith works through love (*agape*). In Gal 5:13, he urges the addressees to serve one another through love (*agape*). In the next verse, the point made in Romans 13 is found again: Following the command to love (*agapao*) one's neighbor is equivalent to the fulfillment of the whole law. Finally, in Gal 5:22, love (*agape*) is described as one part of what is called the fruit of the Spirit.[88]

Two aspects of love (*agape*) are mentioned in Col 3:12–14. Firstly, interpersonal love is called "the perfect bond of unity" (v. 14); and secondly, the addressees are called upon to show compassion and kindness, *because* they are loved by God (v. 12).[89]

---

84. Again, as in 1 Cor 8:1, there is a contrast between knowledge and love. In the larger context of 1 Corinthians 12–14, it is especially the proper use of the gifts of the Spirit and the overarching aim of how to edify the church that are central.

85. And perhaps even more precisely, the kind of love that is visible at the cross; see Riddlebarger, *First Corinthians*, 358–59.

86. Cf. Riddlebarger, *First Corinthians*, 360.

87. For an explanation of this verse see, e.g., Barnett, *The Second Epistle to the Corinthians*, 585–86.

88. That "love" in this verse primarily refers to the love for fellow believers is made clear by the context, beginning in v. 14. There is also a close connection between this verse and 1 Cor 13:4–6. For details see Ridderbos, *Galatia*, 206–7.

89. "God's love in Christ to human beings and their answering love to him are presupposed here as the basis of that mutual love which the readers of the letter are called on to practice. It is by such love that the body of Christ is built up" (Bruce, *Colossians, Philemon, and Ephesians*, 156).

In 1 Thess 3:12, Paul prays that the Lord may cause the addressees to abound in love (*agape*) for one another, and indeed for all men. This two-step approach can be said to be representative for the New Testament authors in general: The first objects of love on the level of human relationships are the co-believers; but it does not stop there, but ultimately includes everyone, even one's enemies.[90] In 1 Thess 4:9, he reminds the addressees that they are taught by God to love (*agapao*) one another.[91] In Titus 3:15, love (*phileo*) for the brother is related to faith.

There are almost a dozen passages in 1 and 2 John that talk about interpersonal love, mostly concentrated in 1 John 3 and 4. Again, we will look at the most important ones:

The simplest foundational statement is found in 1 John 3:23 where the author says that it is the Lord's command that we love (*agapao*) one another. Similar to the Synoptics, John, and Paul, love is described as the summation of the law as a whole. Importantly, however, in the present verse there is a direct link to belief in Jesus as Christ. A similar statement is already found in v. 11 of the same chapter and in 2 John 5.

In the passage that precedes 1 John 3:19–24, 1 John 3:16–18, the author lets the addressees know that they are to lay down their lives for their brethren, just as Christ has given his life for them. The same passage further clarifies that love for the brother means not to close one's heart against him when he is in need. This means that self-sacrificing love does not have to wait until there is an opportunity to literally lay down one's life for the brother's benefit, but that love must be exerted right now in practical (material) help for a needy brother.[92]

First John 4:7–8 shows that knowing God as love leads to love (*agapao*) one another. The author adds that everyone who loves is born of God, whereas the one who does not love does not know God, for God is love. In the next sequence, 1 John 4:10–12, it is stated that we must love (*agapao*) one another, because God loved us so much that he gave his Son. Experience of God's love finds its "natural" response in loving one another.[93] The passage concludes by saying that if we love one another, God abides in us and his love is made complete in us.

90. So also Marshall, *1 and 2 Thessalonians*, 101.

91. It is possible that Paul is not only referring to intellectual teaching, but also to the fact that the believers have been equipped and empowered by God to love one another (see Marshall, *1 and 2 Thessalonians*, 115).

92. Cf. Marshall, *The Epistles of John*, 194.

93. Since God's love aims at all sinners, it is likely that ultimately the love for one

First John 4:19–21 repeats what has already been said in chapter 3. The believers have a command to love (*agapao*) the brother, and one cannot love God and hate the brother. Love of God, then, is necessarily related to love of the brother. This love is grounded in the fact that God first loved humankind.

Hebrews 13:1 admonishes the addressees to exercise brotherly love (*philadelphia*). This is contextually related to showing hospitality, caring for the ill-treated and prisoners, among other things. This is similar to what is found in Matt 25:31–46 as far as the practical expressions of love are concerned. The fact that it is clearly related to the love for fellow believers reflects back on the Matthean passage as well.

Finally, we note that the adjective *agapetos* ("beloved"), when used in the context of interpersonal love, refers to fellow Christians and not to neighbors in general.[94]

One of the most important points that is new in the New Testament passages containing the command to love one's neighbor as compared to the Hebrew Bible is that the love-command can in no way be restricted any more to either the co-Israelite—which in more general terms would be: a member of the same ethnic or religious-ethnic group—or the sojourner as the representative of a rather narrowly defined special group within the community.

In terms of application to the topic of migration, it is certainly the case that there is no limit to what the core principle of love for neighbor may entail on the level of an individual person's private life, also with respect to love for (im)migrants. There are no limits to love in terms of any ethnic or social boundaries. At the same time, it is noteworthy that a general command to love foreigners specifically is not found. Migration policy on the state level is not addressed at all. When this level is addressed in the current situation, one has to take into consideration broader aspects that go beyond an individual's calling to show love. This also means that the personal decision to help (im)migrants must not

another is not restricted to the community of believers, even if this is clearly the primary circle of application (cf. Marshall, *The Epistles of John*, 216).

94. See Rom 16:5, 8, 12; 1 Cor 4:14, 17; 10:14; 15:58; 2 Cor 7:1; 12:19; Eph 6:21; Phil 2:12; 4:1; Col 1:7; 4:7, 9, 14; 1 Thess 2:8; 2 Tim 1:2; Phlm 1, 16; Jas 1:16, 19; 2:5; 1 Pet 2:11; 4:12; 2 Pet 3:1, 8, 14, 15, 17; 1 John 2:7; 3:2, 21; 4:1, 7, 11; 3 John 1, 2, 5, 11; Jude 3, 17, 20; Heb 6:9. In all these cases, the subject of love may also be God or the Christ, not just the respective apostle or author.

undermine this broader framework. No single New Testament text dealing with love for neighbor implies support for illegal actions.

While there is no limit to the exercise of love on the personal level, it is important to take into account that in all larger corpora of New Testament writings, love for fellow believers takes precedence over love for people outside the congregation.[95] This is, however, not a matter of either-or, but rather of first-second. To this may be related the observation that both the Pauline and Johannine texts talking about love locate this theme in the context of the live of the congregation and do for the most part not develop it in the context of an individualistic ethics of virtues.[96] While brothers and sisters in the Lord receive a special position as primary recipients of neighborly love, this is not the case with (im)migrants or foreigners—in contradistinction to a widespread tendency in the current migration debate as far as the priorities of the proponents of liberal immigration policies are concerned.

For a correct interpretation and application of the New Testament love ethics, consideration also needs to be given to the fact that love for neighbor is seen as a response to God's love that the believer receives, or as a fruit of the Spirit; in addition, love for neighbor is seen as something that cannot be detached from the love for God or Christ. This means in the current circumstances—as already observed in our analysis of the parable of the good Samaritan—that while Christian initiatives for helping migrants of all kinds can be rooted in the New Testament, attempts to impose such help on the whole of a (mostly secular) society through law and taxation is a different matter. It also means that a reduction of love to material help, with no connection to the spiritual level in a more holistic approach, is not supported by the New Testament. Also relevant for the topic of the investigation is the observation that love for neighbor in the New Testament cannot be exerted in ways that are opposed to truth and justice. We will come back to this point and elaborate on it in chapter 7.

95. See, e.g., Gal 6:10.
96. See Wischmeyer, *Liebe*, 14.

6. ERASURE OF DISTINCTIONS IN CHRIST:
GALATIANS 3:28, EPHESIANS 2:19

Passages such as Gal 3:28 and Eph 2:19 are also frequently used in the migration debate as arguments for liberal immigration policies.[97] These texts underline the unity of the body of Christ, a unity that transcends ethnic (and other) distinctions.[98] In this way, the New Testament goes beyond the legal texts in the Hebrew Bible, in line with some of the prophetic traditions found in the Hebrew Bible that talk about the unification of foreign peoples in the reverence for YHWH or even the inclusion of foreigners into God's people in eschatological times.

According to Eph 2:19, the gentiles, who before Christ were *xenoi* ("foreigners") or *paroikoi* ("sojourners"),[99] are now full citizens of the kingdom of God, together with the *hagioi* ("holy ones"). It is a matter of dispute whom the latter category is referring to; the main possibilities are Jews, messianic Jews, fellow Christians of other places, or angels.[100] Whatever the exact referent may be, the main point still remains the same: The new people of God is a unity in which distinctions of religious-ethnic background do not matter. By using the term "sojourners," Eph 2:19 can be seen as pointing to the fulfillment of expectations found in a small number of prophetic texts in the Hebrew Bible, according to which the "sojourners" will be included in the new people of God in the eschatological future.[101]

Another important text to be mentioned in the category under review is Gal 3:28. According to this verse, "there is neither Jew nor Greek, there is neither slave nor free, there is not male and female." This means that in the emerging Christian communities, among those who are baptized in Christ (v. 27), there is no difference between "Jews and Greeks" and the other categories that are mentioned, as far as their new identity in Christ and their status before God is concerned; they are "all one in

97. See, e.g., Campese, "¿Cuantos Más?" 294; Escobar, "Refugees," 106; Gonzales, "Sanctuary," 46; Senior, "Beloved Aliens," 32.

98. In other texts, Paul does not *describe* the unity among believers of various backgrounds, but *urges* them to live accordingly; see, e.g., Rom 16:16.
Paynter derives similar conclusions about the overcoming of the importance of ethnic distinctions from her reading of Rom 11:17–18; see "Porous Borders," 126–27.

99. It is unlikely that a precise technical distinction between the two terms is in view; see, e.g., Thielman, *Ephesians*, 179; cf. Lincoln, *Ephesians*, 150.

100. See, e.g., Lincoln, *Ephesians*, 150–51; Thielman, *Ephesians*, 179.

101. See especially Isa 14:1 and Ezek 47:22–23.

Christ Jesus" (v. 28b). It is clear that Paul here expresses the view that in some important ways all fundamental human distinctions are superseded by the new reality of the unity of the body of Christ to which the believers belong,[102] and that in Christ they have full access to God as "sons of God" (v. 26). On the other hand, it is also evident that the mention of the third category, male and female, cannot be interpreted to mean the abolishment of the differences between the sexes in general; the context of the writings of Paul makes this unambiguously clear.[103] This observation, however, in itself cannot be taken as proof that the same is true for the first two elements, the distinctions between Greek and Jew on the one hand, and slave and free on the other. The element of the distinction of male and female is different from the other two in that it is established with creation itself (see Gen 1:27). With respect to the distinction between slave and free, one has to consider that Paul severely undermines the institute of slavery, though he does not venture to abolish it.[104] It is also important to observe that Paul does not question the legitimacy and importance of social distinctions and hierarchies in general.[105] As far as the first distinction (Jew and Greek) is concerned, it can be read in two ways: either as pointing to the (antagonistic) difference between Jews and gentiles, or more broadly to ethnic differences generally, with the distinction between Jews and gentiles only being a specific example of these differences. The alternatives are, however, not mutually exclusive, for even if one opts for the first variant, it could still be argued that by extension ethnic differences in general can be included. As in the case of the other two categories of distinctions, it is clear from other passages that what Paul has in view is not the erasure of the distinctions, but their redemption.[106]

One of the primary ethical consequences of the assertions made in the two texts is that love for the fellow believer must not be limited

102. So also George, *Galatians*, 284.

103. See, e.g., George, *Galatians*, 289–91.

104. See, e.g., George, *Galatians*, 289.

105. See, e.g., Rom 13:1–7. First Cor 11:3–15 shows that differences between genders are seen as important even within the order of the church. First Cor 12:5 is one of the many examples that point to distinctions and hierarchies within the church. In other texts, like Eph 5:22—6:9—although in this case, it is disputed whether it is Pauline—social distinctions and gender distinctions are combined, with a view to life outside of the church.

106. This explains why Paul emphatically points to the continuous differences between Jews and gentiles in Romans 9–11.

by ethnic considerations. Secondly, such texts imply that Old Testament legal regulations must not (or no longer) be used in a way that separates believers based on their respective Jewish or gentile backgrounds.[107] This is borne out in some detail and as a matter of principle in the decisions of the Jerusalem Council referred to in Acts 15. There is no distinction between gentile and Jewish believers, the former are included in God's people and must not be demanded to obey the Jewish law *in toto*, with the exception of some fundamental regulations (see Acts 15:19–20).[108] "In other words, the church decided not to demand cultural assimilation from Gentile believers. It made clear that they were not expected to become Jewish."[109]

In the case of both Eph 2:19 and Gal 3:28, we are not dealing with general anthropological claims; rather, it is all about the new creation of the body of Christ. The passages do not state that ethnic differences need to be overcome or ignored completely. They only argue that such distinctions need to take a backseat and must not be allowed to interfere with the unity of the body of Christ. Also, there is no more room for ethnic pride (or abuse of power based on one's social position or a man's privileged position over women).[110]

The focus on Christian identity before God and on Christian unity implies that if one attempts to relate these passages to (im)migration issues, they would be relevant only for Christian migrants in relation to Christian hosts. And in fact, it is both clear and important that in the

107. Cf. Jervis, *Galatians*, 107.

108. According to one view, these requirements were imposed to avoid causing offence among Jewish Christians against their gentile co-believers and thus to enable fellowship with both conscientious Jews and Jewish Christians who still kept the Old Testament law in high regard (see, e.g., Parsons, *Acts*, 215; Peterson, *The Acts of the Apostles*, 435; Prill, "Migration," 342). It is also argued that the requirements reflect the rabbinic concept of Noahic precepts that were thought to be of such a fundamental nature that they were not only binding on Israel, but on humanity at large or—with regard to some laws—the *ger* (see Bockmuehl, "The Noachide Commandments," 93–95; Parsons, *Acts*, 215; Peterson, *The Acts of the Apostles*, 434). Finally, a case can also be made for the view that the prohibitions aim primarily at the participation in pagan temple feasts (see Petersen, *The Acts of the Apostles*, 433–34). Of course, the various explanations are not necessarily mutually exclusive.

109. Prill, "Migration," 342. In an exegetically unfounded generalization and transfer from the ecclesial to the political sphere, Strine claims that Acts 15 proves that "the nascent Christian movement rejects nationalistic ideology" ("Embracing Asylum Seekers," 488).

110. So also George, *Galatians*, 285.

body of Christ distinctions of ethnic background are relativized. It is also clear, however, that modern mass-(im)migration is to a larger part not connected to these issues. The only connection exists with a view to (im)migrants who identify as Christian believers—proportionally rare in the European immigration context, though somewhat more important in the case of the U.S. immigration context. But even in these cases there is for the most part no direct relationship with the current migration debate, because in this context it is predominantly the state or the national community that is supposed to fill the role of host, not the church. One can argue that there is an additional way in which these texts are relevant for the migration debate, in that ethnic pride at the expense of other ethnic groups outside one's own is delegitimized in principle. This does, however, not add really anything to what can be inferred already from Genesis 1.

An additional point has to be raised: The view that creational differences such as those of ethnicity are irrelevant with respect to a person's standing before God does not imply that such differences can be ignored when it comes to ordering practical life, including the organization of civic life in a state. These are two different aspects of reality that cannot and must not be conflated.

Another text that bears mentioning in this paragraph is Acts 10:34–35, in which the following exclamation is found in Peter's mouth, in the context of his encounter with Cornelius: "I most certainly understand now that God is not one to show partiality, but in every nation the man who fears Him and does what is right, is welcome to Him." This has been interpreted as showing that "the other" is "sacred" and "part of God's human family."[111] However, such an interpretation goes beyond the precise wording of the text, by including everybody in God's family—and thereby arguing for open borders as the only sensible way of dealing with immigration questions. The biblical text, however, contains the restrictive clause "who fears him and does what is right." Similar texts that point to the exemplary faith of foreigners and their inclusion into the Christian community, as can be found (i.a.) in Matt 8:11 or 15:21–28, likewise cannot be directly related to questions of mass-(im)migration involving non-believers.[112] Rather, the focus is on standing before God and access to God, not access to a specific country.

111. Senior, "Beloved Aliens," 30.
112. *Pace* Senior, "Beloved Aliens, 31–32.

The texts that were investigated in this paragraph certainly support the view that in principle it is preferable to build church communities that are comprised of various ethnic—and indeed, social—backgrounds. This point is reinforced by the following observations: the early church in Jerusalem, according to Acts 6:1–7, was composed both of Hellenists and Hebrews. They obviously had their own meetings,[113] and yet they were united under one overarching umbrella, under the leadership of the apostles. It is also noteworthy that there were no "attempts made by the Aramaic-speaking majority to demand cultural or linguistic assimilation."[114] Also the church in Antioch, as can be gleaned from Acts 11:19–21; 13:1–3 was multi-ethnic in character;[115] the same goes for the church in Philippi as depicted in Acts 16:13–33,[116] and the church in Corinth as depicted in Acts 18:2, 7–8.[117] The fact that the mission teams that were headed or composed by Paul also were multiethnic points in the same direction.[118] Such observations need to be considered carefully when organizing church life in multi-cultural or multi-ethnic contexts.[119]

It is, however, not clear that the first Christian congregations were mixed based on the notion that this had to be done as a matter of principle. They may have done so simply due to pragmatic reasons, mirroring reality on the ground rather than creating new realities. It is also possible that in many areas congregations were not mixed, and were not actively seeking to change this state of affairs. Furthermore, the distinction between church and state has to be kept in mind, and therefore no one-to-one transfers can legitimately be made from one realm to the other. Especially, one has to keep in mind that questions of immigration policies are wholly distinct from questions of church building and congregational organization. Inclusion (into the congregational community) of foreigners

113. See Prill, "Migration," 334.

114. Prill, "Migration," 336.

115. So also Prill, "Migration," 336–37.

116. So also Prill, "Migration," 338–39.

117. So also Prill, "Migration," 339. According to Acts 17:4, 12, the situation was similar also in Thessalonica and Beroea.

118. For details see Prill, "Migration," 340.

119. Cf. Escobar, "Refugees," 106. It is often argued that a multi-cultural make-up of the local church prefigures the eschatological situation of a multi-cultural body of Christ or more generally a new humanity (see, e.g., Escobar, "Refugees," 106). The eschatological picture of the body of Christ or humanity in general is, however, not as straightforward as this approach suggests (for more details see the following paragraph).

who have been admitted to a country is not the same as addressing the question of who should be allowed to cross the border.

To conclude this paragraph, we need to consider the encounter of Jesus with a Phoenician woman reported in Matt 15:21–28 (// Mark 7:24–30). While Jesus praises the faith of the woman, he also maintains a blatant distinction between Israelites and non-Israelites, the latter being likened to "dogs" (Matt 15:26–27), pointing to an inferior position which is also recognized by the woman herself. This difference in position also translates into distinctions on the material level: the "dogs" only get the "crumbs from their masters' table" (v. 27). While it is difficult to assess how exactly this passage can or should be transferred into the current situation, it certainly points both to lasting distinctions between "Jews and gentiles" and a questioning of rigorous non-discrimination principles when it comes to practical help for various groups of people.[120] At the same time, Jesus's praise of the woman's faith and his granting of her request shows that whatever distinctions may be applicable, they are put into a broader context of compassion even towards a member of a previous enemy of the people of God.[121]

7. THE FUTURE PEOPLE OF GOD ACCORDING TO REVELATIONS

According to Rev 7:9–17, among other texts, the eschatological people of God will consist of "a great multitude, which no one could count, from every nation and all tribes and peoples and tongues"—that is, it will be multinational and multilingual. Therefore, many commentators claim, the church should strive to mirror this eschatological picture in the here and now.[122] Some add that Christians should work to mirror these realities also in the realm of the general political body.[123] This argument does not, however, stand to scrutiny. First, the eschatological images of both the Hebrew Bible and the New Testament are too vague to use them as concrete prescriptions for a particular policy in terms of ethnic mixing. When John sees people of all nations and languages praising God before

120. Cf. Evans, *Matthew*, 304; France, *Matthew*, 573; Houston, *You Shall Love*, 143.

121. Houston's generalizing conclusion, on the other hand, that "external borders can't protect us" (*You Shall Love*, 143), is not warranted by the text.

122. See, e.g., Carroll, *Christians*, 128.

123. See, e.g., Strine, "Embracing Asylum Seekers," 489.

his throne, it does not mean that they represent multi-ethnic bodies or that they are transformed permanently into multi-ethnic bodies. Almost on the contrary: the fact that nations and languages are distinguishable presupposes some kind of separation between them. Second, the realm of the church cannot simply be identified with the broader society, because the addition of the spiritual domain and the work of the Holy Spirit enables congregations to be formed and to behave in ways that cannot be copied by the outside world. Third, as a matter of principle future states and conditions cannot be taken as automatically or necessarily dictating how life in the current situation on this side of eternity has to be organized.[124] This is broadly accepted in other areas of life. As an example, we can point to the fact that the overwhelming majority of Christians marry, although marriage is not an institution that will be carried on in the world to come.[125] Thus, the question arises as to why one would want to implement an eschatological state in the present age in one realm (question of the importance of ethnic differences), but not in the other (marriage)?

8. SEPARATION FROM NON-BELIEVERS

The general thrust of the New Testament texts is to presuppose the distinctions of nations as the normal condition of communal life in this world, a condition that does not need to be overcome my human means. Acts 17:26 in particular confirms the view that a differentiation of various ethnic groups together with concomitant national structures is seen as a positive institution ordained by God himself. The book of Revelation expects that even in the time of the completion of world history there will be a distinction of various, clearly definable ethnic groups among the people participating in God's salvation.[126] The same book, in chapter 13, also depicts an attempt to establish a unified global state as part of the rule of the (final) anti-Christ.

It is also important to recognize that the New Testament contains a good number of texts that advocate for a distinction between believers and non-believers.[127] This implies that a distinction between "in-group"

---

124. That would amount to an inappropriate conflation of ages.

125. See Matt 22:30.

126. See, e.g., Rev 21:24–26; 22:2.

127. See, e.g., Rom 15:31; 1 Cor 6:5; 2 Cor 6:14–15; 2 John 10–11; 3 John 7.

and "out-group," between "Us" and "Them," is part of the worldview of the New Testament authors and understood by them as divinely ordained. Against this background, the church will not find support in the New Testament when it actively promotes liberal immigration policies that open the doors for immigrants with a non-Christian background or with a background that is even antagonistic towards Christianity.

Based on Rom 13:1–7 and similar passages, Christians will also not support lightly any actions that involve breaking the law of the land. The examples found in the New Testament where Christians do in fact stand up against specific rules or laws are restricted to cultic matters and the preaching of the gospel. Strong and compelling arguments would need to be presented if one would claim that resistance is necessary in other areas as well.

9. BRIEF SUMMARY

As in the case of the Hebrew Bible, the New Testament authors do not provide support for a general openness to foreigners as such, regardless of their religious affiliation, or for a political program promoting large-scale (im)migration / open borders, or prioritizing help to (im)migrants as opposed to help to other persons in need. What we find in the New Testament is something else, something different from both a narrow nationalism and a general cosmopolitan humanitarianism: a prioritizing of help for the brothers and sisters in Christ, regardless of their ethnic background. Beyond this, it also inculcates a love for each neighbor of all ethnic or religious backgrounds as far as relationships *within* a community are concerned, without, however, having questions about the opening of state borders for potential immigrants on its radar. There is also no program for alleviating or even eradicating poverty worldwide. As far as borders and ethnic distinctions are concerned, the few passages that relate to these issues confirm that ethnic and national distinctions are divinely ordained aspects of communal life at least on this side of eternity.

4

Historical Differences between Biblical Times and the Present

1. INTRODUCTION

IN THIS CHAPTER, WE will identify some of the main differences between the situation represented in the biblical texts and the present.[1] These historical differences are often ignored, leading to direct (literalistic) applications of (select) biblical texts.[2] Only if there is a clear idea of these differences will it be possible to abstain from simplistic one-to-one transfers of biblical texts and develop a framework for the hermeneutical task of setting up parameters that allow to cautiously relate biblical texts to the current situation.

The differences can be classified in three main groups: character of the broader context; aspects relating specifically to the migrants; and aspects relating specifically to the receiving society.

---

1. In this chapter, as far as the Hebrew Bible is concerned, it is primarily the "orthodox perspectives" endorsed by the biblical authors that inform our description of biblical Israel. As the biblical texts themselves show, there were other perspectives on the issues under discussion entertained by Israelites with whom the biblical authors disagreed.

2. This is also observed by, e.g., Amstutz, *Just Immigration*, 131. One example among many (in addition to those mentioned in previous chapters) for direct transfers based on a lack of acknowledgment of historical differences is Möller, "Asylum Seekers."

The classification could be done in alternative ways. What is important are the individual elements that will be mentioned in this chapter, not the way in which they are organized. Many of these elements have to do with the religious outlook of ancient Israel on the one hand and with the globalized world-order of today on the other.

The comparison will be mostly between Old Testament texts reflecting the situation during the periods of sovereign statehood of Israel and Judah on the one hand and the present on the other.[3] The situation is considerably more complex in the period of the New Testament. There are various kinds of larger movements of individuals and whole people groups during this period. However, these social realities are not directly addressed in the New Testament texts beyond the level of individual hospitality as far as the question of dealing with foreigners is concerned, and questions of state-related immigration policies are not taken up at all. One also needs to keep in mind that the Jews were not able to direct such issues independently as a sovereign state at that time.

2. GENERAL CHARACTER OF THE BROADER CONTEXT

2.1. Numbers

The numbers of (potential) immigrants are completely different in the case of ancient Israel and in the current situation in the West.[4] As far as the New Testament period is concerned, the situation is more complex; however, texts that talk about hospitality to strangers do not presuppose conditions that are comparable to the modern ones. In addition, there is a *global scope* of the migration movement absent in the situation of ancient Israel and also different from the situation reflected in the New Testament.

While there were mass migrations in what we can loosely describe as "the world of the Old Testament," these were mostly limited to forced deportations, initiated especially by the Assyrians.[5] Reports on people

3. For reasons of convenience, reference to the united kingdom, the northern kingdom of Israel, and the southern kingdom of Judah will be made by using the term "Israel."

4. According to numbers provided by a U.N. report, there were 272 million migrants in 2019, amounting to 3.5 percent of the world population; see McAuliffe and Khadria, *World Migration Report 2020*, 3.

5. For this phenomenon see especially Oded, *Mass Deportations*, 120–90.

immigrating into Israel by their own will in periods in which Israel/Judah could actually be seen as sovereign political entities are relatively sparse. An early example in a canonical reading of the Hebrew Bible is Ruth, a Moabite woman who chooses to move to the village of Bethlehem out of loyalty to her mother-in-law Naomi in the period of the Judges, that is, relatively shortly after the settlement of the various Israelite tribes in the southern Levant. Other cases include the Edomite Doeg during the reign of Saul,[6] the foreign wives of Solomon,[7] or a limited number of Greek mercenaries in the kingdom of Judah at the beginning of the sixth century BC.[8] At no point do we find hints at migration movements that would involve numbers as massive as is the case of the present situation in many areas of the world.

As far as the current situation is concerned, in some parts of the world the number of migrants exceeds even the magnitude of the mass migrations on the European continent in late antiquity. The numbers are so high that a policy of completely open doors would lead to an immediate collapse of the established order at least in the receiving societies and most likely in the sending countries as well.[9]

2.2. Culture and Language

It is probably right to say that "sojourners were not a threat to Israel's national identity."[10] This has to do primarily with the numbers involved, but also with the fact that the cultural differences (including language) between the sojourners and the host society were relatively modest—after all, most sojourners in all likelihood had their roots in the neighboring countries of Israel.[11]

6. See 1 Samuel 21–22.

7. See 1 Kings 11.

8. The latter are not mentioned in the Hebrew Bible; but their existence is attested in the letters of Arad (see Renz and Röllig, *Handbuch der althebräischen Epigraphik I*, 353–82; Smelik, *Historische Dokumente*, 99–104 [ostraca 1, 2, 4, 7, 8, 10, 11, 14, 17]). For an extensive overview over biblical reports on foreigners in Israel, see Zehnder, *Umgang mit Fremden*, 402–98.

9. According to a study published in 2008, 40 percent of adults in the poorest countries would emigrate to another country if they could; see Leeson and Gochenour, "The Economic Effects," 12.

10. Carroll, *Christians*, 97; an identical formulation is found in *The Bible*, 80.

11. A third major reason for the non-threatening character of the existence of sojourners in biblical Israel can be found in the self-assertion of Israel (for more details

The situation looks different in the current situation in the West, in Europe more markedly than in the U.S.[12] In Europe, as far as large-scale immigration from countries outside of Europe is concerned, most immigrants are from the Middle East, North Africa, and Sub-Saharan Africa. In the U.S., on the other hand, the dominant immigrant population is from Latin America (including Mexico), which is not only very close to the already large percentage of U.S. citizens and permanent residents classified as "Hispanics," but also relatively closer in terms of culture, language, and religion even to the still dominant non-Hispanic segments of the U.S. population than are newcomers to western European countries and their "indigenous" populations.[13]

2.3. Ease of Movement and Communication

While moving from one place to another was difficult and slow in antiquity, modern means of transportation like buses, trains, boats, and airplanes make it possible for migrants to reach far shores, often in large numbers. In addition, modern communication technology as well as transportation facilities enable present-day (im)migrants to stay in close contact with their original homelands, which was not possible to the same degree in biblical times.[14] One of the consequences is the establishment of transnational social networks.[15] This affects the degree in which newcomers may feel a need to or are willing to assimilate to the new environment. Related to this is the emergence of new concepts of transnational citizenship, flexible citizenship, or post-national citizenship.[16]

---

on this point see below).

12. For more details see the demographic data below in chapter 6.2.

13. This does not mean that the large influx of Mexican and Latin American immigrants in general, especially in combination with a persistence of an important role of identity-markers related to the countries of origin rather than the U.S., does not pose challenges that have the potential to fundamentally change the character of the U.S. For details see, e.g., Huntington, *Who Are We?* especially pp. 221–56.

14. For the role of mass-transportation see, e.g., Brettell, "Theorizing Migration," 120. For more details on questions surrounding the need to accommodate to the new environment see chapter 5.2.

15. See, e.g., Brettell and Hollifield, "Migration Theory," 17–18; Brettell, "Theorizing Migration," 120.

16. See, e.g., Brettell, "Theorizing Migration," 123; Schmitter Heisler, "The Sociology," 92–97. Under "postnational citizenship," "rights and identities become increasingly decoupled from national citizenship" (Schmitter Heisler, "The Sociology," 93).

2.4. Border Control and Legality

The technical possibility of effective border control in the present situation differs from the situation in antiquity. Though instances of tight border control are also known in antiquity, for example chains of fortresses on the northeastern frontier of Egypt in the Late Bronze age,[17] or extended walls and fortifications on various parts along the borders of the Roman Empire in several phases throughout its history,[18] in many cases ancient borders would be much more porous when compared to modern ones. This certainly applies to the situation in ancient Israel.[19] The potential capability to control borders in modern times is connected with a degree of internal control by the state bureaucracy that is also very likely to be much lower in the case of ancient Israel than it is today in the West. At the same time, one also needs to acknowledge that the technical capability to control borders is not necessarily effective, because of various and changing impediments based on political or human rights considerations, etc.[20]

To the domain of bureaucratic control of migration is related the distinction between legal and illegal immigrants. The statement that the biblical laws "make no distinction between 'legal' and 'illegal' immigrants"[21] is at least partially anachronistic, because the systems to manage migration that were in place then and are applied now are different. Therefore, one cannot deduce that the distinction between "legal" and "illegal" immigrants is "unbiblical" in the current circumstances.

Transnationalism can be defined as the maintenance of activities or occupations that are related by necessity to regular social contact over time across national borders and/ or across cultures (see Portes et al., "The Study of Transnationalism," 217–37).

17. See, e.g., Hoffmeier, *The Immigration Crisis*, 39–45.

18. See, e.g., Brecze, *The Frontiers*.

19. One of many examples in the Hebrew Bible that point in this direction are the movements of Naomi's family as described in the book of Ruth.

20. See Brettell and Hollifield who observe that, "enforcement of immigration law is often constrained by cost or by liberal and human rights ideologies" ("Migration Theory," 9). A case in point is the opening of the borders of Germany for hundreds of thousands of asylum seekers in the fall of 2015. The German chancellor's statement that it would not have been "possible" to control and protect the border can easily be understood as a rhetorical deflection, since on other occasions, both before and after the events that took place in that year, the same borders could and can in fact be controlled and protected, most recently when the borders were closed in the context of the Covid-19 lockdown in the spring of 2020.

21. Carroll, *Christians*, 94; the formulation is slightly toned down in *The Bible*, 77.

2.5. Mass Media

As opposed to the situation in antiquity, current migration movements to the West are heavily influenced by the enormous role of mass media both in the sending and the receiving societies. How exactly mass media shape the discussion and perception of various important aspects of migration is difficult to assess, and varies depending on the specific circumstances and also according to the audience. Two of the more obvious aspects of this influence can nevertheless be identified: The broad availability of movies in the sending countries that depict life in the West in such ways that trigger high expectations of an easy way to material success contribute to augment the number of people who aspire to reach the shores of Western countries. On the other side, focus on individual cases of tragic migrant biographies speak to the emotional dimension of the issue and contribute to move public opinion in the West in the direction of liberal immigration policies.[22] There is a general tendency in most Western countries of mainstream media and governments working together in promoting liberal immigration policies, depicting them as the right humanitarian attitude and positive in terms of both economy and cultural enrichment, while opposing views are framed as xenophobic, right-wing, and the like.[23] In the process, problems caused by immigration are downplayed in various ways.[24] Of course, the picture is not

22. Famous examples are the death of Alan Kurdi at the beginning of September 2015 (see the Wikipedia entry on the "Death of Alan Kurdi") or reports about migrants (also at the beginning of September 2015) at the Keleti train station in Budapest (see, e.g., Lima, "Train Station in Budapest"). In the case of the U.S., media focus on the separation of migrant families at the U.S.-Mexican border in various instances in recent years can be mentioned.

23. See, e.g., Haller, Die "Flüchtlingskrise" in den Medien; Maurer et al., "Auf den Spuren der Lügenpresse," 15–35. The same attitude can be found in theological treatises; see, e.g., Houston, You Shall Love, 131 (deploring the "amalgam in public discourse of Islam, fundamentalism and terrorism," and not recognizing that this "amalgam" has long been replaced both in mainstream media and by the vast majority of Western governments by a narrative that constantly and explicitly rejects this "amalgam").

24. A well-known example for the former are the events on New Year's Eve 2015/16 in Cologne; see also, e.g., Stoldt, "Ende der Schweigekultur." Directives to generally separate the terms "Muslim" and "terror"/"terrorism" at the FBI (law enforcement training material) and the termination of the use of the word "terror" (outside of direct quotations) at the BBC are other examples. During the Obama administration, the Fort Hood attack was not classified as related to terrorism and Islam, in spite of the clear statements of the perpetrator pointing in this direction; furthermore, the mention of ISIS was deleted in a redacted version of the Orlando 911 transcript. Of course,

black and white; there are still opposing voices, and mass media in many cases do report specific problems related to immigration; this does not, however, change the overall tendency just mentioned.[25]

2.6. People Smuggling

In the current situation, migration—as far as migration from third world countries into the Western world is concerned—has become to some (considerable) degree a phenomenon that is often labeled an "industry," with people-smuggling playing an important role on the side of the movement from an original place to the new destination.[26] In some cases, also state authorities, especially in places of transit, are involved in the trafficking/smuggling.[27] These phenomena have no direct counterpart in antiquity.

Financial interests are not restricted to smugglers/traffickers, but are also at play in various ways both in different segments of the sending and receiving communities; these aspects are, however, often more difficult to assess.[28]

---

such incidents are just the tip of the iceberg. As a matter of principle, the Council of Europe in its Resolution 1605 (of 2008) prohibits negative depictions of Islam in school textbooks (see article 9.7.9.); the European Coalition of Cities against Racism in its "10 Points Action Plan" commits to promoting and screening both locally, nationally, and internationally media productions made by groups that are—without further definition or elaboration—classified as "discriminated groups" (point 9); and in its Global Compact for Migration the U.N. commits to a fundamentally positive attitude to migration (see, i.a., articles 13 and 17d; see *Global Compact for Safe, Orderly and Regular Migration, Final Draft, 11 July 2018*).

25. This is often denied by representatives of governments and mainstream media, but without any evidence.

26. See, e.g., the Wikipedia entry on "People Smuggling"; Bouteillet-Paquet, *Smuggling of Migrants*.

27. See, e.g., Beier et al., *Globale Wanderungsbewegungen*, 109.

28. Some aspects will be covered in the section on economic aspects of migration below. In addition, financial interests of NGOs, international organizations and state agencies in the receiving countries dealing with (im)migration can be mentioned, together with many private individuals in the receiving countries benefitting from an expansion of various kinds of businesses through immigration.

2.7. Direct Involvement of Government

In the texts of the Hebrew Bible, government is not visibly involved in the management of immigration into Israel and Judah. Most of the laws that deal with sojourners and foreigners address the native-born individuals, families, or extended communities, not government officials. The same goes for prophetic texts. Regulations concerning the admittance of non-Israelites into the territory of Israel are practically non-existent, with the possible exception of Deut 23:2–9 and some passages in Ezra/Nehemiah. The situation looked different in the Roman Empire; but there are no New Testament texts that directly and explicitly address questions of state regulations of (im)migration.

On the other hand, in the current situation (im)migration is part of central government policy especially in the receiving countries in the Western world, and at least to some degree also in the sending countries and in the countries of transit, although in many cases the tight bureaucratic control and management mechanisms of the West are not in place in developing countries. Government involvement in the West does not apply only to the question of admittance, but also extends to most aspects of the life of new arrivals (such as education and health care, depending on the status of the immigrants also housing, material support, etc.). In many cases, people coming from outside will only have a minimal need to interact with natives on a personal level.[29]

2.8. Remediation of Demographic Problems

In the current situation, with no clear analogue in antiquity, mass-migration is used as a means to address demographic problems both in the sending and the receiving countries.[30] On the side of the sending coun-

29. This has not only to do with the central role of government agencies in the process of admittance and integration, but also in some cases with the existence of diaspora communities which may receive new arrivals coming from places with similar backgrounds.

30. Parallels to situations in antiquity are only very partial. Shortages of food at one place that caused people to emigrate were only temporary and generally not the direct result of a sustained exponential growth of population. Shortages of labor could also occur, for example in the heartland of Assyria when resources were used in various ways outside of that zone as part of the expansion of the empire, or in areas that were heavily affected by military campaigns; the solution was not sought, however, in liberal immigration policies, but in the forced deportation of subjected peoples and their resettlement in areas where labor forces were insufficient (see, e.g., Zehnder, *Umgang mit Fremden*, 141–219).

tries, the fundamental problem that is dealt with through emigration is overpopulation or exponential growth of population;[31] on the side of the receiving Western countries, the fundamental problem are birth rates that are below the replacement rate,[32] which is perceived as problematic especially in terms of the viability of the financing of the social security systems, but also in terms of economic stability or lack of manpower in health care facilities and nursing homes, to name the most important domains. As a response that addresses the challenges on both sides at the same time, the concept of "replacement migration" has been developed and accepted as part of official U.N. policies.[33]

2.9. Democratic Discourse System

While there are some hints in texts of the Hebrew Bible that there were various views in ancient Israel concerning the dealing with foreign persons and foreign cultural (and especially religious) elements,[34] these matters were not part of a public debate in the context of a democratic discourse system as it is the case in the current situation in the West, with immigration questions being especially sensitive and important partisan issues.

2.10. Framework of International Conventions

In the ancient Near East, questions of migration were not handled with the involvement of international bodies such as the U.N. or the European Court of Justice, or in the context of the notion of binding international

31. One of the clearest examples is the continent of Africa. While the continent had about 140 million inhabitants around 1900, which amounted to about one third of the inhabitants of Europe at that time, the situation is in the process of being reversed, with Africa approaching 1.5 billion people—and likely 2 billion in the coming years (as of July 2020, the number is 1.341 billion; see "Africa Population") compared to about 500 million inhabitants of Europe.

32. See the Wikipedia entry on "Sub-Replacement Fertility."

33. See the Wikipedia entry on "Replacement Migration."

34. It is very likely that the numerous legal and prophetic texts referring to the dealing with foreign persons and foreign cultural elements reflect disagreement about these matters, in some instances perhaps more potential forms of disagreement, in other instances acute and real ones. A similar background can be assumed for New Testament texts dealing with hospitality to strangers, though in this case not referring to state policies.

law that could be compared to the present-day world. As a matter of fact, there were some international treaties between various political entities, but regulations concerning aspects of migration were of a different character as compared to today, with the duty to extradite fugitive slaves and protect traveling merchants of foreign countries topping the list.[35] Seen from a modern perspective, such treaties were basically bilateral in character, as opposed to the multilateral and global scope of international law today.

For some decades following the end of World War II, the most important piece of international law dealing with migration issues was the 1951 Refugee Convention (or Geneva Convention). More recently, various laws and regulations set up by the European Union and the U.N. deal with issues related to migration more broadly, focusing primarily on the human rights of migrants.[36] The most comprehensive recent piece of international law—though not legally binding as such unless taken up in national law—is the Global Compact for Safe, Orderly and Regular Migration, the primary purpose of which is not the restriction of migration, but the establishment of orderly channels to manage and facilitate it.[37]

The Israelites, in the period of the united kingdom and subsequently of the kingdoms of Israel and Judah, governed their migration policy to a high degree independently of any outside forces, even in periods when they were semi-dependent on one of the super powers of those days, because these super powers had no primary interest in such questions besides imposing a limited amount of personnel in countries that had become formal vassal-states in order to control their loyal conduct. Of course, things changed dramatically when both the northern kingdom Israel and later the southern kingdom Judah were conquered by the Assyrians and by the Babylonians respectively. Forced deportations of Israelites and Judaeans on the one hand and the import and settlement

---

35. See, e.g., Kestemont, "Les grands principes," 269–78.

36. As opposed to the rights of individual states to sovereignty and protection of identity, although the first element is not negated in principle. Of course, things are more complicated in the case of the European Union, where ultimate sovereignty is (in the process of being) transferred from the national to the Union level, with direct and immense consequences for (im)migration issues. The Schengen-Dublin agreements are the most salient examples of this.

37. For the full text of the final draft of July 11, 2018, see https://refugeesmigrants. un.org/sites/default/files/180711_final_draft_0.pdf [accessed July 3, 2020].

of foreigners into the former kingdom of Israel were among the main consequences of the loss of political sovereignty.[38]

2.11. Migration as Weapon

In some cases, mass-migration is currently used as a weapon of sorts to change the order of the receiving societies. There are three major—sometimes interconnected—facets of this phenomenon. The first is related to the aspirations of considerable parts of the elite establishment in the West with a view to replacing the ethnically relatively coherent nation-states with multiethnic and multicultural societies; as such it will be discussed below in the paragraph on aspects relating to the receiving societies. The second is related to a wish to dismantle Western (White European and American) dominance on a global scale, often related to an idea of establishing justice by enacting some kind of punishment on the West because of its involvement in imperialism and colonialism—as well as slavery—in the past.[39] The third, more clearly recognizable, facet is related to the aim of establishing a global caliphate, an aim consistently and publicly supported and propagated by a large number of influential leaders of the *umma* (that is, the world-wide community of Muslims).[40]

---

38. For biblical summary reports concerning the deportation of Israelites and Judaeans see, e.g., 2 Kgs 17:6 and 25:11; for the settlement of foreigners in Israel see, e.g., 2 Kgs 17:24. In New Testament times, migration issues were basically under the control of the Roman Empire.

39. This wish is attested among some groups in the West, but also among some groups in the rest of the world. As far as non-Western countries are concerned, anti-Western rhetoric by many governments, especially with a left-wing or Islamic orientation, testify to the worldview that forms the background for the potential use of mass-migration as a means to subvert or change the existing order in Western countries. At the same time, it is difficult to find explicit official statements that connect anti-Western sentiment with migration; the connection becomes more easily graspable in practical attitudes, like granting transit to migrants or denial of re-entry of emigrants who are not recognized as having a legal title to stay in the West. As far as specific cases are concerned, one may point to allegations of Russia (in cooperation with Syria) intentionally creating a migrant crisis to destabilize the West (see, e.g., Dearden, "Russia and Syria 'Weaponizing' Refugee Crisis"), or to pressure on Israel to allow the return of Arab refugees and their descendants to places inhabited by them before the War of Independence in 1948 (which would, of course, demographically erase the Jewish character of the state of Israel). Muammar Gaddafi uttered threats that Europe might become "black" if he is not paid large amounts of money to prevent this from happening in 2010 (see, e.g., Willey, "Gaddafi Wants EU Cash").

40. See, e.g., Corcoran, *Refugee Resettlement*. Perhaps most famous are Muammar

In the ancient Near East and the Graeco-Roman world, comparable goals were generally reached by conquest rather than by means of mass-migration with the collaboration of the ruling elites of the receiving societies.[41]

3. ASPECTS RELATING SPECIFICALLY TO THE MIGRANTS

3.1. Motives

While—as we have seen—the biblical texts suggest that immigrants who came to ancient Israel to stay there permanently in most cases very likely did so because of a lack of alternatives for survival, in the current situation what is at stake in many instances is not immediate survival; rather, it is the wish to enhance an otherwise inferior life situation that is the main incentive for migration.[42] The wish is triggered by broad and easy access to—even if often misleading—information about the better life conditions in other parts of the world, for example the West, and

---

Gaddafi's threats that Europe would be Muslim in the foreseeable future because of its large amount of Muslim immigrants in 2006 (see "Muammar Gaddafi 2006—Islam Will Conquer Europe without Firing a Shot," *Youtube*) and Recep Tayyip Erdogan's claim that assimilation of Turkish immigrants in Europe would be "a crime against humanity," a statement made in a speech in Cologne in February 2008 (see, e.g., Press, "Turkish Prime Minister").

41. Minor exceptions like the creation of (basically commercial) outposts of Assyrians in Hatti during the Old-Assyrian period not involving military campaigns do exist; however, they are not comparable to current events in terms of numbers of persons involved and overarching goals.

42. Which is, of course, not to say that matters of life and death cannot be involved in some cases also today. The available statistics from all Western countries, however, make it clear that such cases only constitute a minority of those who actually reach the Western world. As a random example among many, we can point to the fact that only 38 percent of first instance asylum decisions in the European Union in 2019 resulted in positive outcomes (see "Asylum Statistics," *Eurostat*). It is interesting to observe that in Germany, looking at the period from 2005 through 2014, the *"Gesamtschutzquote"* (roughly equivalent to the percentage of asylum seekers who were granted asylum status) jumped from 6.3 percent in 2006 to 27.5 percent in 2007 and remained above 20 percent for the rest of the period (see Fischelmayer and Lederer, *Das Bundesamt*, 47. It is likely that this remarkable break is primarily founded in changes in policies rather than in outward circumstances, since there are no clear differences in the latter that would explain the break (see the relevant data presented by Fischelmayer and Lederer, *Das Bundesamt*, 19).

made possible in its realization by the existence of modern means of mass transportation. Both access to information via modern mass media and access to mass transportation were of course absent in the ancient Near East.

It is also likely that the social-emotional attachment to one's place of origin was generally stronger in antiquity, again leading to an lower degree of inclination to move away from either the place of origin in the case of a settled lifestyle, or from the clan of origin in the case of a more nomadic lifestyle.

Moreover, there are a number of new reasons motivating people to emigrate that are related to concepts foreign to the ancient world, like gender discrimination or sexual orientation.[43]

3.2. Internal Disposition

Partially encouraged by changes in the views on (im)migration in the receiving societies, the number of immigrants who on the one hand intend to stay permanently in their new places of settlement, but on the other hand are not disposed to assimilate to central tenets of the culture and worldview prevalent in the receiving society has grown considerably in the current situation as far as immigration from non-Western to Western countries is concerned. We do not know of large waves of immigrants in ancient Israel who would settle permanently with the intention (or permission) to keep their cultural heritage to a high degree or even with the aspiration to remodel their new environment according to their original cultural system[44]—an attitude which in the present situation may even include the conviction that the culture of the place of origin is not only superior to the one of the receiving society, but in fact the only legitimate one in a global horizon. Such attitudes are not restricted to, but perhaps most visible, in communities with a Muslim background.[45]

43. See, e.g., Houston, *You Shall Love*, 43–44.

44. Attitudes that come close to this can be ascribed only to pre-Israelite Canaanite inhabitants of the land and their descendants, or to various groups of invaders; but none of them would classify as "immigrants."

45. One indicator of this phenomenon is that polls among Muslim immigrants in the West consistently show high numbers of support for Sharia law. Here are three random examples: A 2006 poll in the U.K. reveals that 40 percent of Muslims want Sharia law to be applied in the country (see Hennessy and Kite, "Poll"); a 2010 poll in Austria shows that the majority of Turks want Sharia law incorporated into the legal

Related to this are the cases in which immigrants support the idea of *reconquista*, for example, in southern parts of the U.S. or in Andalusia.[46]

4. ASPECTS RELATING SPECIFICALLY TO THE RECEIVING SOCIETY

4.1. The Religious Character of Ancient Israel

Biblical Israel represents a type of society that has no analogue in the (post-)modern Western states. Israel as we know it from the biblical texts representing the orthodox Yahwistic ideology has a special understanding of her origins and role: a people created and chosen by God, with a land given to her by God himself. Connected to this is the notion that the people has to be loyal to God by keeping his commandments in order not to jeopardize the hold on its land.[47] In this concept, religious and national boundaries are more or less coextensive.[48] All of this is different from any modern Western state.

From a New Testament perspective, the church is the primary locus of a complex prolongation of biblical Israelite society. This means that as far as the specific Old Testament patterns covering such issues as the dealing with foreigners are thought to be transferable to the current situation, it is not the state or society at large that can be the primary stage for such a transfer, but the church. By extension, this is valid also for specific New Testament models of dealing with foreigners. However, since the current church is not an ethnic-political body as was ancient Israel, and since there are differences in historical circumstances that separate the current church both from ancient Israel and the situation reflected in the New Testament, no simple one-to-one transfers are possible even on the church level. The numerous and complex differences between the old and the new covenant—in addition to the inclusion or exclusion of the

system ("Austria: Majority of Turks Want Sharia Personal Law Incorporated into Legal System"); a 2019 poll in France shows that 46 percent of Muslims want Sharia law to be applied in the country ("Poll: 46% of French Muslims Believe Sharia Law Should Be Applied in Country"). One can also point to the proliferation of Sharia courts throughout Europe, especially the U.K.; see, e.g., Puppinck, "The Council of Europe."

46. As far as the Southwest of the U.S. is concerned, see Huntington, *Who Are We?* 221–43, 251–56; cf. also the Wikipedia entry "Reconquista (Mexico)."

47. See, e.g., Lev 25:23.

48. Therefore, a good number of the laws that deal with different types of foreigners concern cultic matters.

level of ethnicity in the definition of the people of the covenant—have the same effect.

4.2. The Scope of the Regulations in the Biblical Texts

This point is directly related to the previous point concerning the religious character of biblical Israel.

As far as the "legal" material in the Hebrew Bible is concerned, both generally and specifically with respect to texts dealing with foreigners, the interest is not so much focused on general civic questions, but mainly on questions that have to do with the specific religious character of the community.[49] The way of thought in which these issues are addressed is not informed by various kinds of (secular) philosophy, political expediency, or economic deliberations, but primarily by theological concepts. This means that all the specific laws dealing with foreigners must be understood as embedded in the larger theological framework defining Israel, for which there is no analogue in any modern state. Moreover, as already mentioned above, one has to take into consideration that these laws are not statutory state law in the modern sense of a law code.[50] The same is true, *mutatis mutandis*, for all the regulations concerning strangers in the New Testament.

It must also be noted that in the Hebrew Bible questions dealing with how to treat foreigners who are already in the country take precedence over questions dealing with who should be admitted to the country, while in the current situation the ethical debate focuses more on the latter questions.[51]

49. As the overview in chapter 2 has shown.

50. See, e.g., Berman, *Inconsistency*, 107–36, 137–98; Lefebvre, *Collections*, 258. A possible exception may be the administration of the internal affairs of the province of Yehud in Persian times, and perhaps the role of the biblical legal material in the administration of the Hasmonaean kingdom.

51. There is broad agreement among Christians that immigrants who have been admitted to a country need to be treated with dignity and love (even though views differ on what this exactly means in practical terms). Major points of dispute concern questions of who is to be admitted in the first place and how illegal immigration must be dealt with.

4.3. The Social Makeup of Ancient Israel

Internal tensions notwithstanding, ancient Israel can likely be described as being more homogeneous than most postmodern Western societies, both in terms of religion, culture, and ethnicity. The differences become embodied on the practical level in the opposition of the principle of *ius sanguinis*, which is compatible with the Israelite model, vs. *ius solis*, which is the expression—either in terms of cause or consequence, or both—of a society that is not marked by a high degree of or emphasis on religious, cultural, and ethnic unity.

The homogeneity that is characteristic of the case of ancient Israel is important from a sociological point of view, since the possibility for immigrants to assimilate to a new environment is dependent on the degree of homogeneity prevalent in the receiving society.[52] In most postmodern Western countries, the Christian heritage that had been an important element in the shaping of a relatively homogeneous society in terms of religion and culture, has lost its special status to a large degree, especially on the official state level, being replaced by a relatively loose net of "values," with "tolerance" and "inclusion" being among the most cherished.[53] It is, however, clear that when such "values" are scrutinized, they turn out to be mainly about questions relating to the *approach* to specific societal challenges, while the questions of the *content* of common foundational tenets of the postmodern societies that could be described in positive terms tend to remain unanswered. The most salient element of this approach is the affirmation of a multicultural acceptance of various worldviews, eschewing the well-known philosophical (and practical) problems of such an approach.[54] More recently, however, there is a manifest acceleration in the establishment of a new set of values in terms of content.

52. For more details see chapter 5.2. below.

53. A random example: The European Commission finances research and education programs devoted to "tolerance and education" for roughly 90 billion Euros in 2020; see "Funding Opportunities for Promoting Tolerance and Education," *European Commission* (2020).

54. The following quote reflects the typical views well: "[I]ntegration is still widely perceived as a one-way process to be shouldered by the migrants, overlooking the responsibilities of the host societies. As long as migrants continue to be viewed as 'threat' to Europe, the focus will remain economic rather than cultural and humane. If the cultural benefits and the enrichment that migrants bring to the host society remain undervalued, it will be challenging to ensure equal opportunities for migrants in Europe and to promote powerful, diverse, and multicultural societies" (Invitation text to the conference on "Promoting Migrant Integration for a Powerful, Diverse and

4.4. Varying Degrees of Self-Assertiveness

There seems to be no corresponding element in ancient Israel to the relatively new ideology in the present situation in the West,[55] according to which the receptive society has primarily responsibilities and not rights,[56] and where it does not matter whether one's ancestors have lived in a country for hundreds of years or whether someone arrived just yesterday.[57] This approach is necessitated by a certain concept of human rights and a strict interpretation of the rules of equality and non-discrimination.[58] An embodiment of this new view can be found in the slogan "No human being is illegal."[59] As opposed to this, there are clear distinctions between the rights of a native-born Israelite, a sojourner (*ger*), and a foreigner (*nokri*) in ancient Israel as far as one can tell from the biblical texts.

A related phenomenon is the aspiration of large parts of the establishment in the West to permanently replace the ethnically relatively

---

Multicultural Europe," held on September 14, 2017, in Brussels; see Avos Melchor, "Promoting Migrant Integration" [accessed July 3, 2020]. For similar rhetoric in the realm of theology and biblical studies see, e.g., Paynter, "'Make Yourself at Home,'" 57 ("Moving from the dichotomy of native 'hosts' and immigrant 'guests' can open one's eyes to the possibility of two-way hospitality; and hence of the enrichment which immigrants bring to a culture").

55. The new view has gained ground gradually since the latter part of the twentieth century. It goes hand in glove with the renunciation of the assimilation principle, though it is distinct from it in theory.

56. See again the quote from the invitation text to the conference on "Promoting Migrant Integration for a Powerful, Diverse and Multicultural Europe."

57. There is some lack in the conceptual consistency of those who promote such views, because they will normally not assert that the principle should be transferred to other parts of the world outside the West.

58. Of course, there are differences between various Western countries in how exactly these issues are handled, and usually some kind of minor distinctions are still made, for example in the form of waiting times for the reception of certain welfare benefits. This does, however, not change the overall tendency described in this paragraph.

59. The slogan is—very likely on purpose—formulated in a way that conflates two distinct levels—a classic example of manipulative language. What is meant is that no one's *place of residence* is illegal; readers are lured into the acceptance of this position by way of a cognitive combination of this position with the undisputed principle that the *existence* of each human being can never be seen as "illegal." The slogan is, however, not only manipulative, but also inconsistent and insincere, because it would normally not be applied to cases like the Falkland Islands (that is, Brits on the Falklands), Palestine (that is, Jews in Palestine), Tibet (that is, Han-Chinese in Tibet), South Africa (that is, Whites in South Africa), to name a few.

coherent nation-states with multiethnic and multicultural societies.[60] Again, there is no equivalent on the side of biblical orthodox views on how Israel should look in this respect.

Such tendencies are not only informed by certain concepts of individual human rights, but also by a sense of historic guilt among considerable segments of the Western elites,[61] and also a kind of spiritual, cultural, and moral void that requires compensation through the "enrichment" by (the representatives of) other cultures.[62] It is interesting to note that such enrichment-rhetoric is not found in the Bible.

4.5. Assimilation

As can be deduced from the chapter on the complexity of views about migration in the Hebrew Bible,[63] a relatively high degree of assimilation is the aim of the integration process of those who want to stay permanently and participate fully in the host society in the case of ancient Israel. While assimilation has been the goal set by the receiving societies in the West until the 1960s, this model is no longer in place and has been replaced by various notions of multiculturalism.[64] This point is obviously directly related to the one mentioned in the previous paragraph.

---

60. This has become the commonly accepted mainstream position in the West. As opposed to a couple of years ago, the furthering of multiculturalism, together with a growing "integration" of the member states of the European Union—which, of course, does not mean anything else than the transfer of power from the national level to the supra-national level of the Union—, is on constant display in official documents and statements of the representatives of the European Union, and generally also of the representatives of its member states in the West (as opposed to the situation in central-eastern Europe).

61. This phenomenon has been on the public radar most recently in the attention given to Western involvement in racism, colonialism, and slavery subsequent to the death of George Floyd. However, the phenomenon is much older; earlier mass-manifestations can be seen in the protests against the Vietnam war and in the 1968 student rebellions.

62. The frequency with which the term "enrichment" is used is one of the clear pointers in this direction. On a strictly spiritual level, it is possible to discern a longing for some kind of inner-worldly redemption or salvation informing these phenomena.

63. See chapter 2 above.

64. See, e.g., Howson and Sallah, *Europe's Established and Emerging Immigrant Communities.*

4.6. The Foundational Myth

Biblical Israel has a foundational myth[65] that is based on migration. The first of the patriarchs, Abraham, as well as his descendants, are conceived of as migrants in the Hebrew Bible, and the beginning of Israel as a nation is connected with the dramatic emigration from Egypt and immigration into—or rather: gradual conquest of—Canaan.[66] Importantly, the experiences of migration of the patriarchs and the emerging people of Israel inform much of the reflection concerning the dealing with foreigners who come to Israel. The Israelites are instructed to use empathy in their dealing with foreigners, remembering their own or their forefathers' experience as foreigners in Egypt.[67] A comparable type of foundational myth cannot be found in the case of modern Western states. The history of the U.S., however, can perhaps be said to bear some resemblance to the Israelite model; but the comparative lack of religious, cultural, and ethnic homogeneity at least since the latter part of the nineteenth century, and especially the absence of a similar direct divine ordination of the processes of emigration and immigration still point to considerable differences between the U.S. and ancient Israel.[68]

4.7. Administration of Immigration on the Central State Level vs. the Local-Personal Level

As compared to the current situation in the West, the situation in ancient Israel is characterized by the absence of a state bureaucratic apparatus administering immigration. In the Western states, the situation is reversed, with constant disputes about the right function of the concomitant institutions, and considerable financial interests of various parties related to them. In ancient Israel—as much as in the relevant texts of the

65. The term "myth" does not necessarily presuppose a specific degree of lack of historical foundation. For details see chapter 5.2. below.

66. See not only the foundational stories from Gen 11:31 onward as far as Abraham, Isaac, and Jacob are concerned, and the books of Exodus through Joshua as far as the emerging people of Israel is concerned, but also numerous echoes throughout the whole of the Hebrew Bible.

67. See especially Exod 22:20; 23:9; Lev 19:34; Deut 10:19; 24:18, 22.

68. Divine ordination was claimed by the early settlers and their descendents (see, e.g., Huntington, *Who Are We?* 63–64). Even without evaluating the merits or problems of this claim, the difference between secondary emulation and original model, codified in the canonical texts of the Bible, is obvious.

New Testament—responsibility for the handling of immigrants is located directly on the local-personal level, whereas responsibility is delegated to a large degree in the modern West, with politicians, bureaucrats, and activists playing the major roles.[69] Some of these agents, especially the bureaucrats, but in many cases also the activists, make a living for themselves through their involvement in the administration of immigration.[70]

5. BRIEF SUMMARY

The lesson to be drawn from the overview of some of the major distinctions between the situation in ancient Israel and New Testament times on the one hand and the (post)modern West on the other hand is that biblical regulations concerning the treatment of sojourners or strangers cannot in any simple way be directly "applied" to current issues of (im)migration.

---

69. Obviously private initiatives exist as well, but they all operate under the larger umbrella of the state administration of immigration, and are often financially supported by the state.

70. See also Carroll: "[A]ncient Israel did not have the kind of government programs and social systems in place that we have today . . . . Help for the needy had to occur at several levels and through various channels: individual families . . . , the community . . . , workplaces of whatever kind . . . , religious centers . . . , and at the city gate" (*Christians*, 91–92).

5

Broadening the Horizon I

Philosophical and Sociological Perspectives:
Migration and Ethnicity, Migration and the
Nation-State

1. PHILOSOPHICAL PERSPECTIVES

1.1. General Philosophical Reflections on Foreignness ("Otherness"): Bernardo Bazan

In a philosophical perspective, the individual "foreigner" is a concretization of the more general phenomenon of alterity or "otherness." It is possible to distinguish between two major types of analysis of this phenomenon:

According to one philosophical view, alterity is an aspect of plurality and (historical) change, which is opposed to the One, the essence, the unchangeable, the eternal; the former is inferior to the latter ontologically and therefore also on all other levels. One has to overcome alterity by seeing differences as manifestations of the One. In this sense, alterity is basically conceived of in negative terms.[1] In many respects, this school of thought, which aims at unity, has found its sharpest representation in the philosophy of Hegel. In his view, the whole universal history is just a process of the self-unfolding of the One, and the "other" is only one

1. See Bazan, "Pensée," 50–51, 53–54. Plato is a prime representative of this philosophical school.

124

moment of the whole. For the benefit of the whole, the "other," the difference, must be overcome. While it can be said that the One manifests itself in the many particularities, especially in the spirits of the peoples, these particularities have their justification only in relation to the universal whole, and therefore ultimately need to be sacrificed to it.[2] Since the particular, alterity, only represents a partial aspect of the universal whole, it must be suppressed, and—if necessary—fought against.[3] The goal of history is the absolute dominance of the one culture that represents the own spirit of the respective dominating power, which is attained through a process of—sometimes violent—assimilation and reduction.

The opposite view finds its classic representation in the philosophy of Thomas Aquinas. While in his ontology all beings are unified through "being," the way of being of each individual is inalienable. Therefore, the principle of community is at the same time the root of individuality.[4] The individual beings have their being based on a creational act by the unlimited Being who in creation expresses his own perfection, exactly by giving room for limited beings besides himself or in addition to himself. Because each individual limited being is an expression of the perfection of the Creator, their particular way of being is something that is of infinite value.[5] In such a view, alterity is founded in the root of being itself and valued positively, as an expression of the richness of creation. The one infinite Being does not totalize, but out of love cherishes the diverse variety of the finite beings.[6] The Creator himself creates limited beings with inalienable alterity, both vis-à-vis each other as well as vis-à-vis himself. Since the Creator does not create the species, but the human individual, in particular acts of divine love, each person has his/her inalienable individuality. It is this individuality, in its uniqueness and difference in relation to other individuals, which is the goal of creation—and not the perfection of the species.[7] This "laissez être" of the infinite Creator vis-

---

2. See Bazan, "Pensée," 62.

3. See Bazan, "Pensée," 63–64.

4. See Bazan, "Pensée," 66.

5. See Bazan, "Pensée," 69.

6. See Bazan, "Pensée," 69.

7. Fornet-Betancourt expresses a similar thought: "[T]he 'stranger' . . . becomes present to us in the diversity of linguistic worlds, worlds of life, religions, traditions, cultures, and horizons of understanding. What is strange exists because plurality exists. Plurality manifests itself in phenomena that represent originals, which cannot be reduced to variations of a single identity" ("Hermeneutics," 212).

à-vis the finite creatures is the model for the relationship between human beings. What is "right" is an attitude that recognizes the fundamental equality of the fellow human being and does not aim at assimilating his/ her alterity, but respects and furthers it.[8]

Relating the two different philosophical approaches to alterity to questions of mass-(im)migration, one can see that the relationship between the two approaches and views on migration is multi-faceted. A position that advocates for migration policies that are as liberal as possible is usually related to multiculturalist views. At first glance, multiculturalism seems to be closer to the Thomist position because of its respect for the variety of cultures. On the other hand, a position that advocates for stricter migration policies usually expects immigrants to assimilate to the culture of the host country, which seems to be closer to the Hegelian position. It is, however, clear that this picture does not reflect the deeper layers of the characteristics of the two positions. As far as the liberal multiculturalist position is concerned: While on the individual level and in the short term it does in fact promote variety and diversity and the respect for a person's alterity, things look quite different on the larger societal level and in the long term—if large number of migrants are involved. In this case, cultural differences are ultimately erased over time to a considerable degree; especially the cultures of the host countries may be exposed to a process of gradual vanishing. Moreover, the basic notions of global responsibility and global citizenship have a strong totalizing component and undermine ethnically based group-differences in the longer term in principle. On the other hand, restrictions to immigration clearly serve to protect alterity, as far as ethnicity is concerned, in principle. When it comes to the assimilationist expectations vis-à-vis immigrants, the result is not an extinction of variety and diversity on the group level, but a change of identity in individuals. The individual is not expected to conform to a universal unitarian model, but to a particular national, ethnic, or cultural identity. In sum, then, the Hegelian position is closer to liberal (im)migration policies, while the Thomist position is closer to strict (im)migration policies. As has become clear in the previous chapters, and as will be demonstrated also in the final two chapters, it is the Thomist position that is much more in line with biblical views on (im)migration than the Hegelian position.

8. See Bazan, "Pensée," 80.

1.2. Philosophical Reflections on Helping Persons in Need: Daniel von Wachter

Against the background of the mass-immigration into Germany in the fall of 2015, the philosopher von Wachter wrote an essay in which he argued that the indiscriminate opening of the borders to masses of immigrants is immoral from a philosophical point of view.[9] Here are his main arguments:

It is morally good to want to help someone who is in need. However, this applies only to individuals who give freely, and there is no duty to do so which would then imply a right of the person in need to receive such help.[10] Things look differently when the helping agent is not an individual, but the state. It is morally different because in this case the agent uses means that are not his own, but are taken from others—the citizens of the respective state—by coercion. As a consequence, the state has neither the obligation nor the right to do this.[11] The situation is aggravated by the fact that internal discord necessarily arises among the citizens of the respective state as to how to allocate means to various groups of people in need.[12]

If people accept the notion that the state is the right agent of doing good in the sense of helping people in need, at least some of them will imagine the number of recipients not to be limited. To them, pointing to limits of accepting immigrants and providing material help becomes immoral, because such limits would restrict something that is inherently morally good. The problem with this attitude, however, is that it does not square with the realities on the ground.[13]

Against such an unrealistic position, von Wachter maintains that a state has a duty to help only towards its own citizens. A major reason for this is that only citizens contribute to the budgets from which the money to support people in need is taken.[14] A state has no right to help non-citizens if these persons only want to improve their material life conditions. It is allowed, though not obliged, to grant asylum to individuals. In such

9. See von Wachter, "Die Öffnung der Grenzen ist unmoralisch."

10. See "Die Öffnung der Grenzen ist unmoralisch," 14.

11. See "Die Öffnung der Grenzen ist unmoralisch," 14.

12. See "Die Öffnung der Grenzen ist unmoralisch," 15.

13. See "Die Öffnung der Grenzen ist unmoralisch," 15.

14. See "Die Öffnung der Grenzen ist unmoralisch," 15. However, other aspects would need to be considered as far as this point is concerned.

cases, however, material support must not exceed the bare minimum for survival. These restrictions apply because the material resources the state uses are not its own. In some cases, a state has a duty to help: if a person is persecuted and his/her life is in acute danger; if this person has no other place to go; if the person will not pose a threat to the host country; if the person will leave once the danger is over.[15] These obligations are in accordance with international law concerning refugees.[16] No single state can be expected to protect all persons in need in a global perspective.[17]

1.3. The Philosophical Background of the Propagation of Open Borders

The opening of borders with few or no restrictions for persons in need, regardless of the specific type of need, is ultimately a socialist concept as far as the macro-level is concerned. The presupposition behind the concept is that there is no ultimate (communal) ownership of a specific group of people on a given territory, including the means of production found on that territory and the profits that result from the use of these means. On the micro-level of individual private ownership, the socialist nature of the concept is normally recognizable only indirectly, because in most cases the expropriation will only take place in the form of raised taxes, by which means property is redistributed from the original inhabitants of a territory to the new arrivals, which amounts to a partial invalidation of the right of private ownership.

From a perspective informed by biblical ethics, this socialist concept may be understandable, especially in an eschatological perspective. On the other hand, the questions of its philosophical cogency as well as questions concerning its ethical deficits need to be given serious attention.[18]

15. See "Die Öffnung der Grenzen ist unmoralisch," 16.

16. See "Die Öffnung der Grenzen ist unmoralisch," 17.

17. See "Die Öffnung der Grenzen ist unmoralisch," 9.

18. For a discussion of these problems see the data collected in chapter 6 and the ethical considerations presented in chapter 7.

2. SOCIOLOGICAL CLARIFICATIONS

2.1. Ethnic Identity

As an ontological matter of fact, people are different in various ways; the identity of every person is different from that of all other persons.[19] Therefore, some kind of "alterity"/"otherness" is the flip side of the coin the other side of which is "identity." The differentiation between "Me" vs. "the others," and by extension "Us" vs. "Them" is a necessary part of the human condition.[20] At the same time, however, it is important to note that the boundaries between "Us" and "Them" (or "the other") are not fix, but constantly "negotiated."[21]

Alterity can be located on a number of different levels, with more than one level at a time, and the markers of identity can vary. Layers of alterity can relate to, for example, family, village, tribe, ethnic group, state, social class, political beliefs, etc. The question is always whom one wants to differentiate oneself against.[22]

Ethnicity can be identified as one important level or part of identity (and corresponding alterity). As with the case of other levels and aspects of identity (and alterity), the boundaries of an ethnic group are not rigidly fixed.[23] It is "dialogic," created, preserved, reaffirmed, and even rejected through a continuous set of contrasts between one's own group and others.[24] Also, there is not necessarily a clear either-or distinction between various ethnic identities. Directly related to this fluidity is the observation that factors that function as markers of an ethnic group vary, dependent on circumstances and on the groups involved.[25] Things that are

---

19. See, e.g., Bazan, "Pensée," 50–51, 53, 62–64, 66, 69, 80.

20. See, e.g., Brett, "Interpreting Ethnicity," 10; Huntington, *Who Are We?* 21.

21. See, e.g., McGrane, *Beyond Anthropology*, 115; Schuster, "Ethnische Fremdheit," 207; Huntington, *Who Are We?* 22–24.

22. See, e.g., Gilissen, "Le statut des étrangers," 10–11.

23. Ethnicity is, however, a less flexible part of identity than other aspects (like language or religion, or all the aspects related to the political, economic, and social spheres); this is also true for gender, and even more for age (see, e.g., Huntington, *Who Are We?* 22–23, 27).

24. Cf. Brettell, "Theorizing Migration," 132.

25. See Roosens, *Creating Ethnicity*, 12, 18; Brettell, "Theorizing Migration," 133–34. Cf. also Scott, "Ethnicity."

important in one case can be unimportant in another. What the main markers are will be discussed below.

Changes in the outward situation always lead to the activation or deactivation of certain layers of ethnic identity and to a change in the specific weight of the various ethnic markers. Also, seemingly peripheral elements can become more important in the process. In more extreme cases, changes in the outward situation can not only result in a change in the relative weight of ethnic markers, but even in the creation of a new ethnic group almost *ex nihilo*.[26]

In principle, almost everything can become an ethnic marker (music, clothing, etc.); there are, however, some factors that have proven to be more important—and are generally accepted as part of the definition of "ethnicity:" common group name, descent, language, religion, territory, history, sense of solidarity, and way of life.[27] It is never necessarily all of these factors that need to be present to establish ethnic identity.[28] The weight of the various factors may vary among the individual members of an ethnic group; also the intensity of the ethnic identification may be different among various individual members of a given group. Both for the group as well as its individual member, both the salient ethnic markers and the intensity of the ethnic identification can change over time.[29] The need for ethnic identification and the attachment to an ethnic group will usually increase in circumstances of rapid and thorough social change and the weakening of other social bonds, or in the face of a strong mixture of people with different backgrounds.[30]

26. In such cases a group did not previously have any real specific distinguishing traits as far as the fundamental markers like language, religion, history, and everyday customs are concerned. A very interesting and prominent example is the creation of a Palestinian people in the context of the Arab-Israeli conflict in the twentieth century.

27. See, e.g., Hutchinson and Smith, *Ethnicity*, 5–6; Jenkins, *Rethinking Ethnicity*, 10; Keyes, "The Dialectics," 7–9; Scott, "Ethnicity;" Smith, *The Ethnic Origins*, 26–28; Zenner, "Ethnicity," 393. As far as the homeland is concerned, actual physical occupation of it is not necessarily required; it can be replaced by a symbolic attachment in which normally past memories play an important role.
Sometimes "culture" is also mentioned. However, it is clear that culture and ethnicity are not co-extensive; an ethnic group may consist of sub-groups with different cultures, and groups sharing a specific culture may consist of more than one ethnic group; also, an ethnic group's culture can change over time (see Cohen, "Ethnicity," 383–87).

28. See, e.g., Levine, *Constructing Collective Identity*, 20.

29. See, e.g., Jenkins, *Rethinking Ethnicity*, 20–21; Reminick, *Theory*, 3, 18; Roosens, *Creating Ethnicity*, 10, 16.

30. See, e.g., Bell, "Ethnicity and Social Change," 171; Kellas, *The Politics of Nationalism*, 84; Reminick, *Theory*, 45–46, 63.

It is a matter of debate how much weight the factor of "common descent," which points to a biological element in the definition of ethnicity, has—if any.[31] The fact that a person cannot randomly choose his/her ethnicity suggests that a biological dimension cannot be ignored completely and that ethnic identity cannot be freely "constructed," even if some degree of choice and change must be acknowledged.[32] The element of common descent can be understood as a manifestation or an extension of kinship—which is a ubiquitous, trans-cultural phenomenon.

An important element in the development of an ethnic or a national identity is a "common myth of descent,"[33] usually consisting of both historical and legendary elements.[34] In historical perspective, such myths in most cases have a somehow religious (or pseudo-religious) dimension. A religious element in the constitution of an ethnic group, especially if it is broadly accepted, proves to be a particularly strong driver of mobilization and historic perseverance.[35] The force of the religious element is heightened if the religion ascribes the respective group a salient position in the cosmic order.[36] Besides religion, clearly distinctive or unique cultural traits, especially if their number is high, will contribute to the intensity of ethnic identification.

Even when ethnicity is defined by the common salient markers just mentioned, it is not generally clear when one has to speak of a distinct ethnic group. For example: Are Germans an ethnic group, or rather Bavarians, Saxonians, etc.? Are Sinti an ethnic group? What about someone living in Prague around 1600 speaking Czech? What about the children of a Czech speaking person who has migrated to another part of the Holy Roman Empire, say to Cologne? What distinguishes an ethnic group (or a people) from a tribe, or a religious community such as, e.g., the Druze?

31. There are those—although in a minority position—who reject any biological element. An example is Allport (*The Nature of Prejudice*, 107).

32. See, e.g., Keyes, "The Dialectics," 6. It seems best to avoid extreme primordial and subjectivist views of ethnicity. As in all human affairs, "there is an interaction between genes and environment, and neither is independent of the other" (Kellas, *The Politics of Nationalism*, 15). Cf. also Brettell, "Theorizing Migration," 131–32; she points to the differences between primordialist, instrumentalist, and situational approaches to the study of ethnicity.

33. Smith, *The Ethnic Origins*, 24–25.

34. Smith, *The Ethnic Origins*, 25.

35. See Smith, *The Ethnic Origins*, 109–25.

36. See Smith, *The Ethnic Origins*, 35.

There are no generally accepted answers to these questions. One possible approach is to assert that an ethnic group (or a people) exists when a large enough number of individuals in a society view themselves as such. Obviously, however, such an answer underlines that there are no fixed boundaries in these matters; one cannot, for example, say how large this group needs to be.[37] The answer to the question of the existence of an ethnic group just given must be qualified, because ethnic identity is not only a matter of the definition of its members, but also of the perception of persons outside the group.[38] Inside and outside ascriptions are interdependent—which does not mean that they are necessarily congruent.[39] One point is clear: For an ethnic group (or a people) to exist it is not necessary that they are co-extant with a nation-state.

Even if a group has established itself as a distinct ethnic group (or a people), it remains subject to constant changes, through a number of processes, like adoption, exogamy, mass deportations, large scale immigration, replacement of the elite after a military defeat, spread of a *lingua franca*, etc. Put in a different way: A state of relative alterity can shift over time and become a state of participation/belonging vis-à-vis a respective referential group, by various processes of assimilation and integration, including cohabitation or cooperation.

Ethnic change is also related to the interplay of individual and collective elements constituting ethnicity. Without the existence of an ethnic group, there is no basis for the corresponding ethnic identification of an individual. On the other hand, an ethnic group can only persist if enough individuals internalize its characteristics and actively participate in its life.[40]

Ethnic groups are not only subject to change, but they can die out, either biologically or culturally (or both). The latter scenario—mostly dragging on for some time—is historically more frequent. It normally happens through assimilation to other cultures. For the persistence of an ethnic group the continuing relevancy of a sufficient number of elements of its mytho-symbolic complex is indispensable. The mytho-symbolic complex needs to be adaptable to changing circumstances and transmitted to all

37. And not in all cases will their aspiration succeed.

38. See, e.g., Jenkins, *Rethinking Ethnicity*, 19: "[E]thnic identity depends on ascription, both by members of the ethnic group in question and by outsiders."

39. See Jenkins, *Rethinking Ethnicity*, 53, 59.

40. Cf., e.g., Reminick, *Theory*, 51.

strata of society and each new generation to fulfill its supportive role. Other factors terminating an ethnic group are internal strife and external invasion (which may be interrelated). Of course, a minimally sufficient biological reproduction is also always necessary for the survival of an ethnic group.

2.2. State and Ethnicity

A distinction needs to be made between state on the one hand and ethnicity and nation on the other. A state is a legal and political entity that operates with force on a given territory, while an ethnic group and a nation are communities of individuals who are bound to each other by a sense of togetherness and—traditionally—by a shared culture.[41] However, the term "nation" also has a political dimension, which may, under certain circumstances, also be the case with respect to ethnic groups. In spite of the differences, there is a connection between state on the one hand and ethnicity and nation on the other, because normally state institutions presuppose ethnic or national forms of group identity.[42]

A state can be composed of various ethnic groups or nations (depending on the definition of the term "nation"), while an ethnic group or nation (again depending on the definition of the term "nation") can be spread across more than one state. The nation-state aspires at making the boundaries of state and nation congruent. This is, however, hardly fully achievable.[43]

41. For the complexity of the relationship between ethnicity and culture see above. As far as the concept of nation is concerned, it can be observed that it is currently undergoing deep changes. For some of the issues involved see the following paragraph.

42. Obviously, the ethnic dimension is in many cases not present. While it has been an important factor in Europe for the last couple of centuries, it is currently eroding on a large scale, through mass-immigration on the one hand and the creation of a common European space by the European Union.

43. There are many, both in the political and in the scholarly world, who view the nation-state in wholly negative terms. An example is Favell, for whom nation-states and their borders are nothing else than artificial constructions (see "Rebooting Migration Theory," 271), invented "to cage and penetrate social and economic interactions that would otherwise be unbounded" ("Rebooting Migration Theory," 273). He sees the European Union as a model that overcomes the traditional boundaries of nation-states in all areas of life, and thereby redefines the meaning and concept of migration (see "Rebooting Migration Theory," 274)—a positive first step towards recasting "the subject of migration in a thoroughly decentered, global perspective" ("Rebooting Migration Theory," 275). Such views are not shared by the present author.

2.3. Nation/Nationalism and Ethnicity

There is considerable overlap in the definitions of "ethnic group" and "nation," and often the terms are used interchangeably. However, it is possible to identify the distinctions between the two terms with some precision:

- As in the case of ethnicity, elements like common descent, language, religion, and territory belong—traditionally—to the objective elements of a nation. And as in the case of ethnic identity, individuals consciously relate to their national background and have some emotional attachment to it.

- The formation and persistence of a nation is—traditionally—dependent on some kind of ethnic kernel, which is mostly given, but can also be constructed to some degree.[44] Connected with the ethnic rootedness of nations is the fact that conceptions about national bonds are most often presented in terms of family-like models.

- As in the case of ethnicity, historical and cultural commonalities play an important role in the formation and persistence of a nation.[45] In most cases, however, religious traditions are less important in the case of nations than of ethnic groups.[46]

- Economic, political, and administrative interconnections play a more important role in the case of nations, whereas descent has—depending on the type of national aspirations—less weight. In the case of nations, co-residency and the concept of a contiguous, shared territory as a present reality are foundational.[47]

- Nationalism can be related to negative views or attitudes toward individuals or peoples who do not belong to one's own nation. This is, however, not an inherent and necessary trait of nationalism. On the other hand, nationalism can be connected with traits that are generally seen as positive, such as the furtherance of democracy, art, economic enterprise, etc.[48]

44. See, e.g., Jenkins, *Rethinking Ethnicity*, 143; Smith, *The Ethnic Origins*, 17–18, 212–14. "There are 'ethnic roots' which determine, to a considerable degree, the nature and limits of modern nationalisms and nations" (Smith, *The Ethnic Origins*, 18).

45. See, e.g., Smith, *The Ethnic Origins*, 14.

46. See Smith, *The Ethnic Origins*, 171, 180–82.

47. See, e.g., Grosby, *Biblical Ideas*, 27; Smith, *The Ethnic Origins*, 135, 183–90.

48. See Seton-Watson, *Nations*, 2, 466–67. There is a tendency for nationalism to

- The two central elements of political nationalism are usually determined as requests for a distinct, contiguous territory, as well as sovereignty and independence. Sometimes, however, a national movement settles for less, like preserving an independent culture or limited political autonomy within a (con)federal state.[49] Requests for a contiguous territory and full independence necessarily lead to serious tensions in societies with considerable ethnic diversity.[50]

- With respect to the affiliation of potential members to a nation, different types of nation (and nationalism) can be distinguished: ethnic nation (and ethnic nationalism); social nation (and social nationalism); official nation (and official nationalism). In the case of an ethnic nation, membership in it is restricted to the members of one ethnic group and thereby regulated primarily in terms of descent. In the case of a social nation, members of various ethnic groups form a nation, and affiliation to it is granted through social and cultural adherence also independently of descent. In the case of an official nation individuals are bound together by the state through the principle of citizenship.[51] Official nationalism is often used politically as an antidote against ethnic or social forms of nationalism.[52] A similar distinction is the one between ethnic nationalism and civic nationalism.[53] The former is rooted in biological necessity, runs in families, and is inherited. In this paradigm, people are born into a particular nationality, which determines interests, sentiments, and a sense of attachment. In the case of civic nationalism nationality is equated with citizenship. It is defined in political and legal terms, and implies a voluntary commitment to certain duties and rights more or less independently of descent.[54] None of these two or three

become more fanatic in cases where religious bindings decrease (see Seton-Watson, *Nations*, 465), although only in the context of Western/Christian societies.

49. See Seton-Watson, *Nations*, 469–70; Smith, *The Ethnic Origins*, 225. An example for the latter, moderate form of nationalism would be Welsh nationalism in the U.K.

50. See Mühlmann, "Ethnogonie," 21.

51. See Kellas, *The Politics of Nationalism*, 3–4, 66.

52. See Kellas, *The Politics of Nationalism*, 218.

53. See, e.g., Huntington, *Who Are We?* 29. He observes that in the current discourse in the West, the civic variant is evaluated positively, while the ethnic (or cultural, or integral) variant is rejected as exclusive.

54. See Scott, "Nationalism." He points to the inherited cultural identity of eastern European countries vs. the civic pride of Americans.

types is normally found in a pure form at the total expense of the others. There is always a tension between the (tendentially inclusive) territorial and the (tendentially exclusive) ethnic principle, the first being related to the *ius soli*, and the latter to the *ius sanguinis*.[55] It would probably be important and helpful to more clearly distinguish between the ethnic and cultural layers of a nation. One can imagine that shared cultural values provide sufficiently strong bonds to support the persistence of a nation even in the absence of ethnic coherence.[56]

Broadly speaking, in modern times the territorial principle has been dominant over the ethnic principle in Western states:[57] Whoever resides on the territory of the nation-state and adheres to the "national" culture is a citizen of that nation, not only an individual who belongs to the respective nation by descent. This comes close to the "social" type of nation. In central and eastern Europe, as well as in the Middle East, the transition to the nation-state took another course, because of the more complex relationship between ethnic groups and states; there was more of a mixture between the territorial and the ethnic concept of nation.[58] In many areas of Asia and Africa the ethnic model of nation is dominant, with two subtypes: In some cases, the dominance of specific ethnic groups results in other ethnic groups not being able to fully participate in the nation; in other cases, because of a relatively even ethical fragmentation, some kind of cultural homogeneity and emotional bonds that transcend ethnic groups need to be designed and implemented. In a number of cases, however, it is doubtful whether the term "nation" can be applied in a meaningful way at all.

- As a developed doctrine, nationalism is only found since the French Revolution, "derived from the eighteenth century notion of popular

---

55. See Kellas, *The Politics of Nationalism*, 91.

56. See Huntington, *Who Are We?* 30–31.

57. This has changed in the last couple of decades, with an ever-growing influence of supra- or transnational models and aspirations.

58. It can be said that in the West, approximately from 1600 through 1800, nationalism served to provide a cultural justification for an already existing political structure. On the other hand, in eastern Europe, in the nineteenth century, nationalism was used to justify the creation of nation-states in politically and economically less developed regions, by redrawing political boundaries in conformity with ethnographic demands (see Scott, "Nationalism").

sovereignty" on the one hand, and from the "cult of individuality, both personal and cultural" on the other.[59] If one does not define the term "nation" too narrowly and connects it to the notion of popular sovereignty or a republican form of government, the phenomenon of "nation" is in fact much older. As Smith observes: "[T]here is considerable continuity of *ends* between pre-modern *ethnie* and modern nations, as the continuing relevance of a reinterpreted past of ethnic identity in the maintenance of nations demonstrates."[60] Even in ancient societies, including ancient Israel and Judah, is it possible to discern a national consciousness which has many parallels to the modern times, although specific differences cannot be denied.[61]

- Nationalism can be akin to a civil religion according to some. According to others, nationalism is secular and there can be at most a functional equivalence between nationalism and religion.[62] It can certainly be observed that the concepts of nation and religion are intertwined in both Islam and Judaism, as well—even if in different ways—in traditional forms of Polish and Irish nationalism, to mention just some examples.[63] Problems will arise by necessity when religious nationalism is imported into societies in which the majority does not belong to this religion.

59. Seton-Watson, *Nations*, 6. According to Smith, however, already towards the end of the seventeenth century "the idea of populations being divided by 'national character' and possessing a common identity" had begun to spread among the educated layers of society in Europe (*The Ethnic Origins*, 11).

60. Smith, *The Ethnic Origins*, 5.

61. See Kellas, *The Politics of Nationalism*, 89–90, 214; Smith, *The Ethnic Origins*, 11–13. With a view to the ancient Near East, Smith states that, "It is *ethnie* rather than nations, ethnicity rather than nationality, and ethnicism rather than nationalism, that pervades the social and cultural life" (*The Ethnic Origins*, 89). On the other hand, one can observe that in the case of ancient Israel and Judah the similarities with modern national concepts of the "sovereignty of the people" are particularly developed. Accordingly, there are those who speak of Israel and Judah as "proto-nations" (see, e.g., Brett, "Nationalism," 143).

62. See Scott, "Nationalism."

63. See, e.g., the movement called "Nation of Islam"—which has no equivalent in "Nation of Buddhism," "Nation of Presbyterianism," etc.

2.4. Race/Racism and Ethnicity

While ethnicity is often seen as an omnipresent element of human culture and social interaction, in some ways "'[r]acial' categories are second-order cultural creations or notions; they are abstractions, explicit bodies of knowledge that are very much more the children of specific historical circumstances."[64] In this sense, the category of race can be understood as "a historically specific facet of the more general social phenomenon of ethnicity."[65]

While ethnic markers cover a wide range of elements beyond common descent, as seen above, it is physical or phenotypical (and/or genetic) characteristics that are often identified as being of primary importance in the identification of races.[66] Their importance is, however, not objectively given, but culturally or socially established as such.[67]

In more recent discussions, some of the elements that were broadly seen as constitutive for the concept of race are questioned, and the constructivist aspect is stressed. Montagu, for example, claims that race is the expression of a "process of genetic change within a definite ecological area," and "a dynamic, not a static, condition"; "it becomes static and classifiable only when a taxonomically minded anthropologist arbitrarily delimits the process of change at his own time level."[68] For Allport, on the other hand, race is a natural category, referring to "hereditary ties" and inherent genetic behavioral "traits" that define human populations.[69] Somewhat similarly, Whitney maintains that popular perceptions of race are valid and parallel to genetic differentiations between subgroups of humanity.[70] As the situation presents itself currently, it can be said that "there is no theoretical, methodological, or political consensus shared across any of the subdisciplines on how to interpret and explicate the realities that constitute race."[71] Perhaps as the dominant position, however, it is possible to identify the one proposed by the American Association of Physical Anthropologists in their official statement on race, containing

64. Jenkins, *Rethinking Ethnicity*, 77.

65. Jenkins, *Rethinking Ethnicity*, 23.

66. See, e.g., Kellas, *The Politics of Nationalism*, 5.

67. See, e.g., Anderson, *Die Erfindung der Nation*, 150.

68. Montagu, *Man's Most Dangerous Myth*, 40.

69. *The Nature of Prejudice*, 107.

70. See Whitney, "On Possible Genetic Bases," 135.

71. Harrison, "Introduction," 610.

the following claims:[72] There is only minimal biological variation between humans; the biological differences can be traced to the interaction between hereditary and environmental factors; pure races do not exist as all human groups reflect significant genetic diversity; there are physical differences between people groups in distinct geographic areas due to an interaction of various genetic and environmental factors; traits traditionally used to define different (racial) groups are transferred independently, hence are not collective traits typical of any group; humans are not adapted exclusively to any particular environment; the genetic composition of human populations changes continually; there is no relationship between physical and behavioral traits nor between genetic background and cultural traits; people, though influenced by heredity, are individuals and as such differ intellectually and behaviorally.—While some of the items found in the statement just point to what is obvious, other elements may be seen as glossing over real and difficult questions, like the relative weight of genetic and environmental factors in the interaction between the two, and whether it is only some or all traits that are (or were) traditionally seen as typical of a specific race that are transferred independently, and so on.

In the case of racism, the racial groups are ascribed unchangeable characteristics, and those groups that are foreign to one's own are seen as inferior. This, in turn, serves to justify existing hierarchical relations or to aspire to the establishment of such relations to the benefit of one's own group.[73] Whether racism is a necessary companion of the categorization of humanity in different races is a matter of debate. There seems to be no compelling reason, however, to support the claim that the recognition of racial distinctions necessarily or intrinsically leads to denigration of or hostility toward members of other races.[74]

One can argue that categories such as ethnicity and race are based on "overgeneralizations about Others."[75] But generalizations in mapping the social sphere are necessary, and not in themselves bad if handled with flexibility. They are necessary to reduce the complexities of the world in ways that make it possible to handle it and go beyond pure individualism

72. See "AAPA Statement on Biological Aspects of Race," 569–70.

73. See, e.g., Jenkins, *Rethinking Ethnicity*, 23.

74. *Pace*, e.g., Gossett, *Race*, 411; Rigby, *African Images*, 1–5; Sadler, *Can a Cushite*, 5.

75. Allport, *The Nature of Prejudice*, 27.

that prevents the development of practical knowledge and of meaningful comparisons between larger entities. One also needs to take into consideration that the perception of ethnic or racial differences as such does not necessarily lead to inter-group animosity,[76] and that even if distinctions based on the categories of ethnicity and race were overcome, some other social distinctions will still remain.

2.5. Migration

2.5.1. General Remarks

The *nature* of migration and its *causes* are closely interconnected. One of the important distinctions is the distinction between the role of push and pull factors. In the cases of *forced migration*, pertaining especially to asylum-seekers and refugees, the search for security is dominant. In the case of *economic migration*, the search for (better) income is dominant. In the first case the push factor is relatively more important, whereas in the second case it is the pull factor that is relatively more important.[77] In many cases, however, the distinctions are fuzzy and combinations of various aspects may be at play. The successful migration of one family member often creates a chain of opportunities for the whole kin network ("chain migration").[78]

2.5.2. The Dealing with Immigrants (and Other Foreigners) by the Majority Ethnic Group

The majority ethnic group has in principle the following possibilities to deal with immigrants:[79]

---

76. *Pace* Allport, *The Nature of Prejudice*, 4, 9.

77. See, e.g., Scott, "Migration, Sociology of."

78. See, e.g., Scott, "Migration, Sociology of."

79. Cf. Bellebaum, "Randgruppen," 55; Grassl, "Grundsätzliches," 45. Schmitter Heisler, referring to Portes, distinguishes three types of responses: "receptive, indifferent, and hostile" ("The Sociology," 89). Listing the various reactions does, of course, not imply any (positive) ethical evaluation.

1. Rejection/exclusion of foreigners, in different ways, for example exclusion from certain political rights, forcing into ghettoes, etc.; expulsion, or even extermination.[80]

2. Attempt at complete assimilation of the foreigners. This model has been given up by the elites in most parts of the Western world.[81]

3. Establishment of a *plural society*, with political domination of the dominant ethnic group, combined with some restrictions for the foreign minorities (concerning mixed marriages; real estate; inheritance; certain public posts, etc.). In this system, life is lived to a large extent within the boundaries of the different ethnic groups, with these groups having a certain position within the ranking system of the whole. This model is not accepted in principle anywhere in the modern Western world.[82]

4. Establishment of a *pluralistic society*. In this system, life is lived beyond the boundaries of the ethnic groups; members of all the ethnic groups (or most of them) have the same possibilities of participation and upward social mobility in a whole that is seen as non-segregated. There are two main variants:

   - *Liberal pluralism*: complete equality of opportunity, complete prohibition of discrimination;

   - *Corporate pluralism*: equality of results, positive discrimination through affirmative action, power sharing, renunciation of the principle of the rule of the majority. Corporate pluralism has replaced liberal pluralism for the most part in the Western world.

5. "*Herrschaftswechsel:*" Conscious subjugation of their own (majority) cultural identity and adaptation to the culture of the immigrants.

---

80. Rejection and exclusion may be based on ethnic prejudice. According to Allport, ethnic prejudice can be manifest in either or all of the five following ways: refusal to communicate; refusal to engage in social intercourse; discrimination; physical attack; genocide (see *The Nature of Prejudice*, 9).

81. See, e.g., Brettell and Hollifield, "Migration Theory," 16; Schmitter Heisler, "The Sociology," 84–85 (cf. also p. 90).

82. This does not necessarily mean that elements of it may not be present in various forms in certain cases.

There are other models of classification concerning the framework of the modern concept of the sovereign nation-state—which is, however, currently subject to considerable changes. For example, the following variants of the inclusion of different ethnic groups in a society can be distinguished: uniform; equivalent; hierarchic.

- Uniform: ethnic affiliation is not taken into consideration on the political and all the other important levels.

- Equivalent: societal-political life is organized in a way that different ethnic groups stand besides each other with politically equal rights.

- Hierarchic: some ethnic groups have more, others less political weight.

These systems are fluid, and variants may be coexisting in different segments of societal life and applied differently to various groups of immigrants.[83]

More recently, a kind of middle concept between 4 (pluralistic society) and 5 ("*Herrschaftswechsel*") has been proposed: *convivencia*, the intercultural transfiguration of both the self and the other, in order to interact and search for the creation of a common shared space, perceived as a dialogue-communion, where identities are not changed or exchanged, but sensitized through the practices of proximity, a process in which the other becomes the "*affin*."[84] This process of intercultural transformation aims at realizing the vision of an intercultural community of worlds that are different and yet in solidarity, constantly being reshaped by the interaction. It is the transformation of a multicultural society into an intercultural community, based on the normative idea of

83. See, e.g., Schmitter Heisler, "The Sociology," 89.

84. Guerra, "A Theology," 257.

mutuality.[85] On the practical level, this model also requires pluralism in the legal sphere.[86]

This approach is related to a principled rejection of the concept of assimilation—in fact, at this point, the rejection of assimilation has become the dominant position in the West, both in secular and religiously inspired discourses.[87] The new approach is informed by anti-Western notions[88] and ultimately allocates a preferential position for the non-Western immigrant who must be given an unconditional right to live his/her culture.[89] In the process, even the notion of "integration" is given up. This approach follows a decidedly adaptionist paradigm. It is not clear

---

85. This model has been developed in some detail by Fornet-Betancourt ("Hermeneutics," 210, 215–22) and Guerra ("A Theology," 245, 255–63), among others. Similar propositions are found in Houston (*You Shall Love*, 144, 153, 159) and Strine ("Embracing Asylum Seekers," 479, 491–93). According to Fornet-Betancourt, the fact that our own way of thinking is historically conditioned and not static is one of the reasons why we must not try "to control the strangers," but rather replace assimilation by recognition ("Hermeneutics," 216–17). What is needed is "a hermeneutics that is both liberated from the habits of colonial thinking and allows itself to be influenced by the strangers" ("Hermeneutics," 217). The guiding vision is that "of an *intercultural* community of worlds that are different and yet in solidarity with each other" ("Hermeneutics," 219). The receiving society has to "work with the strangeness of the stranger in order to achieve an ecumenical reconstruction of the social order in which the strangers *are not deprived of their rights* but that, on the contrary, *are authorized* and *recognized* in their difference in such a way that the guarantee of their physical and vital *integrity* does not depend on their social or cultural *integration*" ("Hermeneutics," 220, italics in the original). As a consequence, not only the notion of assimilation, but also the concept of "*Leitkultur*" has to be given up (see "Hermeneutics," 221). For Guerra, *convivencia* as an "intercultural transformation" means to overcome the mono-logical, mono-cultural, and universalistic domination of Western thought and civilization, taking the faith, live, and journey of migrant communities as a primary source of orientation and inspiration (see "A Theology," 245). He also uses the term "interculturation," defined as "the process where the mutual acknowledgment and a reciprocal interchange of cultural orientations, values, traditions, or behaviors takes place" ("A Theology," 256). Among the specific elements of such a process he mentions full citizenship for the migrants and the promotion of interreligious dialogue (see "A Theology," 262–63). Also Volf advocates for the *convivencia* model (without using the term), applying the metaphor of embrace and rooting it in the Trinity (see *Exclusion and Embrace*, 125–28, 143–47).

86. See Battistella, "Migration," 189.

87. For examples see Battistella, "Migration," 179; Schreiter, "Migrants," 111, 118.

88. In part because Western culture is perceived as tainted by colonialism.

89. See Guerra, "A Theology," 245 (the culture of "the other" is the primary source of orientation); Fornet-Betancourt, "Hermeneutics," 220 (immigrants must be granted "the right to live their culture").

how it would allow for the long-time survival of clearly distinct, fully developed, independent cultures.

It is possible to find a mixture of different approaches in a society; and it is also possible that different groups of foreigners and individuals can be subject to different kinds of treatments.[90] In many circumstances, different groups within the receiving society will promote different goals as to how to deal with foreigners/immigrants or with different groups of foreigners/immigrants (based on class, ethnic differences, political persuasion etc.).[91] Correspondingly, the treatment that foreigners/immigrants experience can vary according to the social compartment in which they live. Moreover, there may be large gaps between official statements about immigration policies and the actual implementation of these policies.

Historically, mixed marriage, adoption (of individuals or whole groups), and the incorporation of immigrants into the army were the most important instruments for the integration of foreigners.[92]

In modern societies the educational system is of special importance for the integration of foreigners. In this domain, however, integration does not happen where foreigners are given educational opportunities as such, but only where they are integrated into the educational institutions that reflect the values of the host culture.[93]

Normally there is an interdependence between some degree of assimilation of foreigners and the willingness of the receiving society to welcome them in a hospitable way.[94]

Both for the possibility of integration (seen from the perspective of the host society) and of assimilation (seen from the perspective of immigrants) the absolute as well as the relative number of foreigners is important, as much as the degree of compatibility of the values of the different groups;[95] cultural proximity will typically be combined with an

90. Cf. Gordon, "Toward a General Theory," 105–6.

91. It is well known, for example, that in the last decades there has been a tendency in Western countries for the elites and the political left to favor more liberal immigration policies than the lower strata of the indigenous population and right-wing parties.

92. See, e.g., Mühlmann, *Homo Creator*, 324–44. "Forgetting" the ethnic background of immigrants who assimilate to the dominant group can be seen as a special case of adoption.

93. This means that courses in the language or religion of the places of origin are not a step of integration, but rather a means to promote segregation.

94. See, e.g., Smith, *The Ethnic Origins*, 150.

95. See, e.g., Gordon, "Toward a General Theory," 102–3; Grassl, "Grundsätzliches,"

open attitude by the receiving society.[96] Economic factors are also important. In times of economic stress, openness towards newcomers will shrink among those who expect a deterioration of their situation because of immigration.

Generally, negative reactions by (parts of) the receiving society are to be expected in cases of economic distress (as mentioned), or when there is a clash of cultural values, or when some groups in the receiving society are frustrated.[97] Also preceding experiences of foreign domination, or the extraordinary social upward movement of foreign groups at the expense of natives often cause negative reactions.[98] At the same time, however, it seems that there is a kind of natural inclination towards skepticism against foreigners as one part of the innate inclination to the formation of groups. On the other hand, at least in some cultures this xenophobic tendency is balanced by a (more xenophile) tendency, especially in the form of interest for the unknown.[99]

2.5.3. Reactions of Immigrants to Being Exposed to a New Environment

In cases in which individuals or groups migrate and find themselves in a minority position vis-à-vis the host society, the question of adaptation/ assimilation or segregation poses itself. In this respect, one has to differentiate in principle between the level of the individual and the level of the collective.

---

43. As far as numbers are concerned: It seems that about 20 percent foreigners in a given society is the maximum percentage that allows for the possibility that the outcome will be a successful integration.

96. See, e.g., Scheuringer, "Begegnung," 9. A historical example is the integration and assimilation of French Huguenots in the Netherlands and Switzerland (as well as other parts of Protestant Europe). On the other hand, not only a larger cultural distance, but also the stress on cultural distinctions by immigrants often reduces the degree of openness on the side of the receiving society. In conflictual situations, there is often a circular argument: Immigrants may say that their attitude which is seen as over-confidential and provocative is a reaction against the negative attitude of the host society, while the latter explains their attitude as a reaction provoked by the behavior of the newcomers.

97. Cf., e.g., Gordon, "Toward a General Theory," 97.

98. See, e.g., Grassl, "Grundsätzliches," 43.

99. See, e.g., Loewenstein, "Wir und die anderen," 13–14.

One option is integration with a high degree of assimilation. It is an option that has come under strong criticism in the current discourse in the West, as opposed to only some decades ago. Assimilation means the adjustment to and adoption of the culture of the new place of residence in most areas of life. As a rule, assimilation is realized in various stages.[100] In cases where the receiving society is very heterogeneous, assimilation to society as a whole is no longer possible.[101] Complete assimilation has tendentially been the exception; as a rule, at least some of the elements that are characteristic of the culture of the place of origin are kept in a modified way.[102]

An alternative option consists in the preservation of the original ethnic identity to the largest possible extent in any given circumstances, or even the heightened development of some of the differentiating markers in contradistinction to the new environment.[103] As a rule, this is an option for individuals only if they can rely on the cultural support of a group being rooted in the same traditions; if such support is absent, the individual will be forced to adjust to the norms of the majority society.[104] Depending on the situation, the wish to preserve the original ethnic identity can be combined with a partial integration into the new environment, or with the withdrawal into quasi-ghettos or peripheral areas.[105] When a non-assimilating ethnic enclave is big enough, it is to be expected that it wants to become an autonomous or even independent political entity.[106] If the distinct ethnic group that wants to preserve its identity is not related to a specific territory, it will likely aspire to obtain special rights and possibly to participate in the power structures of the given state.[107] "[P]ersistent diacritical marks"[108] of a specific group, such as skin color or (textually based) religion, increase the probability that

100. See, e.g., Schuetz, "The Stranger," 499–507.

101. See Banton, "The Direction," 43.

102. So, e.g., Smith, *The Ethnic Origins*, 16.

103. This attitude can be called "alienation"; see Aymer, "Sojourners Truths," 3.

104. See, e.g., Galter, "Zwischen Isolation und Integration," 277.

105. See, e.g., Mühlmann, *Homo Creator*, 333.

106. The history of the Indian subcontinent in the mid-twentieth century or the Balkans since the 1990s provides examples for this. A new phenomenon are the ca. 800 *zones urbaines sensibles* in France and similar zones in other Western countries, where the state has no absolute control over the respective territories any more.

107. Cf., e.g., Bellebaum, "Randgruppen," 56.

108. Smith, *The Ethnic Origins*, 11.

assimilation will not take place.[109] Generally, adaptation of foreigners to a receiving society tends to be the more difficult and slower, the more the original culture and social developmental stage is different from the new environment.[110]

There are many intermediary options between assimilation and segregation/alienation.[111] But in all events, some kind of "accommodation" is necessary, that is, a functional adjustment in those areas of life that are related to the immediate survival in the new environment, but that do not affect the level of deeper values and dispositions.[112] Which path is chosen is dependent on the attractiveness of the values of the sending and the receiving societies.[113] Also important is the question which tangible, concrete advantages are connected with the preservation of old or the adoption of new cultural patterns. But also factors like economic situation, attitude of the receiving society, and geographical location play a role. Finally, individual personal factors must also be taken into consideration.[114]

Among the factors that promote assimilation or integration are a high attractiveness of the dominating culture; social, economic, and political advantages in case of assimilation; a universalistic, non-ethnic orientation both of the sending and the receiving culture; a liberal individualistic order of society; the inclusion of the immigrants' children into the existing educational system; a strong mixture of different groups of newcomers, etc.[115] There is, however, no automatic development of the process. In spite of any of the factors just mentioned—or even as a conscious reaction against them—assimilation or integration can fail to take place.

109. Cf. Schmitter Heisler, "The Sociology," 83.

110. See Scheuringer, "Begegnung," 5.

111. In addition to the categories mentioned here, see also Guerra, "A Theology," 248, 254.

112. See, e.g., Scheuringer, "Begegnung," 7. Aymer defines "accommodation" as one of the four possible attitudes of immigrants, consisting of the adoption of certain aspects of the host culture, while retaining some aspects of one's culture of origin; see Aymer, "Sojourners Truths," 3.

113. See, e.g., Banton, "The Direction," 38.

114. Sunil Bhatia and Anjali Ram point out that immigrant reactions necessarily differ given the history, politics, gender, and other social realities of particular migrants (see "Rethinking," 6). One also has to take into consideration that complex interactions between different ethnic minority groups can affect the processes.

115. See Reminick, Theory, 24–25.

To what degree the absence of assimilation or integration of considerable segments of larger groups of immigrants will put the stability of the receiving society in jeopardy depends on the specific circumstances. It must be kept in mind, however, that the stability of a given society can be subverted also without the presence of non-assimilated or non-integrated immigrants, as, for example, the French Revolution, the Russian Revolution, or the situation in post-World War I Germany demonstrate. Deep ideological divisions in the current situation in the West point in the same direction; they are, however,—as opposed to the historic examples just mentioned—directly linked to questions about mass-immigration.

The integration of foreigners proceeds on different levels and in different stages. One has to differentiate especially between private and official attitudes, inner convictions and outward actions, between various elements of cultural identity (language, religion, etc.) and of social interaction (marriage, places of residence, political and economic participation, etc.).[116] Not only will the degree of adaptation or divergence normally differ with respect to various social sectors (work place; home; religion, etc.) and with respect to the psycho-social level (inner convictions; outward behavior, etc.), but always with respect to different individuals within a group.[117] Also the speed of the process of assimilation or segregation can vary; often, it covers two to three generations. There may be visible institutionalized markers that indicate important steps in the transition, or the transition may be "fluid."

Within the process of adaptation, the first steps are normally related to those areas of life that are crucial for survival and the social upward movement, like language and work, while in the private sphere the old ethnic traditions are preserved.[118] In this phase, one typically finds a dual orientation with a double loyalty. In outward appearance, adaptation to the new codes may be very strong, while the inner solidarity is reserved for the original ethnic group. Individuals in this situation tend to try to promote the values of their original group, also on the political level.[119]

---

116. Cf. Gordon, "Toward a General Theory," 84.

117. This is why generalizations concerning a group will never reveal the whole picture; nevertheless, trends about majorities within a group are possible to detect.

118. See Banton, "The Direction," 33, 35, 44–45; Mühlmann, "Ethnogonie," 25; Mühlmann, *Homo Creator*, 313–14; Reminick, *Theory*, 42; Roosens, *Creating Ethnicity*, 149.

119. See, e.g., Kellas, *The Politics of Nationalism*, 21.

Until recently, such an intermediary state was normally only transitory, especially on the individual level, because a bicultural orientation necessitates a high degree of psychological autonomy.[120] Because of the ease with which the affiliation with the original cultural milieu can be maintained in immigrant communities in the West in the current situation, the necessity to move beyond the intermediary state has decreased sharply. The next step would then normally be either to fully embrace the values of the new dominating culture, or the move on to a more segregationist solution of the challenge.[121] Mixed marriages are especially important for the process of assimilation. In some cases, outward accommodation may take place only for strategic reasons, with the goal of maintaining the original identity as far as the inward disposition is concerned.[122]

The children of immigrants often distance themselves from the culture of their parents' ethnic group; at least, they see their parents' culture no longer as a natural given; rather, it becomes the object of conscious reflection.[123] This does not mean that belonging to this culture is being given up; but belonging is now only possible as a result of a conscious choice, it is no longer self-understood. The heightened consciousness of the foundational characteristics of the culture of the place of the parents' origin in contradistinction to the culture of the host society creates a special tension for this generation.[124] In many cases, the next generation will then relate back to some of the characteristic traits of their original ethnic group.[125]

At practically no point is the process of adaptation and assimilation completely irreversible. A phase of adaptation to the new environment can be followed by a phase of demarcation and re-application of some elements of the original culture.[126] Typically, however, it is not a complete

---

120. See Scheuringer, "Begegnung," 13.

121. Cf., e.g., Reminick, *Theory*, 27–30.

122. See, e.g., Mühlmann, *Homo Creator*, 315–20.

123. See, e.g., Reminick, *Theory*, 36; Roosens, *Creating Ethnicity*, 151.

124. See, e.g., Reminick, *Theory*, 27.

125. In recent years, scholars have claimed that "reactive ethnicity," a rejection of the host culture that goes hand in hand with a heightened expression of ethnic and cultural distinctiveness, arises as a (negative) response to coercion to assimilation imposed by the receiving society; see, e.g., Paynter, "'Make Yourself at Home,'" 45 (with reference to Fiske and Diehl & Schnell). There is, however, no evidence for this assertion.

126. See, e.g., Reminick, *Theory*, 21, 29; Schmitter Heisler, "The Sociology," 86.

reversal, but only a partial one, which allows the respective immigrants to remain as an integrated part in the society of the dominating group.[127]

Things look somewhat differently in the present situation in the West, because it is possible for many immigrants to move directly into more or less independent enclaves of their places of origin established in Western cities, which means that they are only minimally exposed to the culture of the receiving society. In this situation, the diaspora is conceived of as part of transnational identities. The concept of transnational identity in the context of transnational migration is often encouraged today. Within this framework, permanent double orientation or double belonging are seen as positive options. The new paradigm of transnational migration (or "transmigration") suggests that even though immigrants invest in their new society in various ways, they may still continue to participate in the society from which they emigrated. In this way, they "lead dual lives" and move between cultures.[128]

Finally, there is also the possibility of double denial, which means that migrants choose to belong neither to the old nor to the new society. This can be called "marginalization," the alienation both from one's culture of origin and from the culture of the host country.[129]

2.5.4. Concluding Observations

Every kind of close coexistence between different ethnic groups, independent of the question how this coexistence came about in the first place, results in changes in the perception of the other's and one's own cultural patterns and finally in changes in the (ethnic and otherwise) identity of the groups involved—all of them. The same is true for all changes in the outward environment. This also means, among other things, that migration, especially large-scale immigration, always results in a change of the societal system as a whole and affects all parties involved; therefore, also the receiving society and its members will look differently as a result of

---

127. Cf., e.g., Reminick, *Theory*, 33, 43.

128. See Hanciles, "Migration and Mission," 148. Cf. Carroll, *Christians*, 23; Brettell, "Theorizing Migration," 120–21. It is sometimes claimed that transnationalism and assimilation are compatible concepts (see, e.g., Schmitter Heisler, "The Sociology," 97–98). This necessitates, however, a redefinition of what is traditionally understood by "assimilation."

129. See Aymer, "Sojourners Truths," 3.

the process than they did before.[130] Moreover, mass-immigration is always related to changes in the power-structure of the receiving society.[131]

130. See, e.g., Banton, "The Direction," 33, 35; Keyes, "The Dialectics," 18–19.

131. The question is, of course, how "mass" in "mass-immigration" can be defined. In what ways and to which degree the power structure is changed will depend especially on the degree of assimilation of the newcomers.

6

Broadening the Horizon II
Migration and Psychology, Demography, Economy, and Security

1. INTRODUCTION

THE QUESTION OF HOW a biblically inspired attitude to migration and im-migration looks like is primarily an ethical question. For wise and coherent ethical assessments, it is important not only to have—in the context of biblically informed ethics—a thorough understanding of the relevant biblical material, but also of all the extra-biblical data that are relevant to address the issues. Some of these will be dealt with in this chapter. Of course, as pointed out in the introduction to this book, there are further fields that are important, like law, public health, ecology, history, to name a few. For the purposes of the present study, however, it will be sufficient to focus briefly on four of the relevant fields: psychology (including socio-psychological aspects), demography, economy, and security.

As will become clear in the following chapters, the situation in the U.S. is different in important ways from the situation in most European countries. These differences have consequences when it comes to the ethical assessment of the issues involved and to practical steps envisioned to address the challenges connected to mass-(im)migration. Among the most important differences we can identify the following ones:[1] The U.S. has historically, almost from its beginnings as an independent nation,

1. Details and empirical data will be provided in the following chapters.

been a society of immigrants, composed of arrivals with various ethnic and cultural backgrounds from the latter part of the nineteenth century onward. However, acceptance of (larger numbers of) immigrants outside of the Anglo-Saxon (and Dutch, German, and Scandinavian) Protestant parts of Europe was very slow, and until the legal changes of the 1960s the vast majority of the immigrants had a European, Christian background. Nevertheless, the ethnic and racial composition was relatively complex even before then, given the continued presence of descendants of Indian tribes and of African slaves.[2] Since the occurrence of the legal changes in the 1960s, the pool of immigrants has been diversified considerably, with Latin Americans dominating the immigration statistics, followed by East Asians. Tendentially, the new arrivals have quickly integrated into the workforce; culturally, the Latin Americans share Christianity as a religious background with the existing dominating culture, while persons from East Asia have generally integrated into the mainstream American culture even in the cases where a Christian background was lacking. On the other hand, most modern nations in Europe that have become destinations of mass-immigration do not have a historical background of immigration and ethnic complexity that is comparable to the U.S. Moreover, in the current situation a majority of the immigrants are not integrating into the workforce,[3] and establish a counter-culture[4] that is foreign to the traditional cultures of the European nations.

2. PSYCHOLOGICAL ASPECTS

2.1. Introduction

The points mentioned in this chapter are not meant to give a comprehensive overview of all the major issues related to the psychological dimensions of migration. Rather, some aspects are highlighted that point to some of the most important challenges and problems that are connected

---

2. For a helpful summary of the history of immigration see, e.g., Huntington, *Who Are We?* 37–58. He makes the important distinction between immigrants and settlers, a distinction which is obfuscated when it is claimed that "America is a nation of immigrants" (see *Who Are We?* 37–44).

3. For the details see below in the section on economic aspects of migration.

4. Mostly of a Muslim variance; for details see below in the sections on demographic and security aspects of migration.

with many types and cases of migration, both on the individual, but also on the broader social level.

2.2. Eugen Rosenstock-Huessy's Observation

Eugen Rosenstock-Huessy, the famous twentieth-century historian and social philosopher, maintained that for many people in the pre-industrialized world it would be normal, at least in rural settings, where the majority of people lived, to have close contact with only a couple of dozen or at most with a couple hundred of people throughout their whole lifetimes, and to be involved in a very limited number of social commitments only—but commitments that were of lasting character.[5] The situation that developed afterwards is radically different, and causes in many cases—mostly unconscious—psychological stress. Newer findings show that this stress is heightened in cases where the environment in which someone lives is highly diverse in terms of cultural, linguistic, ethnic, or religious backgrounds.

2.3. Diversity and Stress

The most famous study pointing to the connection between diversity and stress on the broader societal level is the one published by Harvard sociologist Putnam in 2007, "E Pluribus Unum: Diversity and Community in the Twenty-First Century." He finds that

> In the short run, . . . immigration and ethnic diversity tend to reduce social solidarity and social capital. New evidence from the US suggests that in ethnically diverse neighborhoods residents of all races tend to "hunker down." Trust (even of one's own race) is lower, altruism and community cooperation rarer, friends fewer.[6]

This thesis is related to a large number of various empirical studies undertaken during the last couple of decades, covering a whole range of different geographical areas and life settings.[7] The most important source, however, is the Social Capital Community Benchmark Survey, conducted

---

5. See Rosenstock-Huessy, *Des Christen Zukunft*, 34.

6. Putnam, "E Pluribus Unum," 137.

7. See Putnam, "E Pluribus Unum," 142–43.

in the year 2000 in forty-one very different communities in the U.S., including interviews with about 30,000 people living in very different situations.[8] The survey shows that, "The more ethnically diverse the people we live around, the less we trust them";[9] "[i]n more diverse communities, people trust their neighbours less."[10] Somewhat surprisingly, "in-group trust, too, is lower in more diverse settings."[11] This means that, "Diversity seems to trigger not in-group/out-group division, but . . . social isolation."[12] There are other negative effects besides trust, among them: lower confidence in local government; lower confidence in one's own influence; lower expectation of communal cooperation; lower engagement in charity and volunteering; fewer close friends; less happiness and lower perceived quality of life.[13] In sum, "inhabitants of diverse communities tend to withdraw from collective life, distrust their neighbours, regardless of their skin."[14] Diverse communities are also less egalitarian, more crime-ridden, and have a higher share of poorer, less educated inhabitants.[15] Putnam observes that the negative impacts of diversity affect all social groups in similar ways: men and women, young and old, whites and non-whites, affluent and poor, conservatives and liberals, etc.[16] It is also important to note that, "Economic inequality . . . does not appear to cause, amplify or obscure the apparent effects of ethnic diversity on social capital."[17] The same goes for the quality of communal infrastructure.[18]

On the other hand, Putnam also maintains that,

8. See Putnam, "E Pluribus Unum," 144–46.

9. Putnam, "E Pluribus Unum," 147.

10. Putnam, "E Pluribus Unum," 148.

11. Putnam, "E Pluribus Unum," 148.

12. Putnam, "E Pluribus Unum," 149.

13. See Putnam, "E Pluribus Unum," 149–50.

14. Putnam, "E Pluribus Unum," 150–51.

15. See Putnam, "E Pluribus Unum," 151. Lower amounts of trust are not only related to diversity, but also to age, specific ethnic groups, as well as lower economic and educational status. At the same time, these factors mostly intersect with diversity (see Putnam, "E Pluribus Unum," 152–53). Interestingly, it turns out that districts that are equal in terms of economic status or crime-rate etc. are still different in terms of trust depending on the degree of ethnic diversity (see Putnam, "E Pluribus Unum," 153).

16. See Putnam, "E Pluribus Unum," 154.

17. Putnam, "E Pluribus Unum," 157.

18. See Putnam, "E Pluribus Unum," 157.

> In the long run, . . . successful immigrant societies have overcome such fragmentation by creating new, cross-cutting forms of social solidarity and more encompassing identities. Illustrations of becoming comfortable with diversity are drawn from the US military, religious institutions, and earlier waves of American immigration.[19]

However, whether the long-term potentially positive effects of diversity really come into effect, is not a given, but dependent on the "success" of a given society to manage higher degrees of diversity. As the data presented in the previous chapter show, the likelihood of a positive outcome will depend on various factors, especially cultural and racial distance between locals and immigrants. Success is not a mere question of time.

Putnam's general claim that "an extraordinary achievement of human civilization is our ability to redraw social lines in ways that transcend ancestry"[20] is certainly right in principle. The same is true for his claim that it is an "emphasis on shared identities that cross racial"—or in fact: other culturally and socially important—"lines"[21] that will help to overcome the challenges of immigration and segregation. But still, the success—and costs—are not predictable and depend on a multitude of factors that are different in each case.

Putnam's assumptions with regard to the long-term effects are questionable when one looks at the parameters by which he determines the positive effects of immigration-driven diversity: enhancement of national cuisine and "culture of all sorts"; enhancement of creativity, resulting in better and faster problem-solving; more rapid economic growth; offset of the impending negative economic effects of the retirement of the baby-boom generation.[22] As far as the cuisine is concerned: It is astonishing that such a point is even mentioned—and continues to be mentioned—in serious debates about migration, since it is so unimportant and since (especially in the age of internet) all kinds of recipes from the whole world are readily available online, and ingredients to use them are also readily available through international trade; in addition, not much enrichment can be said to be added if there are three or five kebab-stands or sushi-bars (to choose two random examples) instead of one in a given district. As far as the general cultural argument is concerned: It is obvious that not

19. Putnam, "E Pluribus Unum," 137.

20. Putnam, "E Pluribus Unum," 161.

21. Putnam, "E Pluribus Unum," 161.

22. See Putnam, "E Pluribus Unum," 140.

all foreign cultural elements can be accepted as positive on moral or aes-
thetical grounds; moreover, many valuable local cultural elements may
come under threat, with potential negative effects on the sense of identity
of the original local population. Better and faster problem-solving may
rather be an effect of intellectual diversity than racial, ethnic, or cultural
diversity;[23] in any case, this is a much too complex issue to be assessed
in general terms. Concerning the economic effects, things are much less
straightforward and again more complicated than Putnam suggests, as
will become clear in the chapter on the economic dimensions of migration below.[24]

Putnam's study, as far as the findings of the short-term effects of increasing
diversity on social cohesion are concerned, have been subject to various
criticisms and double-checking. One of the most important examples of
the latter is a study by James Laurence and Lee Bentley of the University
of Manchester, published in 2016 in the *European Sociological Review* under the title "Does Ethnic Diversity Have a Negative Effect on Attitudes
towards the Community? A Longitudinal Analysis of the Causal Claims
within the Ethnic Diversity and Social Cohesion Debate." Their results
are as follows: In principle, the negative causal effect of increased ethnic
diversity on social cohesion does in fact exist, with some modifications,
however: the effect is higher among *stayers* than among *movers*; especially
among the latter, pre-existing bias concerning ethnic diversity may be an
important factor determining the degree of their disengagement with the
community. Also, other factors like the quality of the community services
need to be taken into account, as much as differences in values that exist
between young single persons without children and elder married home-
owning persons with children. Also, the tendencies are not predictable
for individual cases. All these qualifiers notwithstanding, the general
connection observed by Putnam is confirmed by Laurence and Bentley.

There are many other studies that confirm Putnam's main findings,
among them the following: a 2013 study from Australia (*Journal of Urban
Affairs*: "Ethnic Diversity and its Impact on Community Social Cohesion and Neighborly Exchange"); a 2015 study by the University of North

23. As Putnam himself suggests (see "E Pluribus Unum," 140).

24. Putnam also mentions benefits for the sending countries in the global South
(see "E Pluribus Unum," 141). To what degree this assumption may be justified cannot
be discussed in any detail in the present study; however, some remarks on this aspect
will be made in the section on the economic dimensions of migration.

Carolina examining a number of regions across Europe (*Social Forces*: "Ethnic Diversity, Economic and Cultural Contexts, and Social Trust: Cross-Sectional and Longitudinal Evidence from European Regions, 2002–2010"); and a study by the University of Gothenburg about the situation in Sweden published in 2017.[25]

The findings of these studies can be summarized in the following way: "Flourishing is maximized within communities that enjoy high levels of trust and voluntary cooperation. Social solidarity is not an automatic byproduct of interactions among people. Rather, communal solidarity is a human creation—a byproduct of shared customs and traditions, common moral values and aspirations."[26]

The observations presented in this paragraph point beyond the more specific focus on migration to issues related to diversity and multiculturalism—topics that would need special in-depth treatment which cannot be provided in the present investigation.

2.4. Insights into the Psychological Struggles of Migrants

In a next step, some findings provided by psychology and psychiatry will be scrutinized. The first source in this section is Leon and Rebeca Grinberg's monograph entitled *Psychoanalytic Perspectives on Migration and Exile*.

According to Grinberg and Grinberg, migration generally has a traumatic phase,[27] with *trauma* being defined as an excess of external stimuli which overcome the protective barrier against overstimulation, leading to disturbances in ego functioning, with the potential to threaten the integrity of the personality.[28] It may cause phobic symptoms and other manifestations of anxiety and also result in sorrow.[29] Whether or not at some point the migration event will have traumatic consequences depends upon the subject's previous personality traits and other circumstances.[30] The subject's reactions are not always expressed or visible, but

25. See Strömbäck, "Stabilitet," 1–17.

26. Amstutz, *Just Immigration*, 106.

27. See Grinberg and Grinberg, *Psychoanalytic Perspectives*, 10.

28. See Grinberg and Grinberg, *Psychoanalytic Perspectives*, 11.

29. See Grinberg and Grinberg, *Psychoanalytic Perspectives*, 11–12.

30. See Grinberg and Grinberg, *Psychoanalytic Perspectives*, 12.

the effects may run deep and last long regardless of their expression or visibility.[31]

Besides trauma, Grinberg and Grinberg also use the category of *crisis*. Crisis is defined as temporary disturbance of the regulatory mechanisms in one or more individuals. An individual or collective crisis can be either the cause or the effect of migration[32]—or, of course, both. The authors also state that crises are transition periods that can represent both opportunities for growth as well as the danger of increased vulnerability to mental illness.[33]

The transition from the old to the new surroundings is demanding; if the migrant does not find some kind of "transitional place" and "transition period," the continuity between the self and the surroundings is broken.[34] Migration exposes the individual to a state of disorganization and requires a subsequent reorganization—which is not always achieved.[35]

In a chapter entitled "Migration and Identity," Grinberg and Grinberg state that events such as migration, which cause drastic change in a person's life, can pose threats to the *sense of identity*.[36] The question needs to be addressed how much change an individual can tolerate because it works potentially irreparable harm on his or her identity.[37] The feeling of "sameness" over time and the feeling of "belonging" are identified as two of the most central elements in identity building.[38] The confrontation with a new environment leads to psychological challenges in that primitive anxieties may be triggered, such as fear of being swallowed by the new culture or being torn apart by it.[39] These experiences result from a conflict between the desire to assimilate with others so as not to feel left out or different, and the desire to be different so as to continue feeling the same.[40]

In any event, being in a place where the newcomer has no roots, no history, no ancestry, no personal memories, creates a feeling of *sorrow*.

31. See Grinberg and Grinberg, *Psychoanalytic Perspectives*, 12.
32. See Grinberg and Grinberg, *Psychoanalytic Perspectives*, 13.
33. See Grinberg and Grinberg, *Psychoanalytic Perspectives*, 14.
34. See Grinberg and Grinberg, *Psychoanalytic Perspectives*, 14.
35. See Grinberg and Grinberg, *Psychoanalytic Perspectives*, 14.
36. See Grinberg and Grinberg, *Psychoanalytic Perspectives*, 129.
37. See Grinberg and Grinberg, *Psychoanalytic Perspectives*, 129.
38. See Grinberg and Grinberg, *Psychoanalytic Perspectives*, 132.
39. See Grinberg and Grinberg, *Psychoanalytic Perspectives*, 132.
40. See Grinberg and Grinberg, *Psychoanalytic Perspectives*, 132.

This again will be treated by the immigrant by tending to elements of the past in the physical and/or psychic space to reaffirm his/her sense of identity. The danger of this is that it may prevent the immigrant from incorporating the new and accepting the past as past.[41] The psychological process of accommodation will be easier when important elements of the past can be transferred to the new situation, such as when there is continuity in the work life, when similar social environments exist, etc. Yet even so, migration is a considerable psychological challenge, and demands the acceptance of losses and working through the concomitant mourning process.[42]

In another chapter, Grinberg and Grinberg link the experience of migration to the loss of a stable container, as is the mother for a child.[43] This is aggravated—as sociology confirms—in cases in which the immigrant must confront a new language and unfamiliar customs and behavior.[44] How well a person will cope with these challenges also depends on the previous psychological health which this person brings into the process.

As far as second-generation immigrants are concerned, complicated psychological problems arise, the specific shape of which not only depends on the attitudes of the receptors, but also on how their parents coped with the migration process. Two factors are mentioned by Grinberg and Grinberg: Where the family nucleus was scarred before the migration, pathology becomes apparent or aggravated after the migration.[45] When working through and mourning over the losses linked to migration are delayed, it passes to the second generation.[46]

Psychological challenges are also posed to the members of the receiving society. It is not an easy task for them to incorporate the presence of a stranger in their midst. Especially when larger numbers of strangers arrive, the functioning of the ground rules can be thrown in doubt, the cultural identity of the receiving community or their sense of group identity can be (perceived to be) threatened.[47]

---

41. See Grinberg and Grinberg, *Psychoanalytic Perspectives*, 133.

42. See Grinberg and Grinberg, *Psychoanalytic Perspectives*, 134.

43. See Grinberg and Grinberg, *Psychoanalytic Perspectives*, 137.

44. See Grinberg and Grinberg, *Psychoanalytic Perspectives*, 137.

45. See Grinberg and Grinberg, *Psychoanalytic Perspectives*, 168.

46. See Grinberg and Grinberg, *Psychoanalytic Perspectives*, 168.

47. See Grinberg and Grinberg, *Psychoanalytic Perspectives*, 81.

One factor that is important in determining the reaction of the receptors is whether they were actively participating in the process, either by inviting the immigrant themselves or at least by being informed beforehand and being asked whether they would accept the immigration.[48] If this is not the case, the psychological response will be a guarding off on the side of the receptors or even hostility if the newcomers are viewed as a threat.[49] The immigrant's attitude and conduct will of course modify the receptors' response over time.[50] But then, it is also a cyclical process, because the attitude of the receptors will also influence the development of the reaction of the newcomers.[51] This is a very complex process, in which initial positive feedbacks can be reversed mutually at any stage when expectations are no longer met.[52] Migration will be a productive process when each side functions with sufficient flexibility. This presupposes on the side of the immigrant a nondestructive behavior and the will to assimilate.[53]

Some of the findings presented by Grinberg and Grinberg are corroborated and elaborated by Sluzki. He points to the fact that migration necessarily—as opposed to a matter of individual pathology—causes psychological stress.[54] One of the major factors that triggers stress is the severe disruption in the social network, which occurs regardless of the causes for migration.[55] A more or less substantial part of the previous social network is lost because of the relocation, and the migrants are confronted with a psychologically demanding and lengthy process of re-socialization in the new environment. For extended periods of time, "many interpersonal functions accomplished by the old network remain unfulfilled."[56] If the migration includes several family members, part of the network will be transferred, but not enough to make the transition easy. The family relationships themselves are under considerable stress, because family members are expected to meet psychological needs that

48. See Grinberg and Grinberg, *Psychoanalytic Perspectives*, 82.
49. See Grinberg and Grinberg, *Psychoanalytic Perspectives*, 83.
50. See Grinberg and Grinberg, *Psychoanalytic Perspectives*, 83.
51. See Grinberg and Grinberg, *Psychoanalytic Perspectives*, 83.
52. See Grinberg and Grinberg, *Psychoanalytic Perspectives*, 85.
53. See Grinberg and Grinberg, *Psychoanalytic Perspectives*, 82.
54. See Sluzki, "Disruption," 359, 362.
55. See Sluzki, "Disruption," 359–60.
56. Sluzki, "Disruption," 361.

162 The Bible and Immigration

were filled by other people before, and which they are unable to fill in satisfactory ways.[57] Sluzki's article summarizes the findings as follows: "The
rule is that, when compared to the one left behind, the new network will
remain smaller for a long time, . . . with a lower density and a narrower
repertoire of functions, less multidimensional, reciprocal, and intense.
All this creates a network that may be insufficient and, therefore, prone
to overload,"[58] which leads to crisis.

Some important observations made by Perez Foster need to be added to
our discussion. Perez Foster also points to the loss of social networks that
are related to migration, whatever the cause of the migration may be;[59]
the need to rebuild social networks is a task that is enormously challenging.[60] The energy necessary to learn a new language and to acculturate in
various ways is substantial.[61] The situation is aggravated in cases in which
the immigrant's social status is lower than in the country of origin and if
the migration is not embedded in the network of family.[62] Extra stress
is put on immigrant families if traditional gender roles prevalent in the
places of origin cannot be maintained in the new environment.[63] While
migration itself is likely to cause psychic disorders of various kinds, it is
especially "traumatic or derailing events before, during, or after disloca-
tion that lead to psychological distress of clinical proportions."[64] In many
cases, premigration trauma has long-term effects.[65] Difficulties in the
life conditions in the new environment like poverty, unemployment, or
negative attitudes by the host society aggravate the problems.[66] Children
of migrants are also hugely impacted psychologically by the difficulties
their parents face.[67]

Perez Foster points to two specific problems not mentioned so
far: Because of broader cultural differences, it is important—though

57. See Sluzki, "Disruption," 361–62.
58. Sluzki, "Disruption," 362.
59. See Perez Foster, "When Immigration Is Trauma," 154.
60. Perez Foster, "When Immigration is Trauma," 156.
61. See Perez Foster, "When Immigration is Trauma," 157–58.
62. See Perez Foster, "When Immigration is Trauma," 154, 158.
63. See Perez Foster, "When Immigration is Trauma," 154.
64. Perez Foster, "When Immigration is Trauma," 155.
65. See Perez Foster, "When Immigration is Trauma," 157.
66. See Perez Foster, "When Immigration is Trauma," 157.
67. See Perez Foster, "When Immigration is Trauma," 158.

not easy—"to distinguish idiosyncratic pathology from culture-specific behavior in new immigrants."[68] However, even if such a distinction can be made, the question still remains which of the patterns rooted in the culture of origin can be transferred to the new environment, without creating too many difficulties for the individuals in question or too many irritations for the members of the host society.[69] The second problem concerns the cultural and linguistic expression of psychological distress. Psychological distress is expressed in different ways in different cultures,[70] and persons with a foreign background suffering from psychological distress are able to communicate their views and experiences—at least in some cases—only in a limited way by means of a second language. In addition, the use of a second language may put additional psychological stress on the respective persons.[71]

Finally, the problems of identity formation often detectable in the context of migration deserve some elaboration. For young adults with an (im)migration background identity negotiation is generally more stressful than for other young adults, because they are exposed to competing demands from their family's society of origin on the one hand and the culture of the host country on the other.[72] The conflict is not just about specific cultural practices, but (depending on the cultures involved) even about the primary goal of socialization—whether the focus is on the development of an autonomous individual or on the fostering of interconnectedness and interdependence on the level of family, clan, or larger community.[73] The disruption of their own lives through the process of migration may complicate the role that parents play in the process of identity formation

68. Perez Foster, "When Immigration is Trauma," 159; cf. also p. 160.

69. The same applies for the question to what degree Western perspectives on psychological function and dysfunction need to be culturally adapted (cf. Perez Forster, "When Immigration is Trauma," 160).

70. See Perez Foster, "When Immigration is Trauma," 160.

71. See Perez Foster, "When Immigration is Trauma," 164–65. Perez Forster suggests that these problems need to be addressed by having the immigrants treated by persons who are familiar with the culture of origin and especially with the primary language of the patients (see "When Immigration is Trauma," 166). There are, of course, many other studies that corroborate the findings presented here. For one example see Murphy, who mentions anxiety, depression, and decreased satisfaction as phenomena typically related to migration ("Transnational Ties," 81).

72. See Kisiel Dion, "On the Development of Identity," 302.

73. See Kisiel Dion, "On the Development of Identity," 303.

of their children, often in the sense of attempting to have greater influence on their children's development.[74] Protracted periods of co-residence will further this tendency. When parents perceive a threat to the values of the society of origin by the host culture, they often react by being more restrictive towards their children, which also affects the process of identity formation. In addition, practical challenges will have a large influence on factors that are important for identity formation, like choice of occupation.[75] As far as gender differences are concerned, there is a tendency that "women might be more prone than men to be more conflicted about their sense of cultural identity," while at the same time "the psychological salience of ethnocultural identity" is often higher among women than men.[76]

2.5. Transnationalism and Mental Health

As seen above, in recent years assimilation has been replaced, among other concepts, by transnationalism as an alternative model to define the best aspiration of (im)migrants. It can be seen that transnational ties and practices among new immigrants may in fact influence their mental health in positive ways.[77] It is especially the social support experiences in such a context that "serves to directly decrease emotional distress."[78] Also the strengthening of the sense of ethnic identity may positively affect the mental health of the respective persons.[79] The picture is, however, more complex, because the transnational existence also has negative effects, like inducing frustrating nostalgia, delaying the process of integration that would lead to more positive results on many layers in the long run, and adding emotional burdens through a sense of responsibility for persons in the country of origin.[80]

74. See Kisiel Dion, "On the Development of Identity," 303.

75. See Kisiel Dion, "On the Development of Identity," 304.

76. Kisiel Dion, "On the Development of Identity," 309.

77. See Murphy, "Transnational Ties," 81, 83–84.

78. Murphy, "Transnational Ties," 84.

79. See Murphy, "Transnational Ties," 85.

80. See Murphy, "Transnational Ties," 84. Even the enhanced social support is not only positively connoted, because closer ties with family, for example, also provides more opportunities for tensions and disappointment (see Murphy, "Transnational Ties," 89).

2.6. Psychology and Cultural Difference

The Danish psychologist Sennels has published the results of hundreds of therapeutic sessions with about 150 young criminal Muslims in Copenhagen in 2009 (*Blandt kriminelle muslimer*).[81] According to his findings, the large cultural difference between Muslim immigrants and Western value systems makes integration of these immigrants almost impossible, with the exception of some highly motivated individuals who are psychologically able and willing to sacrifice some of the dominant cultural elements that were defining markers of their personality.[82] Among the salient elements that distinguish traditional Muslim culture from Western values are the importance of honor and the positive evaluation of aggression and retaliation, and the concomitant rejection of compromise and dialogical negotiation. Another area of difference is the low estimation of education and professional achievement among the Muslim immigrants.[83] According to Sennels, it is differences such as these, rather than socio-economic conditions, that explain the large-scale failure of attempts to integrate Muslim immigrants despite huge amounts of money invested in various integration measures.

Sennels's findings are corroborated by German psychiatrist Dogs. He maintains that the main personality traits are established at about age twelve mostly, and age twenty completely, and that it is therefore hardly possible to bring about fundamental and far-reaching changes in the value systems of immigrants from cultures that are much different from the Western countries of destination.[84]

2.7. The Reception of Psychological Findings in Theological Studies of Migration

To some degree, psychological problems related to migration are recognized sporadically also in theological studies of migration. An example is Carroll, who—with a view to the situation of immigrants from Latin America in the U.S.—mentions "the conflicts of heart and mind of the

---

81. An English version was published in 2018 (Sennels, *Holy Wrath*).

82. See Sennels, "Muslims and Westerners."

83. See Sennels, "Muslims and Westerners."

84. See Dogs, "Mit den Migranten kommt eine Zeitbombe" (the interview was done on Sept 16, 2017).

immigrant or descendant vis-à-vis their Latin American heritage and their life in the United States."[85] He continues by observing that their life "is a pilgrimage of joy and sadness, of frustration and self-discovery, of appreciation for the past and anticipation of the future, a life of hybridity."[86]

More detailed reflections can be found in Rodríguez who asserts that the migrants' "suffering usually involves a process of letting go, of displacement and loss, and even mourning in various ways."[87] He continues to describe this process in some detail: the mourning connected to leaving one's country of birth, leaving behind friends and family, not being able to use one's native language and lose daily contact with one's ethnic group; the disappearance of support systems; the leaving behind of one's culture which shapes one's identity and provides a sense of place in the world, and which is related to a specific land through the presence of the ancestors. In addition, there is the stress and anxiety related to learning to navigate a new culture, a new language, a new job (often of lower social status).[88]

Another example is Schreiter's study on migrants and reconciliation, focusing on forced and reluctant migration. He maintains that psychological injuries—of various kinds, depending on the nature and cause of migration—are related both to the leaving behind of the homeland, the experiences during the transit, and the challenges presented by the new environment.[89] According to him, the effects of migration are traumatic in cases of involuntary migration as far as the first two phases (leaving one's homeland, transit) are concerned; but psychological injuries also occur in cases of voluntary migration in terms of the adjustment to the new environment.[90] Of particular importance is Schreiter's observation that trauma experienced by migrants can "become imbedded in the identity of subsequent generations."[91]

---

85. Carroll, *Christians*, 23.

86. Carroll, *Christians*, 24. See also his comments on the patriarch Joseph, whom he calls "an example of the conflicted nature of many immigrants throughout the ages, who struggle with a heart for two cultures" (*Christians*, 60).

87. "A Witness," xii.

88. See Rodríguez, "A Witness," xii–xiii.

89. See Schreiter, "Migrants," 107–8.

90. See Schreiter, "Migrants," 108–10.

91. "Migrants," 112.

2.8. Brief Summary

This section shows that migration poses considerable challenges on the psychological level, both for migrants themselves and members of the receiving societies, and both on an individual, familial, and communal level. The exact nature of the challenges will look differently depending on the specific circumstances, and are especially acute in the short-term and in cases of involuntary migration.

3. DEMOGRAPHY

3.1. General Observations

There is no doubt that immigration, especially large-scale immigration, changes the demography of any given nation. It is also clear, however, that the exact nature of the changes brought about by immigration are difficult to assess, because they interact with other demographic factors in complex ways.[92]

Since in many cases migrants are not old, migration will have an effect on the age structure of the population in the countries affected by migration.[93] One has to remember, however, that the effects in the country of destination will flatten out over time if the numbers of immigrants decrease.

Another topic is sex composition. In those cases in which the immigrant population does not divert in substantial ways from the sex composition prevalent in the country of destination, the size of the immigrant population will not have any remarkable effects on that level. Things look, however, differently if there is a large dominance of one sex over the other among immigrants.[94]

It is often claimed that immigration is important in terms of population size only on a local or national, not on a global level.[95] This assumption is, however, overly simplistic, because the number of actual births per potential parent will not be necessarily the same wherever they live,

92. See, e.g., Smith and Edmonston, *The New Americans*, 76.

93. See, e.g., Smith and Edmonston, *The New Americans*, 101.

94. This is at least true when the immigrants are in child-bearing age or younger. Remarkable cases are the new arrivals from Africa and the Middle East in Europe in the last couple of years, with a vast majority of them being young men.

95. See, e.g., Smith and Edmonston, *The New Americans*, 99.

but will be responsive to the life conditions of their place of residence. The place of residence also effects the availability of potential marriage partners, as well as their ethnic affiliation. Therefore, migration has effects on global population growths, as well as on the ethnic composition of world population. On the other hand, it is also clear that there is no way of predicting with any precision how these elements will be affected by migration.

As far as projections into the future are concerned, a large degree of uncertainty exists with a view to many factors, especially the numbers of immigrants and the percentage of intermarriage; nevertheless, there are some trends that can be identified with some certainty. Projections for the immediate future are more reliable than those looking further ahead in time, even if single major events such as the opening of the borders in Germany in September 2015 can lead to dramatic changes even in the short term.

What is clear is that immigrant groups with persistently high fertility rates will grow disproportionally over time, both in absolute numbers and in relation to other population groups.[96]

According to a widespread view, fertility rates of immigrants and their descendants converge toward the national norm within two generations.[97] There are, however, data that point in another direction. For example, it can be observed that the fertility rates of Hispanic immigrants and their descendants in the U.S. decrease over time, but still remain above average.[98]

In the following section, the major demographic data on six countries will be presented, focusing on the numbers of the relative growth of the immigrant population.[99] The choice of the cases is based mainly on personal familiarity of the present author;[100] in most instances, the countries selected also represent cases of especially accentuated changes of demography related to immigration.

96. See, e.g., Smith and Edmonston, *The New Americans*, 77, 85. Putnam ("E Pluribus Unum," 140) supports the view that "immigrant groups typically have higher fertility rates than native-born groups."

97. See, e.g., Smith and Edmonston, *The New Americans*, 158; cf. also p. 83.

98. See Smith and Edmonston, *The New Americans*, 87, 115.

99. Related issues like changes in age structure and overall population growth or decline will not be investigated.

100. The exception is Sweden.

3.2. Special Case Studies: U.S., Germany, France, Switzerland, Sweden, Norway

3.2.1. U.S.

Here are some of the important numbers showing the demographic changes in the U.S. during the last decades. The first set of data relates to the racial ratios, the second to the percentage of the foreign-born population.

In 1960, the U.S. had a total population of 180.7 million. Out of these, 160 million were White (that is, 88.5 percent), 19 million African American (that is, 10.5 percent), and 1.64 million "other races."[101] In 1990, according to the 1990 census, 75 percent of the population were White, 12 percent African American, 9 percent Hispanic, and 3 percent Asian.[102] In 1995, the U.S. had a total population of 263 million. Of these, 193.6 million were White (that is, 73.6 percent), 31.6 million African American (that is, 12 percent), 26.9 million Hispanic (that is, 10.2 percent), and 8.8 million Asian (that is, 3.3 percent).[103] In 2010, out of a total of 308.7 million people, 223.5 million were White (that is, 72.4 percent); 38.9 million were African-American (that is, 12.6 percent); 50.5 million were Hispanic (that is, 16.3 percent); and 14.7 million were Asian (that is, 4.8 percent).[104]

In 2000, according to OECD data, 28 million out of a total population of 282.2 million were foreign-born (that is, 9.9 percent),[105] while 12.3 percent of the population in the U.S. was foreign-born in 2008.[106] In

---

101. According to the census of 1960; see "National Intercensal Tables: 1900–1990," *United States Census Bureau.*

102. See Smith and Edmonston, *The New Americans*, 114.

103. See Smith and Edmonston, *The New Americans*, 118.

104. See Humes et al., "Overview of Race." The projections made by Smith and Edmonston for that year are relatively far away from the real developments. They expected the percentage of White to be 67 percent, of African American 13 percent, of Hispanic 14 percent, and of Asian 5 percent (see *The New Americans*, 121).

105. See "Stocks of Foreign-Born Population in OECD Countries," *OECD Data.* It is very interesting to note that the projections made by Smith and Edmonston in 1997 proved to be wrong. They worked with five different immigration scenarios, ranging from zero to "very high," but estimated the population of the U.S. for 2000 at a maximum of 281 million even under the maximum immigration scenario (see Smith and Edmonston, *The New Americans*, 95).

106. See Guild, *Security and Migration*, 137.

2017, almost 44 million people out of a total population of 325.7 million were foreign-born (that is, 13.5 percent).[107]

Population estimates by census.gov for 2018, based on the 2010 census, look as follows:[108] Total population was at ca. 327 million people; of these, 13.4 percent were foreign-born; 60.4 percent were White; 13.4 percent were African American; 18.3 percent were Hispanic; 5.9 percent were Asian; 1.5 percent were classified as others; and 2.7 percent were of two or more races.

The clearest indicator of demographic change brought about by migration is the rising growth of the Hispanic and Asian population groups. Another indicator is the increase of the Muslim population.[109] According to statista.com, the number of Muslims in the U.S. has increased from 2.35 million in 2007 (that is, 0.8 percent) to 3.45 million in 2017 (that is, 1.1 percent).[110]

The projections for 2050 made by Smith and Edmonston look as follows: In a medium immigration scenario, the total population is estimated at 387 million; in a high-level immigration scenario, the total population is estimated at 426 million; and in a very high-level immigration scenario, the total population is estimated at 463 million.[111] In any event, the addition to the population of the U.S. through immigration will be considerable, about 80 million out of 387 million in a medium immigration scenario.[112] In a medium immigration scenario, what is expected is an increase of the African American population to 54 million (that is, 14 percent), a growth of the Hispanic population—partially fueled by immigration—to 95 million (that is, 25 percent), and of the Asian

---

107. See "Stocks of Foreign-Born Population in OECD Countries," *OECD Data.*

108. See "Population Estimates, July 1, 2019," *Quick Facts, United States Census Bureau.* Of course, there are important sub-groups within the major categories, which may exhibit differing developments over time.

109. This assumption presupposes that the increase of Muslims is mostly immigration-driven. This presupposition is justified in the absence of evidence for conversion of statistically significant numbers of Americans of other faiths or no faith to Islam. As far as the situation in Europe is concerned, Islam saw a decrease in terms of religious switching between 2010 and 2016, while it grew heavily in the same period both through natural increase and net migration gains (see Hackett, "5 Facts").

110. See Duffin, "Muslim Population in the U.S."

111. See Smith and Edmonston, *The New Americans,* 95.

112. See Smith and Edmonston, *The New Americans,* 122.

population—mostly fueled by immigration—to 34 million (that is, 8 percent).[113]

In all scenarios, the future population will continue to age for the decades to come.[114] However, both absolute and relative numbers of the age groups except for the elderly will grow in different ways depending on the immigration scenario.[115] What is also foreseen is a blurring of traditional ethnic boundaries as a consequence of a growing number of intermarriage; an estimated 21 percent are expected to report multiple ancestries.[116]

3.2.2. Germany

In the last decades, until about 2015, Germany has seen a relatively moderate population growth only—sometimes even phases of minor decline. The numbers are not as precise as in other countries, because official federal censuses have been conducted only intermittently, with the last taking place in 1987. Instead, the German Government relies on extrapolations from sample data collected from a small percentage (around 1 percent) of the population.[117] Germany did, however, participate in the EU-wide census in 2011, which provided data about the country's population. Another difficulty is created by the fact that especially since September 2015, state authorities have only partial control of who enters the country; also, many of the new arrivals have not been accepted as refugees, but are nonetheless not sent out of the country, while many of them do not appear in current population statistics. These aspects notwithstanding, the broad lines are still clear. The population growth in recent years is entirely driven by immigration, with substantial contingents coming from the Balkans and the Near East.

Here is an overview of the development from 1950 until 2018 as far as the number of inhabitants of Germany is concerned:[118] 1950: 69.966 million;

---

113. See Smith and Edmonston, *The New Americans*, 114–15.
114. See Smith and Edmonston, *The New Americans*, 102, 106.
115. See Smith and Edmonston, *The New Americans*, 103–6.
116. See Smith and Edmonston, *The New Americans*, 113, 119, 121, 123.
117. See "Germany Population," *World Population Review*.
118. See "Germany Population," *World Population Review*.

1965: 76.258 million; 1980: 78.283 million; 1995: 81.139 million; 2010: 80.827 million; 2018: 83.124 million.

Statistics for the percentage of foreign-born persons look as follows: According to OECD data, in 1955 the German population consisted of roughly 70 million people (FRG and GDR combined), more or less none of them foreign-born. In 1990, roughly 6 million people out of a total population of 79.75 million were foreign-born (that is, ca. 7.5 percent).[119] In 2000, roughly 9 million people out of a total population of 82.26 million were foreign-born (that is, ca. 11 percent). In 2017, almost 13 million people out of a total population of 82.79 million were foreign-born (that is, ca. 15.7 percent).[120]

The following overview shows where substantial numbers of immigrants have come from in recent years:[121] Turkey, 2000–2017: ca. 640,000; Syria, 2014–2017: ca. 630,000; Iraq, 2010–2017, ca. 280,000; Afghanistan, 2010–2017, ca. 250,000; Iran, 2010–2017, ca. 140,000; Albania, 2013–2017, ca. 120,000; Pakistan, 2000–2017, ca. 106,000; Somalia, 2010–2017, ca. 40,000. The sum total of immigrants from these eight countries alone amounts to 2.2 million persons for the periods indicated.

According to official numbers for 2018 (published by the *Statistisches Bundesamt* [Statistical Federal Office]), 25.5 percent of the population of Germany had migration background, 20.799 million persons out of a total population of 81.631 million; 9.907 million persons or 12.1 percent of the permanent residents were foreigners. 13.5 million persons or 16.5 percent of the permanent residents were foreign-born.[122] For 2019, the numbers look as follows: 26 percent of the population had migration background, 21.246 million persons out of a total population of 81.848 million; 11.2 million persons or 12.4 percent of the permanent residents were foreigners.[123] In 2008, by contrast, only 12.1 percent of the population were foreign-born.[124]

119. See "Migration Profiles: Germany," *UNICEF.*

120. See "Stocks of Foreign-Born Population in OECD Countries," *OECD Data.*

121. See *International Migration Database* (OECD.Stat); interestingly, data about "Immigrants by Citizenship and Age" referring to Germany are not available.

122. See "Jede vierte Person in Deutschland hatte 2018 einen Migrationshintergrund," DESTATIS, *Statistisches Bundesamt.*

123. See "Bevölkerung mit Migrationshintergrund 2019 um 2,1 % gewachsen," DESTATIS.

124. See Guild, *Security,* 137.

For 48 percent of the immigrants in 2018, family reunion was the motive of their move to Germany, while only 19 percent of immigration was work-related; 15 percent immigrated to seek asylum. Education was the main motive for 5 percent of the immigrants.[125]

The trends become even more remarkable if some additional information is taken into account:[126] (1) The vast majority of recent immigrants has only low (if any) professional qualifications; on the other hand, about 150,000 mostly highly qualified Germans leave the country every year. (2) The excess of deaths over births among German persons without migration background is about 1.2 million per year. (3) It is projected that Germans without migration background will be a minority around the year 2050.

The development of the numbers of the Muslim population looks as follows:[127] Estimates for the Muslim population increased from 1,000 or less than 0.01 percent in 1920, to 20,000 or 0.03 percent in 1951, to 1,150,000 or 1.5 percent in 1971, to 1.8 million or 2.9 percent in 1981, to 2.5 million or 3.1 percent in 1991, to 3.2 million or 3.9 percent in 2001, to 4.3 million or 5.22 percent in 2009. According to Pew Research, 4.95 million persons or 6.1 percent of the population of Germany were Muslims in 2016.[128]

3.2.3. France

The situation in France is different from the one in the U.S. (and many other countries) in that a law from 1872 prohibits the French Republic from conducting a census which would make any official distinction between its citizens in terms of race, ethnicity, or religious beliefs. This law does not apply to private surveys or polls, however, so that it is still possible to get some data. INED and INSEE are the most important independent agencies that provide statistical data that cover the "forbidden" areas.

125. See "Jede vierte Person in Deutschland hatte 2018 einen Migrationshintergrund," DESTATIS, Statistisches Bundesamt.

126. Figures are according to Hamer, "Ein Viertel der Deutschen haben Migrationshintergrund."

127. See Kettani, "Muslim Population," 161.

128. See Hackett, "5 Facts."

As in the case of most European countries, population growth after the baby-boomer years in the early- and mid-1960s was driven primarily by immigration and higher birth rates among immigrants.

Here is an overview of the development from 1950 until 2018 as far as the number of inhabitants of France is concerned:[129] 1950: 41.834 million; 1965: 48.747 million; 1980: 53.868 million; 1995: 57.802 million; 2010: 62.88 million; 2018: 64.99 million.

As far as the share of the foreign-born population and the racial composition of the population are concerned, the following data are available: In 1990, according to UN statistics, roughly 6 million out of a total population of 58 million were foreign-born (that is, roughly 10 percent).[130] In 2000, according to numbers gathered by OECD, 4.3 million out of a total population of 60.51 million were foreign-born (that is, roughly 7 percent).[131] In 2004, it was estimated that 85 percent of the population of Metropolitan France was White or of European origin, 10 percent from North Africa, 3.5 percent Black, and 1.5 percent Asian.[132] Numbers for 2008 show a population of 11.8 million foreign-born immigrants and their immediate descendants; this figure accounted for around 19 percent of the total population at that time.[133] In 2009, a marketing company called Solis estimated numbers of ethnic minorities as 5.23 percent Maghrebis, 2.94 percent Black (a majority from Sub-Saharan Africa), and 0.71 percent Turkish.[134] In 2010, 27 percent of newborns in the metropolitan areas of France had at least one foreign-born parent.[135] In 2016, according to OECD data, almost 8 million people out of a total population of 66.6 million were foreign-born (that is, roughly 12 percent).[136]

Looking at religious affiliation provides an additional perspective. France is one of the least religious countries in the world. According to a 2016 survey from the *Institut Montaigne*, 39.6 percent claimed no religion. Slightly more than half (51.1 percent) identified as Christian, 5.6 percent

129. See "France Population," *World Population Review*.
130. See "Migration Profiles: France," *UNICEF*.
131. See "Stocks of Foreign-Born Population in OECD Countries," *OECD Data*.
132. See "France Population," *World Population Review*.
133. See "France Population," *World Population Review*.
134. See "France Population," *World Population Review*.
135. See "France Population," *World Population Review*.
136. See "Stocks of Foreign-Born Population in OECD Countries," *OECD Data*.

as Muslim, and 0.8 percent as Jewish.[137] According to a Pew Research Study of Islam in Europe, however, 5.72 million persons, or 8.8 percent of the French population, were Muslim in 2016.[138]

When these numbers are compared to 1986, a few trends become apparent. The percentage of French people identifying as non-religious has increased exponentially in the thirty years between 1986 and 2016, from 15.5 percent to nearly 40 percent. The other trend is the growth of the Muslim population in France. The Muslim population is expected to continue to increase due to immigration, as well as comparatively higher birth rates than among other population groups.[139]

The detailed numbers concerning the development of the Muslim population over a longer period look as follows:[140] Estimates for the Muslim population increased from less than 1,000 or 0.01 percent before 1900, to 6,000 or 0.02 percent in 1912, to 100,000 or 0.26 percent in 1920, to 120,000 or 0.3 percent in 1924, then decreased to 70,000 or 0.17 percent in 1936, and increased again to 230,000 or 0.55 percent in 1952, to one million or 2 percent in the 1960s, to two million or 3.9 percent in 1975, to 2.5 million or 4.6 percent in 1981, to four million or 7 percent in 1991, to 5 million or 8 percent in 2001, to six million or 10 percent in 2009.

Finally, it can be observed that—despite considerable efforts from the government attempting to curb the trend—segregation in the metropolitan areas is growing. Religious-ethnic segregation has become stronger than socio-economic segregation. It affects mainly immigrants from North Africa, Sub-Saharan Africa, and Turkey.[141]

3.2.4. Switzerland

Among all the European countries observed in this chapter, Switzerland has known the highest relative increase in population over the last decades. As in the other cases, the increase was driven by immigration from the second half of the 1960s onward. It is also the country with the

---

137. See "France Population," *World Population Review.*

138. See Hackett, "5 Facts."

139. See "France Population," *World Population Review.* Conversion comes into play especially in the context of intermarriage.

140. See Kettani, "Muslim Population," 159.

141. See, e.g., Préteceille, "Has Ethno-Racial Segregation Increased," 31.

highest percentage of foreigners and foreign-born permanent residents in relation to the overall population size.

Here is an overview of the development from 1950 until 2018 as far as the number of inhabitants of Switzerland is concerned:[142] 1950: 4.7 million, of which 285,000 (6 percent) were foreigners; 1960: 5.36 million, of which 514,000 (9.6 percent) were foreigners; 1970: 6.2 million, of which 1 million (16.1 percent) were foreigners; 1980: 6.335 million, of which 914,000 (14.4 percent) were foreigners; 1995: 7.1 million, of which 1.364 million (19.2 percent) were foreigners; 2000: 7.204 million, of which 1.424 million (19.8 percent) were foreigners; 2010: 7.87 million, of which 1.766 million (22.4 percent) were foreigners; 2018: 8.545 million inhabitants, of which 2.15 million (25 percent) were foreigners.[143]

As far as the share of the foreign-born population and the ethnic composition of the population are concerned, the following data are available: Roughly 1.4 million out of a total population of 6.674 million were foreign-born in 1990 (that is, 21 percent).[144] Roughly 1.6 million people out of a total population of 7.204 were foreign-born in 2001 (that is, 22.2 percent).[145] And almost 2.5 million people out of a total population of 8.42 million were foreign-born in 2017 (that is, roughly 30 percent).

The official cumulative numbers for the population fifteen years and older for 2013–2017 are as follows:[146] 6.9 million persons, of which just under 5.26 million were Swiss nationals. Italians, Germans, nationals of the Balkan states (Albania, Serbia, Bosnia and Herzegovina, Montenegro, Macedonia, Kosovo), and Portuguese were the largest groups of non-Swiss permanent residents, about 1 million persons all together.

---

142. See "Bevölkerungsdaten im Zeitvergleich, 1950–2018," *Bundesamt für Statistik*.

143. These numbers reflect only part of the real demographic shifts, because since about 1990 it has become much easier to obtain Swiss citizenship. This means that many persons who would previously have appeared in the category of "foreigner" no longer do so from then on, since the respective individuals will have become Swiss citizens.

144. See "Migration Profiles: Switzerland," *UNICEF*.

145. See "Stocks of Foreign-Born Population in OECD Countries," *OECD Data*.

146. See "Ständige Wohnbevölkerung ab 15 Jahren nach Nationalität und Religionszugehörigkeit," *Bundesamt für Statistik*.

The development of the Muslim population looks as follows:[147] Based on census data, the Muslim population grew from 2,703 or 0.05 percent in 1960, to 16,353 or 0.26 percent in 1970, to 56,600 or 0.89 percent in 1980, to 152,200 or 2.21 percent in 1990, to 310,807 or 4.26 percent in 2000. In 2016, according to Pew Research, 6.1 percent of the permanent residents of Switzerland were Muslims.[148]

3.2.5. Sweden

The demographic profile of Sweden has altered drastically due to immigration patterns since the 1970s. The patterns mentioned relating to Switzerland apply here as well. There are no official statistics on ethnicity, so that precise information about this aspect is not easy to get.[149]

Here is an overview of the development from 1950 until 2018 as far as the number of inhabitants of Sweden is concerned:[150] 1950: 7.01 million; 1965: 7.746 million; 1980: 8.316 million; 1995: 8.836 million; 2010: 9.39 million; 2018: 9.972 million.

As far as the share of the foreign-born population and the ethnic composition of the population are concerned, the following data are available: In 1990, according to OECD data, roughly 800,000 out of a total population of 8.527 million were foreign-born (that is, 9.4 percent).[151] In 2001, roughly 1 million people out of a total population of 8.883 million were foreign-born (that is, 11.26 percent).[152] In 2017, almost 1.8 million people out of a total population of 9.995 million were foreign-born (that is, 18 percent). In 2018, almost a third of the population had at least one parent who was foreign born.[153]

147. See Kettani, "Muslim Population," 161.

148. See Hackett, "5 Facts."

149. See "Sweden Population," *World Population Review.*

150. See "Sweden Population," *World Population Review.*

151. See "Migration Profiles: Sweden," *UNICEF.* According to *Statistics Sweden* around 1.921 million inhabitants of Sweden (that is, 20.1 percent) were of a foreign background in 2012. These backgrounds included: the indigenous population of Swedes with Finnish and Sami backgrounds, and foreign-born or first-generation immigrants like Turks, Greeks, Finns, people form ex-Yugoslavia, Danes, and Norwegians (see "Sweden Population," *World Population Review*).

152. See "Stocks of Foreign-Born Population in OECD Countries," *OECD Data.*

153. See Ngo, "Sweden's Parallel Society." According to a 2019 report, as many as

The following overview shows where substantial numbers of immigrants have come from in recent years:[154] Syria, 2010–2017: ca. 140,000; Iraq, 2000–2017, ca. 108,000; Somalia, 2006–2017, ca. 57,500; Afghanistan, 2000–2017, ca. 47,500; Eritrea, 2008–2017, ca. 38,000; Iran, 2000–2017, ca. 30,000; Turkey, 2000–2017: ca. 24,500. The sum total of immigrants from these seven countries alone is almost 450,000 persons for the periods indicated.

The statistics concerning the development of the Muslim population look as follows:[155] Estimates of the Muslim population increased from 1,000 or 0.01 percent in 1951, to 17,000 or 0.2 percent in 1971, to 25,000 or 0.3 percent in 1980, to 100,000 or 1.2 percent in 1991, to 300,000 or 3.41 percent in 2001, to 500,000 or 5.38 percent in 2009. In 2016, according to Pew Research, 8.1 percent of the population were Muslims.[156]

Similar to the situation in France, there are a number of districts around the larger cities that are highly segregated.[157] A number of neighborhoods, designated by police as "especially vulnerable" areas,[158] are marked by parallel social structures that compete for authority with the state. These districts are mostly populated by immigrants. Examples are Rosengård, Seved, and Nydala, immigrant neighborhoods in the southern city of Malmö. Other examples include Rinkeby, Alby, and Tensta in the greater Stockholm area. Among the signs of segregation are the following: In such districts, young girls and even some babies are dressed in modesty headscarves. Cafés are in practice mostly male-only spaces, and restaurants may offer segregated seating, with a curtain, for "families," which is a euphemism for women. In contrast to the near-cashless society elsewhere in urban Sweden, many businesses accept only cash. The overall security situation is poor. As in the case of France, the synagogues in the major cities are under special threat by Muslim immigrants or their

90 percent of the roughly 40,000 migrants who came to Sweden in 2015 and were granted permanent residency were unemployed; see Douglass-Williams, "Sweden: 5,460 of 7,000 of Afghan 'Child Migrants' Were Actually Adults."

154. See *International Migration Database* (OECD.Stat).

155. See Kettani, "Muslim Population," 161.

156. See Hackett, "5 Facts."

157. For the following observations see Ngo, "Sweden's Parallel Society." There are a great many additional sources of various kinds that concur with the observations made by Ngo; see, e.g. Svahnström, "I Danmark."

158. Similar to the French *zones urbaines sensibles* (sensitive urban zones).

descendants, which leads to an exodus of Jews from those areas, some of them moving to other parts of the country, but many of them (especially in the case of France) leaving the country altogether.

The segregationist tendencies are linked to Sweden's institutionalization of multiculturalism which began in 1975, when a parliament led by Olof Palme rejected assimilation in favor of policies that encouraged minorities to keep their separate identities. Mustafa Panshiri, a former police officer and now full-time integration educator, who came to Sweden with his family from Afghanistan when he was eleven, maintains that Sweden fails at explaining what citizenship is: "You don't have to speak a single word of Swedish to become a citizen. There are no expectations."

3.2.6. Norway

Historical landmarks in the demographic development were reached in 1825, when the population of Norway hit 1,051,318 and thereby exceeded one million for the first time in the country's history, and in 1900, when the numbers reached 2,240,032.[159]

Throughout the twentieth century, population growth was steady, with an annual increase between 0.5 percent and 1 percent. The highest annual growth rate Norway has ever seen was in 2015 when there was an increase of 1.25 percent. As in the case of most other European countries, if the population changes were dependent on the number of children born to the average Norwegian woman alone, population numbers would have begun to fall in the second half of the 1960s; but the number of immigrants entering the country has kept the numbers where they are. As of 2019, the annual growth rate in Norway was 0.89 percent, which adds roughly 50,000 people to the population each year. [160]

Here is an overview of the development from 1950 until 2018 as far as the number of inhabitants of Norway is concerned:[161] 1950: 3.265 million; 1965: 3.724 million; 1980: 4.086 million; 1995: 4.367 million; 2010: 4.886 million; 2018: 5.338 million.

As far as the share of the foreign-born population and the ethnic composition of the population are concerned, the following data are available: In

---

159. See "Norway Population," *World Population Review*.
160. See "Norway Population," *World Population Review*.
161. See "Norway Population," *World Population Review*.

1950, there were ca. 46,500 foreign-born persons among the total population of 3.265 million people (that is, 1.4 percent), the largest amount of them born in Sweden (ca. 18,500). The only non-Western countries of birth listed for that year were Poland and the Soviet-Union, together accounting for about 1,700 persons. The number of resident aliens was ca. 15,800 (that is, 0.48 percent), with the largest groups coming from Sweden (ca. 4,600) and Denmark (ca. 3,900). Only one non-Western country was listed, Poland (616 persons).[162] In 1960, there were ca. 62,200 foreign-born persons among the total population of 3.6 million people (1.73 percent), the largest amount born in Sweden (ca. 17,500). The most important non-Western countries and continents of birth listed were Hungary (1358), Poland (1032), the Soviet-Union (954), Africa (830), China (481), and "rest of Asia" (483). The number of resident aliens was ca. 25,800 (0.72 percent), with the largest groups coming from Sweden (ca. 4,300) and Denmark (ca 8,000). Again only one non-Western country was listed, Poland (616 persons).[163]

In 1966–1970, net immigration was at 2,476 persons, 1,709 of them from Western Europe. The largest non-European contingent was from the U.S. (638 persons). Net immigration from Africa was 103, and from Asia 188.[164] In 1971–1975, net immigration was at 4,822 persons, 2,251 of them from Western Europe. The largest non-European contingent was from the U.S. (915 persons). Net immigration from Africa was 195, and from Asia 1,296, with over half of them coming from Pakistan.[165] In 1984, net immigration was at 5,175 persons. The largest contingents were from the U.K. (735), Sweden (267), Germany (257), Poland (228), France (212), and Denmark (204). Africa in total was at 250, Asia in total at 2017, with the largest contingents coming from Pakistan (467), Vietnam (323), and South Korea (298). The U.S. was represented with 175 immigrants, and Colombia with 133. In 2007, net immigration was at ca. 31,100 persons from non-Western countries, and ca. 8,600 from Western countries.[166] In 2016, net immigration was at ca. 27,000 persons from non-Western countries, and negative by about 130 for Western countries.[167]

162. See Bjerve, "Folketellingen 1. Desember 1950."

163. See Bjerve, "Folketellingen 1960."

164. See Sørensen, *Inn- og Utvandring*.

165. See Sørensen, *Inn- og Utvandring*.

166. See "Immigration, Emigration and Net Migration, by Citizenship 2007K1–2020K1," *Statbank Population*.

167. See "Immigration, Emigration and Net Migration, by Citizenship

In 1984, there were a total of almost 98,000 foreigners among the permanent residents of Norway of 4.14 million people (that is, 2.37 percent). Among them were almost 61,000 Europeans, with Danes (ca. 15,000), Brits (ca. 11,700), and Swedes (ca. 9,700) forming the largest contingents. Asians were at about 19,000, with Pakistanis (ca. 8,000) and Vietnamese (ca. 5,000) being the most important groups. Also U.S. citizens formed a sizeable contingent, with just over 10,000 persons.[168] In 1990, ca. 195,000 people (that is, 4.6 percent) out of a total population of 4.233 million were foreign-born.[169] In 2000, according to OECD data, roughly 290,000 people (that is, 6.5 percent) out of a total population of 4.478 million were foreign-born,[170]

In 2017, according to OECD data, almost 800,000 people (that is, 15.2 percent) out of a total population of 5.258 million were foreign-born.[171]

The statistics for the development of the Muslim population look as follows:[172] Estimates of the Muslim population increased from 5,000 or 0.13 percent in 1971, to 50,000 or 1.2 percent in 1991. According to official statistics, the Muslim population changed from 76,621 or 1.69 percent in 2005, to 72,023 or 1.59 percent in 2006, to 79,068 or 1.75 percent in 2007, to 83,684 or 1.85 percent in 2008, to 92,744 or 2.05 percent in 2009. According to Pew Research, 5.7 percent of the population were Muslims in 2016.[173]

As far as future expectations are concerned, the abstract of the most comprehensive recent study on economic developments contains the following passage dealing with demographic aspects, based on two possible scenarios, a "realistic" migration scenario and a zero-migration scenario:

> From the present 5.3 million, realistic migration causes the Norwegian population to pass nearly 8.5 million in 2100, which is nearly twice the 2100-level in the 0-scenario. From 2016 till 2100 the population share of residents with background from countries outside the EEA, North-America, Australia and New

2007K1–2020K1," *Statbank Population.*

168. See Øien, "Folkemengdens Bevegelse 1984."

169. See "Migration Profiles: Norway," *UNICEF.*

170. See "Stocks of Foreign-Born Population in OECD Countries," *OECD Data.*

171. See "Stocks of Foreign-Born Population in OECD Countries," *OECD Data.*

172. See Kettani, "Muslim Population," 161.

173. See Hackett, "5 Facts."

Zealand grows steadily from 10 to 29 percent, whereas the share of natives with at least one parent born in Norway declines from 83 to 64 percent.[174]

3.3. Brief Summary

The data presented in this chapter show that large-scale immigration has been taking place in all of the countries that were surveyed in recent years, with an accelerating increase in the most recent past in terms of the ratio of people with a foreign background. This increase is even more accentuated than the numbers presented above indicate.[175] Since many of the people with immigration background are citizens of the respective states, statistics based on citizenship will not necessarily reflect these trends with any accuracy. Much more telling are visual impressions or name statistics. As far as the former are concerned, no one wandering the streets of any major city in western Europe can fail to see the change in the cultural-ethnic composition that has taken place during the last decades.[176] Sometimes, these changes are visible also in rural areas. As far as name statistics are concerned, it is especially the spread of various spellings of the name Muhammad, particularly among new-born male children, that catches the eye, dominating the lists of names of (new-born) male children in several parts of Europe.[177] In the context of this investigation the question is not whether or in what ways these changes are desirable or problematic; the focus here is only on the fact that these changes do take place.

174. Holmøy and Strøm, "Betydningen."

175. It can be expected that the implementation of the Global Compact for Migration (formally adopted by the United Nations General Assembly on December 19, 2018) will accelerate the speed and scale of demographic transformation through immigration into Western countries even more.

176. A simple way to watch the development without actually travelling is (for example) to do searches on Google Maps, entering search terms like "mosque near xy" or "kebab near xy" and count the usually high number of matches.

177. See, e.g., Sonnad, "England Says." This article is interesting because it points to possible distortions in official statistics, in this case by not adding the various spellings of the name Muhammad. According to Wikipedia, the name Mohamed ranked seventh in Belgium in 2012, and in the Brussels-Capital Region even second; see "List of Most Popular Given Names," *Wikipedia*. According to the *Berliner Zeitung* (May 2, 2019), Mohammed was the most popular name for new-born male children in Berlin in 2018 (see "Namen-Ranking 2018: Mohammed beliebtester Erstname in Berlin").

4. ECONOMIC ASPECTS

4.1. Introduction

The purpose of this section is not to present a comprehensive picture of the economic dimensions of mass-(im)migration to the Western world. The issues are much too complex for such an undertaking.[178] Also, apart from a limited number of instances, this section will not present findings that have not been pointed out before. Rather, it tries to map the field by identifying the main factors at play, and also by presenting some of the salient figures concerning which there is a relatively broad consensus among specialists. In addition, this section will help to rectify one-sided or simplistic perceptions of the economic aspects of mass-(im)migration.[179]

As far as the countries of destination are concerned, data available for the U.S., Germany, and Norway will be studied in some detail. Major considerations for the choice of these three countries are: 1) some familiarity with the situation in these countries based on years-long personal observations by the current writer; and 2) the wish to present cases that

178. One of the complicating factors when it comes to assess the economic aspects of mass-migration are environmental costs. These are routinely not factored in into any of the investigations dealing with economic facets of migration.

179. Three—randomly chosen, but representative—examples are the following ones.

1) Some economists (who subscribe to a globalist worldview) claim that the elimination of policy barriers to the international movement of labor will automatically maximize global wealth; see, e.g., Leeson and Gochenour, "The Economic Effects," 30.

2) Quite widespread is the claim that immigration is necessary to absorb the negative economic effects—especially related to the welfare system (pensions, health care)—of low birth rates in Western countries; see, e.g., Carroll, *Christians*, 22, 30; Kerwin, "The Natural Rights," 198. Somewhat more generally, Campese asserts that, "more immigration . . . is what the labor market and the economy need" ("¿Cuantos Más?" 281); this view is echoed by Kerwin, who states: "In the 1990s, the foreign-born filled 47 percent of the new jobs created. Between 2000 and the first four months of 2004, they constituted 60 percent of the growth in the U.S. workforce. The U.S. economy needs immigrants" ("The Natural Rights," 197–198). See also "Immigration 2009," National Realities.

3) It is frequently claimed that immigrants primarily come to work at jobs that no one else wants; see, e.g., Groody and Campese, "Preface," xx. According to a related argument, immigrants are confined to economic activities rejected by nationals; see, e.g., Battistella, "Migration," 178. See also Campese, who claims that immigrants are the ones "who perform the 3-D jobs—dirty, demanding, and dangerous" ("¿Cuantos Más?" 288). The data presented in this section show that none of these assumptions stands the test of scrutiny.

are reflective of (some of) the major variations that can be found in the current situation in the West.

The overall economic picture presented in this study is likely to be subject to considerable changes in the very near future.[180] The economic (and social) consequences of the Covid-19 crisis (and especially the consequences of the lockdowns implemented in a large number of countries) will affect the economic data of all the countries that are considered in this study—both as destination and as sending countries—dramatically. The same can be said with a view to radical measures under way to fight climate change, and those related to the implementation of the Global Compact for Migration. Moreover, the debt crisis lingering over most Western countries is likely to also produce enormous economic (and social) disruptions. In addition, there are unpredictable political developments that also will change the picture.

It is important to note that economic factors, even if they must be given due weight, cannot in themselves fully explain population movements, in isolation from the social and cultural context in which they take place.[181] In addition, economic reasons for migration are complex in the sense that not only the improvement of the economic situation in absolute terms aspired to by migrants and their sending households, but also in relative terms compared to other households may cause migration.[182]

4.2. Basic Economic Parameters

a) Distinctions must be made between the *national GDP* and an increase or decrease in *GDP per capita*, and between a *quantitative* and a *qualitative* growth of the economy (growth in breadth vs. growth in depth) of a country (or a district, town, etc.). The two distinctions are closely interconnected. The quantitative growth of an economy is—apart from rising production as a consequence of technological progress or other means by which productivity can be enhanced—mostly driven by an increase in population numbers. The growth of construction related industries is one of the most

180. The following list is, of course, not meant to be exhaustive.

181. See Brettell and Hollifield, "Migration Theory," 7; see also Brettell, "Theorizing Migration," 125. Schmitter Heisler notes that, "economic behavior is shaped by the overarching social structures in which people are embedded" ("The Sociology," 88).

182. See Brettell and Hollifield, "Migration Theory," 11.

important quantitative phenomena. National GDP will also grow as a consequence of population growth,[183] unless major parts of the added population are not integrated into the workforce. An increase in the GDP per capita, on the other hand, will in most circumstances only occur if there is also a qualitative dimension to the growth of the economy, like the development of industries or services that go beyond the basic necessities of food, clothing, and housing, and are competitive also on the international market.

Quantitative and qualitative growth can be positively interconnected. For example, an industry may be dependent on a critical mass to develop or use new technologies, which in turn will increase GDP.[184] On the other hand, growth in the size and scale of an economy does not in itself reduce or increase the productivity of labor and capital.[185]

For a sustained increase of GDP per capita, besides factors of the institutional framework, like (for example) the protection of property rights, raising productivity (especially as a result of technological progress) and the growth of capital are necessary.[186]

b) Distinctions also need to be made between tax-payer supported workplaces and jobs created in and by the free market, as well as between work that generates real surplus through the production of goods or the execution of services that bring in capital from outside the national economy, and work for which this is not the case. In those instances where work is funded by taxes or money is shifted from one taxpayer to the other within the confines of the national economy without new products being created, there is no growth in terms of the addition of new values. On the other hand, tax-funded work in a well-organized system will (at least in many cases) contribute to the functioning of the economy as a whole *indirectly*, through the provision of security, health, education, etc.—all necessary preconditions also for the potential real in-depth growth of an economy. The same will be true for many of the services provided

---

183. Increases in the supply of labor mean (under normal circumstances) that more goods and services are produced, which raises GDP (see, e.g., Smith and Edmonston, *The New Americans*, 137).

184. See Smith and Edmonston, *The New Americans*, 150.

185. See Smith and Edmonston, *The New Americans*, 150.

186. See Smith and Edmonston, *The New Americans*, 160.

by private enterprises. It remains, however, the case that in almost all economies jobs exist that do not contribute in any positive way to an economy other than enabling the respective workers to pay taxes and not be dependent on the welfare subsidies provided by the state.

c) Immigration has long-term economic impacts in the receiving societies only if the immigrants and their descendants do not converge toward the general outlook of the native population in terms of education, labor, and consumption preferences.[187]

4.3. Main Challenges in Assessing the Economic Impact of Migration

a) Due to the complexity of economic macro-systems, one has to admit that most observations concerning the economic results of migration need to be understood as approximative and open to constant change. Even sophisticated models can ultimately not factor in all elements at play. The situation is exacerbated by the fact that the relevant data are sometimes difficult to come by, if they are gathered by the respective state authorities (or other organizations) at all. All of this does not mean, however, that it is not possible to observe trends and tendencies, and in some restricted areas even hard data are available.

b) The economic impacts of migration are constantly changing, depending on the variation of the major factors involved, such as the makeup of the immigrant population, changes in the legal framework that affects the economy, general economic trends developing independently of migration, etc.

c) Based on the differences in the outlook of the immigrant population, the legal regulations affecting economic activities, the legal regulations affecting the rights of immigrants (including state benefits available to them),[188] and the general economic condition of a

187. See Smith and Edmonston, *The New Americans*, 158. "In the extreme case in which immigrant descendants never assimilate and have a higher rate of natural increase, the nation to which they have immigrated eventually takes on the same economic characteristics as the one from which they came" (Smith and Edmonston, *The New Americans*, 158 n. 25).

188. Especially health care, education, and unemployment insurance/payments.

country, the economic impacts of migration will in many respects look very differently in various countries of destination (and in fact in many cases also in various parts of a specific country). This is one of the reasons why three specific cases will be studied in this section.

d) According to general economic theory, a net benefit of immigration is possible, but only on a small scale.[189]

e) Immigration is most beneficial economically when there is little direct competition between native-born workers and immigrants,[190] and in cases in which the added workforce pours heavily into export-intensive industries.[191] When there is competition, it will usually lead to either immigrants taking away jobs from native-born residents and reducing their wages,[192] or to high unemployment rates among immigrants. While the wage losses may have positive effects on the economic system as a whole, higher unemployment—whether among native-born workers or immigrants—is always a drain on the economy.[193]

f) It must be taken into account that the comparative[194] lack of knowledge of the culture of a host country in general and its labor market in particular among immigrants, as well as the limits in locally available networks and the lack of fluency in the local language, all constitute economically negative factors, even if they are difficult to quantify. This implies "that the immigrant's human capital has a lower value in the host country than at home."[195] On the other hand, it can be observed that in some cases children of immigrants outperform children of natives, which can have positive effects for the economy.[196]

g) Many goods that are produced by immigrant workers could be imported through international trade, with the same effect of allowing

189. See Hatton and Williamson, *Global Migration*, 290.

190. See, e.g., Smith and Edmonston, *The New Americans*, 141. The downside of this observation is that differences between immigrants and native citizens are often connected to social and cultural factors that make integration more difficult.

191. See Smith and Edmonston, *The New Americans*, 148.

192. See, e.g., Borjas, "Yes, Immigration Hurts."

193. Cf. Hatton and Williamson, *Global Migration*, 290–91.

194. In comparison to the native population.

195. Hatton and Williamson, *Global Migration*, 315.

196. See Hatton and Williamson, *Global Migration*, 316.

a country to specialize in its production and still consume goods that lie outside the frame of what is produced internally.[197] To the degree that this is the case, it appears that free trade is a better solution not only in terms of the avoidance of the social side-effects of migration, but also in economic terms, because the fiscal problems of immigration can be avoided in this way and the degree of competition for native workers is lower or competition is easier to escape by moving to working in nontraded goods and services.[198]

h) As far as the economic—and in fact also the moral—dimensions of immigration are concerned, migration to Western countries is often seen as a migration from poor countries to rich countries. While there is, of course, a *prima facie* justification for such a view, it is nevertheless in need of some qualification: Most Western countries have tremendous amounts of debts on the national and the communal levels,[199] and in many cases also the private households are indebted, on top of the public deficits. This means that in reality the current wealth is borrowed from future generations, and prone to disappear in the near future in many countries. One also has to bear in mind that there is not only a dividing line between rich and poor countries, but also between rich and poor individuals in every country. This observation is important not only in moral terms, but also on the strictly economic level, in the two following ways in particular: It is generally not the poorest people from the sending countries that are able to migrate to the West;[200] and in the Western countries of destination, it is generally the poorest among the native population who are hit hardest by immigration.

197. See Smith and Edmonston, *The New Americans*, 146. Of course, there are goods, and especially services, that are not commutable in this way.

198. See Smith and Edmonston, *The New Americans*, 147.

199. Exceptions exist, but are rare; most notable among them are Norway and Monaco. Norway technically does have yearly deficits in the state budget; but they can be covered in actuality by the oil fund.

200. See, e.g., Amstutz, *Just Immigration*, 84. The situation is, however, complex. For example, if the country of origin is close enough to the country of destination, migration costs are lower, which makes migration more attractive and more accessible for poorer people. This is the case, for instance, for Mexico, Central America, and the Caribbean with respect to the U.S., as opposed, for instance, for Iraq or Nigeria with respect to Europe. It is interesting to observe that poverty rates and mobility rates are not congruent within the European Union (see, e.g., Guild, *Security*, 144).

i) Migration within the European Union is of a special nature on most accounts.[201] Because the present study focuses on questions related to mass-migration from countries outside of the West (including the eastern parts of the European Union), the topic of inner-EU migration will not be considered here.[202]

j) There are also migratory movements from developed to developing countries, for example in the context of ventures of multinational companies. The numbers of persons involved in such movements are, however, considerably lower than those occurring in the reverse direction, and because of the special focus of this study will not be investigated here.

k) It is important to take into account the economic effects of migration not only in the societies of the receiving countries, but also in the societies of the sending countries.

4.4. Answering the Question of the Economic Impact of Migration: Identifying the Main Trends

a) As far as *sending countries* are concerned, there is a mixture of positive and negative effects in strictly economic terms: On the *positive* side (from the perspective of the sending countries) are the remittances sent by the emigrants who succeed in earning enough in their host countries to send back part of their income to the members of the families who stay in the countries of origin. The primary beneficiaries are the direct recipients of these remittances, but positive effects on the broader community can normally be expected as well. The number of countries where remittances amount to double percentages of GDP is limited to mostly smaller countries; the highest numbers can be found (as of 2005) in Honduras and Lebanon, where remittances are (or rather: were) just over a fifth of the GDP.[203]

---

201. Its extent is relatively small (in the low digit percentages; see, e.g., Guild, *Security*, 142). Poles and Romanians are those who move most within the EU for work purposes in absolute numbers, Greeks, Lithuanians, and Latvians in relative numbers (see, e.g., Guild, *Security*, 143–44).

202. It is interesting to observe that the EU treats inner-EU migration and immigration from non-EU countries in markedly different ways (see, e.g., Guild, *Security*, 135).

203. See Guild, *Security*, 139 (OECD numbers for 2005). The statistics look

On the other hand, in countries like Mexico and Nigeria that have
the largest numbers of citizens working abroad, the percentage of
remittances is (or: was) only between 2 and 3 percent of GDP.[204]
Remittances tend to be higher when migration is only temporary.[205]
If they are used to larger extents to finance further emigration, their
positive impact on the economy of the home country decreases.[206]

One of the problems of remittances is their fluctuation according to changes in the economies of the countries in which the
migrants work.[207] In addition, the "presence of hard currency [in
the sending countries] has made prices rise and the cost of land
go up,"[208] among other economic disturbances, like the economic
dependency on migration or the diffusion of consumerism.[209]

b) On the *negative* side of the effects of migration for sending countries, one of the major issues is what is called "brain-drain," the loss
of social capital as a consequence of the emigration of people who
could otherwise make positive contributions to the development
and well-being of their places of origin.[210] Numbers concerning

somewhat differently for the mid-1990s: Yemen and Jordan were the two countries in
which remittances amounted to more than one fifth of GDP, followed by Jamaica and
El Salvador, where they amounted to just over 11 percent (see Hatton and Williamson,
Global Migration, 335).

204. See Guild, *Security*, 139 (OECD numbers for 2005). In the mid-1990s, the
highest remittances in terms of absolute numbers are found in India, followed by
Mexico and Egypt; but in the case of India, these remittances amounted to only 2.17
percent of GDP, and in Mexico only to 1.28 percent (see Hatton and Williamson,
Global Migration, 335).

Rodríguez is an example of those who do not describe the situation in accurate
terms. He claims that, "The remittances they send tend to be the most important and
the most reliable income sources for our economies, especially in countries like El
Salvador, Nicaragua, Guatemala, Mexico, and Honduras" ("A Witness," xii).

205. See Hatton and Williamson, *Global Migration*, 336.

206. See Hatton and Williamson, *Global Migration*, 336.

207. See, e.g., Carroll, *Christians*, 31.

208. Carroll, *Christians*, 31.

209. See Brettell, "Theorizing Migration," 119.

210. See, e.g., Guild, *Security*, 134. One of the negative effects of the emigration
of highly educated people can be a general increase in unemployment (see Leeson
and Gochenour, "The Economic Effects," 23). High education in the country of origin
does not always translate into high-level jobs in the countries of destination, because
(among other factors) diplomas issued by the countries of origin may not be recognized in the countries of destination (cf. Guild, *Security*, 139).

this effect vary from country to country and seem most serious in smaller countries, especially islands.[211] But also in a large country such as Nigeria, for example, only 16 percent of the emigrants have only primary education, while 54.7 percent have tertiary education.[212] According to an OECD statistical overview for 1990, there were fifteen out of sixty-one poor countries in which more than 20 percent of the persons with tertiary education emigrated, six of them with emigration rates of even more than 50 percent for persons with tertiary education (Algeria, Tunisia, Jamaica, Trinidad and Tobago, Guyana). In all of these fifteen countries, with the exception of El Salvador, the ratio of the highly educated emigrants to the total number of emigrants of the respective country was on average about twenty to one.[213] There are clear losses for the sending countries in such circumstances, and the losses are severely compounded by the fact that in all those countries persons with tertiary education would constitute only between 3 and less than 1 percent of the population.[214]

On the other hand, there are various mitigating factors. For example, the existence of diasporas may facilitate transfer of knowledge back into the countries of origin.[215] In addition, the remittances sent back to the countries of origin may compensate for the losses of brain-drain in some cases.[216] In those cases—as can be observed often in the Philippines—in which emigrants return to their country of origin, the temporary brain drain may turn into a brain gain.[217] However, as far as students are concerned, there is a trend among them to be less likely to return home the more they have invested

---

211. See, e.g., Guild, *Security*, 137.

212. See Guild, *Security*, 138–39.

213. See Hatton and Williamson, *Global Migration*, 328–30.

214. See Hatton and Williamson, *Global Migration*, 328. A special case is Mexico: The level of emigration is quite high, but the relative numbers of emigrants with tertiary education is not far apart from the overall percentage of emigrants (see Hatton and Williamson, *Global Migration*, 330).

215. See Leeson and Gochenour, "The Economic Effects," 25.

216. See Hatton and Williamson, *Global Migration*, 336.

217. See Hatton and Williamson, *Global Migration*, 328, 330. The returnees will in many cases not only be able to promote the economic development of a country, but also to contribute to positive societal changes in general.

in their education in the host country.[218] The drain effect seems to be mitigated to some degree also by the fact the skill-scarcity "also provides an incentive for others to acquire skills and education, replacing those who have left. Better emigration opportunities for the highly skilled raises the expected total return to skills."[219] "[G]reater numbers of highly educated emigrants living abroad offer incentives to younger cohorts to complete secondary education at home."[220] Moreover, higher investment in education by top high school students in preparation for emigration will have positive effects on the home country—effects that are intensified if these people ultimately decide not to emigrate.[221] On the other hand, skills learned abroad may not be applicable in the different circumstances of the home country.[222]

There is also a combination of short-term positive and long-term negative effects: While the emigration of parts of the workforce alleviates short-term economic pressure, this also diminishes the need for economic (and indeed, other) reforms which in the long run might have improved the situation in the sending countries.[223]

c) Mass-migration proves not to be an efficient tool to combat poverty on a global level. In most of the sending countries, population growth eliminates possible economic effects of migration in the course of a very short period.[224]

218. See Hatton and Williamson, *Global Migration*, 332.

219. Hatton and Williamson, *Global Migration*, 331. It is a matter of debate how the two conflicting effects can be weighed against each other (see Hatton and Williamson, *Global Migration*, 331).

220. Hatton and Williamson, *Global Migration*, 332.

221. See Leeson and Gochenour, "The Economic Effects," 22–23.

222. See Brettell, "Theorizing Migration," 119.

223. See, e.g., Leeson and Gochenour, "The Economic Effects," 27; Amstutz, *Just Immigration*, 84. In theory, the implicit vote cast through emigration against the existing order may cause authorities to change policies (see Leeson and Gochenor, "The Economic Effects," 25–26); this seems, however, not to be the case in most instances. There may be examples, however, where popular pressure on authorities increased, because citizens of a state were in a position to compare the emigrants' life conditions with those prevailing in the country, such as Moldova in 2009 (see Leeson and Gochenor, "The Economic Effects," 26).

224. For details see "Immigration, World Poverty and Gumballs," *NumbersUSA.com*. The numbers presented in this clip deal with immigration into the U.S., but can be taken as representative for immigration into Western states generally.

Also relevant is the observation that from an economical point of view, aid offered to refugees in locations close to their places of origin is much more efficient than help offered through immigration. One dollar spent for a refugee close to the place of his or her origin is in its effect about equal to seven or thirty, or perhaps even seventy dollars spent for the same recipient in the context of the process of immigration.[225]

d) In the *countries of destination*, mass-immigration is economically negative when a large percentage of the immigrants cannot be integrated into the labor force, but rather are dependent on state-funded means of support. Tendentially, this is the case in the current situation in European countries that have a high proportion of immigrants from Africa and the Middle-East. The problem is aggravated by the fact that there seems to be a correlation between the generosity of a country's welfare system and its attractiveness to persons who are least likely to succeed in the labor market.[226] On the other hand, the economic consequences of mass-immigration look much more positive when a large percentage of the immigrants can be integrated into the workforce, such as in the U.S.

e) Generally, *skilled* immigration is beneficial for the net economy of the receiving country,[227] even though those workers of the native population who are immediate competitors to the immigrants may lose.[228] However, the numbers of people affected are usually relatively low, and because of the education and skills of the affected workers, they will usually be able to find other employment.

f) In the current situation, as far as mass-migration movements to the West are concerned, the majority or the immigrants are not

225. For the general principle see, e.g., von Wachter, "Die Öffnung der Grenzen ist unmoralisch," 16–18. Estimates concerning the exact ratio vary and are of course dependent on the specific circumstances.

226. See Hatton and Williamson, *Global Migration*, 327. It is, however, a matter of debate how strong this correlation really is (see Hatton and Williamson, *Global Migration*, 327).

227. See Borjas, "Yes, Immigration Hurts;" Guild, *Security*, 134; Hatton and Williamson, *Global Migration*, 311. It could be asked, however, how the numbers would look in comparison if the positions had been created by or filled with nonimmigrant workers.

228. See, e.g., Smith and Edmonston, *The New Americans*, 138, 170.

well-educated.[229] As a consequence, to the degree that they find employment, they are competitors for the lower strata of the native population, for whom mass-immigration has negative economic effects, through the loss of jobs and the decrease of salaries.[230] To the degree that the immigrants need to be supported by state subsidies, it is the middle class of the receiving societies that has to carry most of the burden through taxation; but lower classes will suffer as well because of the fact that less public means will be available for them. Regardless of whether the mostly unskilled immigrants are integrated into the workforce or not, their presence is an economic problem for the members of the lower classes of the native population in terms of shortages on the housing market.

g) On the other hand, low-skill immigration has a positive effect on native-born residents with lower skills in the longer term insofar as they are forced to seek higher education or to move to more productive industries.[231] It is also assumed that in response to the relative decrease of the price of unskilled labor, additional capital flows to that economy, which in turn benefits the wage rates and employment of native workers.[232] Moreover, prices for goods and services produced by low-skilled immigrants will drop, which is—at least potentially—beneficial for all native citizens. The increase in numbers of low-skilled workers often has beneficial consequences for domestic skilled labor, because an increase in the number of production workers leads to an augmented demand for supervisors, whose wages will rise.[233] Furthermore, immigration of low-skilled workers allows a destination country to use domestic labor more productively, specializing in producing goods in which the respective nation is more efficient.[234]

---

229. Which is not to deny that immigration by well-educated people exists as well, generally more importantly in the U.S. (and Australia) than in Europe.

230. See, e.g., Leeson and Gochenour, "The Economic Effects," 14; Smith and Edmonston, *The New Americans*, 137, 139, 157.

231. See Smith and Edmonston, *The New Americans*, 144; cf. Hatton and Williamson, *Global Migration*, 291.

232. See Leeson and Gochenour, "The Economic Effects," 15.

233. See Smith and Edmonston, *The New Americans*, 137.

234. See Smith and Edmonston, *The New Americans*, 144.

h) For persons who migrate to Western countries from outside the West, the welfare gains are on average considerable.[235]

i) In the current situation, in Europe more markedly than in the U.S., mass-immigration leads to an increase in national GDP rather than in GDP per capita, and to a quantitative rather than a qualitative growth of the economy.[236]

j) Taking into consideration experiences not just in the last couple of years, but over a longer period, it is evident that there is no intrinsic connection between growth of GDP per capita and immigration. A comparison between two different geographical areas proves the point: The U.S. and Canada are examples of growing economies over an extended period of time where *immigration* was important, while the Scandinavian countries experienced similar growth rates in the post-World War II period with relatively high levels of *emigration*.[237]

k) Claims that mass-immigration does not hurt the economy or is even beneficial for the economy of a specific country of destination can not be verified, since it is not clear how things would have developed without the mass-immigration taking place.

4.5. Special Case Studies: U.S., Germany, Norway

4.5.1. U.S.[238]

The U.S. has seen immigration throughout most of its history, and there is broad agreement that predominantly it has been a net benefit for the country in economic terms. This has to do with the circumstances—prevailing into the beginning of the twentieth century—in which immigration took place: availability of land and capital, high tariffs for imports,

235. See Leeson and Gochenour, "The Economic Effects," 12.

236. As mentioned above, the growth of construction related industries is one of the most important quantitative phenomena. National GDP will grow as a consequence of population growth, unless major parts of the added population are not integrated into the workforce.

237. See Smith and Edmonston, *The New Americans*, 154–55.

238. For a brief description of the two main opposing views on the economic effect of Hispanic immigration see Carroll, *Christians*, 27–30.

combined with shortage of labor,[239] and an immigration population who in the vast majority of cases joined the workforce immediately after arriving to the shores, and the fact that state benefits did not exist or were not available to them.

There are, however, periods in which things looked more complicated. Towards the end of the nineteenth century and onward immigration posed serious economic problems. Because of changing macro-economic parameters immigrants in many cases displaced native-born workers and wage-growth was inhibited;[240] also land prices increased.[241] This led to severe restrictions in the admittance of immigrants in 1921 and onward.[242] Until 1965, immigration continued to be restricted to a considerable degree.[243] During this period, American workers got richer, income inequalities decreased, and unemployment was low for the most part.[244] By keeping work supply down, wages tended to be higher.[245]

Things changed radically from then on. In 1965, Congress passed the *Immigration and Nationality Act Amendments*. Numerical quotas were replaced by a system granting preference for relatives of U.S. citizens and of Legal Permanent Residents. One of the major changes was the admission of non-European immigrants to degrees never previously

239. See, e.g., Rubenstein, "The Negative Economic Impact," 1.

240. See Hatton and Williamson, *Global Migration*, 305; Rubenstein, "The Negative Economic Impact," 1.

241. See Hatton and Williamson, *Global Migration*, 306.

242. In 1921, Congress passed the Emergency Quota Act, which restricted the number of immigrants from any country annually to 3 percent of the number of residents from that same country living in the U.S., based on the numbers of the U.S. Census of 1910. In effect, this put quite drastic numerical limits on immigration, and it also meant that people from northern European countries had higher quotas than people from eastern and southern European countries, as well as non-European countries (though they were no limits on immigration from Latin America and the act did not apply to Asian countries listed in the Immigration Act of 1917). New legislation was passed in 1924, cutting immigration to 160,000 persons per year (see Rubenstein, "The Negative Economic Impact," 1; according to Huntington [*Who Are We?* 57], the ceiling was 150,000 per year). In effect, immigration was down to ca. 50,000 persons per year by the end of the 1920s (see Rubenstein, "The Negative Economic Impact," 1). During the 1930s, a total of about 500,000 persons immigrated to the U.S., in the 1940s about one million (including World War II refugees; see Rubenstein, "The Negative Economic Impact," 1).

243. See, e.g., Carroll, *Christians*, 10–11.

244. See Rubenstein, "The Negative Economic Impact," 1.

245. See, e.g., Xie, "The Effects of Immigration Quotas," 1.

seen in U.S. history. The number of Legal Permanent Residents admitted to the U.S. rose to an annual number of about 600,000 in 1988, soared to almost two million at the beginning of 1991, and has remained relatively stable at an annual average of a little over one million since 1992.[246] Since 1965, around 35.2 million persons were granted Legal Permanent Resident status.[247]

Whether immigration in the last couple of decades has been an economic net benefit to the country is a matter of dispute. The majority view is that it has in fact been a net benefit for the country as a whole, though only very modestly.[248] What is clear is that there are both economic winners and losers of the immigration that took place in the last couple of decades: Those who profit most from immigration are the immigrants themselves and American employers. Employers gain, because sales and profits grow, whereas labor costs fall.[249] Also upper-income natives who hold disproportionally high shares of capital gains, stock options, etc., benefit from mass-immigration.[250] They also gain because they are consumers of goods and services provided by immigrants at relatively lower rates, like, e.g., house-cleaning and private child-care.[251] Immigrants who enter the labor force almost always win, because they normally earn more than in their country of origin.[252] On the other hand, there are those who lose. Those suffering most are Americans with low skills and education,

246. See   https://www.migrationpolicy.org/programs/data-hub/charts/Annual-Number-of-US-Legal-Permanent-Residents [accessed Oct 7, 2019].

247. See Rubenstein, "The Negative Economic Impact," 2.

248. See, e.g., Leeson and Gochenour, "The Economic Effects," 21; Smith and Edmonston, *The New Americans*, 135, 152–53, 171. According to Borjas, the immigration surplus of 2013 was about $35 billion ($437 billion gain for employers, vs. $402 billion wage loss for native workers), which is about 0.24 percent of GDP; see Borjas, "Immigration and the American Worker," 20; according to Hatton and Williamson, the average net gain in recent years was at most 0.1 percent of GDP (see *Global Migration*, 303). It is argued that in absolute numbers the possible migration net gain is not so low in absolute numbers, especially since there are not many other public policies that yield the same amount of gain (so Smith and Edmonston, *The New Americans*, 152).

249. See, e.g., Borjas, "Yes, Immigration Hurts;" Rubenstein, "The Negative Economic Impact," 9.

250. See Rubenstein, "The Negative Economic Impact," 10.

251. See Smith and Edmonston, *The New Americans*, 144.

252. See, e.g., Borjas, "Yes, Immigration Hurts"; Rubenstein, "The Negative Economic Impact," 9–10. Of course, exceptions exist, especially in cases where immigration was not primarily motivated by economic concerns (cf., e.g., Smith and Edmonston, *The New Americans*, 136).

for whom the majority of the immigrants are direct competitors. Rising unemployment rates and wage losses are the most important negative consequences for the lower skilled or lower educated Americans.[253] On the other hand, native-born workers who do not directly compete with foreign workers on the labor market may benefit from immigration.[254] It is, however, a matter of debate whether this is really the case.[255] High-skill immigration also lowered the wage of competing native workers.[256] According to a number of scholars, the mass-immigration that has taken place in the last decades has exacerbated income inequality.[257] The available evidence clearly points in this direction; the question is, however,

253. See, e.g., Borjas, "Yes, Immigration Hurts;" Hatton and Williamson, *Global Migration*, 295–96; Leeson and Gochenour, "The Economic Effects," 17; Rubenstein, "The Negative Economic Impact," 3–5; Wax and Richwine, "Low-Skill Immigration." Cf. also Alan Greenspan's remarks in a 2009 hearing before the Senate Immigration Subcommittee (see https://www.judiciary.senate.gov/imo/media/doc/greenspan_testimony_04_30_09.pdf [accessed Feb 15, 2020]). The size of these impacts is a matter of debate (cf., e.g., Rubenstein, "The Negative Economic Impact," 3; Leeson and Gochenour, "The Economic Effects," 20–21 [arguing for little effect]). Surveys of results presented in various studies can be found in Leeson and Gochenour, "The Economic Effects," 17–19; Richwine, "An Abundance." It can ultimately only be measured on the national level (and over an extended period of time), because workers who lose their jobs as a consequence of immigration often move to other places within the U.S. (or because specific places that used to have many openings—as a consequence of previous waves of immigration—have stopped being available as alternative destinations, without the figures for unemployment going up in the areas where immigrants from outside the U.S. have found employment). Real unemployment numbers are difficult to assess, because many unemployed (whether previously employed or not) do not register as job-seekers, and statistics do normally not clarify whether persons working only part-time do so voluntarily or not. In any event, the fact that immigrants are more likely to participate in the workforce than native-born Americans points to negative job-effects for American workers caused by immigration (see https://stats.oecd.org/Index.aspx?DataSetCode=MIG [accessed Oct 7, 2019]).

It is sometimes proposed that the negative effects of mass-immigration on low-skilled American workers can be amended by redistributing income from those who gain (see, e.g., Smith and Edmonston, *The New Americans*, 140, 146). The problem is, however, that such redistribution would necessitate costly bureaucratic expansion, and that there are no realistic scenarios under which this is politically feasible (cf. Borjas, "Yes, Immigration Hurts."

254. See Rubenstein, "The Negative Economic Impact," 3.

255. See Rubenstein, "The Negative Economic Impact," 5–6.

256. At the same time, consumer prices tend to be reduced and corporate profits increased; see Bound et al., "Understanding the Economic Impact," 1.

257. See, e.g., Hatton and Williamson, *Global Migration*, 305; Rubenstein, "The Negative Economic Impact," 6.

how large the effect of immigration on income inequality is.[258] As far as GDP is concerned: While the national GDP rises when new immigrants are added to the labor force, GDP per capita is actually declining, because a vast number of immigrants earn less than natives.[259] It is also a problem for the U.S. economy as a whole that for the larger part immigrants do not work in export-intensive industries that benefit the national economy as a whole.[260]

Finally, a look at public finances: A study published in 1997 indicates that the current type of mass-immigration negatively impacts public finances, both on the federal, state, and local levels. According to those findings, the average immigrant household receives $13,326 per year in federal spending, while it pays only $10,644 in federal taxes.[261] The fiscal burden varies according to education: An immigrant high school dropout causes a net fiscal drain of $89,000 over the course of his or her lifetime, while for those with a high school degree (and no further education) the net drain amounts to $31,000. On the other hand, immigrants with more than a high school education contribute to the fiscus $105,000 on average.[262] In the year 2000, 19.7 percent of immigrant households received benefits from one or more public welfare programs, while only 13.3 percent of the native households did. At the same time immigration households received larger public education benefits and paid lower

258. According to a study published by the National Bureau of Economic Research investigating wage inequality between 1980 and 2000, only 5 percent of the rise in wage inequality can be related to immigration (see https://www.nber.org/digest/apr09/w14683.html [accessed Oct 7, 2019]). Even if this relatively low number is correct, it would still need to be assessed how much immigration contributes to the structural basis of income inequality, apart from its rise. It is also interesting to note that inequality decreased between 1947 and 1970, in a period of low immigration, and has increased since (see Johnston, "A Brief History"). It can also be observed that inequality is higher in states with high shares of foreign-born populations, such as New York and California, than in states with low immigration numbers (see Rubenstein, "The Negative Economic Impact," 7–8). The influence of immigration on income inequality has to do with the fact that immigrants themselves are overrepresented in the lower- and upper-income brackets (see Rubenstein, "The Negative Economic Impact," 8).

259. See Rubinstein, "The Negative Economic Impact," 8–9. It is evident that an increase in the number of persons who enter the workforce does in itself not rise the GDP per capita; otherwise, most countries in Africa, Latin America, and Asia would be much better off. The mere increase in population numbers, independent of the development of the workforce, is even farther removed from growth in GDP per capita.

260. See Smith and Edmonston, The New Americans, 148.

261. See Smith and Edmonston, The New Americans, 283.

262. See Smith and Edmonston, The New Americans, 334.

taxes.[263] According to another study, the foreign-born population cost the federal government $346 billion in 2007, which is about 13 percent of the federal expenses of that year, and about $9,100 per immigrant.[264] "State and local governments may suffer even more. Immigrants pay proportionately less state and local taxes than federal taxes, but consume services disproportionately funded by state and local taxes—especially social services and public education. Immigration also impacts spending on public infrastructure (roads, bridges, airports) and environmental protection programs. Hospitals, prisons, public school buildings, and mass transit facilities are also in short supply and deteriorating due, at least in part, to immigration-driven population growth."[265]

It can be observed that the economic assimilation rate of immigrants in comparison to native-born residents has fallen over the past decades.[266] This may well indicate that a certain degree of saturation has been reached, which implies that overall immigration in its current form is no longer economically as beneficial as it was in the past. This is at least true for the steadily increasing share of low-skilled immigration.[267] The problem is compounded by the fact that the children of immigrants tend to be overrepresented in the population with low education, which means that immigrants reduce the educational quality of the U.S. labor force.[268]

Here are some of the important numbers:

263. See Hatton and Williamson, *Global Migration*, 308.

264. See Rubenstein, "The Negative Economic Impact," 10. According to Borjas, the fiscal deficit of immigration is at least $50 billion per year (see "Yes, Immigration Hurts").

265. Rubenstein, "The Negative Economic Impact," 10. The fiscal burden on average nonimmigrant households is shared very unevenly across the U.S. California is estimated to exceed the national average by about ten times (see Hatton and Williamson, *Global Migration*, 308).

266. See Hatton and Williamson, *Global Migration*, 318.

267. See Hatton and Williamson, *Global Migration*, 319.

268. See Hatton and Williamson, *Global Migration*, 320. The situation is even worse among illegal immigrants, whose relative importance has increased in the past decades (see Hatton and Williamson, *Global Migration*, 321).

According to OECD data, almost 44 million people out of a total population of 325.7 million were foreign-born in 2017.[269] In the same year, the number of immigrants was 1.13 million persons.[270]

The most important group of immigrants in recent decades have been Mexicans. It is for the large part a low-skilled immigration (almost 70 percent have only primary education, while only about 6 percent have tertiary education).[271] 43.6 percent of the Mexican immigrants are employed in agriculture and industry, 37.4 percent in personal and social services.[272]

4.5.2. Germany

Post-war Germany has known forms of mass-immigration since about the middle of the 1960s, when—under some pressure from the side of the U.S. administration—Germany signed an agreement with Turkey that allowed many Turks to enter Germany as guest-workers. The vast majority of these immigrants became part of Germany's workforce. The same was true for other immigrants, with southern European countries being the most important region of origin. Under the circumstances prevailing for about two decades, immigrants were largely not a burden on public finances through the granting of direct state-subsidies, though the overall economic effect of mass-immigration to the German economy is a matter of debate.[273] The situation changed when legal regulations were introduced that allowed family reunification and when the status of guest-worker was abolished. As a consequence, immigration was no longer bound to the economic demands of Germany. From then on, and with increasing speed after further legal changes that made it easier to apply for asylum, the numbers of immigrants who are directly supported by state subsidies has grown considerably. This trend has reached new—and quite monumental—heights after the de-facto opening of the German borders for asylum-seekers in September 2015.

269. See "Stocks of Foreign-Born Population in OECD Countries," *OECD Data*.

270. See https://stats.oecd.org/Index.aspx?DataSetCode=MIG [accessed Oct 7, 2019].

271. See Guild, *Security*, 139.

272. See Guild, *Security*, 138.

273. See, e.g., Pischke and Velling, "Employment Effects of Immigration," 594–604.

Here are some of the numbers that are relevant for the understanding of the current situation:[274] The federal government of Germany set aside 93.6 billion Euros for the support of asylum-seekers/refugees for the period of 2016–2020. To this amount has to be added approximately the same amount that the states (*Bundesländer*) have to use for the same purpose. This means that around 40 billion Euros are spent annually for the support of new arrivals. The real costs, however, are not known, because it is not clear whether costs for new kindergartens, schools, or police forces, are included in these budgets or not.[275] Certainly not part of the budgets are, for example, costs for additional judges who have to deal with large amounts of court appeals against negative asylum decisions, or costs for the treatment of new diseases that are imported by new arrivals.[276] Perhaps numbers around 80 billion Euros per year are more realistic.[277] According to the federal government's (low) estimates, the costs that are covered by the German state (including the expenses for which the *Bundesländer* are responsible) are about 2,500 Euros per asylum-seeker each month. In the case of unaccompanied migrants who have not reached adulthood the costs are about 5,000 Euros per month. Both the *Institut der Deutschen Wirtschaft* and the *Institut für Wirtschaftsforschung*, however, estimate that the average state expenses for adult asylum-seekers are not 2,500 Euros per month, but more than 4,000 Euros.[278]

Because the majority of the new-arrivals will only be able to work in low-paid jobs or cannot be integrated into the labor force at all,[279] they will be net burdens to the German state for the whole of their lives. According to the financial expert Bernd Raffelhüschen, the average costs for those two million asylum-seekers/refugees who arrived between 2015

---

274. Germany's economy is also strongly affected by the immigration of citizens of other member states of the EU, especially from eastern and southern Europe. However, this aspect will not be investigated further because it falls outside the scope of the focus of this study.

275. Numbers are according to Bok, "Die Flüchtlingskosten."

276. The Kiel-based *Institut für Wirtschafsforschung* assumes that the yearly costs are closer to 55 billion than 40 billion Euros (see Bok, "Die Flüchtlingskosten").

277. Based on the estimates of the *Institut für Wirtschaftsforschung*; see Hans Heckel, "Wer soll das bezahlen?" *Preussische Allgemeine Zeitung* (Oct 14, 2017).

278. Numbers according to Hans Heckel, "Wer soll das bezahlen?."

279. Of the new-arrivals, 59 percent have no high school education. Only 13 percent are employed, mainly in low-paid jobs ("*Praktikant*," "*Hilfskraft*"); numbers are according to Bok, "Die Flüchtlingskosten."

and 2018 is about 450,000 Euros per person for the whole of his or her life, which amounts to about 900 billion in total—though the real costs might be higher.[280]

These numbers are relatively modest when set in comparison to Germany's GDP. According to www.statista.com, Germany's GDP in 2018 amounted to 3.344 trillion Euros.[281] This means that yearly expenses of 80 billion would account for not more than ca. 2.6 percent of Germany's GDP. Things look drastically different, however, if the 80 billion Euros are compared to the German federal budget for 2018, which amounted to 335.5 billion Euros.[282] 80 billion Euros is tantamount to almost 24 percent of the federal budget. It is, however, clear, that the budgets of the *Bundesländer* also need to be taken into account to get a more balanced picture. The expenses of the *Bundesländer* amounted to 374.613 billion Euros in 2018.[283] If the expenses of the federal government and the *Bundesländer* are combined, the total is 710.113 billion Euros, of which 80 billion is about 11 percent—still a considerable amount. In the same year, the official numbers for the debt of the German state amounted to 2.06 trillion Euros (ca. 61 percent of GDP).[284] Another interesting perspec-

---

280. Numbers are according to Bok, "Die Flüchtlingskosten." Already in 2000, for example, according to numbers presented by the OECD, labor participation rates were clearly higher among Germans (72.5 percent) as compared to immigrants (68.5 percent), and unemployment rates substantially higher among immigrants (6 percent) as compared to Germans (2.9 percent); see https://stats.oecd.org/Index. aspx?DataSetCode=MIG [accessed Oct 8, 2019].

There are, as one would expect in a debate that is politically sensitive, heated discussions about the net costs of the mass-immigration of asylum-seekers. Not rarely, certain interested parties try to "hide" some of the costs. An example are media reports in September 2019 about a decrease of the number of persons who receive state subsidies through the "*Asylbewerberleistungsgesetz*." While this observation is obviously true based on the official governmental data, the situation looks differently if one takes into consideration that two out of three asylum-seekers receive state support through the institute of *Hartz-IV*—which means that in fact most asylum-seekers have simply moved from one state support system to another one; see Brückner, "So rechnen Medien die Asylkosten klein." According to Ulfkotte ("Die verschwiegenen Kosten der Zuwanderung") already by the beginning of 2014 immigrants in Germany had received a trillion Euros more from tax-funded programs than they had paid in taxes themselves.

281. See   https://www.statista.com/statistics/295444/germany-gross-domestic-product/ [accessed May 30, 2020].

282. See "Bundeshaushalt 2018," *Bundesfinanzministerium*.

283. See "Länderhaushalte 2018," *Bundesfinanzministerium*.

284. See "Deutsche Staatsschulden 2018," *Deutsche Bundesbank*.

tive can be gained by comparing the net expenses for asylum-seekers to state expenses for "*Sozialhilfe*," the basic minimal social support for people without enough income to survive. Both in 2013 and 2018, these amounted to ca. 25 billion Euros, with the majority of recipients in 2013 probably still being native Germans.[285] This shows that expenses for asylum-seekers have clearly exceeded expenses for German citizens in financial need.

The vast majority of asylum-seekers who arrived in Germany in the last couple of years (both before, during, and after the opening of German borders in September 2015) have not been recognized by German state authorities as refugees—only around 5 percent. This means that most of the asylum-seekers are in fact declared to be economic migrants. Nevertheless, they are—except for isolated cases—not expelled of the country, but granted permanent residency.[286]

As opposed to the situation in the U.S., it is the whole population who has to pay the bills through higher taxes. However, the lower strata are more affected, because of rising competition in the low-skill job segment and especially fierce competition in the housing market,[287] as well as declining shares in public benefits.

4.5.3. Norway

Norway has been an *emigration* country for various periods in its more recent history, the large major wave lasting from the second half of the nineteenth century until the beginning of the twentieth century. *Immigration* into Norway has begun in recent times with the economic growth as a consequence of the large offshore oil and gas exploitation, beginning in the 1970s. Besides immigration of workers,[288] there has been a marked

---

285. See https://de.statista.com/statistik/daten/studie/165616/umfrage/ausgaben-fuer-sozialhilfe-in-deutschland-seit-2005/ [accessed Oct 4, 2019].

286. See Wruck, "Politik ohne Verantwortung."

287. There are seemingly contradicting local developments: In neighborhoods with a concentration of refugees from Africa and the Middle East, the rents may go down because native Germans do no longer wish to live in those areas; see Kürschner Rauck and Kvasnicka, "The 2015 Refugee Crisis," 23. Overall, however, prices for housing are skyrocketing.

288. Work-related immigration has increased again significantly from 2004 onward (see Holmøy, *14 spørsmål*).

increase in the numbers of people seeking asylum during about the last two to three decades.

The relevant numbers pertaining to the current situation look as follows: While male native Norwegians from age twenty-five onward contribute to the public budgets about 3.5 million kroners throughout their life-times, male immigrants from outside of Europe and the Western world are a burden to public budgets, by ca. 6 million kroners per person. The main reasons for this difference are that non-Western residents of Norway have higher rates of unemployment (which results in less taxes paid and more support needed), combined with higher birth rates (which results in higher support expenses to be paid by the state). If one takes into account the costs for the native Norwegians of about 5.4 million kroners per person before age twenty-five, and assumes that the non-Western immigrant has come to Norway only as an adult, the difference between the two groups is reduced from 9.5 million kroners per person to approximately 4 million kroners—which is still considerable. If only asylum-seekers/refugees are compared to native Norwegians, the differences are again even bigger than the numbers just presented would indicate.[289] The numbers look quite different for persons from Western countries and the central-eastern European member states of the EU, who move to Norway primarily for work and begin working normally immediately after arriving in Norway. These people are also more likely to leave Norway again after a certain period, as opposed to immigrants from non-Western countries and asylum-seekers/refugees.[290]

According to data published by SSB (*Norsk statistisk sentralbyrå*, the Norwegian Statistical Central Bureau) for 2017, male youths with migration background are still the biggest group among high school dropouts;[291] full-time employment is the lowest among persons with a non-Western background;[292] unemployment is between 13 and 17 percent higher among people with Asian[293] background as compared to native Norwegians, between 23 and 28 percent higher among people with African background, while people from Europe (not including eastern

289. See Byberg, "Så mye 'koster' en innvandrer."

290. See Holmøy, *14 spørsmål*.

291. See Sandnes, *Innvandrere i Norge 2017*, 94.

292. Sandnes, *Innvandrere i Norge 2017*, 123.

293. "Asian" in these statistics primarily refers to immigrants from the Middle East, including Afghanistan, and Pakistan.

non-EU countries) have even slightly higher employment rates than native Norwegian.[294] Again according to findings presented by SSB, the unemployment rate as of April 2020 amounted to 1.6 percent for native Norwegians, whereas unemployment was at 6.3 percent among immigrants from non-Western countries, and 3.5 percent among persons born in Norway to immigrant parents.[295]

Such trends were visible and analyzed already in a study by NHO (*Næringslivets Hovedorganisasjon,* The Confederation of Norwegian Enterprise) in 2006, where they pointed out the large number of high school dropouts and high unemployment rates among non-Western immigrants, which in the end-results—if those trends were not reversed—would mean the melting away of Norway's oil fund.[296]

According to some estimates, immigration into Norway may cost 250 billion kroners per year, instead of 45 billion that are often mentioned.[297] Perhaps the most realistic conservative estimate will be around 125 billion kroners per year.[298] A wish by one of the major parties represented in the Norwegian parliament to get more detailed information about the net benefits and costs of the various types of immigration to Norway was blocked by the other parties.[299]

The official state budget of Norway shows expenses of 1.325 trillion kroners for 2018.[300] If one assumes yearly net expenses for immigrants of 45 billion kroners, this amounts to ca. 3.4 percent of the budget; if, however, the real expenses are closer to 250 billion kroners, the relative size compared to the state budget would rise to almost 20 percent. With the lower amount of 45 billion kroners, expenses for immigrants would be somewhere mid-way between expenses for higher education (39 billion kroners) and defense (55 billion kroners).

---

294. Sandnes, *Innvandrere i Norge 2017,* 125.

295. See "Employment and Salary," *Statistisk sentralbyrå.* The numbers for the persons with foreign background refer to what is called "country group 2," defined as follows: Eastern Europe outside the EU, Asia (incl. Turkey), Africa, South and Central America and Oceania except Australia and New Zealand.

296. See Tjønn, "NHO."

297. See Gilbrant et al., "Innvandringen er dyrere;" Karlsen, "Ikke-vestlig innvandring."

298. See Lurås, "Elefanten."

299. Gilbrant et al., "Innvandringen er dyrere"; cf. Lurås, "Elefanten."

300. See *Statsbudsjettet 2018.*

One specific aspect of the economic consequences of immigration is highlighted by a study from the University of Oslo that shows that low-skill immigration has reduced social mobility. The results are summarized by the authors as follows:

> The starting point of this paper was the observation that the social gradients in natives' economic outcomes have become steeper over time, and in particular that the intergenerational mobility out of the lower social classes has declined. We have examined whether this development is attributable to skill-biased changes in labor supply caused by the rise in the number of immigrants from less developed countries and Eastern Europe. As these immigrants have been disproportionally recruited to jobs typically held by lower-class natives, the hypothesis is that they have crowded out lower-class natives in the labor market.
>
> Our findings suggest that immigration patterns have indeed been a major force behind changes in the social gradients in adult economic outcomes for natives born in Norway between 1960 and 1980. While immigration from low-income countries has steepened the social gradients in native employment and earnings outcomes, immigration from high-income countries has levelled them. And since immigration from low-income countries has been much larger than immigration from high-income countries, the net effect of the actual immigration to Norway over the past decades has been to reinforce the influence of social background on economic outcomes and thus to reduce social mobility.
>
> While our empirical analysis cannot say anything about the aggregate effects of recent immigration patterns on native outcomes, it establishes without reasonable doubt that it has skewed relative economic success away from the lower and toward the higher social classes.[301]

It is obvious that these findings are in accordance with trends described above concerning the situation in the U.S.

Valuable information can also be deduced from the abstract of the so-called Introduction programme for new immigrants:

> The Introduction programme for new immigrants is an integration policy initiative that all Norwegian municipalities are obliged to offer newly arrived refugees according to the Introduction Act (Act no. 80 of 4 July 2003). . . . The main activities

301. Hoen et al., "Immigration," 27.

in the programme are Norwegian language training and social studies, along with work experience and vocational guidance.

. . .

In 2016, 61 per cent of those who completed or dropped out of the programme in 2015 were employed or in education. This share is 58 per cent in 2015 for those who left the Introduction programme in 2014. For all years dating back to 2011, the share in work or education one year after completing the programme is between 58–63 per cent. The share for men in employment or education slightly increases from the first to the second year after the end of the Introduction programme, and then flattens out or goes down. However, for women who left the Introduction programme in this period increases the share in work or education in all years.

The proportion of women in employment and education is significantly lower than for men. Among women who completed or dropped out of the programme in both 2014 and 2015, 49 per cent were employed or in education one year later. However, the corresponding figures for men in the same years were 66 and 61 per cent.[302]

The information to be gained from this abstract is that in spite of state programs to promote recruitment of persons categorized as "refugees"— the costs of these programs remain unspecified—, around two fifth of these persons would still not (be able to) join the work force after completion of state sponsored courses that should help them in this respect. On the other hand, it also transpires that the programs do have a certain, if limited, effect.

Finally, data are also available concerning the future economic developments affected by immigration, based on various immigration scenarios. The abstract of the most comprehensive recent study, referred to in part already above with regard to demographic aspects, reads as follows:

This report analyses the contribution to the long term growth in national income per capita and fiscal sustainability from migration to Norway throughout this century. The study is a part of a project carried out for the Norwegian Ministry of Finance as well as the government appointed committee *Long Term Consequences of High Immigration* (NOU 2017:2). It applies an updated version of the model DEMEC (described in

302. Lunde and Lysen, "Tidligere deltakere," 5.

chapter 3) to simulate and compare two types of scenarios for
the Norwegian economy. The assumptions underlying the scenarios are identical except for those on migration:

1. The *Migration Scenario* assumes the same immigration and emigration as in the "Main Alternative" in the
   population projections published in 2016 by Statistics
   Norway. We regard this as the most realistic among the
   published projections. Here, the annual net immigration equals about 26 000 from 2020. An increasing
   share of immigrants is assumed to come from Africa
   and Asia.

2. In our alternative "o-Scenario" neither immigration
   nor emigration takes place after 2015.

Studies of economic growth have typically not emphasized
the size of the population. However, compared to most other
countries Norway receives substantial income from production
of crude oil and natural gas, as well as returns to the accumu-
lated savings of these petroleum revenues. These revenues are
completely independent of demography. Thus, excess of births
and net immigration will reduce their value in *per capita* terms.
Moreover, most of these revenues accrue to the public through
the central government. Thus, net immigration implies, *cet. par*,
that parts of the petroleum wealth are transferred from natives
to the extra immigrants. This takes place by raising the tax burden when more inhabitants are entitled to a given standard of
tax financed services and cash transfers within the government
budget constraint imposed by the fiscal rule for spending the
petroleum wealth. Chapter 2 shows that **realistic rather than no
migration implies that the petroleum wealth in some decades
has to be shared by a much larger number of residents. From
the present 5.3 million, realistic migration causes the Norwegian population to pass nearly 8.5 million in 2100, which is
nearly twice the 2100-level in the o-scenario. From 2016 till
2100 the population share of residents with background from
countries outside the EEA, North-America, Australia and
New Zealand grows steadily from 10 to 29 percent, whereas
the share of natives with at least one parent born in Norway
declines from 83 to 64 percent.**
In addition to the effects of population growth, migration affects living standards and government finances through
changes in the composition of the population. Although realistic
migration mitigates the growth in the demographic old-age dependency ratio, **realistic migration reduces the average annual**

growth rate of real national income per capita from 0.5 to 0.3 percent in the period 2016–2060 and from 0.6 to 0.5 percent in the period 2061–2100. The slow growth in both scenarios is due to prolongation of the slow productivity growth experienced since 2005. If growth were about 2 percent—the average over the last four decades—we would have judged the growth effect of migration to be small, especially compared to the large population effect. However, with *the bleak general growth prospects in our projections, realistic versus no migration makes a large difference in relative terms.* For example, reducing annual growth from 0.5 to 0.3 percent raises the doubling time from 139 to 231 years. (It is 35 years with 2 percent annual growth.) In 2060 real income *per capita* is 47 000 2013-NOK (7.8 percent) lower than in the 0-scenario. The corresponding reduction in 2100 is 72 000 2013-NOK (9.6 percent). The share of the income reduction that can be attributed to lower *per capita* value of incomes which are independent of demography, increases from 17 percent in 2016 to 45 percent in 2060 and to 59 percent in 2100. The income generated by production in the non-petroleum industries depends mainly on the population size through employment. Measured in 2013-NOK *per capita*, this income is lowered by 27 000 in 2060 and by 33 000 in 2100 due to realistic rather than no migration. The main reason is that the age- and gender specific average labour income per person is lower for immigrants from Africa and Asia than for natives.

Independent of migration Norway faces a fiscal sustainability problem, mainly caused by population ageing: The deficient tax revenue needed to meet the budget constraint implied by the current fiscal rule grows over time in both scenarios, also as a share of GDP for the mainland economy. However, realistic migration enlarges this measure of the fiscal gap in each year after 2025 by approximately 10 500 2013-NOK per capita, or 2.5 percent of the Mainland-GDP. The most important reason is that the return to the Government Pension Fund is shared by more residents. With respect to the population dependent budget components, migration reduces both incomes and expenditures in *per capita* terms. Net income falls until 2047 and increases thereafter. From 2016 till 2060 the fiscal gap has increased to 4 percent of Mainland-GDP, of which 2.4 points can be attributed to realistic migration. However, this effect is nearly constant, whereas population ageing causes a wider fiscal gap year by year, passing 11 percent of Mainland-GDP in 2100. Thus, realistic migration reinforces the fiscal sustainability problems facing Norway due to population ageing, but the relative importance of migration declines over time.[303]

4.6. Brief Summary

The data presented in this section show that the economic effects of mass-(im)migration are very complex, and in no way in general as positive as asserted by some scholars who advocate for liberal immigration policies. While for the individual migrants—as much as for big capital and big corporations—the economic result will be beneficial in many or even most cases, mass-immigration is a zero-sum game at best for the majority of countries of destination. Tendentially, the results will be more positive if the immigrants can be incorporated into the work force. On the other hand, direct competitors on the labor market among the native population will almost always suffer economically to some degree. The effects of mass-migration on the sending countries are varied. As far as the individual migrants are concerned, the likely beneficial outcomes in terms of economy must be viewed against the background of other factors, especially those mentioned in the section on psychological aspects of migration. In many cases, the positive economic effects will be more than outweighed by the negative results on the psychological level.

5. SECURITY ISSUES

5.1. Introduction

It is of course not possible (and in fact not necessary) in the present context to deal with security issues related to mass-migration to the West in a comprehensive way. It is both necessary and helpful, however, to point out *some* of the important data.[304] The situation obviously varies from country to country. One of the important factors is the make-up of the immigration population, both in terms of relative numbers and

303. Holmøy and Strøm, "Betydningen," 7. Italics and bold script are in the original.

304. Even this limited task is not easy to accomplish, because the relevant data are often not collected at all or hidden. One of the reasons for this peculiar situation is fear by state authorities or other interested parties of stereotyping. Of course, one could ask whether to some degree such fears are rooted in a reverse stereotyping of the broader public.

cultural-ethnic background. For the weight given to individual numbers, it is important not only to compare immigrant related crime or terrorism to the numbers of trespasses committed by members of the native-born population, but also to take into consideration that the immigrants' crimes and acts of terrorism would not have taken place if the respective persons had not been present in the host country at all.[305] At the same time, wherever a connection between immigration and crime or terrorism can be detected, it is always clear—as all available data show—that not all or most immigrants of a specific group are criminals or terrorists.

There are authors advocating for liberal immigration policies who either ignore or downplay security concerns.[306] Some of them argue that security must not be turned into an "idol" or an "absolute good."[307] While there are few who would contest this, the rhetoric constructs a wrong kind of dichotomy which does not reflect the real picture as it will emerge in the subsequent paragraphs. It remains true, however, that measures taken to protect the security of a given country's population should indeed be appropriate and measured, with regards not only to the issues raised by (mass-)migration.

The relative weight of crime and terrorism related to immigration[308] is a matter of debate, with liberal governments and mainstream media in the West, together with the most widespread information platforms such as Wikipedia, claiming that there is generally no link between immigration and increased levels of crime or terrorism.[309] As our case studies will show, this somewhat simplistic assessment needs to be modified.[310]

---

305. This means that even in cases where crime rates cannot be said to be statistically higher in terms of relative proportions, it can still be claimed that they carry a specific weight because they are, in some ways "unnecessarily," added to the crimes that are done by native-born citizens of the various states.

306. See, e.g., Campese, "¿Cuantos Más?" 274; Kerwin, "The Natural Rights," 202–4.

307. See, e.g., Kerwin, "The Natural Rights," 204.

308. In the case of terrorism, the debate is primarily about the role of Islam as a motivating factor, more than the question of the relationship with immigration—although the two aspects are correlated.

309. For Wikipedia see the entry on "Immigration and Crime."

310. Relatively lower statistical numbers for the correlation between immigration and crime are partly based on not counting the children or grandchildren of immigrants who were born in the host country as immigrants. The picture is also distorted when immigrants in general are compared with native persons, without investigating the differences between various groups of immigrants.

As far as the brief study of special cases is concerned, data available for the U.S., Germany, France, Sweden, Norway, and Iceland will be presented. Major considerations for the choice of these six countries are: 1) some familiarity with the situation in most of these countries based on years-long personal observations by the current writer;[311] and 2) the attempt to cast light on cases that are reflective of (some of) the major variations that can be found in the current situation in the West, including a comparison of cases on the extreme ends of the spectrum as far as the situation in western Europe is concerned.[312] The comparison between Sweden, Norway, and Iceland is particularly interesting, because the three countries are similar in general cultural terms, and to some degree also in terms of geographical location,[313] though Iceland is, of course, considerably more isolated than Sweden and Norway.

5.2. Special Case Studies: U.S., Germany, France, Sweden, Norway, Iceland

5.2.1. U.S.

Overall, there is no clear evidence that immigrants *in general* are more involved in crimes than native-born Americans.[314] On the other hand, the activities of brutal gangs like MS-13 and drug trafficking along the border with Mexico are well-established facts.[315]

311. The exceptions are Sweden and Iceland.

312. The label "extreme" does not mean that there are no other countries, not included in the survey, that show unmatched numbers relating to the field of migration and crime. For example, more than 70 percent of the total prison population in January 2016 both in Switzerland and Luxembourg were foreigners, ranking fourth and fifth on the global list of countries that imprison the most foreigners. Monaco with almost 90 percent ranks second (all data according to "The Countries that Imprison the Most Foreigners," *statista.com*). This shows that serious problems related to the intersection of migration and crime exist in countries not studied here.

313. Geographic location is in itself an important factor for migratory patterns.

314. See, e.g., Nowrasteh, "Illegal Immigrants;" Ousey and Kubrin, "Immigration and Crime," 63–84.

315. See, e.g., Carroll, *Christians*, 20. It is unfortunately very difficult to find numbers of criminal offenders indicating their exact nationality (or national background in the case of children and grandchildren of immigrants), the crime rate per capita of a specific community, and the precise character of the offences. Among the countries studied here, especially Norway provides much more detailed information about these important data.

According to the Federal Bureau of Prison, in May 2020 just under one fifth of the prison inmates were foreigners, mostly persons with a Latin-American background, and among them mostly Mexicans.[316] Just under a third of all inmates were ethnically Hispanic, with this number including U.S. citizens or legal residents classified as Hispanic.[317] With the Hispanic population amounting to 18.3 percent as of July 1, 2019, according to official numbers,[318] Hispanics were overrepresented in the prison population. Only 6.3 percent of the prison terms were related to immigration offences, which means that many foreigners were convicted for general and more severe crimes other than immigration offences.[319]

Further information can be gleaned from the report of the Bureau of Justice Statistics covering the decade 1998–2018. Among the highlights the following findings are mentioned:

- In 1998, 63% of all federal arrests were of U.S. citizens; in 2018, 64% of all federal arrests were of *non*-U.S. citizens.
- Non-U.S. citizens, who make up 7% of the U.S. population (per the U.S. Census Bureau for 2017), accounted for 15% of all federal arrests and 15% of prosecutions in U.S. district courts for non-immigration crimes in 2018.[320]

Looking at some details of the report, concerning the fiscal year 2018, the following picture emerges. The statistics of federal arrests by most serious offence in federal judicial districts besides those at the U.S.-Mexican border are as follows: about 63,000 suspects related to non-immigration offenses, which comprise 90 percent of all the offenses. About 18 percent of the suspects in these cases are non-U.S. citizens, which means that they are overrepresented in comparison to U.S. citizens. Regions of origin represented with more than 2 percent are Mexico (9 percent), Central

316. See "Inmate Citizenship," *Federal Bureau of Prisons*. Mexicans comprised 10.6 percent of the prison inmates. The other countries providing statistically notable shares were Colombia, Cuba, and the Dominican Republic.

317. African-Americans accounted for almost two fifth of the inmates (see "Inmate Race," *Federal Bureau of Prisons*), Hispanics for just below one third (see "Inmate Ethnicity," *Federal Bureau of Prisons*).

318. See *Quick Facts, Unites States Census Bureau*.

319. *Pace* Ramón et al., who claim that for the most part "immigrants are in prison for being immigrants, not for being criminals," and that the "prevalence of undocumented and other immigrants is largely the result of immigration enforcement priorities, not necessarily increased rates of overall criminality among immigrants" ("Data on Foreign-Born in Federal Prisons."

320. Motivans, "Immigration."

America (3.3 percent), and the Caribbean Islands (2.4 percent).[321] In the U.S.-Mexico border districts, the picture looks differently. Non-immigration offenses account for only 13.3 percent of the cases, which means that immigration-related offenses dominate vastly. About 17,000 suspects were apprehended in connection with non-immigration offenses. In the U.S.-Mexico border districts, 89 percent of the suspects were non-U.S. citizens. This number, however, does not tell much, because of the dominance of immigration related offenses. Since, however, the number of U.S. suspects apprehended for all types of offenses is lower by about 3,000 compared to the number of suspects of all nationalities apprehended for non-immigration offenses, a certain amount of involvement by non-U.S. citizens can be deduced.[322]

Another table in the same study shows that close to 15 percent of suspects prosecuted in U.S. district courts in 2018 were non-U.S. citizens, especially involving fraud (21.8 percent non-U.S. citizens), drug crime (20.2 percent non-U.S. citizens) and regulatory offenses (42.4 percent non-U.S. citizens).[323]

A comparison between a few randomly selected groups of immigrants reveals that criminality rates are considerably different between various countries of origin. The activities of MS-13 with its roots in El Salvador and of Somali youth gangs in Minneapolis, to mention two examples, point to serious problems with criminality in the respective immigrant communities.[324] On the other hand, immigrant communities from other countries, some of them not less destitute economically than El Salvador and Somalia, do not exhibit the same problems, as can be seen, for example, in the cases of Myanmar (especially the large

---

321. See Motivans, "Immigration," 12. Unfortunately, the statistics do not show whether the non-U.S. citizens were engaged in immigration related or non-immigration offenses. The numbers make clear, however, that non-U.S. citizens must be overrepresented among the suspected offenders, since only 56,747 U.S. citizens were apprehended, while the number of non-immigration offenses was at 62,797.

322. See Motivans, "Immigration," 12 (table 8a). Persons from Mexico (56.9 percent) and Central America (29.8 percent) dominate the statistics. But again, the lack of distinction between immigration related offenses and non-immigration offenses prevents more detailed conclusions.

323. See Motivans, "Immigration," 18 (table 3).

324. For MS-13 see the report produced by Dudley et al., "MS13 in the Americas." For Somali youth gangs see Adan, "Report on Somali Youth Issues," especially pp. 27–32 [accessed June 1, 2020].

community of Karen immigrants) or Slovakia.[325] The differences between these groups of immigrants show that 1) the use of the general rubric "immigrant" without further distinctions is in many cases not helpful, and that 2) purely socio-economic explanations for behavioral patterns in specific groups, ignoring other factors like culture, religion, etc., does not adequately reflect the complexities of the reality on the ground.

As far as terrorism is concerned, the statistics look as follows: There were 130 terrorist incidents with at least one person killed between 1990 and 2018.[326] Of these, the major ones were the following:

- April 19, 1995, Oklahoma City, 168 killed and 650 wounded, classified as "anti-government extremists";
- April 20, 1999, Littleton, fifteen killed and twenty-four wounded, classified as "unknown";
- September 9, 2001, 3,004 persons killed and 21,871 wounded, perpetrated by Al-Qaida;
- November 5, 2009, Killeen, thirteen killed and thirty-two wounded, jihadi attack;
- April 17, 2013, West, fifteen killed and 151 wounded, classified as "unknown";
- December 2, 2015, San Bernardino, sixteen killed and seventeen wounded, jihadi attack;
- June 12, 2016, Orlando, fifty killed and fifty-three wounded, jihadi attack;
- Oct 1, 2017, Las Vegas, fifty-nine killed and 851 wounded, classified as "anti-government extremists (suspected)";
- Feb 14, 2018, Parkland, seventeen killed and seventeen wounded, classified as "white supremacists/nationalists."

What emerges is that the majority of the bigger events were Islamic-inspired attacks; at the same time, it is also clear that the picture is variegated and other sources of terrorism are also important. Of the 130

325. For Burmese immigrants see, e.g., the Wikipedia entry on "Burmese Americans," which points to poverty issues, but does not mention any extraordinary crime issues. For the Slovak immigration to the U.S. see Stolarik, "From Field to Factory," 81–102.

326. See *Global Terrorism Database*. Cf. also *Global Terrorism Index*, *Vision of Humanity*.

incidents that resulted in one or more fatalities, thirty-one are Islamic inspired. These cases can be related to migration in the sense that the spread of Islam is the consequence of migration in recent decades.[327]

5.2.2. Germany

The most important source that will be used here are the data published by the *Bundeskriminalamt* (BKA). Their report for the year 2018 provides the following numbers:[328]

From the beginning of 2015 to the end of 2018, there were approximately 1.521 million registered asylum-seekers, with persons from Syria, Afghanistan, and Iraq contributing the largest contingent, together almost 60 percent (just over 1 million persons) of the total number.[329] A majority of these persons were below thirty years of age (73 percent) and male (65 percent).[330] According to BKA statistics, there were 167,268 criminal suspects among the immigrants[331] in 2017, and almost 600,000 criminal suspects among the non-Germans;[332] the first number amounts to 8.5 percent of all criminal suspects, the latter to 30.4 percent of all

327. Whether the perpetrators were immigrants (in the broadest sense of the term) themselves or native-born offspring of immigrants does not matter much in terms of an assessment of the general connection between terrorism and migration (in contradistinction to the weight that is often attached to this question).

328. As in other countries, a pattern has emerged in recent years in which state authorities, especially the federal government, mostly in collaboration with mainstream media (of which some are state run) misrepresent the picture by obfuscating information about incidents that involve immigrants (or second or third generation descendants of immigrants) on the one hand, and disproportionally focusing on or even inventing anti-immigrant incidents. A well-known example for the former are the events on New Year's Eve 2015/16 in Cologne (mentioned above in chapter 4); a well-known example for the latter are the events around a fictitious anti-immigrant riot in Chemnitz on August 26, 2018, culminating in the sacking of the president of the *Bundesverfassungsschutz* (Federal Office for the Protection of the Constitution) after his exposing the truth about the misinformation spread by the federal government and most of the mainstream media.

329. See *Kriminalität im Kontext von Zuwanderung*, 3, 5.

330. See *Kriminalität im Kontext von Zuwanderung*, 6.

331. "Immigrants" in this context are basically asylum-seekers and refugees; this excludes especially foreign workers from other EU countries.

332. "Non-Germans" is not defined in the BKA publication; it is likely, however, that it comprises immigrants of all sorts who are not German citizens, regardless of their place of birth. Importantly, it can be assumed that persons that are typically called "criminal tourists" without permanent residence in Germany are also included.

criminal suspects.[333] For 2018, the numbers look as follows: 165,769 immigrants (8.6 percent of all criminal suspects), and ca. 589,000 non-Germans among the criminal suspects (30.5 percent).[334] In terms of types of criminal acts, immigrants were particularly overrepresented in crimes against life (murder, manslaughter, etc.; 550 persons, 15 percent of all suspects) and in sexual crimes (5,626 persons, 12 percent of all suspects).[335] While persons from Syria, Afghanistan, and Iraq top the list in absolute numbers, they are in fact less criminal than others in terms of percentage of the number of immigrants from any particular country. Rather, it is persons from Nigeria, Morocco, Somalia, Algeria, Serbia, Turkey, Georgia, Gambia, Guinee, and Tunisia who show the highest percentage of criminal suspects in relation to the number of immigrants from these countries.[336] As far as sexual crimes are concerned, about 54 percent of the offenders came from Syria, Afghanistan, and Iraq.[337] The situation looks similar as far as bodily injuries, criminal assault, kidnapping, robbery, etc., are concerned (46 percent of suspects from Syria, Afghanistan, and Iraq),[338] and also with regards to offences against property and forgery (33 percent).[339] As far as theft is concerned, Syria and Afghanistan top the list, followed by persons from Georgia, Algeria, and Morocco; persons from Iraq are only ranked sixth.[340] Of the solved cases of drug offenses in 2018, 10.3 percent were committed by immigrants,[341] and 8.4 percent of the suspects were immigrants.[342] Of these, the highest shares were persons from Syria (18 percent) and Afghanistan (14 percent), followed by Algeria, Gambia, Iraq, and Morocco (all about 5 percent).[343]

Between 2008 and 2018, knife-related crime has increased by 900 percent, with a direct relation between this development and mass-immigration from Africa and the Middle East.[344]

---

333. See *Kriminalität im Kontext von Zuwanderung*, 7.

334. See *Kriminalität im Kontext von Zuwanderung*, 7.

335. See *Kriminalität im Kontext von Zuwanderung*, 8.

336. See *Kriminalität im Kontext von Zuwanderung*, 10.

337. See *Kriminalität im Kontext von Zuwanderung*, 23–24.

338. See *Kriminalität im Kontext von Zuwanderung*, 29.

339. See *Kriminalität im Kontext von Zuwanderung*, 38–39.

340. See *Kriminalität im Kontext von Zuwanderung*, 34.

341. See *Kriminalität im Kontext von Zuwanderung*, 40.

342. See *Kriminalität im Kontext von Zuwanderung*, 42.

343. See *Kriminalität im Kontext von Zuwanderung*, 43–44.

344. See Kern, "Germany."

There are also many attacks on churches, related specifically to Muslim immigration.[345]

A specific crime connected with immigration are the so-called honor killings.[346] It is impossible to count their numbers with precision, but some tendencies are clear. In the years 2016–2019, there were between thirty-eight and fifty-seven honor killings each year, and between thirty-eight and forty-nine attempted honor killings each year.[347] The ranking of nationalities was the same for almost all of these years: Turks, Afghans, Syrians, Iraqis.[348] For 2019, the detailed ranking looks as follows: fifteen Turks, eleven Afghans, eight Syrians, six Iraqis; four persons from Serbia and Albania, three persons from Tunisia, two persons from Algeria and Bulgaria, one person from the Dominican Republic, Nigeria, Morocco, Pakistan, Iran, Kasachstan, Romania.[349] Official numbers published by the *Bundeskriminalamt* are available only for the period 1996–2005.[350] According to their numbers, there were about seven to ten cases on average per year, with no clear tendency of an increase over time.[351] The markedly lower numbers as compared to the available statistics for 2016–2019 can be related both to a different kind of counting as well as an actual increase of incidents in recent years, the latter being connected to much higher numbers of persons originating from countries in which honor killings are an established part of the respective culture. As far as the ethnic background of the perpetrators is concerned, there is some continuity between the two periods, and certainly a continuity with respect to the general cultural (/religious) background. For the period 1996–2005, the statistics look as follows:[352] Over 90 percent of the perpetrators were born outside of Germany and were not German citizens; a minority were second generation immigrants with Turkish and Kurdish backgrounds;

345. See, e.g., Ellis, "Churches Desecrated."

346. For an introduction into the discussion about definition and character of this crime, see, e.g., Oberwittler and Kasselt, *Ehrenmorde*, 12–40.

347. All data are according to *ehrenmord.de*. The website points to *Spiegel.de* and *terredesfemmes.de* as sources.

348. Only in 2018 were there more Syrians than Afghans.

349. In addition, there was a person whose identity was categorized as "Eastern European," likely belonging to the Sinti and Roma, and one person with a Greek and another with an Italian passport, but likely both with a different ethnic background.

350. See Oberwittler and Kasselt, *Ehrenmorde*.

351. See Oberwittler and Kasselt, *Ehrenmorde*, 74.

352. See Oberwittler and Kasselt, *Ehrenmorde*, 85–86.

in a few cases, the perpetrators had German citizenship, but where ethnically non-German: three with Turkish, two with Kurdish, and one with Lebanese, Afghan, and Aramaic background.[353] While the largest group involved in honor killings were Turks, responsible for about two thirds of the cases, also persons from Arab countries, ex-Yugoslavia and Albania, and Pakistan and Afghanistan are represented on the list.

Turning to the specific category of antisemitic incidents, the following picture emerges: Antisemitic criminal offences have risen sharply in the last couple of years. According to Jewish sources in Germany, a majority of the offences is perpetrated by Muslims (either immigrants or offspring of immigrants), especially the more serious types of offenses; the second most important group of offenders are left-wing extremists; right-wing extremists come in third.[354] In the official statistics of the *Bundeskriminalamt*, however, due to a blatantly deficient system of categorization, the overwhelming majority of offences are falsely connected with right-wing extremists.[355]

The Moshe Kantor Database for the Study of Contemporary Antisemitism and Racism provides the following numbers for the year 2018: Most antisemitic incidents were reported in Berlin, home of the largest Jewish community in Germany.[356] Although the overall numbers for the first six months of 2018 stayed stable on a high level in most parts of the city, in Berlin-Mitte there was a decrease of registered incidents (2018: sixty-three; 2017: eighty-one) while in Friedrichshain-Kreuzberg, antisemitic incidents almost doubled (2018: forty; 2017: twenty-two) during the same period. In March 2018, a Berlin police report revealed that antisemitic crimes in the capital had doubled during the 2013–2017 period, a fact that was connected to the increased number of migrants from the Middle East living in the city. National Antisemitism Commissioner

353. In addition, there was an ethnic German who did a killing as a hitman contracted by a Kurdish-Yazidi man.

354. See Funkschmidt, "Antisemitische Straftaten."

355. See Funkschmidt, "Antisemitische Straftaten." The problem persists. In the *Verfassungsschutzbericht* for the year 2019, all the antisemitic incidents that can not be clearly related to a specific group are classified as "right-wing extremist," which in turn inflates the numbers of right-wing extremist offenses compared to left-wing extremist and Islamist offenses (see Kaiser, "Kaisers royaler Wochenrückblick"). This approach looks disturbing in a country that prides itself to be committed to the principle of the rule of law.

356. See Webman and Naamat, *Moshe Kantor Database*, 71.

Felix Klein also admitted that the statistics presented by RIAS (*Recherche- und Informationsstelle Antisemitismus*) support the feeling among Jews that Muslims are far more involved in antisemitic incidents than official statistics indicate.

Finally, we turn to the issue of terrorism. Germany has had a long history of incidents classified as terrorist since 1968.[357] Until a couple of years ago, the attacks in their majority were carried out either by left-wing extremists in their fight for a revolutionary overthrow of the current liberal democracy, or by groups based in the Middle East related to the Arab-Israeli conflict. In addition, roughly between 1991 and 2006, there were minor attacks by groups of neo-Nazis, after a major more isolated incident in 1980. Since 2011, attacks motivated by Islamic extremism have occurred, with the climax reached so far in the Berlin attack of December 19, 2016, one of the bloodiest attacks in modern German history.

There are members of Islamic terrorist groups among the immigrants.[358] According to the German *Verfassungsschutz*, there were about 26,560 Islamist/jihadist persons in Germany in 2018, or 16,560 if the adherents of *Milli Görüs* and related movements are subtracted.[359] The latter number compares with 10,695 for the year 2013.[360] Several terror attacks have been committed by immigrants in the last couple of years, practically all of them related to Islamist/jihadist inspiration.[361] On the other hand, violent attacks by native born German nationals on asylum-seekers are extremely rare.[362]

As of 2018, Germany ranked 39 with a 4.6 index on the Global Terrorism Index, close to—and just a bit worse—than Israel. The situation

357. See "Liste von Terroranschlägen in Deutschland," *Wikipedia*. The data are based on the *Global Terrorism Database*.

358. See *Verfassungsschutzbericht 2015* (Berlin: Bundesministerium des Innern), 164.

359. See "Islamismus und islamistischer Terrorismus," *Verfassungsschutz*. Cf. also *Kriminalität im Kontext von Zuwanderung*, 57. Some of the persons with terrorist leanings are German converts to Islam; in these cases, the link to immigration is of course only indirect.

360. See *Verfassungsschutzbericht 2015*, 154.

361. See *Kriminalität im Kontext von Zuwanderung*, 57.

362. See *Kriminalität im Kontext von Zuwanderung*, 56 (thirteen violent attacks on asylum centers in 2018).

has decreased over the years, as the following figures show: 2010: 66, 1.85; 2002: 51, 2.46.[363]

5.2.3. France

The one phenomenon that shows security problems related to immigration most clearly are the *zones urbaines sensibles* ("sensitive urban zones"). These are Muslim dominated neighborhoods in which organized criminality has spread beyond state control, in spite of large amounts of money spent to ameliorate the situation.[364]

An exemplary description of the situation in a typical *zone urbaine sensible* was published in 2017 by Mamou. Among others, he mentions the following:

> The French daily, *Le Parisien,* disclosed[365] that, in fact, no-go zones are in the heart of the capital. It seems that the district of Chapelle-Pajol, in the east of Paris, has become very much a no-go zone. Hundreds of Muslim migrants and drug dealers crowd the streets, and harass women for wearing what many of these migrants apparently regard as immodest clothing: Women in this part of eastern Paris complain that they cannot move about without being subjected to comments and insults from men. There are several hundred square meters of pavement abandoned to men alone; women are no longer considered entitled to be there. Cafés, bars and restaurants are prohibited to them, as are the sidewalks, the subway station and the public squares. For more than a year, the Chapelle-Pajol district (10th-18th *arrondissements*) has completely changed its face: groups of dozens of lone men, street vendors, aliens, migrants and smugglers harass women and hold the streets. . . .
>
> Mayor Hidalgo . . . said that this security issue has been "identified for several weeks," and proposed launching an "exploratory process" to combat discrimination against women and a "local delinquency treatment group." . . .
>
> Mentioning no-go zones in France was, until recently, taboo. It was regarded as "racist" or "Islamophobic" . . . to talk about that. In May 2016, Patrick Kanner, France's Minister for Urban Areas, harassed by journalists, finally acknowledged the

363. See *Global Terrorism Index.*
364. See, e.g., Belien, "Sensitive Urban Areas."
365. See Beaulieu, "Paris: des femmes victimes."

truth: "There are today, we know, a hundred neighborhoods in France that present potential similarities with what has happened in Molenbeek." He was referring to the infamous neighborhood in Brussels, under Salafist control, which has become the epicenter of jihad in Europe.

What is new, is that no-go zones are no longer relegated to the suburbs, where migrants and Muslims have usually been concentrated. No-go zones, through mass migration, have been emerging in the heart of Paris, Bordeaux, Toulouse, Marseille, Grenoble, Avignon—districts "privatized" here and there by a mix of drug traffickers, Salafist zealots and Islamic youth gangs. The main victims are women. They are—both Muslim and non-Muslim—sexually harassed; some are sexually assaulted. . . . A 2014 report from the High Commissioner on Equality revealed that in the so-called "sensitive urban areas," nearly one in ten women has suffered physical or sexual violence.[366] Another report handed to the government in September 2016, by the organization "France Médiation" revealed significant details, albeit written in chastened terms: Public areas are "occupied" exclusively by men who "park" there, and women are merely authorized to pass through them . . . .[367]

As in the case of Germany, there is a high number of attacks on churches; on average, two churches are desecrated, demolished, or burnt down every day. In many cases the perpetrators are Muslims with an immigrant background.[368] On rare occasions also clergy are attacked; the murder of a priest during mass in a village near Rouen on July 26, 2016 by two young Muslim men with immigration background is perhaps the best-known example.[369]

Turning to the topic of antisemitism, the following picture emerges: Antisemitism in France has been growing in the last years, and the growth is mostly driven by Muslim immigrants or their descendants, in part also by left-wing groups, in addition to the traditional far-right forms of antisemitism.[370]

366. *Les chiffres clés des inégalités femmes-hommes.*

367. Mamou, "France: No-Go Zones."

368. Of course, the perpetrators are not necessarily first-generation immigrants. See Ellis, "Churches Desecrated."

369. See "Attentat de l'église de Saint-Étienne-du-Rouvray," *Wikipedia.*

370. See Hasten, "Jews Leaving France"; Meotti, "France: Muslims In, Jews Out."

The Moshe Kantor Database for the Study of Contemporary Antisemitism and Racism provides the following numbers for the year 2018:[371] The overall number of recorded antisemitic incidents during 2018 increased by 74 percent with 541 incidents, compared to 311 incidents in 2017. The number of recorded antisemitic violent incidents (attack or attempted attack, homicide or attempted homicide, violence, arson or attempted arson, defacement or vandalism) increased by 89 percent with 183 incidents, compared to ninety-seven in 2017. Within the violent incidents category, antisemitic physical violence against persons increased by 170 percent with eighty-one incidents, compared to thirty in 2017. The number of recorded antisemitic threats (oral threats, threatening gestures or insults, flyers and hate mail, graffiti) increased by 67 percent with 358 incidents, compared to 214 in 2017. During the year, French Jews, who represent less than 1 percent of the French population, suffered 55 percent of all racist physical violence committed in France. This figure is even more striking against the background of government data showing a decrease in overall racist and anti-Muslim incidents.[372] All the violent antisemitic acts in recent years were perpetrated by Muslims.[373] Nevertheless, the role of Islam and Muslim immigrants in the increase of antisemitism continue to be a matter of dispute.[374]

As a result of the wide-spread antisemitic incidents, many Jews are and have been leaving France, with a peak of ca. 7,000 persons in 2015.[375]

Also as far as terrorism is concerned, things do not look bright in France. The Global Terrorism Index shows a steady deterioration of the situation

371. Webman and Naamat, *Moshe Kantor Database*, 67.

372. Racist and xenophobic incidents have decreased by 4.2 percent with 496 incidents, compared to 518 in 2017. Anti-Muslim incidents have reached a record low since 2010 with 100 recorded incidents. Anti-Christian incidents in France were more or less steady with 1,063 recorded incidents, compared to 1,038 in 2017.

373. See Webman and Naamat, *Moshe Kantor Database*, 68.

374. Francis Kalifat, for example, the president of the *Conseil représentatif des institutions juives de France* has often put much of the blame on far-right and far-left extremists (see Webman and Naamat, *Moshe Kantor Database*, 69), while Philippe Val, in a recent manifesto condemning antisemitism, signed by 300 prominent Jewish and non-Jewish dignitaries and celebrities (among them Alain Finkielkraut), denounces what is called the "new antisemitism marked by Islamic radicalization" (see "Manifest 'contre le nouvel antisémitisme'").

375. See, e.g., "Antisemitismus: Immer mehr Juden verlassen Frankreich."

and generally high degrees of threat: 2002: rank 29, index 3.74; 2010: rank 41, index 3.91; 2018: rank 30, index 5.48 points.[376]

From 1990 through 2018, there were just over eighty terrorist attacks that resulted in one or more casualties.[377] In about half of the cases the perpetrators are classified as "unknown," though it is likely that in some of these cases Corsican nationalists were responsible. In almost all these cases the number of victims is only one person. There were five incidents in which the responsible party is identified as Corsican, with all together six victims. In addition, there is one incident with a Basque group as perpetrator (two victims), and one incident with a Breton group as perpetrator (one victim). All other incidents are ascribed to Islamic groups. These groups are responsible for all the attacks that resulted in large numbers of casualties: seven dead and eighty-six injured on July 7, 1995; three dead and ninety-one injured on December 3, 1996; 136 dead and 447 injured on November 13, 2015; eighty-seven dead and 433 injured on July 14, 2016. In the Paris attacks of November 13, 2015, two of the perpetrators, likely Iraqi citizens, entered Europe as refugees with Syrian documents.[378]

An individual incident of recent date worth mentioning is the knife attack of a Muslim convert born in Martinique in the Prefecture of Police in the center of Paris on October 3, 2019, which left four police officers dead.[379] The perpetrator was inspired by ISIS. The attack showed that the terrorist threat had in effect implanted itself into the heart of the French security apparatus.

5.2.4. Sweden

The last time there was an official report breaking down crime rate statistics by immigrant status and origin was in 2005, for the years 1997 to 2001. These statistics confirmed that immigrants were significantly over-represented amongst offenders, in particular committing violent crimes. The foreign-born were four times more likely to be suspects in homicide

---

376. See *Global Terrorism Index.*
377. For all the data see *Global Terrorism Database.*
378. See *Verfassungsschutzbericht 2015,* 166.
379. See Wikipedia entry on the "Paris Police Headquarters Stabbing."

cases than those with Swedish origin, and 4.5 times more likely to be suspects in rape cases.[380]

Since then, Swedish criminologists and politicians have made sure that no new statistics have been released. Not a single recent research study in Sweden has attempted to estimate the causal effect of immigration on sexual assault or homicide. Nevertheless, it is well known that both in Malmö and suburbs of Gothenburg and Stockholm serious issues with crime in connection to immigrant communities do exist. There are two areas in particular in which recent developments in Sweden stand out in comparison to other countries in western Europe: rape and bombings.

As far as the bombings are concerned, they have recently reached levels that are unmatched anywhere else in the developed world outside of war zones. As of October 2019, official statistics pointed to over one hundred bombing incidents only in the course of that same year. The bombings are gang-related, with the gangs being based in immigrant neighborhoods.[381] Gang-related shootings have also escalated, with nine out of ten perpetrators being first- or second-generation immigrants.[382]

Looking at rape, the following picture emerges: Between 2003 and 2010, Sweden moved from position eight (with twenty-five incidents per 100,000 citizens) on the world list to position three (with 63.5 incidents per 100,000 citizens) in 2010, behind only South Africa and Botswana.[383] A BBC report published on August 22, 2018, describes the situation in the following terms, based on data offered by the Swedish public broadcaster SVT:[384] Based on the counting of court convictions by SVT, about 58 percent of men convicted in Sweden of rape and attempted rape over the past five years were born abroad. The picture is more complicated in the sense that Sweden had thousands more reported rapes, with no ethnic breakdown for those.[385] The Mission Investigation Programme, due to be broadcast by SVT, said the total number of offenders over five years was 843. Of those, 197 were from the Middle East and North Africa, with

---

380. Sanandaji, "What Is the Truth."

381. See Neuding, "Bomb Attacks."

382. See Neuding, "Bomb Attacks."

383. In 2003, Sweden was ranked behind Denmark and Belgium when looking at the numbers in Europe. For the numbers see "Crime: Rape Rate," *NationMaster*.

384. "Sweden Rape: Most Convicted Attackers Foreign-Born, Says TV."

385. Of course, the fact that no data are available for these cases is bewildering in itself.

forty-five coming from Afghanistan.[386] The data presented by SVT also revealed that in cases where the victim did not know the attacker, the proportion of foreign-born offenders was more than 80 percent.

A report about the situation in some of the crime-ridden Swedish immigration neighborhoods was published by Ngo in December 2018. Here are some excerpts:

> "I don't go to those places without security," a Swedish journalist tells me when I ask whether she would accompany me to some of her country's "especially vulnerable" areas. The label is given by police to neighborhoods where crime is rampant and parallel social structures compete for authority with the state. To the politically incorrect, these are also known as "immigrant ghettos."
>
> While much attention was focused on Germany during the 2015 refugee crisis, in which more than a million migrants from the Middle East and Africa entered the continent at the behest of Angela Merkel, the country that admitted the most migrants per capita was Sweden. In one year alone, the northern European nation of 10 million added nearly 2 percent to its population. Most of those arrivals were young men. Tens of thousands more have continued to arrive since then.
>
> It is too early to see the long-term impact of the 2015 migrant crisis, but if the past is any indication of Sweden's future, the answer may be found in its "vulnerable" neighborhoods. In recent years, the Nordic state known for scoring among the highest among all nations in quality-of-life indexes has also gained a reputation for gang shootings, grenade attacks, and sexual crimes.
>
> Days before I was due to arrive in Sweden last summer, the country was rocked by mass car burnings across its west coast. Authorities faulted "youth gangs" for the fires, a euphemism for criminal young men of migrant backgrounds. My first visit was to Rosengård, Seved, and Nydala, immigrant neighborhoods in the southern city of Malmö and among the 23 "especially vulnerable" areas across Sweden. At times, ambulances and fire trucks will enter only with police protection. Desperate police have appealed to imams and clan leaders for help when they cannot contain the violence.

---

386. It is routinely pointed out that it is only a small percentage of the people coming from abroad who are convicted of rape. This, however, is not what the debate is about. The real issue is the overrepresentation of men from specific cultural/ethnic backgrounds in the rape statistics.

From Malmö's central train station, I began walking alone to Rosengård . . . . The closer the GPS told me I was to my destination, the more headscarves I saw and the less Swedish I heard. In Rosengård, youths gathered during school hours in streets and parks around the public housing that lined the neighborhood. In fact, fewer than half of ninth-graders here pass enough classes to enroll in high school.

Four hundred miles north, in the country's capital, I witnessed similar social phenomena in some Stockholm neighborhoods. I was more discreet on that trip; journalists have been violently attacked in those areas.

In Rinkeby, young girls and even some babies were dressed in modesty headscarves. Cafés were in practice male-only spaces, and a restaurant in the town center offered segregated seating, with a curtain, for "families," a euphemism for women. Here, there were no H&Ms or other hallmarks of Swedish fashion. Instead, small clothing stores sold Islamic robes, hijabs, and face veils. And in contrast to the near-cashless society I encountered elsewhere in urban Sweden, many businesses here accepted only cash.

In Tensta, another "extremely vulnerable" district near Rinkeby, I stopped by the local administrative office. It is one of the few visible institutions of the Swedish state in the area. Security guards stood at the door. The week before, masked assailants left burning tires outside the office—one of a number of attacks on authorities in the neighborhood. . . .

How did Sweden, on the whole a prosperous and peaceful nation, also develop parallel, segregated societies afflicted by criminality and violence? The starkest reminder of this reality are the numerous grenade explosions and gun murders that have become a regular occurrence across some sections of society. In fact, Sweden's homicide rate is now above the Western European average. . . .

University West sociologist Göran Adamson blames, in addition to poor urban planning, Sweden's state-sponsored multiculturalism for financing separatism through various ethno-religious institutions. "The shrewd thing about multiculturalism is that it has somehow fused with the state," the associate professor tells me. Sweden's institutionalization of multiculturalism began in 1975, ...

Most then choose to remain silent. But some of the loudest dissident voices are coming from immigrants themselves, who experience firsthand the failures and contradictions of Swedish multiculturalism. "We have failed at integration for the past

30 years," Mustafa Panshiri, a former police officer and now full-time integration educator, tells me. Panshiri ... says Sweden excels at welcoming migrants but fails at explaining what citizenship is. "You don't have to speak a single word of Swedish to become a citizen. There are no expectations." That sentiment was repeated by Omar Makram, a 33-year-old refugee from Egypt who entered Sweden at the beginning of the migrant crisis in 2014. He describes government authorities as wholly ignorant or willfully blind, in the name of tolerance, to problematic, regressive cultural attitudes held by some migrants. . . .

The visibility of conservative and fundamentalist Islamic norms I witnessed in "vulnerable" neighborhoods may not mean much by itself, but too often it is linked to violent extremism. A Syrian man who lived in Rosengård is currently in French custody for suspected involvement in both the 2015 Paris attacks and the 2016 Brussels bombings. And it is estimated that in 2012–15 some 300 Swedish nationals traveled to the Middle East to join militant Islamist groups. Of that, around 70 percent came from "vulnerable" neighborhoods, Magnus Ranstorp, the research director at the Centre for Asymmetric Threat Studies at the Swedish Defense University, tells me. Another 2,000 individuals remain on the radar of the Swedish Security Service for being potential jihadists.

In April 2017, an Uzbeki failed asylum seeker used a stolen truck to drive through a crowd of shoppers on a busy Stockholm street. Five people were killed, including an eleven-year-old girl. Fourteen others were injured. The man swore allegiance to the Islamic State the day before the attack. One of his known addresses was in Tensta.[387]

As far as antisemitism is concerned, the picture looks similar to the one found in Germany and France. Overall, Malmö is the city that is hardest hit. Jews are leaving the city, and the Jewish congregation may be dissolved in the foreseeable future.[388] Malmö's Jewish community has declined amid frequent threats and attacks, mostly by Muslims, from 1,200 several years ago to an estimated 800 or fewer members today.[389] Ngo describes the situation in Malmö as follows:

387. Ngo, "Sweden's Parallel Society."

388. See, e.g., Liphshiz, "Malmo."

389. Liphshiz, "Malmo." The article also notes that in the previous year, the Jewish Community of Umea in northern Sweden had dissolved itself primarily over threats by neo-Nazis, but also in connection with harassment by radical Muslims, according

> From Malmö's central train station, I began walking alone to Rosengård. . . . Halfway through my journey, I stopped outside the Malmö Synagogue. I was greeted by a metal security fence and closed-circuit cameras. In 2010, the synagogue was attacked with explosives. And in December 2017, hundreds of protesters in the city chanted for an intifada and promised to "shoot the Jews" after President Trump announced the recognition of Jerusalem as Israel's capital.[390]

The Moshe Kantor Database for the Study of Contemporary Antisemitism and Racism provides the following information about Sweden:[391] On December 9, 2017, a group of immigrants from the Middle East tried to burn down the main synagogue in Gothenburg, Sweden. Three of the men involved were arrested and in June 2018 they were convicted for the attempted arson. Two of them were sentenced to prison and the third, a Palestinian immigrant who wasn't a Swedish citizen, to expulsion from Sweden. He appealed, and on September 12 the court of appeals confirmed his prison sentence, but not the expulsion, with the reasoning that there was a very real danger that the state of Israel would try to seriously harm, even kill, the man if he was sent back to the West Bank after having tried to burn down a synagogue.[392] The Muslim-immigrant connection is not limited to this specific incident. Generally, respondents who identified as Muslim displayed antisemitic tendencies to a significantly higher degree than those who identified as Christian or "other." According to the perception of the Swedish Jews, 40 percent of the perpetrators of antisemitic incidents were Muslims, 27 percent leftists and 18 percent rightwing.[393] This squares well with other findings that show members of Muslim immigrant communities at the top of the list of perpetrators of antisemitic incidents.[394]

to its former leader, Carinne Sjoberg.

390. Ngo, "Sweden's Parallel Society."

391. See Webman and Naamat (eds), *Moshe Kantor Database*, 31–33.

392. This means that the very fact that he had carried out a violent antisemitic crime was the reason he must be allowed to stay in Sweden.

393. The comparative numbers for Denmark look as follows (see Webman and Naamat, *Moshe Kantor Database*, 32): When asked about the perpetrators of antisemitic attacks, Danish Jews said 34 percent were Muslims, 27 percent leftists, and 10 percent rightwing.

394. See, e.g., Wyssuwa, "Scharfe Worte."

The statistics covering terrorism look as follows: According to the Global Terrorism Index, there is a sharp increase of terrorist activities over the last approximately twenty years, starting (as opposed to France) at a very low level. This is how the development looks:[395] 2002: rank 106, index 0.1; 2010: rank 77, index 1.22; 2018: rank 51, index 3.94 points.

Until 2018, there were only nine terrorist attacks that resulted in casualties, in six cases resulting in just one victim, with the perpetrators mostly classified as "unknown."[396] The three most important cases were an attack on April 24, 1975, that left three persons dead and thirteen injured, perpetrated by a socialist group; an attack by anti-immigrant perpetrators on October 22, 2015, that left four persons dead and one injured; and a jihadi attack on April 7, 2017, that left five persons dead and fourteen injured. In recent years, a majority of attacks is classified as "antisemitic," the perpetrators being likely Muslims.

5.2.5. Norway

In the case of Norway, much more precise official data are available than in the cases studied so far.

The official numbers for 2017 look as follows:[397] Overrepresented in general crime rates are persons with the following backgrounds: Kosovo, Lithuania, Russia; Eritrea, Morocco, Somalia, other African countries; Afghanistan, Iraq, Iran, Pakistan, Sri Lanka, Turkey; Chile. The highest crime rates can be found among persons with backgrounds in Kosovo, Somalia, Afghanistan, and Iraq.

The official numbers for 2010–2013 look as follows:[398] Immigrants and descendants of immigrants from the following countries show higher crime rates than native Norwegians: Denmark; Lithuania, Russia, Bosnia, Kosovo; Eritrea, Morocco, Somalia, other African countries; Turkey, Afghanistan, Sri Lanka, Iraq, Iran, Pakistan, Vietnam; Chile, other Latin American countries. The highest rates can be found among persons with backgrounds in Kosovo, Somalia, Afghanistan, Iraq, and Iran. Among other immigrants or their descendants, crime rates are much below the

---

395. See *Global Terrorism Index.*

396. See *Global Terrorism Database.*

397. See Sandnes, *Innvandrere i Norge 2017.*

398. See Andersen, Holtsmark, and Mohn, *Kriminalitet blant innvandrere og norskfødte med innvandrerforeldre, Rapporter 2017/36* (Oslo: Statistisk Sentralbyrå, 2017), 27.

Norwegian average: Western Europe, North America, Oceania, Philippines, India, China.

Theft and violence are those categories where immigrants are over-represented.[399] Non-Western immigrants—among them refugees—are most likely to be involved in those crimes.[400] Criminality is higher among the children of immigrants than among first-generation immigrants.[401]

When it comes to rape, there is an overrepresentation of persons who were born in Asia or Africa.[402] According to a 2009 report of the police department in Oslo, over a period of three years all rapes committed in the context of an assault by persons who were not known to the victims previously were committed by non-Western immigrants.[403]

Finally, some data concerning terrorism. The global index shows some increase of terrorist incidents over the last two decades, but on a very low level compared to the other countries studied in this section:[404] In 2002, Norway was among the most peaceful countries worldwide, ranking 120, with an incident rate of 0.0 points; in 2010, the numbers looked still similar (rank 120, incident rate 0.06 points). No dramatic change is documented for 2018 (rank 123, incident rate 0.15 points). In total, as of 2019 only nineteen terrorist incidents are documented, only four of them with persons killed, in two of the four cases just one person.[405] The only really grave incidents were the two perpetrated by Breivik in Oslo and Utøya, resulting in seventy-seven persons killed and seventy-five injured—and of course, Breivik was not an immigrant.

5.2.6. Iceland

As opposed to all the cases studied so far, Iceland has only a very small immigrant population. At the same time, it is culturally and ethnically close to the other Scandinavian countries, especially Norway. Therefore,

---

399. See Andersen, Holtsmark, and Mohn, *Kriminalitet*, 32.

400. See Andersen, Holtsmark, and Mohn, *Kriminalitet*, 32.

401. See Andersen, Holtsmark, and Mohn, *Kriminalitet*, 41.

402. See *Voldtektsituasjonen i Norge 2018*, 19.

403. See Veum and Zakariassen, "Overfallsvoldtekter."

404. See *Global Terrorism Index, Vision of Humanity*.

405. See *Global Terrorism Database*.

a comparison of crime rates can open a window into how immigration may affect security.[406]

Here are some of the salient data, pertaining to 2014, comparing Iceland and Norway:[407] General crime levels are 35 percent higher in Norway. Use of illegal drugs is 26 percent higher in Norway. Rates of violent crimes are 15 percent higher in Norway. Rates of property crimes are 15 percent higher in Norway. On the other hand, problems with corruption and bribery are 26 percent higher in Iceland.

Compared to Sweden, the salient data look as follows, again pertaining to 2014:[408] General crime levels are 96 percent higher in Sweden. Use of illegal drugs is 5 percent higher in Iceland. Rates of violent crimes are 68 percent higher in Sweden. Rates of property crimes are 31 percent higher in Sweden. Again, on the other hand, problems with corruption and bribery are 4 percent higher in Iceland.

Looking at terrorism, the statistics show that it is almost nonexistent:[409] 2002: rank 120, 0.0 points; 2010: rank 125, 0.0 points; 2018: 130, 0.06 points. Four terrorist incidents are recorded until 2018, with no casualties (either deaths or injuries).[410]

5.3. Brief Summary

The data collected in this section demonstrate that, on the one hand, there is some kind of connection between high immigration rates from certain countries and an increase in crime, antisemitism, and terrorism. On the other hand, it is also clear that explanations for these phenomena must take into consideration a whole range of possible factors. Simple socio-economic explanations will generally not be satisfactory.[411]

406. This would be more difficult when comparing Norway or Sweden with countries that, like Iceland, have very little immigration, but are culturally much more different, like Hungary or Poland.

407. All taken from "Crime Stats," *NationMaster*. The numbers are per capita, that is, relative to the total population size.

408. See "Crime Stats," *NationMaster*.

409. See *Global Terrorism Index, Vision of Humanity*.

410. See *Global Terrorism Database*.

411. This is also true for some other explanations of specific security issues related to immigration in some countries, like, for example, Battistella's claim that the emergence of terrorist cells in receiving countries has to do with a "lack of opportunities for cultural dialogue" ("Migration," 180).

7

General Biblical Reflections Pertaining to the Ethics of Migration

1. GENERAL REMARKS

A CONSIDERATION OF BROADER ethical principles asserted in the Bible is necessary in the theological treatment of issues of migration because a responsible dealing with migration is fundamentally an ethical question. The various principles mentioned in this chapter are not meant to represent an exhaustive list, but will highlight some of the major aspects to be considered. The sequence in which the principles are organized is by no means the only possible one, and some of the points allocated to a specific principle could also be connected to some other principle in addition to the one under which they are mentioned here.

When it comes to the use of the Bible to assess ethical issues, two limitations have to be recognized:

First: While the Bible speaks clearly on some issues, there are many other issues where this is not the case; compare, for example, the cases of prohibition of murder vs. organization of economic life. In the latter cases, there is obviously much "room for prudential judgment."[1]

Second: Because of the historical differences between then and now, that is, the biblical times and the present times, and because of the specific and unique role of ancient Israel, most of the biblical injunctions—apart

---

1. Edwards, "A Biblical Perspective," 1.

from those that refer to unchanging, universal facets of human life—cannot be transferred in a simple one-to-one manner. This is even more true when it comes to matters of "specific policy guidance."[2] In this area, the Bible can only be turned to in the search for "ultimate perspectives, broad criteria, motives, inspirations, sensitivities, warnings, and moral limits."[3] The church must abstain from giving specific directives, but "should seek to clarify and keep wide open the legitimate options for choice, and thus nurture the moral and political ethics of the nation. Their task is not the determination of policy."[4] On the other hand, it may also be necessary at times to denounce government policies that seem to be at odds with the broader perspectives and principles that can be found in the Bible.[5]

These limitations are relevant for the ethics of (im)migration. As we have seen in chapters 2–4, the biblical views on migration issues are very complex and therefore certainly leave room for judgment. And the historical discontinuities and the differences between biblical Israel on the one hand and individual nations and the church on the other do not allow a copy-paste approach. As with most ethical questions, it is necessary to carefully weigh and balance various facets of the issues involved in migration. The Torah regulations, including those concerning the *ger* ("sojourner") apply in any direct way only to ancient Israel. When it comes to addressing questions of a possible transfer, it is necessary to identify the role of a specific Old Testament rule or principle in the original context of the system of ancient Israel as a whole, and take into consideration the effects of the differences between then and now. The Old Testament rules and principles also need to be assessed in light of the changes brought about in the New Testament dispensation.[6] As far as New Testament rules and principles are concerned, a more direct line of continuity with the present exists; but it is still necessary to take into

2. Amstutz, *Just Immigration*, 14.

3. Bennett, *Foreign Policy*, 36.

4. Ramsey, *Who Speaks*, 152. See also Amstutz, who states that, "biblical principles cannot be translated directly into public policies" (*Just Immigration*, 133). He rightly observes: "Despite the acknowledgment that Scripture should not be used to directly advance specific public policies, most of the Evangelical immigration documents that I examined do just that, implicitly if not explicitly. They do so by using specific biblical texts to emphasize certain themes, such as hospitality and compassion, and by selectively using biblical principles to advance particular policy goals" (*Just Immigration*, 131).

5. See Amstutz, *Just Immigration*, 229.

6. Cf. Wright, *Old Testament Ethics*, 442–45.

account the differences between the respective historical circumstances, and to identify those aspects of the New Testament ethical guidelines that are culturally conditioned.

On the other hand, a text like Job 31:15, 32 bases the protection of the alien, together with other *personae miserae*, in a universal creation theology,[7] which is directly applicable in all historic circumstances. Moreover, one needs to keep in mind that Israel, including her ethics, was meant to serve as a model for other nations.

2. HOLISTIC APPROACH

The first principle in addressing an ethical issue is to take into consideration all available data concerning the subject at hand. Since this study is about the use of the Bible in the migration debate, one of the sets of data to be considered is the Bible. The point that is important here is that the perception of the biblical material must not be restricted in any way, for example by only focusing on a limited set of biblical passages, be it Jesus's love command or the Old Testament legal passages dealing with the support of the *ger* ("sojourner")—or, in fact, any other selection of texts. One needs to look at the *entire* canon, through the lens of the major biblical themes of creation, fall, redemption, and new creation.[8]

A broad perception of the biblical material is, however, not enough. It is also necessary to collect as many of the accessible *extra-biblical data* as possible. As mentioned earlier, this includes psychological, historic, economic, and demographic data, among many others. Of course, the context of individual investigations will limit the degree to which such data can be studied and incorporated. The main point, however, is that they need to be considered in *some* way and cannot be ignored in principle if one transitions from a mere descriptive to some kind of prescriptive level.

This twofold broadening of the horizon will have the positive effect of rendering special pleading much more difficult and enhance the acceptance of the complexity of the issues at stake.

That the holistic approach with broad horizons concerning both the biblical material and the extra-biblical data is an important principle in evaluating ethical questions can be seen by comparing migration with a

7. See also Brett, "Forced Migrations," 131.

8. See Wright, *Walking*, 14–21

less-contested topic, for example vegetarianism. To decide the questions whether vegetarianism is ethically preferable to the support of a diet that also includes meat, and whether there is a biblical case for such a position, it would not be good enough to only consider Genesis 1 as far as the biblical material is concerned, and ignore extra-biblical data, or in case of the latter only to look at potential health deficits related to a diet that does not include meat. Rather, as far as the biblical material is concerned, the explicit allowance of meat consumption in Gen 9:3–5, the involvement of meat consumption in the festival of Passover or in peace offerings, the mention of meat consumption in the description of the eschatological meal in Isa 25:6, or the absence of reference to meat consumption in Revelations 20–21, among other texts, would all need to be taken into consideration in addition to Genesis 1. As far as extra-biblical data are concerned, aspects like efficiency of meat production compared to the production of alternative food, energy consumption connected with the transport of meat and alternative food, living conditions of animals nurtured for meat-consumption (also in comparison to living conditions of other animals), among many other factors, would need to be investigated in addition to a study of the relevant biblical texts and the assessment of health issues mentioned above.

3. CREATIONAL ORDER

Creational order is an important point of orientation for the assessment of a broad range of ethical questions[9] in a biblical perspective in general. This applies also to migration issues.[10] Some of the important points were already mentioned in chapter 2, but more needs to be said.

a) Genesis 1 stresses the general aspects of *order* and *distinction*. God loves order, and accordingly his creation is marked by a high degree of order. Creation in important ways consists of the overcoming of chaos, the *tohu wa-bohu* that is mentioned in Gen 1:2. The ethical implication of this trait is that human societal life must be organized in a way that avoids chaos. With a view to the question of immigration, this translates (among other things) into support for

9. Ranging from environmental ethics to gender issues, among others.

10. This is also asserted by, e.g., Paynter, "Porous Borders," 123. She does, however, reduce the importance of the opening chapters of Genesis to the aspect of "diversity and equal worth of the created peoples" ("Porous Borders," 123).

a distinction between legal and illegal immigration. It also cautions against the promotion of large-scale (im)migration, because large-scale (im)migration disrupts order and undermines distinctions on various levels. Migration, then, cannot be the "default position" or the preferred and primary recourse in terms of addressing specific needs, and migration movements must be organized (if at all possible) in ways that prevent chaotic situations from occurring.

b) Genesis 1 underlines God's valuing of life in general and of human life in particular, the causing of which is the fundamental goal of creation. Life takes precedence over all other values that may be at stake in ethical considerations.[11] As the restriction mentioned in Gen 2:16, but even much more the punishments mentioned in Gen 3:16–19 show, life takes precedence over the absence of limits to well-being and other detrimental factors. This translates into a distinction between various factors related to migration, whether they relate to what can loosely be labelled "survival" vs. "better life," with the former having more ethical weight than the latter.

c) According to Gen 1:27 and 9:6, every human being bears the image of God and therefore has indefinite value. This *imago Dei*-principle applies also to migrants, and indeed to illegal immigrants as well. On the other hand, being made in the image of God is also the basis for expectations to discerning and morally good behavior.[12] Also, being created in the image of God does not in itself imply a right to settle wherever one wants. Such a notion would be at variance with the concept of rights to property and ownership, among other things.

d) If all persons are endowed with the dignity derived from their status as bearers of the image of God, this applies, of course, also to the citizens of countries that are destinations of migration movements.[13] Therefore, an ethically responsible manner of handling migration issues can never focus exclusively on the needs of migrants, but also

11. From a view that is informed by the New Testament, one would need to qualify this statement by asserting that it is eternal life or spiritual life that has the highest value.

12. See Hoffmeier, *The Immigration Crisis*, 145.

13. This point is also made by Carroll, with a specific view to the obligation of the migrants: "In addition, immigrants should value the people of this country [i.e., the U.S.] as those made in God's image" (*Christians*, 51).

has to take into consideration the needs of the residents of the receiving societies.

e) Genesis 10, read as a (partial) fulfillment of Gen 1:28 and 9:1, points to the importance of the bonds based on family and ethnicity.[14] Moreover, this notion is related to the concept of nationhood in the sense of specific ethnic groups living on specific territories defined by specific borders. This notion is also recognized as a part of God's creational intentions in Deut 32:8. This provides biblical support for the creational assertion of the distinction of peoples and the assertion of their identity, related to a specific territory with specific borders.[15] From this perspective, mass-(im)migration, as well as the aspiration to create what is currently labeled "multicultural" societies, to the degree that they are in conflict with these principles, are potentially counter-creational and therefore in need of special supportive arguments that would outweigh the creational model. The division of humanity into various ethnic groups related to specific territories naturally also implies that territorial states have certain rights and responsibilities that cannot be dissolved into an overarching global community in general terms.[16]

14. It is, therefore, no surprise that by and large those who want to overcome traditional family structures also want to dissolve ethnically coherent nation-states.

15. For a counter-position see, e.g., Favell, who claims that "the idea that human societies need to construct political borders and institutions that define and constrain spatial mobility" is "abnormal . . . and historically constructed" (Favell, "Rebooting Migration Theory," 271). Favell's view is rejected by Brettell and Hollifield as "counterintuitive" (see "Migration Theory," 21). A position similar to Favell's is found in Houston, who claims that the division between citizens and aliens is "arbitrary" (*You Shall Love*, 130).

16. More on this will be said in the following paragraph on responsibility. Amstutz rightly distinguishes two main influential paradigms by which global politics relating—among other things—to questions of migration are organized and assessed: cosmopolitism vs. communitarianism. He explains: "The first views the world as a unitary global society in which the individual rights of people take precedence over the sovereign rights of territorial states. The second views the world as a society of nation-states in which the primary responsibility of such states is to protect and enhance the rights and well-being of its own people while also caring for all people" (Amstutz, *Just Immigration*, 13). Within this framework, it is the second position that seems to be the biblical one. Amstutz also mentions a third paradigm, called "realism"; it is different from communitarianism in that it does not consider "transnational interests and transcendent moral values that constrain states" (*Just Immigration*, 80–81).

f) It is true that the division of humanity into nation-states can lead to conflict.[17] On the other hand, their abolition does not in itself lead to more peaceful conditions, as numerous historic examples of conflicts within supra-national entities show.[18] Importantly, nation-states can also lead to "cooperation in promoting the common good and in confronting evil and injustice"—in the context of a healthy balance of power.[19]

Even if the global system of nation-states were abolished, divisions between various groups would still exist. Because of the "fragmented nature of global society,"[20] states are important as the entities that—to the degree that they are not "rogue states"—advance human rights and the well-being of individuals generally. As Amstutz observes: "Since a person's humanity is expressed through communal life, and since proximity contributes to stronger social ties, membership in limited communities is especially important to human well-being. Nation-states are arbitrary political creations that include many different ethnic, religious, and social groups. Still, the solidarity of the nation-state . . . can foster legitimate social and political ties that enhance human dignity."[21]

In the current discussion, this dimension is missed in two major ways, which are sometimes interconnected:[22] In one view, migrants are seen as economic participants only and the national society is treated "as a market, a place where strangers work and pursue their economic interest, not a society where people share common bonds and shared responsibilities."[23] In the other view, migrants are seen as human beings in need of help, whom the church or the individual believers have to support regardless of any consequences for or interconnections with the natural order. Such approaches are obviously reductionist.

---

17. On the other hand, there is no reason to assert that borders inherently oppress people (*pace*, e.g., Paynter, "'Make Yourself at Home,'" 56).

18. The constant bitter strives between member states of the European Union about various issues—among them immigration policies—are just one example that proves the point.

19. Amstutz, *Just Immigration*, 101.

20. Amstutz, *Just Immigration*, 99,

21. Amstutz, *Just Immigration*, 101.

22. Such as, e.g., in Crisp, "Love and Borders."

23. Amstutz, *Just Immigration*, 104–5.

g) Controlling the borders is a central and constitutive element of statehood and a precondition to its function as a context for human flourishing. "It is a general characteristic of associations that people are free to leave them but not free to join them."[24] This means that individuals have the right to emigrate, but not the right to immigrate to a particular state.[25] Regulating membership through admission and exclusion is essential in preserving "communities of character"—that is, "historically stable, ongoing associations of men and women with some special commitment to one another and some special sense of their common life."[26] "The distinctiveness of cultures and groups depends upon closure and cannot be conceived as a stable feature of human life without it. If this distinctiveness is a value . . . then closure must be permitted somewhere."[27] "States are . . . like clubs in that membership is entirely up to the members themselves to decide. Admissions policies, like immigration laws, are a significant feature of communal life because they contribute to the maintenance of cohesion and a sense of shared purpose."[28]

In the absence of social solidarity on a global scale, communal solidarity is of paramount importance, and this can only be maintained if migration is regulated, which happens through the nation-state and its control of the borders.[29] Mutual regard, which can only be built within borders, "enables a society to nurture cooperation and trust"; but "mass immigration can easily undermine such cohesion by impeding mutual regard."[30]

h) There is a trend in biblical and theological discussions of immigration to either overlook the creational principles and their implications pointed at above completely, or to downplay them to a considerable degree. Here are some examples, most of them based

24. Brian Barry, "The Quest for Consistency," 284.

25. See, e.g., Amstutz, *Just Immigration*, 88.

26. Walzer, *Spheres of Justice*, 62.

27. Walzer, *Spheres of Justice*, 9–10.

28. Amstutz, *Just Immigration*, 89. He also asserts that the state has the right to control immigration "in order to protect the inherent values, traditions, and aspirations of a community" (*Just Immigration*, 102).

29. See Amstutz, *Just Immigration*, 91. He adds that "the pursuit of social or distributive justice can be undertaken only within a state" (*Just Immigration*, 90).

30. Amstutz, *Just Immigration*, 91.

on a "one-world" view:[31] On Christmas Eve 1948, Pope Pius XII wrote to the U.S. bishops that, "the sovereignty of the State, although it must be respected, cannot be exaggerated to the point that access to this land is, for inadequate or unjustified reasons, denied to needy and decent people from other nations . . . ."[32] The right of the state to regulate its borders is recognized in principle, but it is not given much weight. On the other hand, things are more balanced when one takes into consideration the immediately following clause: "provided, of course, that the public wealth, considered very carefully, does not forbid this." This additional clause leaves more room for the creational principles mentioned above, though it singles out only material aspects ("public wealth") and does not address the importance of (familial and) ethnic bonds, or the cultural ramifications of these bonds.[33] In the encyclical *Pacem in Terris*, issued by Pope John XXIII in 1963, mention is made of citizenship in a universal society and of a worldwide fellowship of men; from this follow a general permission to emigrate and take up residence somewhere else.[34] Without any qualifications, Groody and Campese maintain that there are "natural rights of immigrants."[35] Groody also writes about the necessity to "develop a community that transcends all borders, that sees in the eyes of the immigrant stranger a brother, a sister."[36] According to McKinney, Hill, and Hania, when people are unable to secure "the essentials in life" at home, they have freedom to migrate;[37] since the earth is created for everyone and resources are for the good of all, they also have the right to immigrate wherever such resources can be found.[38] Rodríguez states: "We are called

31. In addition to the specific examples quoted in this paragraph, we may note that almost all the biblical studies supporting liberal immigration policies are marked by a lack of any reference to the importance of the creational order.

32. This statement was later introduced into the encyclical *Exsul Familia Nazarethana* (1952).

33. One also needs to take into consideration that the statements made in this papal letter were addressed to the situation in a specific country, the U.S.

34. *Pacem in Terris*, 25. For a similar view see United States Conference of Catholic Bishops (1996), "A Catholic Framework for Economic Life," 4.

35. Groody and Campese, "Preface," xxiv.

36. Groody, "Fruit," 313.

37. Which in their view is concomitant with an obligation to accept them as immigrants. Importantly, the "essentials of life" are not defined in more particular terms.

38. "Welcoming the Stranger," 53–54.

to see in our migrant brothers and sisters a common humanity and work together for a common solidarity."[39] Senior maintains: "God's embrace reaches to the end of the earth," which is "the ultimate bond that ties the human family together." This constitutes "the challenge to the absolute claims of national or cultural boundaries," and establishes "the right of the migrant to cross the border."[40] While it is the universality of mankind, based on "God's embrace," that is stressed, with the concomitant (at least seemingly) unfettered right to migration, there is still the implicit possibility of accepting at least a relative claim to national and cultural boundaries—even if he does not elaborate on how they would be defined or maintained.

i) While creational orders, including ethnicity and nationhood, must not be ignored, the picture is nevertheless more complex. For Christians, the identity of an individual believer is a combination of natural categories such as family and ethnicity on the one hand and the new "being in Christ" on the other; moreover, Christians see themselves as citizens not only of an earthly nation, but also of the kingdom of God which transcends all national boundaries and identities—factors that become visible in a special way in the context of migration.[41] The flip-side of the same coin is the fact that in many cases local churches in countries of destination take on the role of the extended family for immigrants.[42]

Factors such as these do in fact necessitate some nuancing in the weighing and application of creational principles. As a consequence, one must be guarded against a narrow perspective that decides matters exclusively based on creational principles, without taking into account the trans-familial and trans-ethnic (or trans-national) aspects of the Christian identity.[43] There is no room for giv-

---

39. Rodríguez, "A Witness," xvi.

40. "Beloved Aliens," 32.

41. Cf., e.g., Carroll, *Christians*, 37. Schreiter ("Migrants," 113) points to the multi-cultural character of the church.

42. See, e.g., Carroll, *Christians*, 36 (with a view to the situation in the U.S.). It is certainly right to say that immigrants who "are brothers and sisters in Christ . . . deserve all the respect and attention this fact should engender" (Carroll, *Christians*, 38).

43. Carroll seems to be aware of the tension mentioned here when he states that one must not "deny the many contributions of culture or the importance of a specific identity, but . . . put these concerns into perspective. Perhaps these things have to be held a bit more loosely so that we can . . . engage those from other backgrounds

ing *absolute priority* to natural entities such as family, ethnic group, or nation in a biblical perspective. However, the trans-familial and trans-ethnic aspects of the Christian identity cannot simply undo or replace the creational principles.[44] As a comparative example, one can point to the fact that just because the new *familia Dei* established among the followers of Jesus introduces a new reality, it does not as such undo the natural family—which is the reason why the vast majority of Christians continue to marry and raise natural families.

On the other hand, it is important to note that the fact that the church is multiethnic and multicultural does not determine how a local church needs to reflect this principle; even less can it be used as a prescription of how to organize broader societal life at the local or national level. Moreover, mass-migration is in no ways a necessary instrument to teach lessons about the pilgrimage-like nature of life with God. The fact that among the immigrants also Christians are found cannot be taken as the one decisive factor that determines immigration policies in general, especially since resources are limited and the natural realm (of ethnic attachment) cannot be ignored.

j) Ignoring creational order in the realm of ethnicity and nationhood is sometimes related to the notion that countries of destination, especially in Europe, might experience some kind of re-evangelization as a consequence of large-scale immigration,[45] which—given

and cultures" (*Christians*, 115). This is certainly right, but the question is how far one should go in "holding these things loosely." There is a clear tendency in his book not to give enough weight to creational principles.

44. Often the balance between the two sides is not maintained. See, e.g., Paynter ("'Make Yourself at Home,'" 56) who (referring to Reed) rightly asserts that "national borders cannot be sacralised with biblical legitimacy," but only mentions undefined "social benefits" as factors that could legitimize borders, not the deeper aspects of order, identity-creation and -protection, and promotion of solidarity mentioned above.

45. See, e.g., Carroll, *Christians*, 39. McKinney et al. note that, "new arrivals can enrich, enliven and energise the local (and national) churches they join" ("Welcoming the Stranger," 54). Escobar notes that, "Such people in transition are open to becoming believers" ("Refugees," 103; cf. also p. 105), while Prill claims in general terms that immigrants embrace Christianity following their arrival (see "Migration," 332). Carroll applies this aspect also explicitly to the U.S.: "[C]ould what we are witnessing in this country be part of a new, divinely directed global phenomenon? Is God bringing millions of Hispanics to the United States to revitalize the Christian churches here and to present to those who do not yet believe the opportunity to turn to Christ in their search for a new life?" (*Christians*, 40). Similar statements are found in "Immigration

the importance of the concepts of the kingdom of God and eternal life—might put into question the creational principles mentioned above.

There are two observations that need to be taken into consideration to assess this claim. On a general level, as with the points of tension mentioned above, one needs to abstain from conflating spiritual and natural realms of life and having the former replace the latter. Natural bonds based on familial, ethnic, cultural, and historic ties still play a role in life on this side of eternity, even if it is fully right to admit that the spiritual domain is important as well, and in some respects in fact more important than the natural domain.[46] More specifically, the claim that a large-scale re-evangelization is taking place in the West is simply not borne out by any available statistics. In the case of western Europe, for example, overall church attendance has not grown, in spite of mass-immigration, and the number of non-Christian immigrants turning to the Christian faith is minimal.[47] On the other hand, it is interesting to note that there is a broader revival of Christian roots exactly in those eastern European countries that do not follow the policies of their western counterparts and are largely closed to immigration from Muslim countries.[48]

2009," National Realities.

46. A typical example that demonstrates that natural aspects cannot be ignored even in the context of an overriding spiritual element are mixed marriages between Christians from different ethnic and cultural backgrounds. The special challenges present in these relationships, in some cases leading to divorce, proves the point. This claim is based on personal observations (I was not able to find statistics on this issue); the anecdotical nature of the observations precludes any far-reaching conclusions. On the other hand, there are statistical indications for the fragility of cross-cultural marriages in general; see, e.g., Crippen, "Working with Intercultural Couples."

47. While there are obviously Muslims both worldwide and also in Europe who convert to Christianity, reliable numbers are difficult to come by. None of the reports that mention the conversion of Muslims to Christianity in Europe offers numbers that are higher than a couple of thousands—which is very little compared to the fast growth of the Muslim population in Western countries. The clearest data are provided by Pew Research, relating to the situation in the U.S. According to their findings, the number of Muslims in the U.S. who leave Islam is outweighed by the number of converts to Islam; see Mohamed and Podrebarac Sciupac, "The Share."

48. See, e.g., Mazurczak, "Eastern Europe's Christian Reawakening." The situation is, of course, complex, and it is not predictable whether the trend will change in the foreseeable future.

k) As we have noted in chapter 3, it is often pointed out that in the church there is no distinction based on ethnic or national identity, especially not in an eschatological perspective. From this the conclusion is drawn that Christians should work to mirror these realities in the realm of the general political body. This argument does not, however, stand to scrutiny. Some arguments were already presented in chapter 3. Here, some more will be added. First, the eschatological images of both the Hebrew Bible and the New Testament are too vague to use them as concrete prescriptions for a particular policy in terms of ethnic mixing. Second, the realm of the church cannot simply be identified with the broader society, because the addition of the spiritual domain and the work of the Holy Spirit enables congregations to be formed and to behave in ways that cannot be copied by the outside world. Third, future states cannot be taken as automatically or necessarily dictating how life in the current situation on this side of eternity should be organized. This is broadly accepted in other areas of life. As an example, one can point to the fact that the overwhelming majority of Christians marry, although marriage is not an institution that will be carried on in the world to come. Thus, the question arises why one would want to implement an eschatological state in the present in one realm (question of the importance of ethnic differences), but not in the other (marriage)?

4. RESPONSIBILITY

a) The case for open borders or liberal immigration policies is mostly connected to the notion that in some way the receiving nations have a responsibility to alleviate the suffering of members of other nations. On the other hand, proponents of more restrictive migration policies point to the responsibility of the state to maintain order, which includes border control.[49]

---

49. It is interesting to observe that the notion that nations (or nation states) have a direct and unavoidable responsibility to admit migrants in need is often presupposed without further justification beyond such general principles as, for example, "hallowing bare life"; see, e.g., Bretherton, *Christianity and Contemporary Politics*, 126–74. Another variant is the concept of "equitable burden-sharing" in which the countries of the North have to bare their fair share of the burden (Houston, *You Shall Love*, 10).

b) In the context of theological statements, one often encounters the view that the world belongs to all humans, regardless of borders, and that the shared bond of humanity trumps specific ethnic or national affiliations. From this a responsibility of materially affluent states towards people from less affluent states is deduced. Here are some examples: In their article on "Welcoming the Stranger," McKinney, Hill, and Hania insist that space and resources must be shared, and that the transformation of the shared space must be accepted.[50] According to Kerwin, there is a general "right to economic migration," with "corresponding responsibilities" on the side of the countries of destination.[51] He also requests that one should receive migrants "whenever possible."[52] Carroll, referring to the Doha Round, points to "the moral obligation of more powerful nations to help move the entire world forward."[53] An extensive plea in support of global responsibility is provided by Battistella. He maintains that there is "a common responsibility toward others regardless of their ethnicity or nationality. Such responsibility is grounded on the notion of common belonging to the human family . . . and on the sacredness of human dignity."[54] He adds that, "The temptation of sovereignty is to feel free from obligations toward foreigners . . . even irregular migrants,"[55] and that "the equal worth of all people . . . cannot be diminished by such accidents as the place of birth or the nationality of the parents."[56] He also posits that, "the introduction of the humanitarian principle pushes the ethical reflection beyond the realist approach [that national culture needs to be protected, that states have a—primary—duty towards their citizens], questioning the current divide among states and economies as unjust."[57] Elaborating on the aspect of human dignity, Battistella argues, referring to *Gaudium et Spes*,[58] that because of the universal character of human dignity,

---

50. McKinney et al., "Welcoming the Stranger," 54.

51. Kerwin, "The Natural Rights," 193.

52. "The Natural Rights," 195.

53. Carroll, *Christians*, 33.

54. Battistella, "Migration," 177.

55. "Migration," 181.

56. "Migration," 186.

57. "Migration," 186. Because of this, it is unacceptable to include human rights "in a cost-benefit analysis" ("Migration," 187).

58. An encyclical commissioned by Pope John XXIII.

persons must be granted to migrate when dignity is not available in one's own country, in the context of a global responsibility to make available "to all persons everything necessary for leading a life truly human."[59] It is only in the pursuit of "the (universal) common good" that "the state has the right to regulate migration."[60] Battistella adds that, "The duty of the state towards migrants, and therefore the limitations of the state in its migration policies, derives from the larger community to which all belong, the human family." Because of a "collective responsibility," "solidarity is not an option, but a duty."[61] As a consequence, "interdependence must be transformed into solidarity, based on the principle that the goods of creation are meant for all"; "the stronger and richer nations must have a sense of moral responsibility for the other nations."[62]

The most fundamental problem with this view is the confusion of realms: the church in her specific character, resulting in particular responsibilities, is not the same as the state or the larger body politic of any given ethnic or national group.

c) While the theological statements quoted above are mostly grounded in theological assertions of a shared humanity, arguments for the responsibility of Western states towards immigrants from other countries are often based on non-theological perceptions of differences in prosperity and stability. Sometimes, such arguments are augmented by references to history. A primary example is the case of the U.S., with its long historic traditions of immigration. Another, somewhat different, example is Norway. For many Norwegians, besides general humanitarian considerations, the fact that their ancestors were granted entry to foreign countries in the past to seek a better life, especially in the U.S., means that they are under a moral obligation to open their borders to migrants who seek a better life in Norway today.

---

59. "Migration," 188.

60. "Migration," 188. See also Campese, "¿Cuantos Más?" 289–90.

61. "Migration," 189.

62. "Migration," 189. The last quote takes up a formulation coined by Pope John Paul II (*Sollicitudo Rei Socialis*, art. 39). See also Campese, who bases his universalist notion of responsibility on the fact that "catholicity . . . [is] one of the primary characteristics of our Christian community" ("¿Cuantos Más?" 290).

Such arguments are not without problems. To begin with the case of Norway: One has to keep in mind that there is no direct link between the past history of emigration and the present circumstances. Among other things, the agents are different, because in the current situation it is not about Americans seeking opportunities in Norway; also the social-economic systems are different, because in the current situation Norway with its highly developed welfare system offers much more in publicly funded support for immigrants than the U.S. did when Norwegians arrived there in the past. There are also specific Old Testament perspectives that make such direct historical lines look unconvincing. There is, for example, the principle that children must not be held accountable for the crimes of their parents.[63] Also, Israelites did not claim a right to settle in Assyria or Babylonia at later periods as part of a claim to compensation. Turning to the U.S., three points have to be borne in mind: First, historic cases of immigration are different from current ones in that new arrivals had no access to government-financed means of social welfare; second, immigration was historically always strictly controlled and admission never simply granted to all persons in need; and third, on a general note, historical patterns cannot be allowed to dictate current ethical decisions.

As far as the general connection between higher degrees of prosperity and stability in a country and its responsibility in terms of immigration policies is concerned: It is ethically not justifiable to make this consideration the sole decisive factor, without also considering the responsibility of agents on the side of the sending countries, especially their governments and elites. One also has to take into account that the ultimate divide is not between rich and poor countries, but between rich and poor people in practically all countries.[64] Finally, one needs to consider that the perceived wealth of Western countries is heavily relativized by the huge debts—in most cases both public and private—that these countries find themselves in.

d) According to another argument, Western states, especially the U.S., because of their foreign and economic policies, are at least "partly responsible for the migration of people from Third World

---

63. See especially Deut 24:16; Ezekiel 18.

64. Things look more complex when it comes to general levels of stability.

countries"; therefore, it is argued, they also need to show responsibility to these persons by allowing them access into their countries as immigrants.[65] There are, however, many problems with such statements. For example, it is often very difficult to draw direct lines of causality between specific actions by Western countries and migratory incentives, or to even quantify such connections, especially when other factors, many of them relating to conditions in the sending countries that are not related to external influences, are also taken into consideration. Moreover, those who are responsible for certain policies in the U.S. or other Western states with regard to sending countries are for the most part not identical with those segments of the population in the countries of destination that will have to deal with the sometimes challenging consequences of mass-immigration—which poses serious ethical questions. On a more general level, as mentioned in the previous paragraph, from an Old Testament perspective one has to take into consideration the principle that children must not be held accountable for the crimes of their parents, as well as the fact that Israelites did not claim a right to settle in Assyria or Babylonia at later periods as part of a claim to compensation.

e) With regard to ancient Israel, we can observe that responsibility, as far as the administration of immigration and the looking after immigrants are concerned, is not primarily located on the level of a centralized state bureaucracy, but predominantly directly on the level of individual families or local communities. This responsibility is restricted to individual cases—the *ger* ("sojourner") is always mentioned in the singular when his support is in view. For broader and more distant issues of economic need, Israel is not called to open her borders to masses of immigrants, but to grant loans to distant peoples.[66]

f) The New Testament texts that touch on the subject of the state and its responsibilities do not envision that the state is a "charity" of sorts which is supposed to work for the relief of suffering people all over the planet; rather, the state has the divinely ordained—and much more limited—role of guarantor of order within its borders

65. Campese, "¿Cuantos Más?" 291.
66. See Deut 28:12.

(especially by punishing wrongdoers) and of defender against enemies attacking its borders.[67]

g) One of the implications of this definition of the role of the state is the notion of national sovereignty, which also means that a state may sovereignly regulate migration and do it in a way that is beneficial for its citizens, which means that foreigners can be denied admission, punished or expelled if they do not abide by the laws.[68]

h) The Bible does not support the view that there is a general human capability to fix all societal problems, from which a corresponding general responsibility could be deduced. This is important for the migration debate because the reason that causes people to migrate is very often some kind of societal problem in their place of origin. Once the idea of a human capacity to overcome such problems is questioned, it becomes clear that neither migration nor other ways of addressing the specific needs might be sufficient to solve the problem; and it also becomes clear that there will never be a definitive solution for such problems in a long-term perspective.

i) In the Bible, responsibility is layered. Israel is not called to open her doors for all the needy of the world. More particularly, no text in the Hebrew Bible supports the idea of global responsibility directly associated with the domain of state governance, with the possible exception of the special case of the rule of the Messiah. Rather, specific help is given (as seen above: not through state agencies) first to the Israelite brothers, then to the *ger* ("sojourner")—who is always envisioned as belonging to a group of people that is limited in number, and who, because of his assimilation, is no longer fully "other." The same kind of help is not extended to other groups of foreigners. Israel is also not called to send free gifts to other nations. Rather, the Israelites are promised that in the case of their obedience to the laws of YHWH, they will receive his blessing, which will enable them

---

67. See especially Rom 13:3–4. See also 1 Pet 2:13–17; Titus 3:1. Carroll, however, together with many others, maintains that state measures "designed to organize and appropriately deal with . . . immigrants should reflect the virtues of kindness, generosity, and patience" (*Christians*, 98). To this, he adds in *The Bible* (82): "The key is to explore options and to ground these measures in divine compassion and wisdom, not in a punitive, exclusionary spirit. All these reflections underscore that migration matters are inescapably systemic" (of course, the last phrase reflects a dominant topic within the current social justice debate).

68. See Edwards, "A Biblical Perspective," 2.

to lend to others (see Deut 15:6; 28:12)—not to hand out free gifts in foreign aid, or to let whole people groups come in. The Hebrew Bible does not support a type of help either that would endanger the survival of Israel as a culturally and religiously distinct entity. Evidently the specific aspects mentioned in this paragraph are not directly addressed in the New Testament, primarily because the notion of a nation of God defined in territorial, ethnic, and political terms has no equivalent in the New Testament.[69]

All of what can be observed in the case of biblical Israel is different from notions prevalent in the current debate in the West, where those advocating for liberal immigration policies stress the world-wide humanitarian responsibilities of potential receiving societies, and grant much less weight to rights that members of the receiving societies might have in terms of self-determination, protection, economic security, ethnic and cultural identity, etc.

The layering of responsibility can be seen in the love command. In the Hebrew Bible, there are commands to love the neighbor, in first place; then, there is the command to love the *ger* ("sojourner"). There is, however, no command to love either the *nokri* ("foreigner") or any foreign nation or even the world's nations in their entirety. Similarly, YHWH hears the cry of the Israelite slaves in Egypt, but not the cry of other slaves in a comparable way. This layering is also found in the New Testament: love of the brother takes precedence over love for other persons—although the latter is commanded as well.

The distinctions made in the Bible between the dealings with different kinds of foreigners can be translated into distinctions— broadly speaking—between refugees and economic migrants. "Because they are fleeing persecution and violence, refugees have moral precedence over regular migrants."[70]

The layering described in this section implies that responsibility ("Verantwortung") is related to specific areas of answerability ("Verantwortlichkeit"), which can only exist in the context of manageable boundaries.

---

69. This fact cannot be used as an argument that the New Testament tacitly overcomes these notions. We are rather dealing with corpora of texts that address different levels.

70. Amstutz, *Just Immigration*, 231.

The layering of responsibility can be quite easily understood in the context of a practical everyday example that compares well with the discussion about migration issues: It is obviously wrong for parents to neglect their own children in the process of taking care of the homeless people in their neighborhood.

j) Ultimately, the related concepts of (quasi-)open borders and global responsibility[71] require some kind of global political administration. This is, however, not a biblical concept—with the possible exception of the rule of the Messiah. Besides this, the only clear biblical reference to a successful attempt to establish a global political administration outside of the rule of the Messiah is found in Revelations 13, envisioning the rule of the Antichrist. Historical attempts to establish an administration with global aspirations do not provide any positive argument in support of the pursuit of this project. How catastrophic an attempt to establish a unified global political entity in the current circumstances would be can only be ignored if one closes the eyes completely to the psychological dynamics of power, the intrinsic incompatibility of the various cultures, ideologies, religions, etc., in addition to all historical lessons.[72] Sin permeates human life, and therefore there will be conflict in social and political life also without the nation-state.[73]

It must also be noted that the joint principles of (quasi-)open borders and global responsibility are not applied equally across the globe, but predominantly addressed as demands to the West. The partial application of a principle that aims to be global opens, however, the door for all kinds of misuse.[74]

---

71. Which is in conflict with the notion of layered responsibility.

72. Of course, this does not mean that the system of nation-states does not have serious flaws, with greed, lust for power and resources, as well as racist and dehumanizing views of "the other" as constant dangers that have the potential to cause conflict. However, such conflicts are not a *necessary* outcome of the nation-state system, and all these flaws will not simply disappear with the dissolution of nation-states. It does not seem that proponents of a globalist one-world ideology have really thought through all the consequences that its implementation would have.

73. So also Amstutz, *Just Immigration*, 101.

74. There are obviously other countries outside of the West in the current situation that are marked both by prosperity and stability; the Gulf states would be one example, Japan (together with some further East Asian states) another.

k) At this point, there is no other institution besides the nation-state which can take responsibility in effective ways and advance human rights in general and protect both migrants and non-migrants in particular.[75] Attempts to combine some measure of nation-state autonomy with some measure of global administration (at this point especially through various branches of the U.N.) in important ways prove disastrous again and again. This means that a decisive step would need to be taken to build a fully equipped global state in the short term to administer all issues related to governance—with all the negative implications mentioned in the previous paragraph.

l) In this context, it is also important to observe that the Sermon on the Mount which is often identified as the very kernel of New Testament ethics must not be interpreted in terms of a direct blueprint for policies of state agencies, but rather marks the goals and aspirations that guide the followers of Jesus in their private lives.[76]

m) Sometimes, though not too frequently, it is also mentioned in biblical and theological discussions of migration that immigrants have responsibilities as well. Carroll, for example, states that "there is also a responsibility that the sojourner must accept."[77] What this might mean in more specific terms is fleshed out later, indirectly, by pointing to the situation in ancient Israel where the law assumes that the sojourner moves "toward the host culture (Israel): learning its ways and its language and respecting its laws and taboos."[78] This is in fact an important point. One might add that it would certainly not be unethical to expect such behavior—*mutatis mutandis*—also from current migrants.

5. LOVE

Both from a biblical perspective and from a perspective of theological ethics some of the ethical requirements that are related to love are also

---

75. See, e.g., Amstutz, *Just Immigration*, 83.

76. This has been stressed most clearly by Martin Luther and reflects the majority position in the newer exegetical community; see, e.g., Crump, "Applying the Sermon on the Mount," 3–14.

77. Carroll, *Christians*, 99.

78. Carroll, *Christians*, 100.

related to justice, and vice versa. This is not surprising, because in various contexts love and justice are complementary rather than mutually exclusive concepts. It is important for the consideration of the implications of love for assessing (im)migration issues that love surpasses justice, but cannot invalidate or push aside justice.

a) There are those who suggest that the command to love the neighbor decides all questions about immigration in the sense of opening the borders of the receiving countries in the West as wide as possible, unless particular circumstances would not allow it technically.[79] In some cases, allowing a migrant to cross the border may in fact be the best solution and the one that is most in line with the principle of love. However, as the following paragraphs will show, things are much more complex.

b) Love and compassion are obviously central biblical ethical concepts.[80] There is, moreover, no doubt that love must also be shown to migrants, including illegal immigrants, since there is no biblical boundary to the love command. However, love and compassion are mandated in the Bible on the individual level (and the church level in the New Testament), not the level of civil authorities.[81] The state is here to uphold justice, not to exercise love, mercy, or compassion,

79. See, e.g., Crisp, "Love and Borders." Indirectly referring to migration, Pope John Paul II in his World Day for Peace Message of January 1, 2001, claims that, "In order to build a civilization of love, dialogue between cultures must work to overcome all ethnocentric selfishness and make it possible to combine regard for one's own identity with understanding of others and respect for diversity" (see "Quotes from Church Teachings on the Rights of Migrants and Refugees," *United States Conference of Catholic Bishops*; interestingly, the exact quote does not appear in the official Vatican edition of this speech).

Sometimes, the point about the importance of love for handling migration issues is made not by referring to the biblical love commands directly, but to some related text that may express the principle indirectly. For example, Carroll takes up the biblical injunction to "give drink to our enemies," inferring from this text: "This is a strong word to those who are suspicious of certain immigrants" (*Christians*, 124), suggesting that the right attitude is one of principled openness. In reality, however, there is no direct or necessary link between extending help to enemies, which is a matter of personal behavior in one's private life, and immigration policies, which is a matter of the organization of public life. Also, if there are objective reasons to be suspicious of *some* immigrants or *certain groups* of immigrants, there is no biblical reason to simply ignore these reasons.

80. See the notes on love in chapters 2 and 3 above.

81. So also Edwards, "A Biblical Perspective," 2.

according to Romans 13 and other New Testament passages dealing with these questions.[82] Love and compassion "cannot serve as the foundation of a legal system."[83] In the case of the state and state legislation, the function of love is restricted to temper, in specific cases (for example of punishments), as opposed to serving as a general guideline. To lovingly offer the other cheek is meant for individuals, but inappropriate for governments. If state authorities were to follow this line of behavior, their actions would be detrimental for the citizenry for which they bear responsibility. The church is in fact called to focus on love and compassion; but this is not true for the state which is responsible for the upholding of justice and order.

In the Bible, love as such, based on the recognition of the neighbor as bearer of the image of God, does not in any direct way serve as a general justification for the subversion of the rule of law and the promotion of illegality.

c) Love, as we have seen earlier, is layered in the sense that there is distinction between primary recipients (co-Israelites; brothers and sisters in Christ), secondary recipients (ger, "sojourner"), and tertiary recipients (everyone else).

d) Love, from a perspective of biblical ethics, cannot be shown ultimately only to a randomly selected specific group—outside of the distinction made between Israelites and non-Israelites and Christians and non-Christians. However, in many theological treatments of the dealing with (im)migrants this is exactly what happens: The (im)migrants as a group, mostly regardless of the specific category in which they would fall, are deemed worthy of special love. However, there is no biblical justification to show more love to migrants in principle than to members of the population of the country of destination. Of course, there is the special concern the Bible shows for weak members of society, in biblical terms the widows, orphans, and sojourners. As far as the ger ("sojourner") is concerned, this special concern is expressed in terms of "love" in Lev 19:34 and Deut 10:19. This does not, however, elevate immigrants above other groups of people in need. First, not all modern immigrants can in any direct and simple way be identified with the biblical category of the ger. Second, also the widows and orphans are envisioned as

82. See, e.g., Edwards, "A Biblical Perspective," 2.

83. Amstutz, *Just Immigration*, 180.

recipients of love, because they are naturally included in the command to love one's neighbor—a command that precedes the command to love the *ger*. On a pragmatic level, it is obvious that in most Western states that function as places of destination for large migratory movements, there are various important groups of needy people that must not be ignored. This is ethically important, because resources are always limited, which means that resources allocated to help migrants will not be available for the support of other people in need. The ethical problem becomes even more serious when one considers that the needy people in the places of destination have no other recourse than their own countries, whereas in the case of migrants also the sending countries have a responsibility to support them. While this support may in most cases not be readily accessible, the responsibility of the governments and leading classes of the sending countries must nevertheless not be taken out of the equation.

To the degree that one can presuppose a biblical "option for the underprivileged," one will need to analyze carefully in each situation who the underprivileged are.[84] It cannot simply be presupposed that the weak persons being in need of protection are always (or primarily, or even exclusively) the (im)migrants.[85] This is lost in the migration debate when migrants per se are imagined virtually exclusively as weak and victims.

The question, ultimately, is not whether one should extend love to migrants, but whether in a specific situation migration is the best way to extend practical help, taking into consideration all the costs (both material and otherwise) for various parties that are related to it, in the context of the limitation of resources. To put it this way: Love for migrants is not the same as love for migration or advancing migration as necessarily the best solution to a real problem in any given situation.[86] What love means in practical terms must be

84. Importantly, the underprivileged persons in a specific context are not necessarily identical with the persons who are worst off financially.

85. This is what happens regularly on the side of those who argue for liberal immigration policies; see, e.g., Wesleyan, The Justice Principle.

86. Referring to conversations that pastors in Mexico have with members who want to migrate to the U.S., Hagan notes that, "evangelical pastors often attempt to discourage the migration of their members before ultimately granting approval" ("Faith," 14). This example shows that one can in fact love someone and nevertheless not simply support the wish for migration.

decided on a reading of the vast biblical material that addresses this issue, and in consideration of the specific circumstances in which it is to be applied.[87] On this side of eternity, other aspects—like the protection of creational order—have to be given weight as well. In addition, there is a distinction between what can be expected from an individual and from the state.[88]

e) In several texts of the New Testament, love is defined in terms of "imitation of Christ" (*imitatio Christi*). This does, however, not mean that the self-giving love of Christ can and should be imitated by his followers in all respects, because the sacrifice of Christ is unique.

f) While it is an act of love when someone invests personal resources (both material and immaterial) to help others, things look differently when the state is involved. To use other people's money is not an act of love, nor is there love when the state forces citizens to do something.[89]

   Biblical love for the *ger* involves personal relationship and therefore cannot be delegated to a bureaucratic apparatus. This is made clear, among other things, by the fact that the *ger* in all of the legal and prophetic texts of the Hebrew Bible is mentioned in the singular, never in the plural.[90]

g) One can also not talk about love when support for liberal immigration policies is based on using immigrants as means to achieve certain goals that are not intrinsic to their existence and their own best interests, like enlarging the voter base of a political party or using migrants to do certain types of work that no one else would be willing to do under the conditions in which employment in this

---

87. As a matter of principle, loving someone in biblical terms does not necessarily mean to comply with the specific wishes of the recipient of love.

88. All of these considerations are often not taken into account in adequate ways. An example is Volf, *Exclusion and Embrace*, 31.

89. Cf. Edwards, "A Biblical Perspective," 4. In fact, when a state is "generous," it will be costly for many among its citizens.

90. The only exception in the legal texts are those passages that look to the experience of the Israelites as sojourners in Egypt. In the prophetic texts, the only exception is Ezek 47:22; this text, however, is not about helping the *ger*, but contains an eschatological announcement that the sojourners will also participate in the allotment of the land.

branch is "offered," or use immigrants to compensate birth deficits that endanger the functioning of the welfare state.[91]

h) Love in biblical terms cannot be reduced to the giving of material things; rather, it includes care for the neighbor as a whole, including the spiritual dimension, and is always connected with the love of God and therefore in itself spiritual. This is normally overlooked in discussions about love for immigrants.

i) Love can also be expected on the side of the migrants. It is not an act of love when illegal immigrants force their presence on others and benefit from a foreign country's welfare system. It is also not an act of love when illegal immigrants put migrants who abide by the laws in a position of relative disadvantage. It is also not an act of love when migrants leave their families behind or when families send their (minor) children ahead. Finally, it is not an act of love when immigrants do not respect the hosts; it is probably appropriate to identify (far-reaching) assimilation as the clearest and highest form of respect.

6. JUSTICE

Next to love, justice is one of the central focal points of biblical ethics. Generally speaking, it can be maintained that in the Bible, love does not destroy justice, but goes beyond it, based on a personal choice made by individuals. Justice is relevant for the migration debate in a number of ways:

a) According to Hoover (and many others), "the moral viability of any community," which is to be identified (in other words) with its justice,[92] "is intimately tied to how it treats its most vulnerable

91. The last point was already mentioned in chapter 4. Examples for the exploitation of the labor force of migrants—in addition to the blatant abuse of migrants in the context of sex trafficking—can be found, among others, in their disproportional employment in underpaid sectors like harvesting in agriculture or domestic services like cleaning and home-nursing of elderly people (see, e.g., Costa, "Employers Exploit Unauthorized Immigrants"). An example for the use of immigrants as an instrument to enlarge a party's voter base are strategies pursued by the Democrats in the U.S. to enlist immigrants as supporters together with a coalition of other minority groups (see, e.g., Williams, "Why Clinton Is Enlisting Undocumented Immigrants").

92. Even if the word "justice" is not mentioned, it seems probable that the use of

members."[93] This is important and directly applicable to immigrants in the sense that it is unjust to exploit them (see especially Deut 24:14–15).[94]

On the other hand, while the point made by Hoover is in principle acceptable, it has to be nuanced in various ways. First, illegal immigrants are not "members" of a community in the normal sense of the term, so the principle cannot be applied to them without qualifications. Second, as pointed out earlier, one cannot automatically identify the "most vulnerable" with immigrants. They may be among those groups who qualify for this descriptor, but often this is not the case.[95]

b) As Schreiter (and many others) point out, immigrants experience "a host of injustices regarding housing, employment, and forms of social welfare."[96] This may certainly be true, though it is necessary in such debates to make sure that general statements of this sort are supported by reliable statistical data. It is, moreover, important that it is defined with more precision what exactly constitutes injustice in the realms mentioned here. Sometimes, making distinctions between groups of people is qualified as unjust discrimination; this is, however, a matter of worldview and ideology. What is also important for our discussion is the observation that possible kinds of injustices in the realms identified by Schreiter and others are by no means restricted to immigrants, and that in some cases the fact that immigrants are treated differently may have just and acceptable reasons.

c) Justice demands that the interests and needs of all sides involved in instances of mass-(im)migration need to be taken into consideration. This is not the case when it is only the world-wide humanitarian responsibilities of potential receiving societies that are stressed and the rights that members of the receiving societies might have in terms of self-determination, protection, property rights, economic

the phrase "moral viability" comes very close to it.

93. "The Story," 170.

94. See, e.g., Hoffmeier, The Immigration Crisis, 157.

95. For example, when strong advocacy groups succeed in steering the public opinion to prioritize support for immigrants over other groups in need, and substantial public funds are directed for the benefits of immigrants.

96. "Migrants," 118.

security, cultural identity, etc., are not given much weight.[97] In the process, it does factually no longer really matter whether one's forebears lived in a certain place for hundreds of years or whether one arrived only yesterday—which is obviously not just.[98] How would it be just that newcomers get the same welfare benefits (or in some cases: more) as those who have paid into the system for many years and whose ancestors have lived in a place for centuries, and built a country with a lot of sacrifice?[99]

What is at stake here is the question of respect of ownership: A country belongs primarily and in a special way to its citizens; if another group is coming into the country that is then largely supported by the state, this means that (indirectly, through taxation) what belongs to the original owners is being taken away from them. If this would happen on the individual level, it would be seen as unjust by most observers. What is at stake is the basic distinction between "mine" and "yours." This distinction is clearly affirmed in the Bible both with respect to material goods and with respect to immaterial goods, like marriage; see especially the prohibitions against theft, coveting, and adultery. Obviously, this distinction is not (and must not be) automatically invalidated when the realm of the individual is replaced by the realm of the collective.

d) Problems with justice arise also on the level of international and national law, in two main respects. First, the Geneva Convention on the one hand and laws regulating asylum in Western states on the other hand have been the main gateway for the permission of large numbers of persons to cross the borders; in reality, however, only a minority of the migrants in the last decades have actually qualified for the status of refugee according to national and international law, and asylum laws as such do normally not give positive entitlement for the immigration (including permanent settlement) into a country. The second point, in the case of Europe, is the breaking of the agreements of Schengen and Dublin by most European

97. One example among many is O'Neill's demand to give priority to migrants' rights over other, less exigent claims, for instance property rights (see "'No Longer Strangers,'" 231).

98. Interestingly—and pointing to a lack of logical coherence and ethical quality—this view is applied almost exclusively to the Western immigration destinations.

99. Put another way: It is not just that people who have never paid into the social security receive as much as people who have.

governments.[100] The respective governments, then, have in fact accepted the suspension of the law, both domestic and international, which amounts to a *coup d'état*, against the interests of their own people and the due process of law.[101]

It is also not just not to send back those immigrants who have no legal title to stay.

e) It is not just that receiving societies are expected to adapt culturally to people coming from outside. One reason for this is that with such an adaptation the notion of communal ownership, including the right to historical identity, would be denied.[102] This also means that it is not acceptable that immigrants get a free pass for a certain amount of time as far as their adaptation to the legal ethos of the host country is concerned.[103]

f) It is especially unjust to neglect members of the native population who find themselves in need of help in some way or another because of the focus on help for migrants.

g) It is not just to downplay the responsibility of the governments and elites of those countries from which large numbers of persons want to emigrate. This, however, often happens, and the consequences of the negative actions of such agents are too readily put on the shoulders of third parties who are not involved in the creation of the problems that cause people to migrate.

h) It is not just for governments in the receiving states to spend taxpayers' money inefficiently. However, this is what happens when as a matter of principle immigration is treated as the preferred option to help people in need somewhere in a foreign country, compared

---

100. See, e.g., von Wachter, "Die Öffnung der Grenzen ist unmoralisch," 8–9.

101. The situation has changed as a consequence of the Global Compact for Migration, which legalizes the practices that have already been used for a while, and even expands them.

102. Which is also against the U.N. Charter Chapter 1, Article 1, Part 2, and the U.N. Declaration of Human Rights, Article 15. The injustice becomes especially acute when receiving states are forced to adapt culturally to migrants, while the sending countries retain their identity.

103. Against, for example, Carroll, who states that, "The majority culture in the US should anticipate that the adaptation by immigrants to the laws and legal ethos of the United States will take time" (*Christians*, 95).

especially to material aid being channeled into places near the countries of origin of larger migration movements.

i) Justice may suffer from the fact that those who decide immigration policies in the receiving countries are not the same as those who are most affected by the consequences of mass-immigration, especially as far as competition on the labor and housing markets, access to public services, tax increases, etc., are concerned. By the same token, it is not just that those employers who gain from the access to cheap labor through immigration are not the same as those who are affected negatively by mass-immigration in the ways just described.

Most of the points mentioned so far can be related to the following observation: Mass-(im)migration is bound up with an unjust process in which relative prosperity is redirected from middle- and lower-class citizens of the receiving Western states to the elites both in the sending and receiving states and for the profit of transnational corporations, combined with a loss of self-determination on the side of the middle- and lower-class citizens of the receiving Western states.[104]

j) On a transgenerational level, it is not just to hold the present generation responsible for real or alleged wrongdoings of their ancestors. This is, however, exactly what happens when, for example, some European nations or the U.S. are pressured to open their borders to atone for past wrongdoings in the context of colonialism or imperialism. It is, of course, also not just to hold only some nations responsible for past wrongdoings, real or alleged, and not others. With a view to a just assessment of colonialism in the nineteenth century, aspects like population explosion in Europe (as opposed to the situation in the vast majority of the destination areas, but similar to the current situation in the global South that causes mass-migration in the reverse direction) and the aim to modernize (and liberate, especially from slavery as far as Africa is concerned) other parts of the world need to be taken into account.

---

104. This is, of course, not to say that mass-immigration is the only or necessarily the primary factor causing the deterioration of the living conditions of middle and lower class citizens in Western states in the current situation.

k) In a similar vein, it is not just to select among those countries that are economically capable to absorb larger amounts of migrants only Western countries.[105]

l) It is not just—and, as noted above, even less compatible with love—to *use* other people, in the narrow sense of the word, be it for demographic purposes or labor purposes. Of course, one could argue that the immigrants themselves would not mind to be used in such ways, especially if they are treated decently enough and may benefit economically. However, as the previous chapters have shown, especially the section on psychological aspects of migration, even if immigrants may benefit economically, they still pay a high price due to the psychological effects of the uprooting they experience.[106]

m) Justice demands to make distinctions between legal and illegal immigrants, especially because the illegal immigrants jump the queue at the expense of those seeking to enter the country legally, putting the latter in a position of relative disadvantage.

On a more general level, it can be maintained that a state cannot condone law breaking of any kind, since this would send the wrong message and embolden future acts of law breaking in potentially different areas, and as such the breakdown of law and order in general with its devastating consequences.[107]

n) Justice requires that everyone follows the laws, including migrants. This again speaks against the acceptance of the concept of illegal immigration. Even if it is a matter of survival, the Bible does not open the way to take matters in one's own hands—rather, it encourages persons in such situations to trust God's provision.[108]

o) Finally, there are two cases in which justice is mentioned in the context of migration where the use of the concept seems questionable:

Rodríguez maintains that "thousands of migrants have died along the U.S.-Mexico border," which in his view constitutes

105. The need for justice among states of the world (see Amstutz, *Just Immigration*, 130) demands that states are not treated differently in this way.

106. Of course, as for many other arguments, it is important to make distinctions between migrants who flee for their lives and others who seek better economic opportunities. Clearly this specific argument does not pertain to the first group of migrants.

107. See, e.g., Edwards, "A Biblical Perspective," 8.

108. See, e.g., Prov 6:30–31. However, as already pointed out, migration in most cases is not about starving or immediate physical danger to life.

"injustice."[109] It seems, however, that the enforcement of border control and border security cannot be called unjust as such; but real injustice could in fact be identified when the enforcement takes place in unpredictable ways and in ways that treat similar cases in different ways.

p) A broader point is made by Gutiérrez (and many others), designating poverty as such, which in many cases leads to migration, as an injustice, and suggesting that the poor are not responsible for their situation themselves.[110] The following comments are in place: Deliberations about the character and deeper causes of poverty go beyond discussions of migration. Also, one cannot exclude as a matter of principle that in some cases poverty could be—at least in part—the result of bad choices of those affected by it. It also needs to be kept in mind that migration is not necessarily the best answer to problems of poverty, and that persons in the sending countries who cause poverty through corrupt and unjust actions must be held accountable.

7. TRUTH

Truth is another of the central elements of biblical ethics. This is important for the migration debate in various ways, as the following overview will show.[111]

a) The data presented above,[112] together with many other findings not mentioned in this study, point clearly to huge demographic consequences and to negative net results of mass-migration in many areas as far as the receiving societies are concerned (financial, social, security related), sometimes also as far as the sending societies are concerned (brain drain, declining incentives for change), and generally for the migrants themselves (psychological effects of uprooting). It is not acceptable under the principle of truth to manipulate

---

109. "A Witness to Hope," xi.

110. "Poverty," 78.

111. Examples for the individual items listed in this section can be found in previous chapters of the book.

112. See especially chapter 6.

information about real numbers and real consequences.[113] On the other hand, positive exceptions do in fact exist, and must not be overlooked.[114]

b) A look at the real numbers of people wishing to migrate to the West shows that opening the borders to all of them would not be feasible.[115] This means that some kind of restrictions need to be set in place. More generally, the truth needs to be faced that resources that can be made available to help people in need are restricted.

The question as to where the boundaries of what is feasible are must not be ignored.

c) It is difficult to think of any historic example where mass-(im)migration has not led to the destabilization of the receiving societies.[116]

d) The guilt complex in Western societies that forms an important motivating factor for liberal immigration policies cannot be reconciled with a fair and accurate assessment of history. The dark picture of the West builds on a one-sided perspective that focuses almost exclusively on what is perceived as unjust, and lacks both the necessary empathy for different values playing important roles in the past, and especially a comparative angle that would show that the concept of a special amount of guilt of the West relative to negative aspects of other cultures and nations cannot be sustained.[117]

---

113. This is, however, exactly what happens; governments or state agencies often hide the truth about various aspects of immigration, as we could observe in some examples provided earlier. See also von Wachter, "Die Öffnung der Grenzen ist unmoralisch," 6–7.

114. It must be mentioned explicitly that the negative and problematic sides of migration are related mostly to *mass-migration*, not to migration as such.

115. See, e.g., Heinsohn, "Der Bericht zur Flüchtlings-Weltlage."

116. This destabilization was sometimes intended by the sending societies. The events that led to the fall of the (western) Roman Empire in late antiquity bear many resemblances with circumstances prevalent in the West today (see, e.g., Holland, "Migrants Sank the Roman Empire").

117. Of course, a book-length study would be needed to explore this point. One particularly salient example is slavery. While the involvement of some European states in the trans-Atlantic slave trade is a well-known fact, the picture gets completely distorted if one does not consider that slavery—and sometimes on a much larger scale—took place in practically all cultures throughout all of human history, and that it is exactly the abolition of slavery initiated by the West that is the historical exception; see especially Flaig, *Weltgeschichte der Sklaverei*; Walvin, *Atlas of Slavery*.

e) Among the negative effects of mass-immigration in the West—more prevalent in Europe, but not unknown in the U.S. as well—are the spread of anti-Semitism and misogyny, in the current circumstances primarily found among Muslim immigrants. A result of this is the gradual disappearance of Jews from many countries in Europe. This shows that an advocacy for liberal immigration policies cannot be framed in general terms of "openness toward 'the other,'" because the immigration of some "others" lead to the emigration of other "others."

f) Arguments for liberal immigration policies are often based on the need for temporally limited help, especially if the migrants are classified as "refugees." However, in reality it is generally not about temporally limited help, but about permanent immigration resulting in full citizenship.[118]

g) One of the major areas in which truth is commonly lacking is the area of classification of migrants. In many cases, migrants generally are called "asylum-seekers" and "refugees,"[119] while in reality many of them—in most circumstances, as far as mass-migration to the West in the last decades is concerned, even an overwhelming majority of them, as pointed out above—are in fact economic migrants and not refugees or people with a legitimate claim to asylum according to the standards of international law.

h) In the current situation, people smuggling is an important element of mass-migration. In addition, this phenomenon is to some degree related to the schemes of individuals with a political agenda, most famous among them George Soros.[120] Related to this point is the observation that it is generally not the weakest groups of persons and those finding themselves in the most desperate situation who are able to migrate to the West.

---

118. Crisp's model is an example of a contribution not making this visible; see "Love and Borders."

119. See, e.g., McKinney et al., "Welcoming the Stranger," 53.

120. The homepage of Soros's Open Society Foundations says under the heading "Immigration:" "We support a range of groups that work on immigration issues, from local and state organizations that provide frontline legal advice to individuals seeking asylum or facing deportation, to national groups such as the National Immigration Law Center, United We Dream, and the Black Alliance for Just Immigration that advocate for fundamental reform."

i) Part of the general tenor among those who argue for liberal im-
    migration policies is the assertion that assimilation by those who
    immigrate cannot be expected. However, it can be observed—and it
    has long been pointed out by sociologists—that if those who come
    and stay do not assimilate, what is promoted is segregationism, and
    eventually even—depending on the circumstances—unfriendly
    take-over and new varieties of colonialism or conquest.

j) Negative developments of the sort described in the last paragraph
    must be expected especially in cases where the cultures or values
    of various groups are not compatible. The mutual incompatibility
    of (parts of) certain cultures is another truth that must be recog-
    nized. For example, a society will either promote the concept of full
    equality of women, or condone FGM and forced marriages—but it
    cannot embrace both at the same time.

k) One element of the truth about migration is the fact that various
    groups advocating for liberal immigration policies often have partic-
    ular interests, as pointed out above: a number of state governments
    in the West want to meet demographic challenges threatening the
    social welfare systems through the importation of young persons
    who are seen as potential taxpayers, future contributors to the social
    security institutions, and workforce for positions that cannot be eas-
    ily filled with natives; big companies welcome the import of cheap
    labor; various political parties aim at the broadening of their voter
    base through the addition of large numbers of immigrants to the
    electorate; NGO's are interested in growing their importance and
    their financial weight through the public focus on migration and the
    arrival of a large number of immigrants who need to be taken care
    of; large amounts of research money granted by scholarly societ-
    ies, individual states or the European Union, provide an incentive
    for academics to deal with migration issues, usually in support of
    liberal immigration policies.

    Generally, one can say that greed is often a major motivating
    factor playing a role on all sides of migration processes (persons in
    the sending states, migrants, persons in the receiving states).

l) As mentioned earlier, the claim that large numbers of immigrants
    become Christians and thereby re-evangelize the West, especially

Europe, does not conform to realities on the ground.[121] This is not to deny, however, that *some* immigrants do in fact become Christians and may have a positive spiritual contribution to make for the church at large.

8. WISDOM

Biblical ethics in many cases entails an approach that is informed by the application of wisdom. This principle can also be applied to questions relating to migration.

a) While the principles mentioned above—especially creational order, love, and justice—are important, the dealing with questions of migration in the light of the application of wisdom demands an even broader perspective. Wisdom is interested in taking notice of all kinds of information that help understand a phenomenon—in this case, the phenomenon of migration—better, in order to deal with it in the best possible way.

b) Even if one takes—for good reasons—the understanding of every person, including (im)migrants, as bearers of the image of God as the starting point for addressing issues related to (im)migration, or even if one begins with the command to love one's neighbor, the question still remains as to *how* persons are to be treated in conformity with the *imago Dei*-principle, or *how* persons are to be treated with love. To answer such questions, wisdom is necessary, because whereas the "what?" is clear, the "how?" will always depend on an informed analysis of the specific circumstances.

c) A wisdom approach will take into consideration that *imago Dei* and love command are not the only biblical principles that are related to issues of (im)migration. All the relevant—sometimes competing— principles need to be balanced in the context of sober deliberations. The principles of creational order, of the rule of law, and the search for the good of *all* parties involved are some of the principles that need to be taken into account.

---

121. There is (as pointed out earlier) no mass-conversion of Muslim immigrants in the West in general or in Europe in particular.

d) Searching for the good of all parties excludes suicidal attitudes and policies. However, serious problems with security affecting individual citizens of host countries, as much as demographic developments pointing to the replacement of native populations in host countries do not stand the test of furthering the general good. The "application" of select Old Testament laws and select biblical principles that have in view personal behavior towards individuals misses the goal.

e) Among the principles that have to be considered is also the realistic analysis of potential negative consequences, based on observations of the past and experiences made in comparable situations. Wisdom forbids to quickly denigrate such observations and experiences with the applications of labels like "fear"—which is often related to the realm of pathologies—and "prejudice"—which connotes ignorance and bigotry.[122]

f) The application of wisdom in the migration debate demands a sensitivity to the realities of the historical situation in which migration takes place, and adaptation to it. This means, for example, in the case of the U.S., that the fact that large-scale immigration has happened in the past does not in itself prescribe what the right procedures are in the present circumstances or in the future.[123]

g) Wisdom also suggests to take seriously fundamental insights provided by sociological and psychological research, which shows that the immigration of large numbers of persons in a short amount of time and the cultural distance between natives and newcomers have negative impacts. One needs to go even one step further by acknowledging that cultures may be incompatible, because they support conflicting ideas in core areas affecting communal life. At a minimum, such a notion cannot be excluded or ignored as a matter of principle, but needs to be investigated carefully. Against this background, one must realize that it is wiser to direct migration

122. As a negative example, one can point once more to Carroll's statement that "those measures designed to organize and appropriately deal with . . . immigrants should reflect the virtues of kindness, generosity, and patience instead of being motivated by fear and prejudice" (*Christians*, 98).

123. *Pace*, e.g., Carroll, *Christians*, 98 ("Immigration is inseparable from the history of the nation and is fundamental to its identity"). One also has to bear in mind that the historic case of the U.S. is different from most other nations and can therefore not be transferred to them or imposed on them automatically.

movements in ways in which people—granted there is no other solution than migration—migrate to countries with a similar cultural
background to their own. Of course, the situation will look differently if the reason for leaving one's country is the wish to break with
this country's culture.

h) As far as refugees with a different cultural background are concerned, the best long-term solution is repatriation, while the least
desirable solution is third country resettlement. The latter is not
the most desirable option "because of the great cultural, social,
and economic challenges that refugees must overcome in becoming fully integrated into a new society,"[124]—and also because of the
problems for receiving societies. Even if refugees are not accepted as
immigrants, some kind of assistance would still need to be given to
them.[125]

i) It is obviously unwise to let people in (especially in larger numbers)
if it can be established that they want to change the democratic system and legal order of the receiving society.

j) Wisdom demands that the root causes that lead to mass-migration
need to be addressed, rather than ignoring them and simply accepting and managing the phenomenon of mass-migration with all its
negative side-effects. Besides greed, economically unsustainable
growth in population in the sending countries, rampant corruption and conflictual, unstable political circumstances in the sending
countries, as well as uneven barriers in international trade hurting
developing countries are among the most obvious ones.

k) Wisdom also suggests that state policies towards foreign nations are
handled in a coherent way. If Western states that are countries of
destination of large numbers of migrants, including persons who are
recognized as refugees and given asylum, entertain normal relationships with sending countries as if things would basically look alright
in these places, there is an obvious lack of consistency. Either such
a country—for example Turkey—is dealt with as a normal partner,
and consequently persons from such a place are not recognized as
refugees; or such a country is treated as a state that lacks respect for
human rights, and then people from this place are granted asylum

124. Amstutz, *Just Immigration*, 107.

125. See, e.g., Amstutz, *Just Immigration*, 109.

(until the situation in the respective country improves). But to combine the two attitudes does not make any sense.

l) Wisdom suggests to consider carefully historical experiences with mass-immigration such as the ones mentioned in the previous paragraph on "Truth." One also has to address the question as to why never before in history open-border policies have been implemented by any Christian state or promoted by any mainstream Christian group.

9. DISOBEYING STATE LAW

Against assigning a decisive role to Rom 13:1–7 and its circumscription of the state's responsibilities, it is sometimes argued that this passage does not dispense us from assessing the quality and justice of the current legislation on immigration.[126] This is certainly right and an uncontested part of how democratic systems function. Existing positive law must always be assessed critically from a Christian perspective. The fact that laws can be changed and do change does not, however, as such subvert the obligation to follow existing laws in principle. On the other hand, some do in fact go one step further and maintain that since current legislation on immigration is so bad, it is alright to trespass it and follow God's higher standards by breaking these laws.[127] In order to prevent the creation of countless cases in which subjective, personal preferences function as a basis for the acceptance of law-breaking—a scenario that clearly has no

---

126. See, e.g., Carroll, *Christians*, 123–24. More specifically, Carroll maintains that Romans 13 cannot be taken as the primary angle, because one has to assess current legislation based on whether it is "charitable to the immigrant" enough according to biblical standards (*Christians*, 123). According to him (and many others), the current laws are wanting, not "good . . . and practical and efficient" (*Christians*, 124). He also states that there is a "right to disagree" and seek "to change legislation" (*Christians*, 125). Carroll adds that one must begin not with Romans 13, but with Romans 12, where Christians are called "not to be molded by the 'patterns of this world' . . . which would include being shaped by the nation's political ideologies . . . with regard to immigration" (*Christians*, 124). It is not difficult to see that the last point does not provide any clarification, because a "nation's political ideologies" can also be found in laws and initiatives that promote liberal immigration policies. Very similar views are found, e.g., in Wesleyan, The Submission Principle; Gonzales, "Sanctuary," 40.

127. See, e.g., Carroll, *Christians*, 125: "Christians must respond to a higher authority . . . and to a higher law and set of values. There will be times when these two authorities will not agree. This is such a time."

support in the New Testament—it would certainly be safer and wiser to be more cautious and acknowledge a conflict between state law and God's will tendentially only in cases of clear, direct, and explicit contradiction between a specific state law and a specific biblical command.[128] That such a case could be made for laws that restrict immigration has yet to be demonstrated.[129] The biblical examples of a divinely sanctioned breaking of laws usually entail either the preservation of life (such as in the case of the midwives in Exodus 1 or the wise men in Matthew 2), or the refusal to participate in idolatry (such as in Daniel 3 and 6) or the freedom to proclaim the gospel (such as in Acts 4).

10. SPECIAL CALLING

There is a difference between venturing to build a solid biblical ethical assessment of migration issues and the realm of following a personal calling in one's life—in the case of Christians: one's life with the Lord. On the latter level, it may well be that someone feels to be called to serve immigrants in a special way. However, such a personal calling does not invalidate or replace the general biblical ethical considerations mentioned above, and it cannot be used as the guiding principle to unilaterally determine broader state (or church) policies. A personal calling to serve (im)migrants will have its place besides other people's callings, for example callings to serve the elderly, protect the life of unborn children, etc. Persons who feel called to serve (im)migrants will then, naturally, also have to accept that other Christians may have other callings connected to the same broader issues related in some way or another to (im)migration, like protecting the borders to prevent damage to their communities by criminal intruders,[130] or investing resources to help people in need

128. Principles such as "to do good rather than harm, and to give life rather than kill" (Gonzales, "Sanctuary," 42) are not useful in making ultimate distinctions between laws that must be obeyed and laws that must be resisted, because what "doing good" and "harm" entails is dependent on the specific situational context, and killing is sometimes necessary to protect society from harm.

129. Hoffmeier makes a similar point: "Clearly the person who fears God and believes that he is sovereigny [sic] controlling the course of human events will be motivated by conscience to follow the edicts of the state unless there is a very clear conflict with the teachings of Scripture. Based on this clear instruction, I believe that citizens and foreigners should be subject to a nation's laws, and this applies to immigration laws" (*The Immigration Crisis*, 142).

130. This statement does, of course, not imply that all or the majority of immigrants

to make (im)migration unnecessary in the first place, or educating the broader public about worldviews and ideologies that are imported into the West by some specific groups of (im)migrants, some of which may not be contributing to the common good or may even be dangerous to the well-being of the receiving communities in general and/or the church in particular. All these different callings relate to different aspects of the reality of current migration issues, and none of these aspects should be ignored, even if discussions about their respective weight and the best ways to handle them are both inevitable and necessary.

The distinction between various personal callings and the ethical treatment of specific issues in a broader context can be illustrated by applying it to another example: In the case of the question of abortion, some may be called to support pregnant women struggling with practical challenges to care for a (perhaps "unplanned") child, while others may be called to educate the broader public about the medical realities at play in abortion procedures, while yet others may be called to do research about the psychological consequences of abortions for women who have gone through the process, etc. These personal callings are not mutually exclusive, and none will replace a comprehensive analysis of the phenomenon on the ethical, theological, philosophical, or judicial level, and action on the political level.

---

are criminal intruders.

8

The Application of the Bible
to Current Issues of Migration

Tentative Suggestions

a) Addressing issues of mass-(im)migration from a biblical perspective should begin with the acknowledgment that questions about *how* to help people in need are not a core gospel issue, where only one approach can be accepted as the right one; rather, it is an ethical issue that requires careful acknowledgment and balancing of the various factors involved, in the context of a rational debate, and an assessment based on (biblically inspired) wisdom.[1] Concepts like creational order, rule of law, ethnic and national identity are factors that must be taken into consideration besides the material life-conditions of individuals and groups in search for a better life.

b) As with all ethical questions, it is important to have a precise knowledge of the (complexity of the) biblical material. This material cannot be reduced to single principles like love or *shalom*. While such principles are important, they need to be understood in ways that are congruent with their original biblical contexts and cannot be defined along conceptual terms that are imposed on the Bible from outside. Immigration policies must not be constructed based on a

---

1. A similar point is made by Amstutz: Because balancing is necessary, one has to use "care and caution," in a spirit of "humility and tentativeness," and not align oneself with specific policies (*Just Immigration*, 217).

handful of randomly selected biblical passages taken out of context and embedded in wholly different circumstances.[2] What is needed is a look at the entire canon through the lens of the major biblical themes of creation, fall, redemption, and new creation.

c) Also the current circumstances to which the biblical material will be related need to be investigated in all their dimensions. In order to accomplish this, it is necessary to look at the current situation from all possible angles.

d) Looking at all aspects includes a consideration of the consequences of mass-(im)migration not just for the receiving societies, but also for the sending countries. It also includes an assessment of the responsibilities of governments and elites in these countries.

e) Looking at all aspects includes the investigation of the impact of mass-(im)migration on all dimensions of personal and societal life, such as economy (incl. costs and benefits), ecology, culture, social cohesion, law (and the rule of law), human rights, security and crime, psychological and physical health, religion, and politics (including questions of sovereignty and citizenship).

f) With respect to all these aspects, attention must be given both to the micro-level (individual migrant and his/her family) and the macro-level (macro-economic and demographic dimensions; institutions; state policy).

g) As far as perspectives of interests are concerned, attention must be given to all parties involved, which are the (im)migrants, members of the receiving societies, and members of the sending societies.

h) Looking at all aspects includes both to learn from past instances of mass-(im)migration and to make projections for the future (long-term perspective).

i) It is important to make distinctions between different kinds of migration and different groups of (im)migrants, as well as differences pertaining to the social and cultural fabric of the receiving societies. This includes primarily distinctions between economic migrants and persons who leave their places of origin because of life-threatening situations, and distinctions between illegal and legal (im)migrants.

---

2. So also Edwards, "A Biblical Perspective," 9. He adds: "Rather, carefully discerning applicable principles better fits the situation" ("A Biblical Perspective," 9).

The doors will generally be more open to legal immigrants and to refugees who are fleeing a life-threatening situation. Those migrants who harbor hostile attitudes towards the potential host society must not be admitted permanent citizenship.

j) Since migration is almost always, in some way or another, a disruptive process, it should not be used as a primary or preferred remedy to address social problems, especially not problems related to poverty; alternative ways of improving difficult situations must be explored. This does, of course, not mean that there are no circumstances in which migration is in fact the only viable or best solution. In any case, the element of disruption has to be taken very seriously, because—from a broader societal viewpoint—a functioning society is a very fragile entity, in which changes related to any of the major factors can have devastating effects, as is obvious in many countries in the world, both throughout history and today.

k) The two most important factors on the social level that must be considered when decisions have to be made about the admission of migrants are numbers per time and cultural difference. The higher the numbers (per time) and the bigger the cultural difference, the more difficult it will be to integrate the newcomers into the existing social fabric of the receiving society.

l) Assimilation must not be discarded in principle as the desired goal of admitting foreigners into a host country; rather, it is the normal way to minimize social disruption and to prevent phenomena like segregation, ghettoization, and struggles between rivaling groups. However, things have become more complex in the sense that from a traditional Christian perspective there are many elements of the (post)modern Western societies that are not worth assimilating to.

m) Questions about "how to help best?" are important, because the resources really are limited. This means that the means need to be allocated in the most efficient ways possible. In most cases, (im)migration will not be the most efficient option. It also means that it is necessary to soberly assess which persons deserve most help, considering the long list of those who are in need—a list that is in no way restricted to (im)migrants.

n) On the list of persons in need are persecuted Christians. They should in fact be high up on the list—especially for Christians—because in many cases Christians are not only discriminated against in various ways, but threatened and attacked physically, incarcerated, and even killed.[3] Such types of attacks on persons' lives take precedence over purely material needs. Since non-Christians often are not very much interested in the persecution of Christians, it should be a primary concern for Christian congregations and organizations to invest all kinds of resources in the help and support of persecuted Christians. Since many secular organizations in the West focus on the support of (im)migrants, Christian congregations and organizations might consider not doing the same, but stepping in where no one else pays attention, and redirect their engagement to the help of persecuted Christians. As a result, there will be a kind of division of labor that ensures that various kinds of people in need receive help.

o) It is not difficult to see that the organization of (im)migration issues on the state level leaves many problems unresolved and is one of the major sources of severe political division in most Western countries.[4] Delegation of integration programs to state agencies proves to be ineffective; the use of taxpayer money for migration issues creates internal tensions; and the use of other people's money without their explicit consent to implement social programs is ethically problematic. Because of all this, the situation might be improved by shifting considerable parts of (im)migration policies to private agents who are committed to help (im)migrants by investing their own financial means and resources of time, by building personal relationships with (im)migrants and being around them in various ways to guarantee their integration into the host society. The way forward is to emulate the example given in the Old Testament legal texts to the degree that this is possible in the present circumstances. The use of other people's money should be minimized as a matter of principle.

In addition, especially in cases where the admission of larger number of potential immigrants and/or of potential immigrants whose ability or willingness to integrate might be questionable, democratic referenda about immigration policies should be held to give the people a voice in the decision-making process. It is not

---

3. According to generally accepted statistics, Christians are the biggest single group of persons persecuted in a global perspective; see, e.g., Caldwell, "Christians."

4. Cf., e.g., Carroll, who rightly observes that, "No legislation can satisfy everyone, nor will it be without its own inherent problems" (*Christians*, 16).

ethically responsible to exclude those people who will be most affected by government decisions from having a direct say in issues that will thoroughly and lastingly change their lives.

p) Within the church, openness to and acceptance of (legal) immigrants should be the normal attitude, unless very severe reasons arise that would necessitate a reconsideration of this posture in specific circumstances. Churches will also be supportive of immigrants who have been admitted to a country as fellow neighbors and bearers of the image of God. This, however, does not mean that churches should lobby generally or in principle for liberal immigration policies. The distinction informing this double-sided approach is the distinction between admittance (at the border) and integration (within the borders). It is related to the distinction between the role of the church vs. the role of the state, between the natural order and the spiritual realm, and between earthly citizenship and heavenly citizenship.

q) As a matter of course, all admitted immigrants must be protected from exploitation and other unjust forms of treatment. The biblical prescription for a just treatment of immigrants is, however, not to be confounded with a program for liberal immigration policies.

r) The biblical flight stories cannot be used to support the argument for liberal immigration policies, because they have no direct connection with the current phenomenon of mass-(im)migration. On the other hand, there is in fact a lesson that can be learned from these biblical stories, namely that a side-by-side of various sovereign states is important. Only such a system can guarantee that there is a place of refuge in case that persecution of some kind or another breaks out in a country. The abolition of borders in the context of a globalized one-world order would render the concept of "flight" as such impossible.

s) Positions and principles brought into the migration debate must be thought through their logical end. This is especially important when considering the "open-borders"-option, or the concept of cultural relativism. It implies, in particular, that the questions of where the limits of the available resources for help for people in need are and where the limits of the absorption capacities for newcomers in any given country lie must not be evaded.

Brief Summary and Conclusions

THE MAIN FINDINGS OF this book can be summarized in the following points:

a) Evangelicals and other Christians who address (im)migration questions from a biblical perspective in many cases use the Bible in a one-sided, simplistic, and eclectic way; they also often tend to ignore extra-biblical data that are important for the ethical assessment of migration issues.

b) The biblical views on (im)migration issues cannot be reduced to the slogan "welcoming the stranger," especially in cases of *mass-(im)migration*.

c) The Bible may function as a source of inspiration to address many of the crucial questions related to (im)migration; it can, however, not be used as a prescriptive text that determines in a straightforward and definitive way matters of policies.

d) The Bible does not promote a general right to be received as an immigrant—rather, it promotes an obligation of the host to treat immigrants who have been admitted well.

e) The *imago Dei*-concept and love for neighbor are two of the outstanding biblical principles that need to inform the dealing with questions about migration; the principles have to be applied equally to migrants and non-migrants. How these principles are best applied must be the subject of informed discussions; they do not in themselves dictate liberal immigration policies.

f) A consideration of all the available pertinent extra-biblical data is needed to address questions related to (im)migration. These data show that in most cases mass-(im)migration has many questionable or negative side-effects for various participants.

g) Factors like creational order, rule of law, ethnic and national identity are aspects that must be taken into consideration besides the material life-conditions of individuals and groups in search for a better life.

h) It has to be acknowledged and taken into consideration that in most cases migration is a disruptive process—and therefore not a preferred option.

i) Inspired by biblical precedent, but also in line with common sense, it is important to distinguish between the various types of migrants and not attempt to treat them all in the same way. Migration that is caused by persecution and other life-threatening circumstances, as well as migration that is caused by divine ordination is to be viewed more positively than other forms of migration. In the latter case, alternative forms of help must be explored. In addition, in various circumstances *temporary* admittance to a host country is one of the options that can be considered, as opposed to the binary choice between rejection and *permanent* admittance. Migrants with hostile attitudes towards a potential host country cannot be admitted as permanent citizens.

j) Assimilation is the normal expectation connected with the admission of migrants who want to stay at a new place permanently.

k) In the reception and integration of immigrants, personal voluntary involvement should take precedence over state enforced measures as far as possible.

l) The Bible does not lend support for illegality in the handling of immigration.

m) It must be acknowledged and taken into consideration that the situation in various Western countries that serve as destinations for large numbers of migrants is different in many respects.

Bibliography

Adan, Shukri. "Report on Somali Youth Issues." *City of Minneapolis, Department of Civil Rights.* https://www.minneapolismn.gov/www/groups/public/@council/documents/webcontent/convert_272143.pdf

Allport, Gordon. *The Nature of Prejudice.* Reading, MA: Addison-Wesley, 1979.

Amstutz, Mark R. *Just Immigration: American Policy in Christian Perspective.* Grand Rapids: Eerdmans, 2017.

Anderson, Benedict. *Die Erfindung der Nation: Zur Karriere eines folgenreichen Konzepts.* Frankfurt am Main: Campus, 1996.

Avos Melchor, Eva. "Promoting Migrant Integration for a Powerful, Diverse and Multicultural Europe." EPALE Upcoming Events (June 2017). https://epale.ec.europa.eu/en/content/promoting-migrant-integration-powerful-diverse-and-multicultural-europe

Avrahami, Yael. "בוש in the Psalms: Shame or Disappointment?" *JSOT* 34 (2010) 295–313.

Aymer, Margaret. "Sojourners Truths: The New Testament as Diaspora Space." *The Journal of the Interdenominational Theological Center* 41 (2015) 1–18.

Banton, Michael. "The Direction and Speed of Ethnic Change." In *Ethnic Change*, edited by Charles F. Keyes, 32–52. 2nd ed. Seattle: University of Washington Press, 1982.

Barnett, Paul. *The Second Epistle to the Corinthians.* NICNT. Grand Rapids: Eerdmans, 1997.

Barry, Brian. "The Quest for Consistency: A Skeptical View." In *Free Movement: Ethical Issues in the Transnational Migration of People and Money*, edited by Brian Barry and Robert E. Goodin, 279–87. University Park, PA: Pennsylvania State University Press, 1992.

Battistella, Graziano. "Migration and Human Dignity." In *A Promised Land, a Perilous Journey*, edited by Daniel G. Groody and Gioacchino Campese, 177–91. Notre Dame, IN: University of Notre Dame, 2008.

Bazan, Bernardo C. "Pensée de la totalité, pensée d'altérité." In *L'altérité: Vivre ensemble différents*, edited by Michel Gourgues, Gilles-D. Mailhiot, 49–83. Recherches, nouvelle série 7. Paris: Cerf, 1986.

Beaulieu, Cécile. "Paris: des femmes victimes de harcèlement dans les rues du quartier Chapelle-Pajol." *Le Parisien* (May 18 and 21, 2017). https://www.leparisien.fr/paris-75/paris-75018/harcelement-les-femmes-chassees-des-rues-dans-le-quartier-chapelle-pajol-18-05-2017-6961779.php

Beck, Chad Thomas. "Sanctuary for Immigrants and Refugees in Our Legal and Ethical Wilderness." *Interpretation* 72 (2018) 132–45.

Bedford-Strohm, Heinrich. "Den Fremdling sollt ihr nicht bedrücken." www.bayern-evangelisch.de/downloads/ELKB-Landesbischof-Migration-und-Flucht-aus-der-Sicht-christlicher-Ethik-2014.pdf

Beier, Christoph, Dirk Messner, and Hans-Joachim Preuss, eds. *Globale Wanderungsbewegungen: Beiträge der internationalen Zusammenarbeit zum Umgang mit Flucht und Migration.* Wiesbaden: Springer Nature, 2020.

Belien, Paul. "Sensitive Urban Areas." *Washington Times* (January 16, 2008). https://www.washingtontimes.com/news/2008/jan/16/sensitive-urban-areas/

Bell, Daniel. "Ethnicity and Social Change." In *Ethnicity: Theory and Experience*, edited by Nathan Glazer and Daniel Patrick Moynihan, 141–74. Cambridge: Harvard University Press, 1975.

Bellebaum, Alfred. "Randgruppen. Ein Beitrag zur Soziologie sozialer Probleme und sozialer Kontrolle." In *Soziale Randgruppen und Aussenseiter im Altertum*, edited by Ingomar Weiler and Herbert Grassl, 47–57. Graz, Austria: Leykam, 1988.

Bennett, John C. *Foreign Policy in Christian Perspective.* New York: Scribner's Sons, 1966.

Berman, Joshua A. *Inconsistency in the Torah: Ancient Literary Convention and the Limits of Source Criticism.* New York: Oxford University Press, 2017.

Bhatia, Sunil, and Anjali Ram. "Rethinking 'Acculturation' in Relation to Diasporic Cultures and Postcolonial Identities." *Human Development* 44 (2001) 1–18.

Bjerve, Petter Jakob. "Folketellingen 1. Desember 1950." *Norges Offisielle Statistikk* XI 236. Oslo: Statistisk Sentralbyrå, 1956. https://www.ssb.no/a/histstat/nos/nos_xi_236.pdf

———. "Folketellingen 1960." *Norges Offisielle Statistikk* XII 140. Oslo: Statistisk Sentralbyrå, 1964. https://www.ssb.no/a/histstat/nos/nos_xii_140.pdf

Blenkinsopp, Joseph. *Ezra–Nehemiah: A Commentary.* OTL. Philadelphia: Presbyterian, 1988.

Bockmuehl, Markus. "The Noachide Commandments and the New Testament Ethics: With Special Reference to Acts 15 and Pauline Halakhah." *RB* 101 (1995) 72–101.

Bok, Wolfgang, "Die Flüchtlingskosten sind ein deutsches Tabuthema." *Neue Zürcher Zeitung* (Sept. 15, 2017). https://www.nzz.ch/meinung/kommentare/die-fluechtlingskosten-sind-ein-deutsches-tabuthema-ld.1316333

Borjas, George J. "Immigration and the American Worker: A Review of the Academic Literature." *Center for Immigration Studies* (April 2013) 1–26.

———. "Yes, Immigration Hurts American Workers." *Politico* (September/October 2016). https://www.politico.com/magazine/story/2016/09/trump-clinton-immigration-economy-unemployment-jobs-214216,

Bound, John, Guarav Khanna, and Nicolas Morales. "Understanding the Economic Impact of the H-1B Program on the U.S." *NBER Working Paper Series* No. 23153 (February 2017) 1–62 and I–IV. https://www.nber.org/papers/w23153.pdf

Bouteillet-Paquet, Daphné. *Smuggling of Migrants: A Global Review and Annotated Bibliography of Recent Publications.* United Nations Office on Drugs and Crime. New York: UNODC, 2011. https://www.unodc.org/documents/human-trafficking/Migrant-Smuggling/Smuggling_of_Migrants_A_Global_Review.pdf

Breeze, David John. *The Frontiers of Imperial Rome.* Barnsley: Pen & Sword Military, 2019.

Bretherton, Luke. *Christianity and Contemporary Politics: The Conditions and Possibilities of Faithful Witness*. Oxford: Wiley-Blackwell, 2010.

Brett, Mark G. "Forced Migrations, Asylum Seekers and Human Rights." *Colloquium* 45 (2013) 121–36.

———. "Interpreting Ethnicity: Method, Hermeneutics, Ethics." In *Ethnicity and the Bible*, edited by Mark G. Brett, 3–22. Biblical Interpretation Series 19. Leiden: Brill, 1996.

———. "Nationalism and the Hebrew Bible." In *The Bible in Ethics: The Second Sheffield Colloquium*, edited by John W. Rogerson et al., 136–63. The Library of Hebrew Bible/Old Testament Studies 207. Sheffield, UK: Sheffield Academic Press, 1995.

Brettell, Caroline B. "Theorizing Migration in Anthropology." In *Migration Theory: Talking across Disciplines*, edited by Caroline B. Brettell and James F. Hollifield, 113–59. London: Routledge, 2008.

Brettell, Caroline B., and James F. Hollifield. "Migration Theory." In *Migration Theory: Talking across Disciplines*, edited by Caroline B. Brettell and James F. Hollifield, 1–29. London: Routledge, 2008.

Brettell, Caroline B., and James F. Hollifield, eds. *Migration Theory: Talking across Disciplines*. London: Routledge, 2008.

Bruce, Frederick Fyvie. *The Book of the Acts*. NICNT. Grand Rapids: Eerdmans, 1988.

———. *The Epistles to the Colossians, to Philemon, and to the Ephesians*. NICNT. Grand Rapids: Eerdmans, 1984.

———. *The Epistle to the Hebrews*. NICNT. Grand Rapids: Eerdmans, 1964.

Brückner, Thorsten. "So rechnen Medien die Asylkosten klein." *Junge Freiheit*, September 17, 2019. https://jungefreiheit.de/politik/deutschland/2019/so-rechnen-medien-die-asylkosten-klein/

Brueggemann, Walter. *Genesis*. Interpretation. Atlanta: John Knox, 1982.

Bruner, Frederick Dale. *Matthew*. Grand Rapids: Eerdmans, 2004.

Bultmann, Christoph. *Der Fremde im antiken Juda: Eine Untersuchung zum sozialen Typenbegriff "ger" in seinem Bedeutungswandel in der alttestamentlichen Gesetzgebung*. FRLANT 153. Göttingen: Vandenhoeck & Ruprecht, 1992.

Byberg, Øystein. "Så mye 'koster' en innvandrer." *Finansavisen* (March 31, 2017) https://finansavisen.no/nyheter/politikk/2017/03/saa-mye-koster-en-innvandrer

Caldwell, Zelda. "Christians Are Most Persecuted Groups in the World, Study Says." *Aleteia*, May 6, 2019. https://aleteia.org/2019/05/06/christians-are-most-persecuted-group-in-the-world-study-says/

Campese, Gioacchino. "¿Cuantos Más?" In *A Promised Land, a Perilous Journey*, edited by Daniel G. Groody and Gioacchino Campese, 271–98. Notre Dame, IN: University of Notre Dame, 2008.

Carroll R., M. Daniel. *The Bible and Borders: Hearing God's Word on Immigration*. Grand Rapids: Brazos, 2020.

———. *Christians at the Border: Immigration, the Church, and the Bible*. Grand Rapids: Brazos, 2013.

———. "Immigration and the Bible." *Missio Dei* 19 (2010) 1–21.

———. "Welcoming the Stranger: Toward a Theology of Immigration in and Empirical Deuteronomy." In *For Our Good Always: Studies on the Message and Influence of Deuteronomy in Honor of Daniel I. Block*, edited by Jason S. DeRouchie et al., 441–61. Winona Lake, IN: Eisenbrauns, 2013.

Castillo Guerra, Jorge E. "A Theology of Migration." In *A Promised Land, a Perilous Journey*, edited by Daniel G. Groody and Gioacchino Campese, 243–70, Notre Dame, IN: University of Notre Dame, 2008.

Cohen, Ronald. "Ethnicity: Problem and Focus in Anthropology." *Annual Review of Anthropology* 7 (1978) 379–403.

Corcoran, Ann. *Refugee Resettlement and the Hijra to America*. Washington, DC: The Center for Security Policy, 2015.

Cortés-Fuentes, David. "The Least of These My Brothers: Matthew 25:31–46." *Apuntes* 23.2 (2003) 100–109.

Costa, Daniel. "Employers Exploit Unauthorized Immigrants to Keep Wages Down." *The New York Times* (September 3, 2015). https://www.nytimes.com/roomfordebate/2015/09/03/is-immigration-really-a-problem-in-the-us/employers-exploit-unauthorized-immigrants-to-keep-wages-low.

Cowles, C.S., Eugene H. Merrill, Daniel L. Gard, and Tremper Longman III, eds. *Show Them No Mercy*. Grand Rapids: Zondervan, 2003.

Crippen, Cheryl L. "Working with Intercultural Couples and Families: Exploring Cultural Dissonance to Identify Transformative Opportunities." *American Counseling Association, VISTAS Online, Article 21* (2011). https://www.counseling.org/resources/library/vistas/2011-v-online/Article_21.pdf

Crisp, Thomas. "Love and Borders" (unpublished paper). https://drive.google.com/file/d/0B-l5_gDI4DLbOVZ4RV85cU5vOGc/view

Crump, David. "Applying the Sermon on the Mount." *Criswell Theological Review* 6 (1992) 3–14.

Dearden, Lizzie. "Russia and Syria 'Weaponizing' Refugee Crisis to Destabilise Europe, NATO Commander Claims." *Independent* (March 3, 2016). https://www.independent.co.uk/news/world/middle-east/russia-and-syria-weaponising-refugee-crisis-to-destabilise-europe-nato-commander-claims-a6909241.html

Dever, William G. *What Did the Biblical Writers Know and When Did They Know It?* Grand Rapids: Eerdmans, 2001.

Dihle, Albrecht. *Die Griechen und die Fremden*. München: Beck, 1994.

Dogs, Christian Peter. "Mit den Migranten kommt eine Zeitbombe, die nicht zu integrieren ist." https://www.youtube.com/watch?v=9xI-H8c8uSw

Douglass-Williams, Christine. "Sweden: 5,460 of 7,000 of Afghan 'Child Migrants' Were Actually Adults, Only 68 Out of 7,000 Have Jobs." *jihadwatch.org* (December 17, 2020). https://www.jihadwatch.org/2020/12/sweden-5460-afghan-migrants

Driver, Samuel R. *A Critical and Exegetical Commentary on Deuteronomy*. ICC. New York: Scribner's Sons, 1916.

Dudley, Steven, Héctor Silva Ávalos, and Juan José Martínez. "MS13 in the Americas." *InSight Crime: The Center for Latin American & Latino Studies*. https://www.justice.gov/eoir/page/file/1043576/download

Duffin, Erin. "Muslim Population in the U.S. 2007–2017." *Statista* (April 29, 2019). https://www.statista.com/statistics/786165/muslim-population-in-the-us/

Dyck, Jonathan E. "The Ideology of Identity in Chronicles." In *Ethnicity and the Bible*, edited by Mark G. Brett, 89–116. Biblical Interpretation Series 19. Leiden: Brill, 1996.

Edwards, James R. "A Biblical Perspective on Immigration Policy." *Backgrounder, Center for Immigration Studies* (2009). https://cis.org/Report/Biblical-Perspective-Immigration-Policy

Ellis, Christian. "Churches Desecrated in Ongoing Attacks across Europe." *CBN News* (April 16, 2019). https://www1.cbn.com/cbnnews/us/2019/april/churches-desecrated-in-ongoing-attacks-across-europe

Escobar, Samuel. "Refugees: A New Testament Perspective." *Transformation* 35.2 (2018) 102–8.

Evans, Craig A. *Matthew*. New Cambridge Bible Commentary. New York: Cambridge University Press, 2012.

Faust, Avraham. "Ethnic Complexity in Northern Israel during Iron Age II." *PEQ* 132 (2000) 2–27.

Favell, Adrian. "Rebooting Migration Theory." In *Migration Theory: Talking across Disciplines*, edited by Caroline B. Brettell and James F. Hollifield, 259–78. London: Routledge, 2008.

Feder, Yitzhaq. "Defilement and Moral Discourse in the Hebrew Bible: An Evolutionary Framework." *Journal of Cognitive Historiography* 3 (2016) 157–89.

Feigin, Samuel I. "The Captives in Cuneiform Inscriptions." *AJSL* 50 (1933/34) 217–45.

Fischelmayer, Michael, and Harald Lederer. *Das Bundesamt in Zahlen 2014: Asyl, Migration und Integration*. Nürnberg: Bundesamt für Migration und Flüchtlinge, 2015.

Flaig, Egon. *Weltgeschichte der Sklaverei*. 2nd ed. Beck'sche Reihe. München: Beck, 2011.

Fornet-Betancourt, Raúl. "Hermeneutics and Politics of Strangers." In *A Promised Land, a Perilous Journey*, edited by Daniel G. Groody and Gioacchino Campese, 210–24. Notre Dame, IN: University of Notre Dame, 2008.

France, Richard Thomas. *The Gospel of Matthew*. NICNT. Grand Rapids: Eerdmans, 2007.

Funkschmidt, Kai. "Antisemitische Straftaten." *Evangelische Zentralstelle für Weltanschauungsfragen* (11/2018). https://www.ezw-berlin.de/html/15_9950.php

Galter, Hannes D. "Zwischen Isolation und Integration: Die soziale Stellung des Fremden in Mesopotamien in 3. und 2. Jahrtausend v. Chr." In *Soziale Randgruppen und Aussenseiter im Altertum*, edited by Ingomar Weiler and Herbert Grassl, 277–301. Graz, Austria: Leykam, 1988.

Geldenhuys, Norman. *Commentary on the Gospel of Luke*. Grand Rapids: Eerdmans, 1983.

George, Timothy. *Galatians*. NAC 30. Nashville: Broadman & Holman, 1994.

Gerhardsson, Birger. "Agape and Imitation of Christ." In *Jesus, the Gospels, and the Church: Essays in Honor of William R. Farmer*, edited by E. P. Sanders, 163–76. Macon, GA: Mercer University Press, 1987.

Gilbrant, Jørgen, Steinar Solås Suvatne, and Gunnar Ringheim. "Innvandringen er dyrere enn de fleste er klar over." *Dagbladet* (April 30, 2019). https://www.dagbladet.no/nyheter/innvandringen-er-dyrere-enn-de-fleste-er-klar-over/71021800

Gilissen, John. "Le statut des étrangers à la lumière de l'histoire comparative." *Recueils de la Société Jean Bodin pour l'histoire comparative des institutions* 9 (1958) 5–57.

Glanville, Mark R. *Adopting the Stranger as Kindred in Deuteronomy*. Ancient Israel and Its Literature 33. Atlanta: SBL, 2018.

Gonzales, Justo L. *For the Healing of the Nations*. Maryknoll, NY: Orbis, 1999.

———. "Sanctuary: Historical, Legal, and Biblical Considerations." *Apuntes* 5.2 (1985) 36–47.

Gordon, Milton M. "Toward a General Theory of Racial and Ethnic Group Relations." In *Ethnicity: Theory and Experience*, edited by Nathan Glazer and Daniel P. Moynihan, 84–110. Cambridge: Harvard University Press, 1995.

Gossett, Thomas. *Race: The History of an Idea in America*. New York: Oxford University Press, 1997.

Grassl, Herbert. "Grundsätzliches und Methodisches zur historischen Randgruppenforschung." In *Soziale Randgruppen und Aussenseiter im Altertum*, edited by Ingomar Weiler and Herbert Grassl, 41–46. Graz, Austria: Leykam, 1988.

Grinberg, Leon, and Rebeca Grinberg. *Psychoanalytic Perspectives on Migration and Exile*. New Haven, CT: Yale University Press, 1989.

Groody, Daniel G. "Fruit of the Vine and Work of Human Hands." In *A Promised Land, a Perilous Journey*, edited by Daniel G. Groody and Gioacchino Campese, 299–315. Notre Dame, IN: University of Notre Dame, 2008.

Groody, Daniel G., and Gioacchino Campese, eds. *A Promised Land, a Perilous Journey: Theological Perspectives on Migration*. Notre Dame, IN: University of Notre Dame, 2008.

Groody, Daniel G., and Gioacchino Campese. "Preface." In *A Promised Land, a Perilous Journey*, edited by Daniel G. Groody and Gioacchino Campese, xix–xxvii. Notre Dame, IN: University of Notre Dame, 2008.

Grosby, Steven E. *Biblical Ideas of Nationality, Ancient and Modern*. Winona Lake, IN: Eisenbrauns, 2002.

Guild, Elspeth. *Security and Migration in the 21st Century*. Cambridge: Polity, 2009.

Gutiérrez, Gustavo. "Poverty, Migration, and the Option for the Poor." In *A Promised Land, a Perilous Journey*, edited by Daniel G. Groody and Gioacchino Campese, 76–86. Notre Dame, IN: University of Notre Dame, 2008.

Hackett, Conrad. "5 Facts about the Muslim Population in Europe." *FactTank Pew Research Center* (November 29, 2017). https://www.pewresearch.org/fact-tank/2017/11/29/5-facts-about-the-muslim-population-in-europe/

Hagan, Jacqueline. "Faith for the Journey." In *A Promised Land, a Perilous Journey*, edited by Daniel G. Groody and Gioacchino Campese, 3–19. Notre Dame, IN: University of Notre Dame, 2008.

Haller, Michael. *Die "Flüchtlingskrise" in den Medien: Tagesaktueller Journalismus zwischen Meinung und Information*. OBS-Arbeitsheft 93. Mainz-Kastel: mmw. druck und so . . . GmbH, 2017.

Hamer, Eberhard. "Ein Viertel der Deutschen haben Migrationshintergrund." *pi.news.net* (December 9, 2020). http://www.pi-news.net/2020/12/bevoelkerungsaustausch/?utm_source=rss&print=print

Hanciles, Jehu J. "Migration and Mission: Some Implications for the Twenty-First Century Church." *International Bulletin of Mission Research* 27 (2003) 146–53.

Harrison, Faye V. "Introduction: Expanding the Discourse on 'Race.'" *American Anthropologist* 100 (1998) 609–31.

Hartley, John H. *Genesis*. NIBC. Peabody, MA: Hendrickson, 2000.

Hasten, John. "Jews Leaving France." *Aish HaTorah* (April 12, 2014). https://www.aish.com/jw/s/Jews-Leaving-France.html

Hatton, Timothy J., and Jeffrey G. Williamson. *Global Migration and the World Economy: Two Centuries of Policy and Performance*. Cambridge: MIT Press, 2005.

Heinsohn, Gunnar. "Der Bericht zur Flüchtlings-Weltlage." *Achgut.com* (March 7, 2020). https://www.achgut.com/artikel/der_bericht_zur_fluechtlings_weltlage

Hennessy Patrick, and Melissa Kite. "Poll Reveals 40pc of Muslims Want Sharia Law in UK." *Telegraph* (February 19, 2006). https://www.telegraph.co.uk/news/uknews/1510866/Poll-reveals-40pc-of-Muslims-want-sharia-law-in-UK.html

Hess, Richard S. "War in the Hebrew Bible: An Overview." In *War in the Bible and Terrorism in the Twenty-First Century*, edited by Richard S. Hess and Elmer A. Martens, 19–32. Winona Lake, IN: Eisenbrauns, 2008.

Hoen, Maria, Simen Markussen, and Knut Røed. "Immigration and Social Mobility." *IZA Discussion Paper Series*, Paper No 11904 (November 2018) 1–30.

Hoffman, Yair. "The Deuteronomistic Concept of the Herem." *ZAW* 111 (1999) 196–210.

Hoffmeier, James K. *The Immigration Crisis*. Wheaton, IL: Crossway, 2009.

Holland, Gerald. "Migrants Sank the Roman Empire. Now, They're Sinking the U.S." *Shreveport Times* (June 12, 2018). https://www.shreveporttimes.com/story/opinion/2018/06/12/migrants-sank-roman-empire-now-theyre-sinking-u-s/690658002/

Holmøy, Erling. *14 spørsmål og svar om kostnader ved innvandring*. Oslo: Statistisk sentralbyrå, 2015.

Holmøy Erling, and Birger Strøm. "Betydningen for demografi og makroøkonomi av innvandring mot 2100." *Rapporter* 2017/31. Oslo: Statistisk sentralbyrå, 2017. https://www.ssb.no/nasjonalregnskap-og-konjunkturer/artikler-og-publikasjoner/_attachment/327853?_ts=15f779396d0

Hoover, Robin. "The Story of Humane Borders." In *A Promised Land, a Perilous Journey*, edited by Daniel G. Groody and Gioacchino Campese, 160–73. Notre Dame, IN: University of Notre Dame, 2008.

Houston, Fleur S. *You Shall Love the Stranger as Yourself: The Bible, Refugees, and Asylum*. Biblical Challenges in the Contemporary World. London: Routledge, 2015.

Howson, Carlton, and Momodou Sallah. *Europe's Established and Emerging Immigrant Communities: Assimilation, Multiculturalism or Integration*. Stoke-on-Trent, UK: Trentham, 2009.

Hubbard, Robert L. *The Book of Ruth*. NICOT. Grand Rapids: Eerdmans, 1988.

Humes, Karen R., Nicholas A. Jones, and Roberto R. Ramirez. "Overview of Race and Hispanic Origin: 2010." *2010 Census Briefs* (U.S. Census Bureau, 2011). https://www.census.gov/prod/cen2010/briefs/c2010br-02.pdf

Huntington, Samuel P. *Who Are We? The Challenges to America's National Identity*. New York: Simon & Schuster, 2004.

Hutchinson, John, and Anthony D. Smith, eds. *Ethnicity*. Oxford Readers. Oxford: Oxford University Press, 1996.

Jacob, Benno. *Das Buch Genesis*. Berlin: Schocken-Verlag, 1934.

Jenkins, Richard. *Rethinking Ethnicity*. London: SAGE, 1997.

Jervis, L. Ann. *Galatians*. NIBC. Peabody, MA: Hendrickson, 1999.

John Paul II. *Message for the Celebration of the World Day of Peace, January 1, 2001* (Rome: 2001). http://www.vatican.va/content/john-paul-ii/en/messages/peace/documents/hf_jp-ii_mes_20001208_xxxiv-world-day-for-peace.html

Johnston, Matthew. "A Brief History of Income Inequality in the United States." *Investopedia* (June 25, 2019). https://www.investopedia.com/articles/investing/110215/brief-history-income-inequality-united-states.asp

Kaiser, Boris T. "Kaisers royaler Wochenrückblick." *Junge Freiheit* (July 11, 2020). https://jungefreiheit.de/debatte/kommentar/2020/kaisers-royaler-wochenrueckblick-66/

Kaminsky, Joel S. "Did Election Imply the Mistreatment of Non-Israelites?" *HTR* 96 (2003) 397–425.

Karlsen, Rita. "Ikke-vestlig innvandring koster Norge anslagsvis 250 milliarder—årlig." *Human Rights Service* (November 12, 2018). https://www.rights.no/2018/11/ikke-vestlig-innvandring-koster-norge-anslagsvis-250-milliarder-arlig/?fbclid=IwAR2xE5kfNSYlR1AHYSsBRNfxoZfynyG35IkqFXjc3hgW_NH9LFzZgio9MfQ

Keener, Craig S. *The Gospel of Matthew: A Socio-Rhetorical Commentary*. Grand Rapids: Eerdmans, 2009.

Kelek, Necla. "Zwangsehen werden bei uns Alltag." *Der Tagesspiegel* (December 15, 2017). https://www.tagesspiegel.de/berlin/soziologin-necla-kelek-zwangsehen-werden-bei-uns-alltag/20697098.html

Kellas, James G. *The Politics of Nationalism and Ethnicity*. 2nd ed. New York: Palgrave Macmillan, 1998.

Kern, Soeren. "Germany: Stabbings and Knife Crimes at Record High." *Gatestone Institute* (February 28, 2019). https://www.gatestoneinstitute.org/13802/germany-stabbings-knife-crimes

Kerwin, Donald. "The Natural Rights of Migrants and Newcomers." In *A Promised Land, a Perilous Journey*, edited Daniel G. Groody and Gioacchino Campese, 192–205. Notre Dame, IN: University of Notre Dame, 2008.

Kestemont, Guy. "Les grands principes du droit international régissant les traités entre les états proche-orienteaux de XVe-XIIIe s.av.J.C." In *Mesopotamien und seine Nachbarn: Politische und kulturelle Wechselbeziehungen im alten Vorderasien vom 4. bis 1. Jahrtausend v. Chr.*, edited by Hans-Jörg Nissen and Johannes Renger, 269–78. Berliner Beiträge zum Vorderen Orient 1. Berlin: Dietrich Reimer Verlag, 1982.

Kettani, Hossain. "Muslim Population in Europe: 1950–2020." *International Journal of Environmental Science and Development* 1.2 (2010) 154–64.

Keyes, Charles F. "The Dialectics of Ethnic Change." In *Ethnic Change*, edited by Charles F. Keyes, 4–30. 2nd ed. Seattle: University of Washington Press, 1982.

Kisiel Dion, Karen. "On the Development of Identity: Perspectives from Immigrant Families." In *Cultural Psychology of Immigrants*, edited by Ramaswami Mahalingam, 299–314. Mahwah, NJ: Lawrence Erlbaum Associates, 2006.

Kitchen, Kenneth A. *On the Reliability of the Old Testament*. Grand Rapids: Eerdmans, 2003.

Koenig, Denice C. "What Does the Bible Say about Refugees?" *World Vision* (June 19, 2019). https://www.worldvision.org/refugees-news-stories/what-does-bible-say-about-refugees

Köstenberger, Andreas J. *A Theology of John's Gospel and Letters*. Grand Rapids: Zondervan, 2000.

Krauss Stuart. "The Word 'GER' in the Bible and Its Implications." *JBQ* 34 (2006) 264–70.

Kürschner Rauck, Kathleen, and Michael Kvasnicka. "The 2015 Refugee Crisis and Residential Housing Rents in Germany." *IZA Discussion Paper Series*, Paper No. 12047 (December 2018) 1–31.

Leeson, Peter T., and Zachary Gochenour. "The Economic Effects of International Labor Mobility." In *The Economics of Immigration*, edited by Benjamin Powell, 1–37. Oxford: Oxford University Press, 2015.

Lefebvre, Michael. *Collections, Codes, and Torah: The Re-characterization of Israel's Written Law*. The Library of Hebrew Bible/Old Testament 451. London: T. & T. Clark, 2006.

Lemon, Jason. "Ann Coulter Suggests Donald Trump Should Be Charged for Employing Undocumented Migrant Workers." *Newsweek* (August 12, 2019). https://www.newsweek.com/ann-coulter-suggests-trump-charged-employing-undocumented-migrant-workers-1453864

Levine, Hal B. *Constructing Collective Identity*. Frankfurt am Main: Lang, 1997.

Lima, Mauricio. "Train Station in Budapest Cuts Off Service to Migrants." *New York Times* (September 2, 2015). https://www.nytimes.com/2015/09/02/world/europe/keleti-train-station-budapest-migrant-crisis.html

Lincoln, Andrew T. *Ephesians*. WBC 42. Nashville: Thomas Nelson, 1990.

Liphshiz, Cnaan. "Malmo, Sweden Jewish Community May Disappear In 10 Years Over Security Concerns." *Fast Forward* (June 26, 2019). https://forward.com/fast-forward/426474/malmo-sweden-jewish-community-may-disappear-in-10-years-over-security/

Loewenstein, Bedrich W. "Wir und die anderen." In *Mit Fremden leben*, edited by Alexander Demandt, 9–23. München: Beck, 1995.

Lunde, Harald, and Jinghui G. Lysen. "Tidligere deltakere i introduksjonsordningen 2011–2015." *Rapporter* 2018/38. Oslo: Statistisk sentralbyrå, 2018.

Lurås, Helge. "Elefanten i statsbudsjettet: Her er tallene for hvor mye innvandringen koster hvert år." https://resett.no/2019/05/19/elefanten-i-statsbudsjettet-her-er-tallene-for-hvor-mye-innvandringen-koster-hvert-ar/

Lussier, Ernest. *God Is Love According to Saint John*. New York: Alba House, 1977.

Mamou, Yves. "France: No-Go Zones Now in Heart of Big Cities." *Gatestone Institute* (May 23, 2017). https://www.gatestoneinstitute.org/10404/france-no-go-zones

Marshall, I. Howard. *1 and 2 Thessalonians*. NCBC. Grand Rapids: Eerdmans, 1983.

———. *Acts*. TNTC 5. Downers Grove, IL: IVP Academic, 1980.

———. *The Epistles of John*. NICNT. Grand Rapids: Eerdmans, 1978.

Maruskin, Joan M. "The Bible: The Ultimate Migration Handbook." *Church & Society* 95.6 (2005) 77–90.

Mathys, Hans-Peter. "Fremde Religionen in der Bibel." In *Christliche Theologie und Weltreligionen: Grundlagen, Chancen und Schwierigkeiten des Dialogs heute*, edited by Hans J. Münk and Michael Durst, 25–54. Fribourg: Paulusverlag, 2003.

Matthews Victor H., and Don C. Benjamin. *Social World of Ancient Israel 1250–587 BCE*. Peabody, MA: Hendrickson, 1993.

Maurer, Marcus, et al. "Auf den Spuren der Lügenpresse: Zur Richtigkeit und Ausgewogenheit der Medienberichterstattung in der 'Flüchtlingskrise'." *Publizistik* 64 (2019) 15–35.

Mazurczak, Filip. "Eastern Europe's Christian Reawakening." *First Things* (January 17, 2014). https://www.firstthings.com/web-exclusives/2014/01/eastern-europes-christian-reawakening

McAuliffe, Marie, and Binod Khadria, eds. *World Migration Report 2020*. Geneva: International Organization for Migration, 2019.

McGrane, Bernard. *Beyond Anthropology: Society and the Other*. New York: Columbia University Press, 1989.

McKinney, Stephen J., et al. "Welcoming the Stranger. New Testament and Catholic Social Teaching Perspectives on Migrants and Refugees." *The Pastoral Review* 11.6 (2015) 50–55.

Meotti, Giulio. "France: Muslims In, Jews Out." *Gatestone Institute* (November 15, 2017). https://www.gatestoneinstitute.org/11311/france-muslims-jews

Michaels, J. Ramsey. *1 Peter*. WBC 49. Waco, TX: Word, 1988.

———. "Apostolic Hardships and Righteous Gentiles: A Study of Matthew 25:31–46." *JBL* 84 (1965) 27–37.

Michel, Otto. *Der Brief an die Hebräer*. Kritisch-exegetischer Kommentar über das Neue Testament 13. 14th ed. Göttingen: Vandenhoeck & Ruprecht, 1984.

Milgrom, Jacob. *Leviticus 23–27*. AB 3B. New York: Doubleday, 2001.

Möller, Karl. "Asylum Seekers and Refugees: Some Biblical and Theological Reflections." *Whalley Deanery Synod Talk* 2014 (2014). https://karlmoeller.files.wordpress.com/2014/02/asylum-seekers-and-refugees-whalley-talk2.pdf

Mohamed, Besheer, and Elizabeth Podrebarac Sciupac. "The Share of Americans Who Leave Islam Is Offset by Those Who Become Muslim." *Fact Tank Pew Research Center* (January 16, 2018). https://www.pewresearch.org/fact-tank/2018/01/26/the-share-of-americans-who-leave-islam-is-offset-by-those-who-become-muslim/

Moloney, Francis J. *Love in the Gospel of John*. Grand Rapids: Baker Academic, 2013.

Montagu, Ashley. *Man's Most Dangerous Myth: The Fallacy of Race*. New York: Columbia University Press, 1945.

Moo, Douglas J. *The Epistle to the Romans*. NICNT. Grand Rapids: Eerdmans, 1996.

Motivans, Mark. "Immigration, Citizenship, and the Federal Justice System, 1998–2018." *Bureau of Justice Statistics*. https://www.bjs.gov/index.cfm?ty=pbdetail&iid=6666

Müller, Hans-Peter. "Gott und die Götter in den Anfängen der biblischen Religion." In *Monotheismus im alten Israel und seiner Umwelt*, edited by Othmar Keel, 99–142. Biblische Beiträge 14. Fribourg: Schweizerisches Katholisches Bibelwerk, 1980.

Mühlmann, Wilhelm Emil. "Ethnogonie und Ethnogenese: Theoretisch-ethnologische und ideologiekritische Studie." In *Studien zur Ethnogenese, Bd. 1*, 9–27. Abhandlungen der Rheinisch-Westfälischen Akademie der Wissenschaften 72. Opladen: Westdeutscher Verlag, 1985.

———. *Homo Creator: Abhandlungen zur Soziologie, Anthropologie und Ethnologie*. Wiesbaden: Harrassowitz, 1962.

Murphy, Eleanor J. "Transnational Ties and Mental Health." In *Cultural Psychology of Immigrants*, edited by Rawaswami Mahalingam, 79–92. Mahwah, NJ: Lawrence Erlbaum Associates, 2006.

Neuding, Paulina. "Bomb Attacks Are Now a Normal Part of Swedish Life." *The Spectator* (October 26, 2019). https://www.spectator.co.uk/2019/10/bomb-attacks-are-now-a-normal-part-of-swedish-life/

Ngo, Andy. "Sweden's Parallel Society—A Case of Mass Immigration without Assimilation." *National Review* (December 20, 2018). https://www.nationalreview.com/magazine/2018/12/31/swedens-parallel-society/

Nihan, Christophe. "Resident Aliens and Natives in the Holiness Legislation." In *The Foreigner and the Law: Perspectives from the Hebrew Bible and the Ancient Near East*, edited by Reinhard Achenbach et al., 111–34. BZAR 16. Wiesbaden: Harrassowitz, 2011.

Nowrasteh, Alex. "Illegal Immigrants and Crime—Assessing the Evidence." *cato.org* (March 4, 2019). https://www.cato.org/blog/illegal-immigrants-crime-assessing-evidence

Oberwittler, Dietrich, and Julia Kasselt. *Ehrenmorde in Deutschland 1996–2005*. Polizei + Forschung 42. Köln: Luchterhand, 2011.

Oded, Bustenay. *Mass Deportations and Deportees in the Neo-Assyrian Empire*. Wiesbaden: Reichert, 1979.

O'Neill, William. "'No Longer Strangers' (Ephesians 2:19): The Ethics of Migration." *Word & World* 29.3 (2009) 227–33.

Oswalt, John N. *The Book of Isaiah, Chapters 1–39*. NICOT. Grand Rapids: Eerdmans, 1986.

Ousey Graham C., and Charis E. Kubrin. "Immigration and Crime: Assessing a Contentious Issue." *Annual Review of Criminology* 1 (2018) 63–84.

Parsons, Mikeal C. *Acts*. Paideia Commentaries on the New Testament. Grand Rapids: Baker Academic, 2008.

———. *Luke*. Paideia Commentaries on the New Testament. Grand Rapids: Baker Academic, 2015.

Paynter, Helen. "'Make Yourself at Home': The Tensions and Paradoxes of Hospitality in Dialogue with the Bible." *The Bible and Critical Theory* 14 (2018) 42–61.

———. "Porous Borders and Textual Ambiguity: Why Old Testament Israel Is No Model for Modern Nationalism." *Journal of European Baptist Studies* 20 (2020) 117–30.

Perez Foster, RoseMarie. "When Immigration Is Trauma: Guidelines for the Individual and Family Clinician." *American Journal of Orthopsychiatry* 71.2 (2001) 153–70.

Peterson, David G. *The Acts of the Apostles*. The Pillar New Testament Commentary. Grand Rapids: Eerdmans / Nottingham: Apollos, 2009.

Pischke, Jörn-Steffen, and Johannes Velling. "Employment Effects of Immigration to Germany: An Analysis Based on Local Labor Markets." *The Review of Economics and Statistics* 79 (1997) 594–604.

Pitkänen, Pekka. "Ethnicity, Assimilation and the Israelite Settlement." *Tyndale Bulletin* 55 (2004) 161–82.

Portes, Alejandro, et al. "The Study of Transnationalism: Pitfalls and Promise of an Emergent Research Field." *Ethnic and Racial Studies Review* 22 (1999) 217–37.

Press, Elizabeth. "Turkish Prime Minister Says 'Assimilation Is a Crime against Humanity'." *the local.de* (February 11, 2008). https://www.thelocal.de/20080211/10293

Préteceille, Edmond. "Has Ethno-Racial Segregation Increased in the Greater Paris Metropolitan Area?" *Revue française de sociologie* 52, Suppl. (2011) 31–62.

Prill, Thorsten. "Migration, Mission and the Multi-ethnic Church." *ERT* 33.4 (2009) 332–46.

Puppinck, Grégor. "The Council of Europe Is 'Greatly Concerned' by the Application of Sharia in Europe." *European Centre for Law and Justice* (February 2019). https://eclj.org/religious-freedom/pace/le-conseil-de-leurope-sinquite-grandement-de-lapplication-de-la-charia-en-europe

Putnam, Robert D. "E Pluribus Unum: Diversity and Community in the Twenty-First Century." *Scandinavian Political Studies* 30.2 (2007) 137–74.

Ramón, Cristobal, et al. "Data on Foreign-Born in Federal Prisons Says Little about Overall Immigrant Criminality." *bipartisanpolicy.org* (March 6, 2018). https://bipartisanpolicy.org/blog/data-on-foreign-born-in-federal-prisons-says-little-about-overall-immigrant-criminality/

Ramsey, Paul. *Who Speaks for the Church?* Nashville: Abingdon, 1967.

Reminick, Ronald A. *Theory of Ethnicity: An Anthropologist's Perspective.* Lanham, MD: University Press of America, 1983.

Renz, Johannes, and Wolfgang Röllig. *Handbuch der althebräischen Epigraphik I.* Darmstadt: Wissenschaftliche Buchgesellschaft, 1995.

———. *Handbuch der althebräischen Epigraphik II/1.* Darmstadt: Wissenschaftliche Buchgesellschaft, 1995.

Richwine, Jason. "An Abundance of New Academic Studies Find Negative Impacts of Immigration." *Center for Immigration Studies* (June 14, 2019). https://cis.org/Richwine/Abundance-New-Academic-Studies-Find-Negative-Impacts-Immigration,

Ridderbos, Herman N. *The Epistle of Paul to the Churches of Galatia.* NICNT. Grand Rapids: Eerdmans, 1978.

Riddlebarger, Kim. *First Corinthians.* Lectio Continua. Powder Springs, GA: Tolle Lege, 2013.

Riemer, Sebastian. "Was Flüchtlinge uns bringen ist wertvoller als Gold." *Rhein-Neckar-Zeitung* (June 11, 2016). https://www.rnz.de/nachrichten/heidelberg_artikel,-Heidelberg-Was-die-Fluechtlinge-uns-bringen-ist-wertvoller-als-Gold-_arid,198565.html

Rigby, Peter. *African Images: Racism and the End of Anthropology.* Oxford: Berg, 1996.

Rodríguez, Oscar Andrés. "A Witness to Hope." In *A Promised Land, a Perilous Journey*, edited Daniel G. Groody and Gioacchino Campese, xi–xvii. Notre Dame, IN: University of Notre Dame, 2008.

Roosens, Eugeen E. *Creating Ethnicity: The Process of Ethnogenesis.* Frontiers of Anthropology 5. London: SAGE, 1989.

Rosenstock-Huessy, Eugen. *Des Christen Zukunft oder Wir überholen die Moderne.* Moers: Brendow Verlag, 1985.

Rubenstein, Edwin S. "The Negative Economic Impact of Immigration on American Workers." *NPG* 162 (2016) 1–12.

Sadler, Rodney Steven. *Can a Cushite Change His Skin? An Examination of Race, Ethnicity, and Othering in the Hebrew Bible.* Library of Hebrew Bible/Old Testament Studies 425. London: T. & T. Clark, 2005.

Sanandaji, Tino. "What Is the Truth about Crime and Immigration in Sweden?" *National Review* (February 25, 2017). https://www.nationalreview.com/2017/02/sweden-crime-rates-statistics-immigration-trump-fox-news/

Sandnes, Toril, ed. *Innvandrere i Norge 2017.* Statistiske analyser 155. Oslo: Statistisk sentralbyrå, 2017. https://www.ssb.no/befolkning/artikler-og-publikasjoner/_attachment/332154?_ts=16290131a1050

Scheuringer, Brunhilde. "Begegnung mit dem Fremden." In *Die Fremden*, edited by Gottfried Bachl, 1–17. Schriftenreihe des Instituts für Wirtschaftswissenschaften an der Rechtswissenschaftlichen Fakultät der Universität Salzburg 10. Regensburg: Transfer, 1993.

Schmitter Heisler, Barbara. "The Sociology of Migration." In *Migration Theory: Talking across Disciplines*, edited by Caroline B. Brettell and James F. Hollifield, 83–111. London: Routledge, 2008.

Schreiner, Thomas R. *1, 2 Peter, Jude.* NAC 37. Nashville: Broadman & Holman, 2003.

Schreiter, Robert. "Migrants and the Ministry of Reconciliation." In *A Promised Land, a Perilous Journey*, edited by Daniel G. Groody and Gioacchino Campese, 107–23. Notre Dame, IN: University of Notre Dame, 2008.

Schuetz, Alfred. "The Stranger: An Essay in Social Psychology." *AJS* 49.6 (1944) 499–507.

Schuster, Meinhard. "Ethnische Fremdheit, ethnische Identität." In *Die Begegnung mit dem Fremden*, edited by Meinhard Schuster, 207–21. Colloquium Rauricum 4. Leipzig: Teubner, 1996.

Scott, John. "Ethnicity." In *A Dictionary of Sociology*, edited by John Scott. ebook. 4th ed. Oxford University Press, 2014.

———. "Migration, Sociology of." In *A Dictionary of Sociology*, edited by John Scott. ebook. 4th ed. Oxford University Press, 2014.

———. "Nationalism." In *A Dictionary of Sociology*, edited by John Scott. ebook. 4th ed. Oxford University Press, 2014.

Seibel, Manuel. *Das Matthäusevangelium.* www.bibelkommentare.de

Senior, Donald. "Beloved Aliens and Exiles." In *A Promised Land, a Perilous Journey*, edited by Daniel G. Groody and Gioacchino Campese, 20–34. Notre Dame, IN: University of Notre Dame, 2008.

Sennels, Nicolai. *Holy Wrath: Among Criminal Muslims.* Helsingborg: Logik Förlag, 2018.

———. "Muslims and Westerners: The Psychological Differences." *New English Review* (May 2010). https://www.newenglishreview.org/Nicolai_Sennels/Muslims_and_Westerners%3A_The_Psychological_Differences/?fbclid=IwAR1iGoGNnbJEFBHYSEcmqpVrMZBNaewi_MHosl-lBR4kwAOJQXFgBvagAS8

Seton-Watson, Hugh. *Nations and States: An Inquiry into the Origins of Nations and the Politics of Nationalism.* Boulder, CO: Westview, 1977.

Sluzki, Carlos E. "Disruption and Reconstruction of Networks Following Migration/ Relocation." *Family Systems Medicine* 10.4 (1992) 359–63.

Smelik, Klaas A. D. *Historische Dokumente aus dem alten Israel.* Göttingen: Vandenhoeck & Ruprecht, 1987.

Smith, Anthony D. *The Ethnic Origins of Nations.* Oxford: Blackwell, 1986.

Smith, Gary V. *Isaiah 1–39.* NAC 15A. Nashville: Broadman & Holman, 2007.

Smith, James P., and Barry Edmonston. *The New Americans: Economic, Demographic, and Fiscal Effects of Immigration.* Washington, DC: The National Academic Press, 1997.

Smith, Mark S. *The Early History of God: Yahweh and Other Deities in Ancient Israel.* 2nd ed. The Biblical Resource Series. Grand Rapids: Eerdmans, 2002.

Sonnad, Nikhil. "England Says Oliver Is the Most Popular Boy's Name, But It's Actually Muhammad." *Quartz Daily Brief* (September 20, 2017). https://qz.com/1082778/popular-baby-names-muhammad-is-actually-the-most-boys-name-in-england-and-wales-not-oliver/

Sparks, Kenton L. *Ethnicity and Identity in Ancient Israel: Prolegomena to the Study of Ethnic Sentiments and Their Expression in the Hebrew Bible.* Winona Lake, IN: Eisenbrauns, 1998.

Stein, Robert H. *Luke*. NAC 24. Nashville: Broadman, 1992.

Stenschke, Christoph. "Migration and Mission in the Book of Acts." In *The Church and Its Mission in the New Testament and Early Christianity: In Memory of Professor Hans Kvalbein*, edited by David E. Aune and Reidar Hvalvik, 163–80. WUNT 404. Tübingen: Mohr Siebeck, 2018.

Stolarik, M. Mark. "From Field to Factory: The Historiography of Slovak Immigration to the United States." *The International Migration Review* 10 (1976) 81–102.

Stoldt, Till-Reimer. "Ende der Schweigekultur um kriminelle Nordafrikaner." *Zeit* (January 17, 2016). https://www.welt.de/politik/deutschland/article151089556/Ende-der-Schweigekultur-um-kriminelle-Nordafrikaner.html

Strine, Casey A. "Embracing Asylum Seekers and Refugees: Jeremiah 29 as Foundation for a Christian Theology of Migration and Integration." *Political Theology* 19 (2018) 478–96.

Strömbäck, Jesper. "Stabilitet i en föränderlig värld: medieanvändning och social sammanhållning." In *Larmar och gör sig till*, edited by Ulrika Andersson et al., 1–17. Gothenburg: Göteborgs universitet, SOM-institutet, 2017. https://www.researchgate.net/publication/317004052_Stabilitet_i_en_foranderlig_varld_medieanvandning_och_social_sammanhallning/link/591da79d45851540595D858b/download

Suh, Joong Suk. "Das Weltgericht und die Matthäische Gemeinde." *NovT* 48 (2006) 217–33.

Svahnström, Jöran. "I Danmark säger de 'ghetton', I Sverige heter det 'utsatta områden.'" *Borås Tidning* (January 16, 2018). https://www.bt.se/ledare/svahnstrom-i-danmark-sager-de-ghetton-i-sverige-heter-det-utsatta-omraden/

Sørensen, Knut Ø. *Inn-og Utvandring for Norge 1958–1975*. Statistiske Analyser 33. Oslo: Statistisk Sentralbyrå, 1977. https://www.ssb.no/a/histstat/sagml/sagml_33.pdf

Thielman, Frank. *Ephesians*. Baker Exegetical Commentary on the New Testament. Grand Rapids: Baker Academic, 2010.

Thiessen, Matthew. "The Function of a Conjunction: Inclusivist or Exclusivist Strategies in Ezra 6.19–21 and Nehemiah 10.29–30?" *JSOT* 34.1 (2009) 63–79.

Tigay, Jeffrey H. *Deuteronomy*. JPS Torah Commentary. Philadelphia: The JPS Society, 1996.

Timmerman, Christiane, et al., eds. *Gender and Migration: A Gender-Sensitive Approach to Migration Dynamics*. CeMIS Migration and Intercultural Studies 3. Leuven: Leuven University Press, 2018.

Tjønn, Halvor. "NHO: Hele oljeformuen kan gå tapt." *Aftenposten* (June 12, 2006). https://www.aftenposten.no/norge/politikk/i/eEjwy/NHO-Hele-oljeformuen-kan-ga-tapt

Tverberg, Gail. "12 Negative Aspects of Globalization." https://oilprice.com/Finance/the-Economy/12-Negative-Aspects-of-Globalization.html#

Ulfkotte, Udo. "Die verschwiegenen Kosten der Zuwanderung." https://archive.org/details/DieVerschwiegenenKostenDerZuwanderungUdoUlfkotte

Vang, Carsten. "The Non-Prophetic Background for the King Law." In *Paradigm Change in Pentateuchal Research*, edited by Matthias Armgardt et al., 207–23. BZAR 22. Wiesbaden: Harrassowitz, 2019.

Van Nguyen, Thanh. "In Solidarity with the Strangers: The Flight into Egypt." *The Bible Today* 45 (2007) 219–24.

Veum, Eirik, and Gaute Zakariassen. "Overfallsvoldtekter begås av ikke-vestlige innvandrere." *NRK* (April 15, 2009). https://www.nrk.no/norge/voldtektsmenner-ikke-vestlige-1.6567955

Villiers, Gerda de, and Jurie le Roux. "The Book of Ruth in the Time of the Judges and Ruth, the Moabitess." *Verbum et Ecclesia* 37.1 (2016) 1–6. http://www.scielo.org.za/pdf/vee/v37n1/26.pdf

Volf, Miroslav. *Exclusion and Embrace: A Theological Exploration of Identity, Otherness and Reconciliation*. Nashville: Abingdon, 1996.

Wachter, Daniel von. "Die Öffnung der Grenzen ist unmoralisch." http://von-wachter.de/papers/Wachter_2016-Einreisende.pdf

Waltke, Bruce K. *Genesis: A Commentary*. Grand Rapids: Zondervan, 2001.

Walton, John H. *Genesis*. The NIV Application Commentary. Grand Rapids: Zondervan, 2001.

Walton John H., and J. Harvey Walton. *The Lost World of the Israelite Conquest: Covenant, Retribution, and the Fate of the Canaanites*. Downers Grove, IL: IVP Academic, 2017.

Walvin, James. *Atlas of Slavery*. London: Routledge, 2014.

Walzer, Michael. *Spheres of Justice: A Defense of Pluralism and Equality*. New York: Basic, 1983.

Wax, Amy, and Jason Richwine. "Low-Skill Immigration: A Case for Restriction." *American Affairs* I.4 (2017). https://americanaffairsjournal.org/2017/11/low-skill-immigration-case-restriction

Webman, Esther, and Talia Naamat, eds. *Moshe Kantor Database for the Study of Contemporary Antisemitism and Racism, Antisemitism Worldwide 2018, General Analysis*. Tel Aviv: Kantor Center, Tel Aviv University, 2019. http://www.kantorcenter.tau.ac.il/sites/default/files/Antisemitism%20Worldwide%202018.pdf

Whitney, Glayed. "On Possible Genetic Bases of Race Differences in Criminality." In *Crime in Biological, Social, and Moral Contexts*, edited by Lee Ellis and Harry Hoffman, 134–49. New York: Prager, 1990.

Willey, David. "Gaddafi Wants EU Cash to Stop African Migrants." *BBC News* (August 31, 2010). https://www.bbc.com/news/world-europe-11139345

Williams, Weston. "Why Clinton Is Enlisting Undocumented Immigrants Who Can't Vote." *The Christian Science Monitor* (August 15, 2016). https://www.csmonitor.com/USA/Politics/2016/0815/Why-Clinton-is-enlisting-undocumented-immigrants-who-can-t-vote

Wischmeyer, Oda. *Liebe als Agape: Das frühchristliche Konzept und der moderne Diskurs*. Tübingen: Mohr Siebeck, 2015.

Witherington III, Ben. *Paul's Letter to the Romans*. Grand Rapids: Eerdmans, 2004.

Wright, Christopher J. H. *Old Testament Ethics for the People of God*. Downers Grove, IL: InterVarsity, 2004.

———. *Walking in the Ways of the Lord: The Ethical Authority of the Old Testament*. Leicester, UK: Apollos, 1995.

Wruck, Gerhard. "Politik ohne Verantwortung für die Zukunft." *secrets-of-africa blogspot* (October 13, 2014). http://secrets-of-africa.blogspot.com/2014/10/gerhard-wruck-politik-ohne.html

Wünch, Hans-Georg. "Gast, Mitbewohner, Fremdling, Ausländer: Zur Begrifflichkeit des 'Fremden' im Alten Testament." In *TSR Jahrbuch 2013*, edited by Alfred Meier and Hans-Georg Wünch, 81–104. Wölmersen: Theologisches Seminar Rheinland, 2013.

Wyssuwa, Matthias. "Scharfe Worte für alte Erkenntnisse: Antisemitismus in Schweden." *FAZ.net* (December 16, 2017). https://www.faz.net/aktuell/politik/ausland/antisemitische-angriffe-in-schweden-15339526.html

Xie, Bin. "The Effects of Immigration Quotas on Wages, the Great Black Migration, and Industrial Development." *IZA Discussion Paper Series*, Paper No. 11214 (December 2017) 1–66.

Zehnder, Markus. "The Annihilation of the Canaanites: Reassessing the Brutality of the Biblical Witnesses," in *Encountering Violence in the Bible*, edited by Markus Zehnder and Hallvard Hagelia, 263–90. Sheffield, UK: Phoenix, 2013.

———. "Anstösse aus Dtn 23,2–9 zur Frage nach dem Umgang mit Fremden." *Freiburger Zeitschrift für Philosophie und Theologie* 52 (2005) 300–314.

———. "A Fresh Look at Malachi II 13–16." *VT* 53 (2003) 224–59.

———. "Literary and Other Observations on Passages Dealing with Foreigners in the Book of Deuteronomy: The Command to Love the *Ger* Read in Context." In *Sepher Torath Mosheh: Studies in the Composition and Interpretation of Deuteronomy*, edited by Daniel I. Block and Richard L. Schultz, 192–231. Peabody, MA: Hendrickson, 2017.

———. "Love in the Bible, and Law, Justice, and Mercy." In *Biblical Ethics: Tensions between Justice and Mercy, Law and Love*, edited by Markus Zehnder and Peter Wick, 15–66. Gorgias Biblical Studies 70. Piscataway, NJ: Gorgias, 2019.

———. Review of *Adopting the Stranger as Kindred in Deuteronomy*, by Mark R. Glanville. *EJT* 29 (2020) 79–81.

———. *Umgang mit Fremden in Israel und Assyrien: Ein Beitrag zur Anthropologie des "Fremden" im Licht antiker Quellen*. BWANT 168. Stuttgart: Kohlhammer, 2005.

———. *Wegmetaphorik im Alten Testament*. BZAW 268. Berlin: de Gruyter, 1999.

———. "Why the Danielic 'Son of Man' is a Divine Being." *BBR* 24 (2014) 331–48.

Zenner, Walter P. "Ethnicity." In *Encyclopedia of Cultural Anthropology* 2, edited by David Levinson and Melvin Ember, 393–95. New York: Brown, 1996.

Øien, Arne. "Folkemengdens Bevegelse 1984." *Norges offisielle statistikk* B 573. Oslo: 1985. https://www.ssb.no/a/histstat/nos/nos_b573.pdf

Articles and books without author name

"10 Points Action Plan." *European Coalition of Cities against Racism*. https://www.eccar.info/en/10-point-action-plan

"AAPA Statement on Biological Aspects of Race." *American Journal of Physical Anthropology* 101 (1996) 569–70.

"Africa Population." https://www.worldometers.info/world-population/africa-population/

"Antisemitismus: Immer mehr Juden verlassen Frankreich." *Deutsche Welle* (March 1, 2019). https://www.dw.com/de/antisemitismus-immer-mehr-juden-verlassen-frankreich/av-47748019

"Asylum Statistics." *Eurostat*. https://ec.europa.eu/eurostat/statistics-explained/index.php?title=Asylum_statistics

"Attentat de l'église de Saint-Étienne-du-Rouvray." *Wikipedia.* https://fr.wikipedia.org/wiki/Attentat_de_l%27église_de_Saint-Étienne-du-Rouvray

"Austria: Majority of Turks Want Sharia Personal Law Incorporated into Legal System." *Europenews* (2010). http://europenews.dk/en/node/29130

"Bevölkerung mit Migrationshintergrund 2019 um 2,1 % gewachsen." DESTATIS, Statistisches Bundesamt. https://www.destatis.de/DE/Presse/Pressemitteilungen/2020/07/PD20_279_12511.html

"Bevölkerungsdaten im Zeitvergleich, 1950–2018." *Bundesamt für Statistik.* https://www.bfs.admin.ch/bfs/de/home/statistiken/bevoelkerung.assetdetail.9466629.html

"Bundeshaushalt 2018." *Bundesfinanzministerium.* https://www.bundesfinanzministerium.de/Content/DE/Bilderstrecken/Infografiken/2017–09–26-Eckwerte-Bundeshaushalt-2018/2017–09–26-Eckwerte-Bundeshaushalt-2018.html;jsessionid=CF5DE2EE18D021A4531F599DCDFD39BD?notFirst=true&docId=120658#photogallery

"Burmese Americans." *Wikipedia.* https://en.wikipedia.org/wiki/Burmese_Americans

"A Catholic Framework for Economic Life." *United States Conference of Catholic Bishops* (1996).

Les chiffres clés des inégalités femmes-hommes dans les quartiers prioritaires et les territoires ruraux. Études du Haut Conseil à l'Égalité entre les Femmes et les Hommes, No. 2 (Avril 2014). http://www.haut-conseil-egalite.gouv.fr/IMG/pdf/hcefh_etude_02–2014–04-egater-2.pdf

"Committee to Study the Migration of Workers." *Christian Reformed Church* (2008). https://www.crcna.org/sites/default/files/Migration.pdf

"Crime: Rape Rate." *NationMaster.* https://www.nationmaster.com/country-info/stats/Crime/Rape-rate#2003

"Crime Stats, Compare Iceland and Norway." *NationMaster,* https://www.nationmaster.com/country-info/compare/Iceland/Norway/Crime#2014

"Crime Stats, Compare Iceland and Sweden." *NationMaster,* https://www.nationmaster.com/country-info/compare/Iceland/Sweden/Crime#2014

"The Countries That Imprison the Most Foreigners." *Statista.com.* https://www.statista.com/chart/4285/the-countries-that-imprison-the-most-foreigners/

"Death of Alan Kurdi." *Wikipedia.* https://en.wikipedia.org/wiki/Death_of_Alan_Kurdi

"Deutsche Staatsschulden 2018." *Deutsche Bundesbank.* https://www.bundesbank.de/de/presse/pressenotizen/deutsche-staatsschulden-783598

ehrenmord.de. http://www.ehrenmord.de/faq/wieviele.php

"Employment and Salary." *Statistisk sentralbyrå.* https://www.ssb.no/en/arbeid-og-lonn/statistikker/innvarbl

"France Population." *World Population Review.* http://worldpopulationreview.com/countries/france-population/

"Funding Opportunities for Promoting Tolerance and Education." *European Commission* (2020). https://ec.europa.eu/info/policies/justice-and-fundamental-rights/combatting-discrimination/racism-and-xenophobia/eu-funding-tackle-racism-and-xenophobia/tolerance-and-education_en

"Germany Population." *World Population Review.* http://worldpopulationreview.com/countries/germany-population/

Global Compact for Safe, Orderly and Regular Migration, Final Draft, 11 July 2018. https://refugeesmigrants.un.org/sites/default/files/180711_final_draft_0.pdf

Global Terrorism Database. https://www.start.umd.edu/gtd/search/Results. aspx?page=1&casualties_type=&casualties_max=&country=217&count=100&e xpanded=no&charttype=line&chart=overtime&ob=GTDID&od=desc#results- table

Global Terrorism Index, Vision of Humanity. http://visionofhumanity.org/indexes/ terrorism-index/

"Immigration." *Open Society Foundations.* https://www.opensocietyfoundations.org/ what-we-do/regions/united-states

"Immigration 2009." *The National Association of Evangelicals.* https://www.nae.net/ immigration-2009/

"Immigration and Crime." *Wikipedia.* https://en.wikipedia.org/wiki/Immigration_ and_crime#Crime

"Immigration, Emigration and Net Migration, by Citizenship 2007K1–2020K1." *Statbank Population.* Oslo: Statistisk Sentralbyrå. https://www.ssb.no/en/statbank/ table/11327/tableViewLayout1/

"Immigration, World Poverty and Gumballs." *NumbersUSA.com.* https://www.youtube. com/watch?v=LPjzfGChGlE

"Inmate Citizenship." *Federal Bureau of Prisons.* https://www.bop.gov/about/statistics/ statistics_inmate_citizenship.jsp

"Inmate Ethnicity." *Federal Bureau of Prisons.* https://www.bop.gov/about/statistics/ statistics_inmate_ethnicity.jsp

"Inmate Race." *Federal Bureau of Prisons.* https://www.bop.gov/about/statistics/ statistics_inmate_race.jsp

"Islamismus und islamistischer Terrorismus." *Verfassungsschutz.* https:// www.verfassungsschutz.de/de/arbeitsfelder/af-islamismus-und- islamistischer-terrorismus/zahlen-und-fakten-islamismus/islamistisches- personenpotenzial-2018

International Migration Database. OECD.Stat. https://stats.oecd.org/Index. aspx?DataSetCode=MIG

"Jede vierte Person in Deutschland hatte 2018 einen Migrationshintergrund." *DESTATIS,* Statistisches Bundesamt. https://www.destatis.de/DE/Presse/ Pressemitteilungen/2019/08/PD19_314_12511.html

Kriminalität im Kontext von Zuwanderung—Bundeslagebild 2018. Wiesbaden: Bundeskriminalamt, 2019.

"Länderhaushalte 2018." *Bundesfinanzministerium.* https://www. bundesfinanzministerium.de/Content/DE/Standardartikel/Themen/ Oeffentliche_Finanzen/Foederale_Finanzbeziehungen/Laenderhaushalte/2018/ Entw_Laenderhaushalte_Dez-2018.pdf?__blob=publicationFile&v=2

"Liste von Terroranschlägen in Deutschland." *Wikipedia.* https://de.wikipedia.org/ wiki/Liste_von_Terroranschlägen_in_Deutschland

"List of Most Popular Given Names." *Wikipedia.* https://en.wikipedia.org/wiki/List_of_ most_popular_given_names#Male_names_4

"Manifest 'contre le nouvel antisémitisme." *Le Parisien* (April 21 and May 2, 2018). https://www.leparisien.fr/societe/manifeste-contre-le-nouvel-antisemitis me-21-04-2018-7676787.php

"Migration Profiles: France." *UNICEF.* https://esa.un.org/miggmgprofiles/indicators/ files/France.pdf

"Migration Profiles: Germany." *UNICEF.* https://esa.un.org/miggmgprofiles/indicators/files/Germany.pdf

"Migration Profiles: Norway." *UNICEF.* https://esa.un.org/miggmgprofiles/indicators/files/Norway.pdf

"Migration Profiles: Sweden." *UNICEF.* https://esa.un.org/miggmgprofiles/indicators/files/Sweden.pdf

"Migration Profiles: Switzerland." *UNICEF.* https://esa.un.org/miggmgprofiles/indicators/files/Switzerland.pdf

"Muammar Gaddafi 2006—Islam Will Conquer Europe without Firing a Shot." *YouTube.* https://www.youtube.com/watch?v=WCGYKSEsYFM

"Namen-Ranking 2018: Mohammed beliebtester Erstname in Berlin." *Berliner Zeitung* (May 2, 2019). https://www.bz-berlin.de/berlin/mohammed-beliebtester-erstname-in-berlin

"National Intercensal Tables: 1900–1990." *United States Census Bureau.* https://www.census.gov/content/census/en/data/tables/time-series/demo/popest/pre-1980-national.html

"Norway Population." *World Population Review.* http://worldpopulationreview.com/countries/norway-population/

"Paris Police Headquarters Stabbing." *Wikipedia.* https://en.wikipedia.org/wiki/Paris_police_headquarters_stabbing

"People Smuggling." *Wikipedia.* https://en.wikipedia.org/wiki/People_smuggling

"Poll: 46% of French Muslims Believe Sharia Law Should Be Applied in Country." *i24news* (September 19, 2019). https://www.i24news.tv/en/news/international/europe/1568920086-poll-46-of-french-muslims-believe-sharia-law-should-be-applied-in-country

"Population Estimates, July 1, 2019." *Quick Facts, United States Census Bureau.* https://www.census.gov/quickfacts/fact/table/US/PST045218

Quick Facts, United States Census Bureau. https://www.census.gov/quickfacts/fact/table/US/IPE120218

"Quotes from Church Teachings on the Rights of Migrants and Refugees." *United States Conference of Catholic Bishops.* http://www.usccb.org/issues-and-action/human-life-and-dignity/migrants-refugees-and-travelers/quotes-rights-migrants-refugees.cfm?platform=hootsuite

"Reconquista (Mexico)." *Wikipedia.* https://en.wikipedia.org/wiki/Reconquista_(Mexico)

"Refugee Highway Partnership." *World Evangelical Alliance.* https://www.refugeehighway.net/wea-task-force.html

"Replacement Migration." *Wikipedia.* https://en.wikipedia.org/wiki/Replacement_migration

"Southern Baptist 2018 Resolution on Migration." http://www.sbc.net/resolutions/2288/on-immigration

"Ständige Wohnbevölkerung ab 15 Jahren nach Nationalität und Religionszugehörigkeit." *Bundesamt für Statistik.* https://www.bfs.admin.ch/bfs/de/home/statistiken/bevoelkerung/sprachen-religionen.assetdetail.7666353.html

Statsbudsjettet 2018. https://www.statsbudsjettet.no/Statsbudsjettet-2018/Satsinger/?pid=83811

"Stocks of Foreign-Born Population in OECD Countries." *OECD Data.* https://data. oecd.org/migration/stocks-of-foreign-born-population-in-oecd-countries. htm#indicator-chart

"Sub-Replacement   Fertility."   *Wikipedia.*   https://en.wikipedia.org/wiki/Sub-replacement_fertility

"Sweden Population." *World Population Review.* https://worldpopulationreview.com/ countries/sweden-population/

"Sweden Rape: Most Convicted Attackers Foreign-Born, Says TV." *BBC News* (August 22, 2018). https://www.bbc.com/news/world-europe-45269764

'*und der Fremdling, der in deinen Toren ist:' Gemeinsames Wort der Kirchen zu den Herausforderungen durch Migration und Flucht.* Hannover: Evangelischer Pressedienst, 1997.

Verfassungsschutzbericht 2015. Berlin: Bundesministerium des Innern.

Voldtektsituasjonen i Norge 2018. Politiet, Kripos. Hustrykkeriet Kripos, 2019. https://www.politiet.no/globalassets/04-aktuelt-tall-og-fakta/voldtekt-og-seksuallovbrudd/voldtektssituasjonen-i-norge-2018.pdf

"A Wesleyan View of Immigration." *The Wesleyan Church* (2013). https://www.wesleyan. org/a-wesleyan-view-of-immigration.

Ancient Document Index

Leviticus

16	25n20
16:29	24
17	24
17–25	71
17:8–9	25
18:21	37n54
18:25, 28	25n17
18:26	24
19:4	37n54
19:10	24
19:33	24
19:34	10n29, 21n5, 24, 27, 122n67, 256
20:2	24, 37n54
21:14–23	51
22:18–25	24
22:25	31
23:33	24
24:10–12	40
24:16	24
24:22	24, 25n21
25:23	66, 117n47
25:35	30n34
25:45	26
25:47–55	26
26:1	37n54

Numbers

9:14	24, 25n21, 71
10:29–32	40
11:4	40
12:1	40
15:14–16	24, 71
15:16	17–18, 19, 25n21
19:10	24, 71
20:16–21	67
21:1–3	40
21:3	36n48
21:14–21	41
21:21–31	40
21:33–35	40
25	40
31	40
32:12	40
33:50–56	36–37
35:11–16	17
35:15	24
35:20–30	17

Deuteronomy

1:16	22
2:1–9, 19, 29	41
2:5, 9, 19	62n126, 62n128
2:6	65n143
2:10–12	63n134
2:12, 22	62, 63n133
2:20–23	63n134
2:21	62, 63n133
2:26–36	40
2:34	36n48
3:1–13	40
3:6	36n48
3:9, 11	63n134
4:16–19, 23, 25	37n54
5:7–9	37n54
5:14	21, 25n19
6:10–11	63n135
6:14	37n54
7:1–5, 16	36–37, 50, 54
7:2, 26	36n48
7:25–26	36n50
8:19	37n54
9:4–5	36n50
10:18–19	14n42, 22
10:18	23
10:19	27, 122n67, 256
11:16, 28	37n54
12	36n47
12:2–3, 29–31	37n54
13:3, 7, 14	37n54
13:13–19	37
14:1–2	37n54
14:21	22, 23, 29
14:28–29	22
15:3	29–30, 33
15:6	252
16:1–7	23
16:11, 14	22, 23
16:22	37n54
17:3	37n54
17:14–20	46
17:15	29
18:9–14, 20	37n54